April 2nd 1997
With all my love
Pam

Huxley

Also by Adrian Desmond

THE HOT-BLOODED DINOSAURS
THE APE'S REFLEXION
ARCHETYPES AND ANCESTORS
THE POLITICS OF EVOLUTION
DARWIN (with James Moore)
HUXLEY: THE DEVIL'S DISCIPLE (Volume One)

Huxley: Evolution's High Priest

ADRIAN DESMOND

MICHAEL JOSEPH
LONDON

MICHAEL JOSEPH LTD

Published by the Penguin Group
27 Wrights Lane, London W8 5TZ
Viking Penguin Inc., 375 Hudson Street, New York, New York 10014, USA
Penguin Books Australia Ltd, Ringwood, Victoria, Australia
Penguin Books Canada Ltd, 10 Alcorn Avenue, Toronto, Ontario, Canada M4V 3B2
Penguin Books (NZ) Ltd, 182–190 Wairau Road, Auckland 10, New Zealand

Penguin Books Ltd, Registered Offices: Harmondsworth, Middlesex, England

First published by Michael Joseph 1997
1 3 5 7 9 10 8 6 4 2

Typset in 11/12.5 pt Monophoto Sabon
Printed in England by Clays Ltd, St Ives plc

A CIP catalogue record for this book is available from the British Library

ISBN 0 7181 38821

Contents

Illustrations

Acknowledgments

AGAIN MY HOME CRITIC Nellie Flexner deserves special credit for reading the volume and improving its intelligibility. Jim Moore was always on call, and happily obliged my telephone enquiries about blasphemy trials or Bishop Wilberforce's grandmother. Bernie Lightman kindly read and commented on the 'Afterword' and parts of the text.

I owe a great debt to Huxley's great-granddaughter Angela Darwin, who allowed me to read her in-press book of letters between the Huxley women. *Your Affectionate Sister* is a tremendous resource which I could not have done without. She has gone on feeding me transcriptions and bracing herself for questions of the kind: 'Did Nettie allude to the socialist mob attacking Hal's bus in 1886?' 'Was the Birmingham caucus mooted in Huxley's letters home?' 'Why did Nettie change vicars?' 'Did she mention Oscar Wilde turning up one night?' (Imagine the stir caused by this velveteen embodiment of the new Hedonism, whose salvation by sin was a snub to Huxley's rational Puritanism!) The queries went on and on, I am afraid, but Angela was very understanding.

My research centred on the 5,000 Huxley letters in the Archives of Imperial College, London. Anne Barrett's help here was above and beyond the call of duty; she supplied information and could produce esoteric articles on tap. I actually used the 54 reels of microfilm of these letters, kindly furnished by Research Publications Ltd, PO Box 45, Reading RG1 8HF. These allowed me an intimacy with Huxley's daily correspondence which could not otherwise have been attained. I am grateful to Cristina Ashby at Research Publications for her generosity.

Many scholars and Huxley family historians discussed their

specialities with me: Jim Moore talked on aspects Darwinian and ideological; Bernie Lightman on points agnostic; Ralph Colp on medical matters; Eric Hollowday on microscopes; Sophie Forgan on that 'fungoid' growth of buildings (as H. G. Wells had it) at South Kensington; Jim Strick on spontaneous generation; Mario di Gregorio on Huxley's marginalia; Giacomo Scarpelli on points Italian; William Collier on John Collier; and Martin Cooke on Henrietta Huxley. Others who rallied or supplied material include Ruth Barton, Peter Bowler, Derek Freeman, David Knight, Ron Rainger, Marsha Richmond and Sonia Uyterhoeven. While Jim Secord and Evelleen Richards at the Huxley Centenary Conference at Imperial College in 1995 convinced me to wrap up my major conclusions in a separate section. A reflexive 'Afterword' connects the narrative text to the latest Huxley historiography.

To the following libraries, archivists and scholars I extend my thanks for access, help and hospitality, or for permission to quote from manuscript material: the American Philosophical Society for supplying a microfilm of their Huxley letters; John Thackray at the British Museum (Natural History); Perry O'Donovan of the Darwin Letters Project, Cambridge University Library; Frank James at the Royal Institution; Gill Furlong and Victoria Lane at University College London Manuscripts Library; C. A. Piggot, Royal Botanic Gardens, Kew; Christine Weideman, Yale University Library; Mary Sampson, The Royal Society; Joan Grattan, The Milton S. Eisenhower Library, Johns Hopkins University; Stella Newton, Oxford University Museum; Gillian F. Lonergan, Co-Operative Union, Manchester; Jennifer Jeynes, South Place Ethical Society; Solene Morris, Darwin Museum, Down House; AnneMarie Robinson, University of London Library; the British Library; and the Wellcome Institute for the History of Medicine, London.

A number of the illustrations have never been published before. For help in obtaining them and for permission to publish I am grateful to Sir Andrew Huxley, Clare Huxley, Richard Milner/Michael Huxley, William Collier and Hilary Buzzard. Likewise my thanks go to the Archives at Imperial College for the liberty to use many photographs from their collection.

Sir Andrew again graciously consented to my publishing extracts from his grandfather's letters.

Finally my editor Susan Watt increased the comprehensibility of the final product. My thanks to her and the Michael Joseph/Penguin team.

The Apostle Paul of the New Teaching

T. H. HUXLEY WAS DUBBED *The Devil's Disciple* in volume one. Of course it was a provocative subtitle with multiple meanings. The Devil was Darwin. But, as in George Bernard Shaw's play, Huxley turns out to be doing the Lord's work: the moralizing 'agnostic' (he coined the word) was ridding society of its idolatry and establishing a new evolutionary priesthood.[1]

The young hothead had harnessed the forces of liberal Dissent on his way to the presidency of the Parliament of Science, the British Association for the Advancement of Science. He was the self-perceived poor boy, one of Thackeray's thrusting blades, trying to turn all that 'symbolic capital' – the medals and kudos – into real cash.[2] His conversion of knowledge into a paying commodity was a major step in the making of a salaried scientist.

Evolution's High Priest takes us from 1870 to Huxley's death in 1895. It shows the Darwinians in place, underpinning the new social order. As the bottom dropped out of history and the Victorians peered, horrified, into the unfathomable abyss of geological time,[3] it was the silver-haired Huxley who cast a stabilizing anchor from the evolutionary ship.

That social order was increasingly professional as the second industrial revolution got under way. Northern capital was flowing into London, and the steel barons were investing in more than the stockmarket.[4] Quakers and Congregationalists, munitions manufacturers and factory free-traders were funding Huxley. These social alignments become more explicit in this volume, as we get beneath the scientist's neutral veneer.

The Victorian era was 'hinged' about 1870 with the industrial retooling. So was Huxley's life. He moved to the forerunner of

Imperial College, honed a new laboratory biology and started training schoolmasters for the industrial regions. It was the beginning of that base-up reconstruction which ensured science's take-off. Money was switching from charity to education, the street arabs were being swept into schools, the Divinely ordered society was becoming Darwinianly ordered and the middle classes were beginning to look to Nature for their ultimate explanations. Huxley was there, at every turn. The *Times* thought the Victorian period unfathomable without taking him into account, and the *Pall Mall Gazette* saw his hand 'in all the moving subjects of the day'.[5]

Huxley's blistering satires on Anglican supernaturalism and Oxbridge privilege have helped to distort our view of the Victorians. Just as Oscar Wilde parodied Huxley's Puritan generation, so Huxley caricatured Bishop Wilberforce's day. He saw strangled priests around evolution's cradle and wickedly lampooned Gladstone's first-century beliefs; and he finally made Christ himself rebuke Victorian Christianity. This was delicious black propaganda for his rival scientific priesthood. And successful too: he persuaded sceptical, Classically-trained politicians that science was essential to an industrial nation. It became an arm of the State, controlled by Huxley. But his scientists incorporated all their mid-Victorian prejudices into the new civil service biology. The slamming lab doors shut out the women and workers and priests. Inside the lab, the new man, having trouble with the 'new woman', could bolster Darwin's gendered and class image of evolutionary 'reality'.

Biography gets us around the sepia image of a static, strait-laced Victorian age.[6] We can plot one man's trajectory through a seething century – indeed, understand why the laces slowly straitened as the old radicals became the new reactionaries. We find Huxley deflecting the spotlight from his own ideological assumptions. He made 'neutral' science a moral Saladin's sword. And a political one: he recast Darwinism in the middle of the 'Great Depression' (1874–96) to contain his workers' Leftward drift – turning open-competition radicalism into a darker 'Social Darwinism'.

So in *Evolution's High Priest* the sets change. I still use what Jim Moore – my co-author on *Darwin* – cannily called a 'ciné theory of narration'.[7] Too cannily, perhaps, for *Huxley*'s scene-painting style left some imagining that it was a misplaced attempt in postmodern times at *cinéma vérité*. But *Huxley* is no fly-on-the-wall documentary of the Darwinian coup. The ciné analogy was meant to evoke a highly-mediated celluloid construct, where the camera pans across a stage (context) to catch actors reading lines, while pulling focus periodically to reveal the lavish 'sets' which give their words meaning. It invites readers to become film critics and discuss an intricately reconstructed image.

Although the Director's voice is disguised (it only intrudes in an 'Afterword'), I regard *Huxley* as a contribution to the new contextual history of science. It looks at evolution's use in order to understand the class, religious or political interests involved. It raises questions about new practices and new workplaces. How did the vicarage view of a designed, happy world in 1830 become the cold, causal and Calvinistic evolutionary vista 40 years later – that passionless cosmos reflected in an impersonal laboratory?[8] Put simply, *Huxley* shows the external world changing with the social world. The 'General' was marketing the 'new Nature' to give his low-status professionals more esteem in an Oxbridge-dominated culture. This is a story of Class, Power and Propaganda.

Not for nothing did the *Daily News* call him the 'Apostle Paul of the new teaching'. His singular sort of science – based on a non-miraculous, cause-and-effect Nature – was for battering down seminary doors. Evolution cradled within an agnostic framework seems obvious today, precisely because we have inherited the victor's mantle. But it was far from obvious in 1870. Then the public schools shunned science as useless and dehumanizing. Their world was of character-forming Classics and Theology. Oxford and Cambridge were finishing schools for prosperous Anglicans. Against 145 Classics Fellowships at Oxford in 1870, there were four in science.[9] The stacked odds explain Huxley's single-minded assault on the ivy edifices. And by the time the knighted legions stood over his grave in 1895 there had been a total re-evaluation of knowledge. Science and the middle-class professionals were in. Evolution had become 'natural'.

This is the human story behind these sea-changes. Huxley continued to be crushed under an inverted financial pyramid, chocked with boozy relations. The sober Darwinian was trying to hold the lid down, trying to usher in a new scientific morality as the gin-sodden floozies threatened scandal. Here was the reverse side of Huxley's public face. And it remains partly disguised. Huxley's extended family is unknown to historians, and my account throws up more questions than answers. Given the tragedy of his daughter Marian's illness (in chapter 8), one wonders what lay behind his sister-in-law's shriek 'No wonder you drove Mady mad.' Was this just the deranged raving of a widow high on chloral and gin? More needs to be done on the relationship of these talented Victorian daughters with their pressured, patriarchal fathers.[10] If nothing else, tragedy and trauma provide a continuity after 1870 as the rational tornado worked like ten men to support dozens of dependants.

The sexagenarian scourge continued to fascinate, just as the *enfant terrible* had. There was more to Huxley than a brilliant early-peaking scientist. He continued to change hats, becoming the supreme cultural critic – part political fixer in private, part matinée idol in public; charismatic from his holier-than-thou agnosticism, authoritative from his command of the 'new Nature'. He had his finger on the pulse; or rather he speeded up the pulse, making the Victorian heart thump with his goading talk of the 'sin of faith'. It explains why Beatrice Webb, arriving late on the scene, should consider him 'greater as a man than a scientific thinker'.[11]

But we cannot snap judge so chimerical a character. He had the confidence to remake himself with the times. The idiosyncratic *enragé* of *The Devil's Disciple* becomes the stern moralizer. The self-perceived 'plebeian' transforms into the powerful Privy Councillor. The scientific radical rebukes Liberal Prime Ministers and takes tea with Tory ones. And every now and then the scowling mask shatters, to reveal a smile (so rarely captured in photographs). It was the beam of a brilliant boy, having arrived in Olympus to find it intellectually empty. The last two photographs typify the contrast: the public face of the Privy Councillor, and the endearing – and disarming – 'phiz' that was, perhaps, ultimately the man.

1870–1884

Marketing the 'New Nature'

1

The Gun in the Liberal Armoury

NETTIE WAS DAY-DREAMING. At Liverpool in 1870, she was riding in the Mayor's 'great gilded swinging coach', amid the glitz and pomp. Beside her was Hal, the city's guest of honour, lionized as President of the British Association for the Advancement of Science. Suddenly she went cold, fearing that she would wake up and 'see the whole affair transformed into rats mice & a pumpkin as Cinderella did'.

But the bubble was not to burst, nor would she return to rags. Thomas Henry Huxley's rise from slum doctoring to Prime Minister of Science was real. Potent forces had created a new phenomenon, a star spokesman, a cultural critic who took Nature as his text. Huxley was the celebrity of the moment whose 'noble phiz' graced *Vanity Fair* and the *Illustrated London News*.[1]

Those sweeping forces were religious as much as secular. Huxley's Darwinian naturalism welled up with a rising radical Dissent. The Northern industrialists, muddy-booted chapel-goers, swore by science and technological progress. Theirs was a wheeze-and-snort Dissent to undermine the miraculous props under the Anglican throne. While Dissenters talked of the 'sin of conformity', Huxley stretched it to the 'sin of faith'.[2] He took Dissent to its 'agnostic' limit, discarding the last idolatrous trace.

Dissent was still eating away at the Church's State privileges. Even Oxford and Cambridge, so long the symbols of wealth and rank (a tassled cap had remained a sign of noble birth at Oxford until 1870), were losing their Anglican monopoly. On 16 June 1871 Gladstone finally repealed the hated Tests Acts, letting non-Anglicans take degrees at the ancient universities. Here was all that Dissenters had demanded for 50 years – with the exception of disestablishing the

Church, severing it from the State. (And Huxley still regarded 'the preservation of this Establishment' as unjustified.[3])

He was riding the Dissenting crest. The industrial barons were his family friends – steel tycoons who had come up the hard way, through the machine shops. These were the hard men who breathed open competition and enthused over Huxley's Great technocratic Britain. They had been marginals, like Huxley – men excluded from Oxbridge, the bench, the elite hospitals, indeed all aspects of the power of the State: but now they too were moving to the centre with their honorary LLDs and knighthoods for services to industry and Empire. It was telling that Hal and Nettie retreated to Sir Joseph Whitworth's 'lovely' Derbyshire pile after the 1870 BAAS presidential campaign. Here they spent five days relaxing, marvelling at the great iron machinery 'invented by himself'.[4] This marriage of Dissenting technology and marginal academia was the Victorian counter-culture come of age.

Whitworth was the embodiment of Northern industry – self-made son of a Congregationalist minister, a one-time journeyman-mechanic whose precision tools had made machine industry possible. The Crimean fiasco had him devising the devastating Whitworth .45 rifle for the War Office. A gruff committee-hating inventor still getting used to his baronetcy, he was happy to offer the Huxleys a wing of his Matlock mansion. His factory was turning out arms to extend Britannia's imperial reach. Special Whitworth steel was used to manufacture cannon and £100,000 of the profits went into science scholarships. Whitworth was a man for that dining coterie, the X-Club – John Tyndall (another friend) lectured on Whitworth's guns, and the Club's mathematician William Hirst was ultimately offered a directorship in the company. With Huxley articulating a radical Dissenting cause-and-effect view of the universe, they got on famously. The Huxleys spent two more 'truly enjoyable' days at Sir Joseph's Manchester town house.[5] Then it was off to Thomas Ashton's cotton mill before coming back to London. The journey was symbolic of Huxley's ideological trajectory.

Technology was making its extraordinary impact on the Victorian age. In 1871 the Huxleys had a nearby Underground, Marlborough Station, which meant that Sunday-evening guests arrived dappled in soot. In 1872 the mayors of London and Adelaide talked by telegraph, spanning the world in an electric click where Huxley's letters had once taken months. The machines lured a new generation. Young Jim – son of Huxley's 'broken down' and asylum-bound brother James – remained at the Royal School of Mines at Uncle Hal's expense. No high-flyer, he persevered at chemistry and metallurgy and would become an analytical chemist in a Sheffield steelworks. The industrial connections were riveted by marriage; the beaux were no longer doctors, even if 'Modern medicine', as Huxley said in industrial Manchester, was 'a kind of engineering'. Twenty-five-year-old Alice Cooke, daughter of Hal's tipsy sister Ellen, was walking out with Arthur Heath, who worked on the Great Northern Line.[6]

But Britain's industrial lead was vanishing. The prospect of losing their world supremacy shocked the mid-Victorians, and the flames of panic were fanned by Huxley's ginger group. He claimed that every 'third-rate, poverty-stricken German university' carried out more research than Oxford or Cambridge, overplaying this as the cause of her industrial might.[7] And yet there was no denying that Prussia's polytechnic schools were breeding a new dedicated industrialist, when Oxbridge disdained the factory manager (indeed, had barred him as a Dissenter to this time). Huxley's activists could now claim to speak in the national interest; the State needed them, needed their technical programmes and their expertise.

The theme was aired at Huxley's Working Men's College in Southwark. This self-betterment tech gave Huxley his 'plebeian' platform. He lured sympathetic speakers across the Thames: the *Fortnightly*'s editor John Morley, and the charismatic Yankee Unitarian Moncure Conway, that 'queer specimen of a latter day prophet', to discuss co-education among the sexes. The self-inflated poet Francis Palgrave came here to bemoan the national decline. With Germany moving ahead, Britain might be 'no longer the premier power', Principal Huxley piped up after Palgrave's warning, but we could 'become a greater nation' by developing every individual's faculties.[8]

Science would make the full man, hone his critical faculties, and it was in the national interest. This was Huxley's pitch in the 1870s. After a Transatlantic trip Whitworth too warned Manchester's foundrymen about America's capacity, pointing out the futility of matching her machines if 'you have not intelligent hands to work them'. The marginals – non-Oxbridge academics and chapel industrialists – were hammering on the government's door, demanding aid for training the 'intelligent hands'. The *Spectator* reminded Gladstone that the state had a duty to support science no less than to print money, and some saw the two as synonymous.

The clamour persisted during the Franco-Prussian war in 1870. Germany's was the 'most wonderful military engine ever seen on the face of the earth', Edwin Lankester told *Nature* readers. But then they were 'a scientific people', he added, rubbing it in. Every incident was played up to jolt a prickly government, including the capsizing of the revolutionary – and unstable – revolving-turret warship HMS *Captain* in 1870, which showed the need for physicists in the docks.[9] The tumult had its effect. Gladstone set up a Commission on Scientific Instruction, headed by the Duke of Devonshire, the President of the Iron and Steel Institute. Huxley, co-opted as a Commissioner, was tasting real power.

T. H. Huxley knew a family stability that the other Huxleys lacked. Home was a microcosm of advanced Victorian society, with an Anglican mother supporting an agnostic father. By 1870 the decade of baby-rearing was over. 'Babs' – the last baby, Ethel – had been baptized to Hal's usual growl, even though Nettie justified it as a vaccination against sin. A succession of ungodly Xs had compliantly stood as godparents: Busk for the lamented Noel, Hooker for Leonard, the Lubbocks for Nettie and Ethel, and Tyndall for Harry. This religious difference between husband and wife seemed surprisingly frictionless, as it did between Hal and the liberal Dean Stanley or Nettie's emancipist vicar Llewelyn Davies. For a supposedly anti-Christian bulldog, Hal had his Broad Church backers inside the family and out. Didn't he head a workers' college courtesy of the Christian Socialists? They supported his intellectual reformation and valued the bulldog's domesticated side. The publisher Alexander Macmillan saw 'so much real Christianity in Huxley that if it were parcelled out among all the men, women, and children in the British Islands, there would be enough to save the soul of every one'.[10]

Father was a mix of fun and formality. Incongruously, for a chap famous for his plebeian prose, he was called 'Pater' by the children (pronounced *Patter*). That was how he had referred to his own father, but it was a hard word which said something of his rising respectability. That brought its own worries: the higher he went, the greater his trepidation at the antics of the relations. Sister Ellen was unregenerate; a governess now, she was still begging and boozing. Her pay plus Hal's allowance 'ought to be sufficient for her wants', Nettie said, 'but somehow it never is'; and her own blowsy daughter Nelly bounced between gin and men in a 'deplorable, wasted life'. The lack of any welfare net had the overstretched *paterfamilias* helping where he could. When his old messmate Archie McClatchie died '& left a couple of boys without any adequate provision', Huxley pulled strings to get them into the Medical Benevolent College. The caring streak betrayed his own precarious past. At least brother George's widow, Polly, was off the family books now. In 1870 she married the ruddy-faced Patrick Duffy, a tax inspector. Nettie knew that pride and prejudice would bar 'any intimacy between Hal and him'.[11] There was a certain pique that an Irish Catholic had taken George's place. Polly too would slowly become estranged.

For the Agnostic Pope, intent on proving that Darwinians were not degenerates, drunken sisters and debauched nieces were to become a threat. An agnostic's respectability was always doubted, and it came as a surprise to bishops' wives that Huxley was 'an affectionate father'! Even the domestics held him in suspicion. The master, trying to prise the inebriate cook from the kitchen floor with 'Bridget . . . you ought to be ashamed of yourself', was put down with, 'I am not ashamed of myself, I am a good christian woman. I am not an infidel like you'.[12] That was the problem. For a man edging into society by preaching a new scientific morality, whose Sunday dining guests were the high and mighty, there could be no scandal.

Huxley's black eyes fixed on that unique colloquium, the Metaphysical Society, where the cardinals of knowledge decided the meaning of life. Unlike Darwin's his mind wasn't a whirl of evolutionary physics so much as existentialist metaphysics. On the second Tuesday each month he left his museum to go into conclave. The Metaphysical saw the great theologians and thinkers, politicians, poets and Positivists, men of science, letters and of the cloth, gather to ponder the great Victorian imponderables, the reign of law versus the grace of God, cosmic determinism versus free will. The society lacked only a Jew and a Muslim to make its denominational zoo complete, and like any zoo it was part forum for conservation in a changing world and part circus. As the two best debaters, Huxley and his opposite, the engaging Anglo-Catholic W. G. Ward, staked their positions, they developed a respect for one another that grew into personal warmth.[13] Of course the society never got past a hearty armistice.

Huxley thrived on the '"Oecumenical" freefight' on a Tuesday night. His 'new Nature', self-contained and evolving unaided, pulled the supernatural supports from a static Anglican (and Catholic) society. By 1870, as the Dissenters came in from the cold, Huxley's professionals were pushing a causal, determined science onto the cultural agenda. Here was the source of the Victorian 'crisis of faith': new social groups pitching for power in the name of the 'new Nature'. And the key issue – Free Will and future redemption versus cosmic uniformity – was the overriding concern at the Metaphysical. Agnosticism helped Huxley elude his detractors. It presented the man of science as non-aligned; it deflected any inquest from his own axiomatic beliefs (and Nature's undeviating causality was as unprovable as the Holy Ghost). And it allowed Huxley to take the offensive. He would sit scratching cartoons of his antagonists before cross-examining them in that 'rich and resonant voice'. Always he would steer the debate back onto the miraculous 'in the manner of a great criminal lawyer'. He traded on Hume's *reductio ad absurdums*; if the soul was immortal, it must be 'ingenerable', and thus have existed for an eternity independent of us. Or if it was somehow connected to our mental faculties, wouldn't animals have one? Hence Huxley's mocking Metaphysical paper, 'Has a Frog a Soul?'[14]

It was so congenial. It should also have been *in camera*, a private conclave of Church and Science. But word was out, and 'A lady told my wife all about these propositions of mine [against the soul's immortality]', he reported. Not that it mattered, for 'I cannot well be blacker than I am in the general mind'. Or greyer as society liberalized. A pale grey if Gladstone is to be believed. The Prime Minister apparently told Huxley's old Haslar Naval Hospital messmate and physician Dr Andrew Clark of the 'pleasure he had derived from your discourses'.[15] But the lion-hunting Clark would have said that. He was using Huxley to get into the Society himself.

That miraculous claims should be subjected to scientific scrutiny was a leitmotif of *Lay Sermons*. This potboiling book with a moral message 'will enrich you', Tyndall told Huxley (keeping his priorities straight). The riches were elusive, even with a reprint in four months, a cheap abridged edition in 1871, and a French translator lined up by Matthew Arnold.[16] But it was success enough for Huxley to start planning a series of volumes.

In America the response was as good, with the liberal *Nation* declaring Huxley a safe scientific guide. The *Nation* was moving for the South's post-war reconstruction, but in a bleak Montgomery, turned into a carpetbagging 'den of thieves', Huxley's sister Lizzie wondered whether the *Sermons* would not shatter the safeguards further. She wanted to know 'how far you carry your proposition of the regenerating effect of human discovery', and 'What you displace . . . by it'. It was a religious probing by the sister who had given him his religious training. 'I w^{d} have given any thing to be able to look up from the page, and ask you the questions', she said.[17]

America beckoned. He 'has had very pressing solicitations', Lizzie heard. Huxley was in the van of the Transatlantic science movement. He was on the committee of E. L. Youmans' International Science

Series – books which would give 'popular expression to the leading advances of thought'.[18] The American Youmans, despite bad sight, had gone into publishing, and he met many of his authors around Huxley's table. Huxley himself was slated to write the first, *Bodily Motion and Consciousness*. Not that it saw the light (nor did another, *The Races of Mankind*), but the series was Huxley to a tee. Its spirit was proselytizing, its territory was Darwinian, and its red covers promised a natural legitimation of social progress. Here were the pastors of science extracting moral and secular values from evolution and the 'Phenomena of Human nature'.[19] And with 40 million Americans it promised to be a lucrative business.

How much so became plain when Huxley hosted his New York publisher William Appleton at the Athenaeum in 1871. Appleton & Co. was a huge concern: its school department could sell a million copies of a single title. America shared Britain's love/hate relationship with Huxley and the firm was desperate for a publicity tour. American intellectuals were behind him. The Badlands explorer Ferdinand Vandiveer Hayden was typical in lapping up the latest Huxley article each time he returned to civilization. In 1870, back from Santa Fe and publishing his maps of Dakota and Nebraska, the chief of the US Geological Survey of the Territories saw Huxley's views being 'rapidly embraced among the Scientific and other Professional men of this Country'. Huxley was begged to make the crossing. Rumours were already sparking lunatic letters declaring that such 'ignorant jackanapes' as Huxley and Tyndall would be 'kicked out' if they dared to show their 'impudent faces on the American Continent', so Hal and 'brother John' were keen to get going. 'Perhaps in three or four years', Nettie told Lizzie, who had not seen her brother since 1846.[20]

The word 'evolution' became common currency in the 1870s. For a decade 'Darwinism' had been the term to cover a multitude of sins. But the 'Darwinians' had been an undifferentiated lot, who clustered for strength and tended to make little distinction between life's genetic development and Darwin's explanation of Natural Selection. Attracting radicals, atheists, socialists and free-traders, 'Darwinism became notorious as much for the friends it kept as for its political enemies'.[21] But at the end of the 1860s the groups were peeling off, emphasizing their internal differences. It was no coincidence that as the word 'evolution' came in and the dissidents fell out, Huxley devised his 'agnosticism' to legitimate only the secular and naturalistic end of the spectrum.

The lost souls were departing. The spiritualists and socialists regrouped behind that perpetual dissident Alfred Russel Wallace. (In 1869 Wallace suggested that the savage had an over-endowed brain for his simple life: so much grey matter was a spirit-bequeathed preadaptation for a civilized cooperative life. Wallace – the co-inventor of Natural Selection – had removed man from its arena.) The Spiritualists marched off to the Millennium.[22] The providential evolutionists went off in another direction, behind the Catholic St George Mivart, for whom life was a fulfilment of God's plan. After the shake-out, Darwinism remained an umbrella organization, and even Huxley diverged on key points. In the 1860s he had harped on the 'living fossils', creatures which had persisted unchanged through geological time. Where Darwin had nature select from tiny variations, Huxley had been happy with larger jumps; where Darwin transported his species to islands by wind and raft, Huxley had invoked drowned continents. At times all they seemed to share was a faith in evolutionary naturalism.[23]

Given Huxley's own deviance, the problem is to understand how and why he designated other evolutionists as heretics. Take University College's pathology professor and rising star H. Charlton Bastian. He was just as materialistic, just as committed to nature's continuum. So much so that he insisted on the continuous chemical production of microbes at the fount of life, feeding Darwin's adaptive spread. In the 1860s Bastian too was part of that nebulous 'Darwinism', one of the new generation, younger than the young guard, and initially supported by Huxley.

'Transubstantiation will be nothing to this if it turns out to be true', Huxley laughed as Bastian went public on spontaneous generation in 1870. Was the simplest life continually being generated from organic chemicals, all around us? Bastian's bottles of boiled hay bristled with microbes after a few days, and this evidence was good enough for part of London's medical community, traditionally an evolutionary hotbed. When the slanging started, the sharp Bastian traded on the clinician's superior experience. The doctors too could lay claim to experimental expertise, and they posed a professional threat to Huxley and Tyndall. Bastian ignored Huxley's advice 'not to publish till all results [were] retested'. This stung, and Huxley saw Bastian 'going out of his way to be . . . offensive'. In the territorial jockeying, Bastian was tarred as 'a clumsy experimenter & an uncritical reasoner',[24] and Huxley pushed deep into a study of *Penicillium* and yeast to suggest that Bastian's spontaneously appearing bacteria were part of the mould's life-cycle. He wooed the electorate, travelling to Leeds and Bradford 'turning an honest penny out of Yeast',[25] and converting his talks into a *Contemporary* essay. Darwin's inner circle presented itself as more reliable than the established doctors.

The young guard was codifying Darwinism, hardening it into a Nicene creed. What had been nebulous became specific and doctrinal about 1870. Only by establishing a creed could the idea of a 'heretic' become real. A one-off matter-to-life event, deep in primeval times, was acceptable. Tyndall's purplest prose which made us children of the cosmos was acceptable. But a rival medical profession trading on the endogenous chemical production of fever-producing poisons and parasites was not (Huxley and Tyndall were singular in adopting the new germ theory of disease). Bastian was an Emperor Julian pointing back to the discredited transformism of the pagan years. Lamarck's crudities (as many saw them) had been kept alive through the dark ages at University College by Bastian's disreputable teacher, the atheist and reputed homosexual Robert Grant. Grant's 'advocacy was not calculated to advance the cause', said a prejudiced Huxley (intent on putting Darwinism on a more respectable footing). The Frenchman Lamarck had believed that life's evolutionary 'ascent' required a continual replenishment at the base. And the 78-year-old Francophile Grant was happy to see Bastian's atoms 'select their partners and waltz off in a quaternary danse of life' (note his French *danse*).[26] But old has-beens and young upstarts were no longer considered part of 'the cause'. 'Pope Huxley' was beginning to use his considerable powers of excommunication.

The General was angling for a new barracks. The Royal School of Mines in Piccadilly was cramped and he needed space, a certain sort of space. For a professional clawing power – no Darwin, with his country house for experiments, no clergyman in his pastoral realm – only the state could provide a rival laboratory space. The laboratory: it was a novel concept which signalled a new approach to education. Huxley's men denied Oxbridge claims that the Classics moulded a gentleman's character. Truth did not come from incestuously recycling Greek texts; it had to be found out, experimentally. The *arriviste* teachers contrasted this direct probing of 'reality' with Oxbridge pedagogy. It was their strategy for cultural domination; their truths would come from the 'new Nature'. The Department of Science and Art now had 30,000 students countrywide and the 1870 Education Act meant proliferating schoolmasters who needed training. More than anything Huxley needed a laboratory where they could be taught the practical Truths of the 'new Nature'. Their knowledge was to make all other ''ologies ... so much book-wormery'.[27]

But a lab meant moving from Central London. Jermyn Street was a glorified geology museum. It had forced Huxley to knuckle down to taxonomic practice; and in arranging the fossils he had become a dedicated palaeontologist.[28] But it gave him no practical facilities. This was the more embarrassing because the vaunted superiority of science lay in its experimental verification.

By default he had come to see sprawling South Kensington as his only option. That strange *sui generis* suburb in the west, all empty plots, building tips and museums, was being turned into a Germanic 'culture centre' with the proceeds of Great Exhibition. The new Albert Hall stood at its north border, while the lot at the bottom was earmarked for the Natural History Museum. It met Huxley's territorial ambitions. With Richard Owen set to get his 'temple' here – that Romanesque Cathedral of Nature to snub the pagan Renaissance – Huxley could face the 'old fool', matching him building for building. It meant swopping Piccadilly for an unmade Exhibition Road (as it became).[29] But the drawbacks were outweighed by the prospect of labs and a proper red-brick science school. The move would symbolize the intellectual shift in the nineteenth century – the switch from museum display to that new knowledge-manufacturing site, the laboratory.[30]

He had close links with the empire-building Henry Cole, Secretary of the Department of Science and Art and South Kensington's effective creator (Cole even coined the name 'South Kensington'). And powerful allies inside the Whitehall machine had become family friends: the Liberal Minister and former Governor of the Bank of England, George Goschen, lobbied for him in Gladstone's Cabinet, while Lucy Goschen had the children to Admiralty parties. Hence one ironmaster's voice in the Commons exaggerating about 'Professor Huxley's anatomical preparations [having to be] made in a dark closet about eight feet square'.[31]

But Huxley had his own political machine. On the Devonshire Committee he was joined by X-Clubber and Liberal MP John Lubbock and his old examiner William Sharpey, with *Nature*'s editor Norman Lockyer as Secretary. Huxley led witnesses to condemn the cramped Jermyn Street, and he out-manoeuvred his old boss Murchison, the imperial swell with the Belgravia trappings. (Murchison had wanted to remain with the Geological Survey close to London's clubland.) Murchison died in 1871, and with this stiff-lipped military geologist went a world of upper-class values, and the last major obstruction. The Committee recommended the amalgamation of the Royal School of Mines with the Royal College of Chemistry and their removal to South Kensington. Still Huxley pushed for more: he had always seen zoology and botany united at a deep cellular level, and a botany department would make it 'a proper Biological School'. 'It would be glorious', he told Hooker.[32]

His strategy paid off. The *Times* saw him inveigling the Committee, and no protest of innocence could shake the feeling that his aim was 'an imposing National College of Science'.[33] Even if the call for laboratories came in a period of national frustration about American advances and the German war-machine, the net result was more State power to Huxley's group. Huxley, the mover and shaker who audited the accounts and signed the cheques, who recast the prospectus and liaised with commissioners, had always been powerful beyond his teaching status. This proved it.

The government-built 'Science Schools' at South Kensington was the first fruit of the politicking. Costing £66,000, with a 186-foot frontage, the four-floor building shouted science's importance. It had been intended as a Royal Navy school, but big labs could be made out of the long rooms designed for naval models. With creamy terracotta, ornate arcades and figures depicting the seven ages of man, it was a match for Owen's projected museum over the road. Huxley would be facing the 'old-fashioned' temple from his modern laboratory,[34] and two more different symbols could not be imagined.

In summer 1871 scaffolding still shrouded the edifice. The bewhiskered professor glowed in the building's red mottled tints. The *Times* thought the façade 'a sight good for eyes tired of the endless stucco'.[35] Inside he crossed the mosaic marble floor laid by convict labour and swept up the huge central stairwell to his top floor. Peering over the balcony, he looked onto the glass dome of the 54-foot lecture theatre below, whose 60-foot ceiling would give his mellifluous voice its accentuating echo. On the top floor was his joy: a 60-foot laboratory, based on the Berlin and Bonn models. This was to be his biological seminary where he could turn the trainees 'into scientific missionaries to convert the Christian Heathen'.[36]

If science was only '*trained and organised common sense*' (someone who saw himself as a self-educated 'plebeian' would say that) then common sense would need training and organizing. Here he could mobilize the teachers who would return to the factory towns. When the first batch arrived for their practicals in June 1871, the interior was still unfurnished.[37] As an interim measure, he had to requisition the ground floor of the South Kensington Museum (the forerunner of the Victoria and Albert). He jerry-built a lab here. Tables and apparatus were set up, preparations readied, 20 cheap, £6 microscopes laid on.[38] So much groundwork that Gladstone's Minister for Education was faced with a £750 bill. But he did sanction the employment of three demonstrators, each paid £100 for the six-week session.

The General's one-man army was a thing of the past. In came the succession of brilliant assistants. The adoring Michael Foster from University College, Professor William Rutherford, who had set up its own physiology labs at King's College London. And that bellicose giant, Ray Lankester. Like so many aspiring sons of Dissenting reformers, Ray had rung the social changes with a First from Oxford. The Congregationalist's son typified that second-generation social-climb to Oxbridge,[39] clambering into the Anglican seat of power where the boys dissipated their fathers' Nonconformist values. Not that Ray had anything but contempt for Oxford's 'disgusting toadying' elitism.[40]

Edwin and Phebe's son was naturally an adept microscopist, and the 23-year-old followed his hero Huxley with papers on monkey brains, fossil fishes and the invertebrate's cell layers. In 1870 the tyro had already published a crushing rebuke to the Darwinian apostate St George Mivart.[41] A freethinking evolutionist, and a fighting critic of Oxford's 'medieval folly',[42] the belligerent Ray was passed over at Oxford for a Readership in Anatomy (it did not help that his father had just blasted Oxford's Classicism in the *Quarterly Journal of Science*). So Ray – the boy who had played truant to hear Huxley lecture – toured the German pathology labs learning the latest staining techniques and returned fresh from Haeckel's Thuringian hills to his 'father-in-science' in June 1871.

He joined the team to drill the first 38 masters and solitary schoolmistress. They were to be introduced to microscopes and taught the conventions in a crash course. Ironically, given the patronizing attitudes about the unsuitability of petticoats, the school-marm took the end-of-term prize. Lankester thought that the shock would spur the men on, so long as they did not set up a 'trades union' closed shop.[43] But there could be no lock-out.

The ramshackle beginnings reflected the scaffold-and-navvy state of South Kensington. Everywhere were shirt-sleeved Royal Engineers, drafted in by the War Office as free labour.[44] Swarms of squaddies completed the picture of regimented science on a war footing. South Kensington was militarized down to its very foundations (put in by the sappers).

Territorial rivalry with a wealthy Church accounted for Huxley's 'military metaphor' – that portrayal of rational science vanquishing the forces of obscurantism. It was a martial image he shared with street religions such as the Salvation Army. But *real* uniforms, those gave the image its authority and science its national purpose. Huxley likened himself to a shilling 'recruiting sergeant', enlisting men 'into the army of science'.[45] The blaze of red at South Ken gave this real meaning. And the Departmental barracks had more than shillings to give away: it had Whitworth's £100,000 in scholarships.

Military precision was admired by the Department's desk-bound head, Henry Cole. It was he who put the Crimean veterans into his top brass. First came Lieutenant John Donnelly, a Royal Engineer who had shown such initiative in clearing the site that Cole drafted him in as adjutant. The ebullient Donnelly would rise through the ranks without ever leaving South Kensington. With Huxley's backing he become the 'Secretary for Science', and he repaid his debt: 'why should you have [another] assistant?' he joked, mimicking the Treasury penny-pinchers. 'Is it not a complete waste of the money of the State? If you can black your own boots why should you not? No; there is no authority . . . Therefore if I were you I should engage Parker'.[46] And so Huxley took on W. K. Parker, professor-to-be at the College of Surgeons and an anatomical pedant with a wandering style (like a dog going home, sniffing everywhere, laughed Huxley). But he knew every millimetre of a bird's skull, and such confounding detail had won him a Royal Medal. Huxley's own team was becoming a crack unit.

The professionals played up their 'expertise' and linked it to national prestige, trying to make science indispensable. Their hijacking of the Devonshire bandwagon led to jibes about the 'Brompton pluralists' creating jobs for the boys. They wanted an expanded professional role: the replacement of Classics-trained advisers, a Ministry of Science, proper science schooling, even experts on public health authorities and as juries in cases involving insanity.[47]

Huxley's anthropological science too would follow Britannia's long reach. The Colonial Office in 1870–1 began its photographic round-up of the natives. Dispatches in diplomatic bags told of Huxley's needs, and governors photographed to his specifications, standing aborigines beside a rule. From Cape Town, Australia, Sierra Leone, the Falklands, West Indies, Ceylon, Formosa and Tierra del Fuego came sorry accounts of conquest, accentuated by photos of dejected faces. Here were Kandyan chiefs and Cape Town bushmen stripped naked in convict chains. Some enlightened governors would only photograph subjects unclothed with their permission; indeed, the missionaries having pointed out their shame, a few refused.[48]

Nothing like it had been tried. With the ladies gone from the societies, these brooding images could be used to render Huxley's talks on the geography of mankind more graphic. The London Stereoscopic and Photographic Company even sold its own 'extraordinary photographs', pandering to public voyeurism on Victoria's far-flung peoples.[49] Unclothed black men and women (white nudity was unthinkable) reinforced the image of the moral inferiority and child-like innocence. Ironically the new anthropology saw these peoples in a pre-Darwinian light as Stone Age survivors. They represented the infancy of the human species. They were the emotional tykes of the Empire who needed stern guidance. Paternal responsibility was another attitude ushered into science by evangelicalism. But at the end of the day, Huxley's collation was part of a Colonial Office project to stamp the subject races as an aid to British rule.

Science pushed into the over-civilized areas at home as brusquely. As the Oxbridge colleges lost their religious bar, liberals such as Revd Benjamin Jowett tried to put science into the exams. Jowett had liberally kicked old Anglicanism in *Essays and Reviews* – and been liberally kicked back (he lost his fees for ten years as Greek Professor for heresy). The changing times told as he became the new Master of Balliol[50] and put Huxley up on his Oxford forays. Perhaps he put Huxley up for more. It was only the 'tremendous shindy' started by Revd Edward Pusey, the High Anglican who had charged Jowett with heresy, that stopped Oxford's revisionists nominating the agnostic for a Doctorate of Civil Laws in 1870. Darwin got it in order to keep a worse devil out, 'oh Coryphaeus diabolicus'.

At Cambridge too Huxley's word counted. He named the man for Trinity's new Praelectorship of physiology. Michael Foster, still grieving the death of his young wife and with 'two little bairns' to support, got the job. With the Tests Bill going through there was nothing to stop a Baptist-turned-agnostic. He joined that second-generation migration to the old seminaries, even though his father had set his heart on seeing him in a chair at University College.[51] With Foster went the London expertise to found a physiology lab in the virgin territory of the fens.

And at that birthplace of English academic physiology, University College, Huxley was just as active. When wealthy philanthropists wanted to do 'something more for science', he had them endow chairs here.[52] As an examiner, he boomed the need for physiological practice among its medical students, and he was in the thick of the politicking to establish a Faculty of Science.[53] Huxley put his money, or at least his son, where his mouth was. Len climbed out of the Gower Street tube daily and walked past UC's classical portico to his class at University College School. It seemed the natural choice, sharing the 'godless college's' Nonconformist origins and progressive regime. The boy did not have his father's lightning mind, but he was 'a miracle of steady perseverance' and topped his class.[54]

The old world scornfully eyed the new. In 1871 Professor Huxley presented the prizes at Charing Cross Hospital (in his own student days, that had been a clergyman's lot). His teacher, the tweedy Wharton Jones, that relic of Burke-and-Hare antiquity, still revelled in his protégé's success, even as he recoiled at a sullying ape ancestry.[55]

It was a typical reaction. The new science was a mix of lofty moral message and dirty substance. Huxley's postbag was full of letters from strangers who had 'great esteem towards you', but who drew the line at 'those "Lay Sermons &c on the Origin of Species"'. Kindly religious folk in awe of his 'great gifts' begged him not to get involved with Darwin's monstrous *Descent of Man*.[56] But radical social theory and evolution were all of a piece now, tied tightly in the *Fortnightly* and *Contemporary*, and there would be no spiking the Whitworth gun in liberalism's army.

Darwin's latest double-decker on mankind's ape ancestry and sexual selection was causing consternation. All pointed ears, hairy embryos and artful baboons, *The Descent of Man* combined anatomy and anecdote to establish that the morality of 'primeval men' grew from the social instinct of apes. A sad Emma Darwin saw her old husband 'again putting God further off'. For the sensitive even the title smacked of scientific man's descent into Hell. Hooker wished that Darwin had simply called it *The Origin of Man*. But the book was still titillating, and ladies had 'to order it on the sly!'[57]

The grand detour of Darwin's life was over; the affable naturalist had finally declared himself on the evolution of mind and morality. It had taken him 33 years to summon the courage for *The Descent of Man*, waiting until a cushioning Huxleyan community had made it quite safe. The poison had been drawn by *Man's Place* and Tylor's and Lubbock's ruminations. By now a flood of papers had inured the public: Wallace on the selection of savage morality and Galton on the selection of civilized character, Walter Bagehot on the evolution of prehistoric politics and W. R. Greg on the evolutionary fate of the low-birth-rate bourgeoisie.[58] These men, the last two an economist and mill owner, threaded class and politics into biological evolution and Darwin sealed the trend, weaving a white, wealthy, male outlook into the fabric of the *Descent*. Reviewers groaned with 'wrath, wonder, and admiration' at his lumpy tome, and predicted as usual that if morals were born of brute instinct 'a revolution . . . will shake society to its very foundations'.[59]

Talk of 'revolution' said more about the nation's nerves in 1871. The *Descent* had been published as those 'bloody Frenchmen' were being crushed at the climax of the Franco-Prussian war. Huxley had wanted the Germans to 'give that crowned swindler' Louis Napoleon and the whole syphilitic Second Empire 'such a blow' that they would 'never recover'. But by the time the *Descent* appeared even he wished the 'infernal war' at an end. Darwin's and Huxley's Russian translator Vladimir Kovalevskii, the nihilist who used science to undermine Tsarist Orthodoxy, had stayed at Downe and sat Huxley's lectures in the winter of 1869–70. Now he could be found carrying proofs of the *Descent* through the Prussian lines to the Dantonesque fortress of Paris. Russia, there too was a problem, a country reneging on the Crimean peace agreement. 'The Russian row is beginning', said Huxley, fearing a wider war. 'Bad days are I am afraid in store for all of us'.[60]

At such a time the *Descent* hit the bookstalls. Four months of siege had left the Parisians starving. The ravenous képi-hatted revolutionaries had even eaten the elephants in the zoo. With peace in February 1871 the Metaphysical antagonists Cardinal Manning and Huxley pulled together on their Paris Food Fund, adding to the 10,000 tons shipped across the Channel.[61] Unfortunately, as the reviewers got their teeth into the *Descent*, the Reds were distributing the parcels. Paris fell to the Communards in March 1871. Kovalevskii settled down to work in the Paris Muséum, laughing at British hysteria about the alleged 'brigands, assassins, [and] socialists' in control.[62] But the hysteria grew.

Huxley thought Darwin's timing 'too bad' because he was bogged down in more metaphysical warfare and 'You know I can't show my face anywhere in society without having read' the book. Not that he was left a free moment for promotion. But the press thought the timing atrocious because of the red skies: 'it is reckless', thundered the *Times*. Darwin expected 'execution' as a minimum, as he told Mivart just before the reactionary bloodbath in the French 'Sodom and Gomorrah'. For Mivart Good and Evil would lose their meaning and authority collapse if morals were made evolutionary products: 'God grant we in England may not be approaching a religious decay' of the sort 'which Frenchmen are now paying for in blood & tears!' he moaned to Darwin.[63]

European palaeontologists had already strung together bitty fossils to draw up genealogies for rhinos, pigs and elephants. With his publicist's flair, Huxley fixed on one creature, meaningful in an equestrian age. London was a din of iron-hoof clopping, a city congested at 8 am. by ten-horse buses and cabs. Ironically the trains had only increased the need for town horses and short-stop travel. On Fridays the swells arrived in hansoms at the Royal Institution to see Huxley. An equine pedigree was above all safe: a model of faithful subservience, the horse showed Nature in yoke. Huxley took 'one of the most beautiful animals in the world' and drew up the ultimate bloodstock. It was appealing, judging by the fact that Tyndall was 'torn to pieces by women in search of tickets'.

From a single-toed stallion, he worked back via the ass-like *Hipparion* with pronounced dew-claws to the three-toed *Anchitherium* of Miocene times. He cast further, past the tapir-ish *Palaeotherium* to an undiscovered five-toed agouti-shaped ancestor. His was a history of streamlined growth and toe-reduction, the making of society's 'exquisite running engine'.[64] He skirted the precise cause of this specialization towards one tip-toe, and it was left to Kovalevskii in the Commune, plunging into the 'adapt-or-die' Darwinian process, to explain it. He saw the Miocene forest ponies being forced onto the first grassy plains.[65] The old spread-toed tapir-like browsers gained long-striding legs on the hard meadows, and long grinders for grazing the tough grasses. No one had seen such a detailed calculus as he correlated toes and joints with survival potential. This was the palaeontology of the future.

The Descent of Man hardly diverted the public from the war. What did, the *Times* said, was the creation of a London School Board (not surprisingly with women voting for the first time in British history). With half the nation's children running loose, the Education Act enabled the setting up of education authorities (school boards) to sweep the street arabs into a countrywide system of schools. Radical London gave every ratepayer the vote in its school board election. The religious sects organized to return candidates. The women's bandwagon was unstoppable, given the chance to roll at last, and the first woman doctor, Elizabeth Garrett, ran in Marylebone. Huxley moved from the educational heights to the guttersnipes. He too contested Marylebone, running with a trade-unionist and carpenter William Cremer on a dream ticket, scientific training and artisan opportunity.

Huxley only had time for four rallies during the November 1870 hustings. London schooling was notorious, and on the platform he claimed that farmers would not rear pigs under such slum conditions. His star-studded (all-male) committee featured the X-Club's Tyndall, Lubbock and Busk, University College professors, J. S. Mill, Tom Hughes and endless foot-soldiers who traipsed from door to door. Two ragamuffins – 'a deputation from Huxley's Committee, or perhaps the Committee itself' – turned up at the house of the Endowed Schools Commissioner Arthur Hobhouse and asked him to be treasurer. He agreed, but first had to put £5 into the kitty.[66]

Unlike rivals, Huxley took no adverts in the papers, and he had few hours for canvassing. When he could manage it Nettie went 'with him in the evg to "stump"'. Here he fleshed out his educational scheme: science and modern studies for both boys and girls, 'drill' to get the street urchins healthy and housekeeping to teach the domestics their trade (applauded by a pernickety Nettie and the middle classes). 'I hope for Marylebone's sake he will be at the top of the poll – for his own at the bottom', said Foster, knowing what success would mean in lost time.[67] But everybody pulled, and Knowles, the new editor of the *Contemporary Review*, leaked extracts of Huxley's forthcoming essay on 'The School Boards' to the press.

The female vote, usually Huxley's, was siphoned off by Elizabeth Garrett's slick machine. He was up against his former pupil, and her supporters 'organised a complete system', Nettie reported, 'working down street after street & house after house'. Nettie admired her: she is a 'charming lady-like woman', 'one of those who does credit to us instead of damaging as many women do the cause they advocate'.[68] Garrett was triumphantly returned for Marylebone. And so was Huxley – in second place.

London's board saw labour, secularism and women well served, but even better served were the Anglicans, Methodists, Baptists, Congregationalists and Catholics, who ensured that factionalism prevailed. Many of the radical Dissenters, however, were secularists, some more so than Huxley. Nowhere could match 'Heterodox Hackney', and none admired Hal more than its Congregationalist delegate Revd James Picton. Hackney revelled in 'slummy' secularism. Its fanatics observed so close a 'connexion of cleanliness with godliness', a wag observed, 'that they abjured the former with the latter'. On Sundays the inns reverberated to speakers who would 'resolve Christ into a Solar Myth' or, in Picton's case, Christianity into Pantheism. Picton fancied that Huxley had underrated 'the revolution which modern discovery is working' on 'religious thought'.[69]

But if the *Lay Sermons* were casting their spell on society's underbelly, turning Congregationalists into Pantheists, Huxley was doing something else with the kids in the board's care. He wanted them taught the Bible. Hackney was bewildered.

Many Churchmen fought to keep the schools religious. The Board had the power to exclude theology altogether, but Huxley knew that making headway meant making compromises. He opted for selective Bible-reading, 'without any comment', to instil moral principles. He agreed with Birmingham's radical MP George Dixon 'the inexpediency of attempting to exclude Bible reading' altogether. But it had to be selective: the Old Testament was as much vice as virtue. Who would want the lasciviousness of Lot's daughters or Joseph's seduction taught? 'As a French friend of mine observed, the stories of "Madam Potiphar et les demoiselles Lot" are not edifying for children'.[70]

On the one hand this was the Huxley who had sent a Bible to his godson Tom, Lizzie's boy. Having been a footloose 'young prig' himself, he was not about to make others stand in moral isolation in a religious world. They 'should be brought up in the mythology of their own time', while being given the skills to question it. They should learn to recognize the 'moral beauty' in all religions. In the *Contemporary* he warned the radical fire-bombers against 'burning your ship to get rid of the cockroaches!' Education was a more targeted toxin to eradicate the sectarian pests. Foster understood: strong medicine was needed to purge the extremists, and the *Contemporary* bait would prove 'Poisonous to snakes' of all shades.[71]

But it smelt of betrayal to out-and-outers, and the issue was to haunt him for life. Very few achieved Moncure Conway's degree of sympathy. For all of Huxley's vaunted familiarity with the 'dirt-eating' ways of the world, he remained curiously idealistic: 'he really believed that the Bible was to be read in the schools as he himself would use it', Conway noted, 'for its good English, its poetry, historical value, selected ethics. He had a vision of heretical Huxleys instructing innumerable little Huxleys'.

The big Huxley held out 'to the disquiet of sundry of our liberal colleagues'. Still, the Sultan Schamyl in him rose at a sniff of doctrinal theology in school. He was the powerful pragmatist again. 'Fanatics on all sides abuse me', he said, 'so I think I must be right'.[72]

Because he occasionally sent small sums to the secularist George Holyoake and sought legal protection for freethinkers, agitators had Huxley pegged as an ally. But the agnostics were fighting their own professional corner. They had their agenda – creating a quasi-autonomous, state-paid scientific caste. No longer did they need this street-level secularist constituency. Holyoake, reporting Huxley's speeches in the American press and his *Reasoner*, celebrating 'your reign to the uttermost ends of the earth', never really understood. He asked Huxley to chair a meeting on the anniversary of the socialist Robert Owen's birth. But while Huxley praised Owen for having the 'courage . . . to work out his theory [of infant education] into a practical reality', his sympathy stopped there.[73] It led to a terrible disappointment when he compromised on the Bible.

Life was becoming topsy-turvy. Having snarled at patronage for so long, he found himself dispensing it in January 1871. George Eliot and Thomas Carlyle both approached him to get friends onto the School Board staff.[74] Huxley had a prodigious capacity for work, but he never seemed to know his limit. Between January and May 1871, as he reconstituted himself into the Board's administrative dynamo, he ran seven concurrent or consecutive courses. Workers' lectures, talks on biology at the London Institution; a Royal Institution course on Bishop Berkeley and the folly of contemplating the unknowable. Like an old-time Providentialist he would gallop up to a northern mining parish for a sermon weaving geological evolution and industry – telling of the aeons that the club mosses took to compact into the country's wealth, coal. Aeons, too, spellbound the children as he explained the origin of their world. In between came advanced physiology students and regular classes. The lectures continued literally *ad nauseam*. He was beginning to be sick. The public was fooled because the talks seemed to flow like 'conversation'. Giving them was 'perfectly easy to Huxley', everyone thought.[75] No one realized the strain.

Nor did home insulate him; the house was becoming a meeting place for the world's intellectuals. Do pop over, he wrote to James Knowles: 'Turguenief, the Russian [novelist], Tyndall, & I hope one or two other good folk are coming to dine with us'.[76] The 'good folk' were now the great. From the Underground the others trooped, Matthew Arnold and Herbert Spencer. And a sculptress: the dinners were rounded feasts, with painters and musicians for leavening. Huxley's wit was yearly in demand at the Royal Academy toasts, and the house welcomed the up-and-coming talent. Briton Riviere, whose syrupy scenes of sick children would come to typify Victorian sentimentalism, was cultivated by Nettie, who penned letters like hospital dispatches. The tall Jess (14) and frail 13-year-old Marian ('Mady') were arty. They would take the Underground to drawing classes at the new Slade School of Fine Art at University College. Mady was the skittish tease among the girls, waiting for Frank Darwin to visit to be on her 'dignity with him!' 'No more kissing, I can tell you', Huxley reported back to Darwin.[77]

The house was about to become their own home. After renting for 16 years, the Huxleys at 46 were finally to own a property. They could scarcely afford it (Hal was just breaking even) but another bank loan would see them through. Knowles now switched his publisher's for architect's hat. Having built Tennyson a house and made it fit for a Laureate, he planned to make Huxley's fit for a professional. In March 1871 Knowles obtained a 99-year lease on 4 Marlborough Place, minutes away in St John's Wood, and started an extension which would dwarf the original cottage.[78]

How to recoup was another matter. The Home Secretary had Huxley sitting (unpaid) on two Commissions. The BAAS President who had cursed epidemics as the 'bloodiest of all wars', and the father who had watched his own blond-tousled child die, had added the Contagious Diseases Committee to the Devonshire.[79] More aggravated (and unpaid) sittings overloaded him at the School Board. He ran its first Education Committee, which was to turn a few ragged schools into a London-wide system of education. After four gruelling months, on 13 June 1871, it published a 50-page plan for London's schooling, covering everything from optimum size to evening classes, and a broad curriculum spanning geography and history to six years of simple object-based science.[80]

The one-man think-tank dominated the meetings, building that ladder from the gutter to the university (his phrase which fired the nation). It was a massive job, and there weren't enough hours in the day. 'I fear for Huxley', Hooker told Darwin; 'his wife tells me' he 'is running a fearful rig of work . . . his love of exercising his marvellous intellectual power over men is leading him on – and on – and on – God knows to where'. Even Huxley saw the absurdity of being worked to death on 'two Royal Commissions & the School Board all sitting at once'.[81] Things had to calm down.

He was making Science rival Classics in the schools, usurping its prestige. Mass education also created a need for new textbooks. These had been the prerogative of country parsons and dame-school matrons, but Huxley's experts would edge them out. Only the 'interpreter of nature', he argued, could really popularize the 'scientific blue books' (academic monographs). And so grand schemes were hatched for a series of ninepenny 'science for beginners'. The best men were on board. The Owen's College chemist Henry Roscoe sent the proofs of his *Chemistry Primer* in August 1871 and chivvied Huxley for his scene-setting *Introductory Science Primer*.[82] But he was over-extended; the pages lay blank.

He was seizing up, like a millipede wondering which leg to move next. So many Commissions and controversies across such a broad front got in the way of construction. To Foster he was 'a brilliant David forbidden to build the Temple on account of the blood of the Philistines on his hands'.[83] At the British Association in Edinburgh it was the new President, Sir William Thomson, who had Huxley on his feet. Huxley loved giant intellects, and none was larger than Thomson's. They had been elected Fellows of the Royal Society together and enjoyed their affable sparring. Thomson had even invited Huxley on a Hebridean cruise, as if he had the time.[84]

But the Scottish physicists stood four-square against the London naturalizers. Not for them Tyndall's belief that mundane Earthly matter could generate 'all terrestrial Life'. Huxley had pinned his own Presidential faith on the chemical origin of primeval protoplasm. But for many the notion that 'dead matter' could crystallize into the 'germs of life' was preposterous. Thomson disliked Darwin's chancy natural selection, and he saw the Londoners' self-creating universe fasten man to Fate. It would deprive him of free will and redemption in a better world. But his own solution hardly helped. Thomson suggested that spore-bearing meteorites had seeded the cooled planet when it 'was ready to become a garden'.[85] The audience was shocked; a few laughed, thinking it was the start of 'some good joke'. And none roared more than Huxley: 'What do you think of Thomson's "creation by cockshy"', he asked Hooker. 'God almighty sitting like an idle boy at the sea side & slinging aerolites [at] . . . a planet!'[86] Shuffling the problem of origins off into the heavens showed the difficulty now for a Providentialist to get around Evolution.

Pater was forever jumping up. September found him still in Scotland, in St Andrews, supposedly relaxing. But he had little real rest. While the family swam and golfed, Hal went off to the Elgin fossil beds, the ancient tombs of his *Stagonolepis* 'crocodiles', there to sift 'tons of Elgin sandstone for bits of my dearly beloved reptiles with dear old Gordon of Birnie – the jolliest old brick of a Scotch minister'. A sackful of vertebrae meant more work. But the children were happy. Jess was enjoying herself 'much as I once used to', Nettie said revealingly, 'only unlike me . . . she has never known "hard times"'.[87] Even Hal was lured onto the 'Royal and Ancient' course by Thomson's colleague Professor Tait, only to be 'hopelessly bunkered three or four holes from home'.

Holidays were punishing rotas, and what snared Pater at St Andrews was scholasticism. Like any self-righteous sectarian, he was fully engaged in a religious age. He exploited society's prejudices against Papism, and made Science speak with a Protestant tongue. He had a 'sectarian keenness of scent for heresy',[88] and even on vacation sniffed his way into St George Mivart's *Genesis of Species*. This was liberal Catholicism come to meet Evolution, to make it progressive and directed. Only the production of preadapted organs could explain what Darwin's chancy mechanism couldn't – an incipient wing. Did natural selection have flight in sight, asked Mivart. If not, and if there was no functional value to half a wing, how could a whole one develop? For Huxley such problems were of no account in a book tainted by Catholicism. A hardening Vatican had given scholastic theology supreme authority over modern science, and the chaffing Mivart – the liberal caught between two infallible popes – had been forced to make the old Jesuits sanction evolution. Seeing the sixteenth-century Father Suarez pressed into service put the glow on Huxley's face. The cold warrior 'dived' into a dozen Latin folios in the university library, chasing Mivart's 'corky exposition of Catholic theology'. Huxley was making sure that 'Frater Suarez would have damned [Mivart] forty times over'.[89] He was keeping the Pope Catholic.

A prickly Darwin could only see the 'scorn & spite' in Mivart's review of *The Descent of Man*. He wanted revenge '& all the more, as I own I felt mortified'. Darwin was oversensitive. He felt betrayed by Huxley's pupil, and Huxley's policing was swift. Mivart was 'clever & not a bad fellow', but he was 'insolent to Darwin & I mean to pin him out'. A Manichaean Calvinist like Huxley needed a reactionary Catholicism. He needed a Jesuit militia to threaten Britain's modernity. It was Huxley's populist pitch: Science was protecting society against the menace of an infallible Papacy. A reconciliation between liberal Catholicism and providential Evolution threatened Huxley's naturalistic power base. Hence the relish at showing Suarez in all his orthodoxy, never the evolutionist: 'Only fancy my vindicating Catholic orthodoxy against one of the Papists themselves'. Darwin laughed until his 'stomach was contracted into a ball'.[90]

Knowles slotted 'Mr. Darwin's Critics' into November's *Contemporary*, when the season was back in swing. 'What a wonderful Essayist he is', said Hooker, passing the proofs to Darwin, this 'defender of the faithful'. Darwin, extending the imagery, thought 'it would be a sin & shame' not to reprint it in Huxley's next opus. Others were beginning to take all this religious imagery seriously. They were characterizing the 'faithful' as a Darwinian 'sect', which, like all beleaguered sects, had sought security in their Election. Or so one reviewer painted them. Those not born-again in Darwin were cast into a Dantean 'limbo of heretics'. Mivart was being excommunicated by bell, *Origin* and candle – publicly ostracized by Huxley, Hooker, Lankester and Flower to stiffen the resolve of the ranks.[91] Agnosticism had gone past Protestantism to become the hallmark of Huxley's profession – Nature pared to the bone, stripped of the last idolatrous trace in this 'New Reformation'. Huxley's supposedly non-aligned agnosticism kept showing its radical Dissenting roots. A secular, uniform Nature was now the unquestioned foundation of the Darwinian Temple.

This was one of five back-to-back reviews drafted on his holidays – so many social commentaries, sectarian interjections and demands for State aid that he returned from Scotland on 29 September 'as tired as two dogs'. Even so he dashed to Manchester within days to discuss exams as a Governor of Owen's College, then to lobby the government from that home of municipal socialism, Birmingham.[92] Talks were refined on the hoof, but the hooves were tiring as he drove himself on. The new opiate 'chloral' helped his sleep, but for the first time he had to cancel a public appearance for fear of dropping.

After lectures he would sit for hours on the School Board. The monumental task of establishing free primary schooling in London had become bogged down in religious bickering. Hardliners, throwing the fat into the fire, wanted the board to pay the fees of children at the existing Anglican and Catholic schools as well. Huxley dug in for a trench war, lampooning this 'outdoor relief' for the rich. The *Times* flapped at his anti-Catholic invective, but the Dissenters saw it as 'high time that *English Science* spoke out' against the 'impudence of the Ultramontanes'.[93] Huxley's speeches grew stirring and passionate until Gladstone took note. The cynical thought it a step to Parliament. But it was a school board, not a springboard, he told the *Daily News*, and 'not even the offer of a seat in the House of Commons' would lead him to forsake his 'proper occupations' again.[94] The grants were blocked to abbey and church schools. London was committed to a secular education.

It was a sign of the diminishing hold of the churches on education. But seven months of wrangling took its toll. Hobhouse wanted the board to switch 'its attention from Heaven to Earth'. So did Huxley. He was frustrated. 'I *cannot* and *will* not' sap 'my energies & waste my time in faction fights & administrative details', he swore.[95] He began clutching at fossil bones, desperate to pull himself out of the quagmire. He was losing precious time, and the wealthy Hobhouse, fearing he would resign, quietly offered him £100 a quarter from his own pocket to keep going. But Huxley turned the cash down to remain a free agent.

He only scrambled onto a higher plane to suffer more. From the chair of the School Board he switched to the chair of the Metaphysical Society, where the sects were locked in a more ethereal struggle. An agnostic on the throne caused consternation among the Catholics here too. 'Nothing could be better', Hooker crowed with Gillrayish crudity; it 'will send a bellyache all round the table. I think I now see the A. Bishops all bolting to the "Cabinets" with their aprons up & breeches down'.[96] F. D. Maurice turned up to read his misty paper encapsulating the quandary of the age, 'On the Words "Nature," "Natural," and "Supernatural"', and then left, never to reappear.

In an age of sects, sectarianism was at the root of Huxley's reviewing to an extent never really appreciated. A roll-call of his unpublished reviews revealed that the Catholic Mivart was not his only target; Huxley submitted papers on Anglican ritualism to the *Quarterly* and on the 'eloquence' of preachers (as he put it sarcastically) to the *Nonconformist Review*.[97] This was saturation publishing, and still the demands came in.[98]

It was too much. He staggered out of his London Institution lectures on mind and body in December, 'seedy to the last degree'. Mind might be a glorious epiphenomenon, like a steam whistle on a loco 'without influence upon its machinery', but Huxley's was whistling a warning. His hurtling express was careening off the rails. The machinery was 'grumbling like an ungreased block'. 'Don't know what is the matter with me except dyspepsia and a strong desire to do nothing', he told Hooker. 'D— everything an inch high and a year old – especially every Governmental thing'. That said it all: the School Board, Metaphysical strain, commissions, the chairs (Foster addressed him as 'The President of Most of the Societies'),[99] lectures on everything from consciousness to coral – the lot had drained him. By the end of 1871 he was crumpling. His diary, usually a splotchy mass of dates with the Victorian greats, from Gladstone to Elizabeth Garrett, fell blank. The listlessness of November gave way to depressions in December. He ran down to Brighton 'for a day or two to see if the sea breezes will set me up'. 'You will be right in a jiffy', Tyndall jollied him.[100] But he wasn't.

Incessant nausea left him looking haggard. On 3 January 1872 he admitted defeat. It seemed that 'weariness, incapacity & disgust' had got the better of him. The doctors said there was nothing organically wrong but they predicted a collapse if he carried on. Nettie was miserable about him, '& for once, he felt [that taking a rest] was a reasonable thing to do'. As usual, 'rest' meant work elsewhere. The Navy already had him studying a 'detestable grub', a maggot of the moth *Ephestia* which 'has been devouring Her Majesty's stores of biscuits at Gibraltar'.[101] So he contemplated a recuperative cruise via Gibraltar to the Mediterranean.

A day or two later his cavalier attitude shattered. 'Hal's health, his capital, suddenly failed'. The crash 'came all at once', Nettie said; 'he literally was unable to give his lectures, scarcely to write his letters'.[102] It left him momentarily incapacitated, unable even to stir from his seat. At short notice Nettie, ever the guardian, got him two months' leave from the School of Mines. Then she booked immediate passage on the steamer *Malta* to take him away from the winter fogs to Egypt.

He sent his resignation to the School Board on 6 January, only to have the Chairman Lord Lawrence try to refuse it. Even Huxley's opponents were mortified. He towered above them all in intellect, the Congregationalist minister Benjamin Waugh said, but never made them feel small. Waugh, the future founder of the Society for the Prevention of Cruelty to Children, had been antagonistic at the start; but he too had gravitated to this man whose 'motive in every argument, in all the fun and ridicule he indulged in', had been the welfare of the children.[103] Still, Huxley went.

The haste astonished everyone. 'Lowe will have to be quick if he wants the benefit of my discretion, piety & learning', Huxley said the next day on hearing that the Chancellor wanted a word, 'for I mean to be off by the P&O on Thursday'.[104]

So he left Nettie to deal with the children, Knowles to get on with the house, Foster to take over 'the SK lectures to womankind',[105] the Commissions to take care of themselves, Mivart to stew in his own juice, and stand-ins all over London to cover for him. He did the unimaginable, just stopped at the beginning of term and took an impromptu holiday.

2

From the City of the Dead to the City of Science

P&O'S LINER WAS A far cry from the creaking, slack-canvas *Rattlesnake*. 'Fogs & calm' beset them but the sturdy steam pumps pushed them through. The Biscay swell was as horrid as ever, making the *Malta* 'very lively', and Huxley couldn't sleep. Past the Lisbon cliffs they ploughed, the last gale blowing them 200 miles in 16 hours into Gibraltar. He was on deck at 8 am. on a 'lovely morning', 16 January 1872, to see the Rock loom up.

Huxley began to revel in the leisure as he 'strolled into the market & devoured red oranges'. Then he presented his Admiralty letter and inspected the dockyard stores, only to find that 'nothing could be better in point of cleanliness & order'.[1] So he visited HMS *Hercules*, where the grumbling below deck about maggoty food was growing ominous. The flour was pure when it left Deptford, so he investigated the nearby sacks of cocoa and fruit, and finally traced the source of contamination: the moth eggs were being blown onto the flour from unpurified cocoa.

The former surgeon's relations with the top brass had equally changed. He was rowed over to the *Minotaur* to have breakfast with Rear-Admiral Hornby, commander of the Flying Squadron, whose warships could reach any trouble spot from Africa to India. Huxley enjoyed his new-found status, dining with colonial administrators and admirals. Hornby had him ferried to Tangier with the Bishop of Gibraltar. A week out and what a difference: he was 'wandering about Tangier', watching the Moors. His was a more admiring eye now, like Burton's, looking favourably on the Muslims in defiance of his own idolatrous culture. As he painted mosques his eye would catch 'a stately moor' wearing his *Haik* 'exactly in the manner of the

Roman toga . . . hung in wonderfully graceful folds'. Britannia's reach was huge, and even in Morocco he had his contacts. 'Left Hooker's letter with Sir John D. Hay', he noted. Sir John was the consular minister and expert on the Barbary coast (although Hooker had been more interested in his daughter). The family had Huxley to dinner nightly and a son took him riding to Cape Spartel near the Cave of Hercules. But even here a depressed Huxley thought that 'the springs of [his] machine were finally smashed' and it reflected in his doom-laden sketches of medieval berber camps. The foul weather made him worse; 'rained Cats & dogs', he wrote, as his gloomy painting began to blotch.[2]

The Fates followed him on the *Nyanza* steaming for Malta. The Mediterranean was 'disagreeable, cold & wet'. His eight hours at Malta were 'rainy and cold', and he was blown on to Alexandria by gales. In Egypt on 1 February the downpours made a mockery of the travel brochures. Alex was a 'muddy hole', and so he took the 8 am. train the next morning up the Delta. From the windows the sleet made it seem more like a blustery Lincolnshire than a wondrous Nile, except for the palms reflecting in the pools.

At Cairo he checked into the palatial Shepheard's Hotel. Through its arabesque lobby passed all the Raj expats. With an English hotel, and almost English prices (14*s* a week), came more English rain. Walked in the bazaar '& went to bed early', he commented sourly. The disgruntled air gave way as he took a donkey and servant 'mosque hunting' the next morning. Always it was religion with him – before the pyramids, before the museum, before even the fossil-rich limestones. He went up to the Citadel, built by Saladin below the Mokattam hills, to take a kaleidoscopic view of the city's white domes. He saw Muhammad Ali's 'grand mosque', newly finished in an out-of-keeping Ottoman style. Through the crowded narrow streets of the Old City he ventured to the huge Sultan Hassan Mosque with its marble columns and fountain courtyard. Then to the beautiful eighth-century Tulun Mosque, where he sat in the enormous courtyard sketching the arches and wood friezes.[3] The noise, the smells, the competing chants from the minarets; the tasselled merchants, the crush of donkeys and traders: whatever the weather, it was the East.

Despite the British presence – the British hotels and British doctors (Dr James Grant, physician to the ruler, the Khedive, kept an open house for English savants) – the Nile was as deliciously mysterious as ever. Here the Orient merged into mystery, and only the matter-of-fact British thought to demystify the river by discovering its source. The impeccable Speke and outrageous Burton had done their job, describing Lakes Victoria and Albert as the White Nile's source, giving the great artery its imperial pedigree. As Huxley mooched around Cairo, a bumptious American reporter Henry Stanley was with Livingstone 2,500 miles to the south on the shore of Lake Tanganyika, having greeted him with the line that would become an imperial pun, 'Dr Livingstone, I presume?' And a weak, lion-savaged Livingstone was shortly to set off on his last journey to see if the Lualaba entered the Nile.

The Nile was a national obsession. The opening of the Suez Canal in 1869 made Egypt the strategic gateway to India. P&O was rebuilding its entire fleet for the Suez run and abandoning its Cape stations. So Egypt was both an easy and an exotic destination. It was also a *de facto* British outpost (becoming a partly official one three years later, when an opportunist Disraeli bought £4 million worth of shares in the French Suez Canal company from the bankrupt Khedive).

With cruise liners sporting lavish décor, and rail lines laid from Alexandria to Rodu, travel was more a 'question of time and money' than slog and slave, as the brochures put it.[4] Palace hotels were springing up to cater to Thomas Cook's trainloads. But most of all Egypt was a fashionable sanatorium for the intrepid who wanted to get away from the genteel spas. The pyramids promised a romantic resort for the wealthy who feared leisure. Here they could heal their congested lungs in the desert air, while losing no time to become more cultured.

Professor Huxley too was something of a national obsession. Doors opened even here. Sir William Gregory, erstwhile Chairman of the Commons Committee on the British Museum and the new Governor of Ceylon, escorted him round Bulaq Museum on the 5th, and the next day took him in his private train through the ancient capital of Memphis to see the world's oldest hewn-stone monument, the step pyramid at Sakkara. The museum housed Auguste Mariette's fabulous treasures, disinterred by his army of 3,000 diggers – Hyksos statues and scarabs, mummies and Meidum paintings. Of course, what stopped Huxley was a 'Sculpture in true bas relief from Memphis' showing 'man leading the apes!' 'Visit again & study carefully', he jotted in his diary.[5]

One afternoon he was in Cairo's City of the Dead, investigating the ornamented tombs of the Caliphs; another on Windmill Hill, littered with ancient potsherds. But much of his time was spent on the Mokattam hills to the east, looking at the limestone strata, drawing sections and ferreting in quarries of nummulite fossils.

Reports went back to Nettie, more about the terrain than the state of his brain. 'Cairo he says more than answers his expectations and at last he was in sun shine'. Unknown to Hal she had his doctor Bence Jones request a further month's leave, and 'I hope that he may see the wisdom of indulging himself'. She coped alone as the Marlborough Place tip was turned into an eight-bedroom home. She would visit it with Knowles and the builders to discuss baths and kitchen pipes. She met every crisis as the small house was expanded to include drawing room, dining room and bedrooms. Delays dogged them; London's planning authority, the Board of Works, halted the building because the extension went a foot over the approved plans. Then the labour costs overshot the estimate and Tyndall had to deposit £100 in Huxley's account.[6]

While Nettie was sitting on the Underground train, taking Jess and Marian to the Slade drawing classes, Hal was sketching in Cairo's Coptic churches. Here Christianity reached back to the third century. There were none of Llewelyn Davies' crucifixion scenes, only icons of a gentler beatific form. Then he popped back to the museum, to see 'the two statues recently discovered . . . at Meidum – 3rd Dynasty – 4800 B.C.' He had no schedules, no fixed itinerary, for once time was his own. When he should have been racing to give his Monday lectures he was taking a donkey across the desert to paint the remaining Wonder of the World, Cheops' pyramid.

It was too expensive to go up the Nile alone. But he fell in with fellow Athenaeum member Frederick Ouvry, the President of the Society of Antiquaries. (The Athenaeum was as much a social focus at Shepheard's as in Pall Mall.) He and a pleasant diplomat's son, Charles Ellis, had taken one of the shallow-draught houseboats, or *dahabiehs*, and invited Huxley along.[7] So on 15 February a fresh wind caught the big forward triangular sail and carried him at seven knots past the Meidum pyramid. Hal sat on deck, sketching, only diverted by a passing felucca boat, or a jackal scavenging on the bank. They saw their first pelicans. The days became hotter, the nights bright and moonlit. They stopped to buy oranges and bread in villages and to get a glimpse of rural life. And back on the boat they watched the dropping sun silhouette the palms with blood-red rays. At last Hal had his therapeutic heat.

They were 400 miles up the Nile by the 23rd. He arrived at Thebes in the evening and ambled about Karnak by moonlight. The great temple had been cleared of peasant huts by Mariette: here it stood, unbelievable, its hypostyle hall the largest in the world, 5,000 square feet, its 60-foot columns dwarfing the visitors with their flickering lights. The collapse of a mighty Pharaonic civilization seemed more real in the stillness, with only bats flapping through the ruins. In the fresh air of the morning Huxley rode with an old guide into the arid Valley of the Kings. First to the ramshackle temple of Kurna (Seti I), 'then to Kings tombs up an amazingly hot valley – visited Belzoni's, Bruces and No 9'. Belzoni's excavation (the tomb of Seti I) was on every tourist's itinerary; 'awe-inspiring', Flinders Petrie would call its paintings of the Book of the Dead. He rode over the hot sandy ridge, his donkey knowing each step, then across a 'plain to the Memnonium' (the Ramasseum, with its huge fallen statues of Rameses II). On he passed, to be surprised by the two stately 65-foot Colossi of Memnon, standing alone on the edge of the desert, all that remained of a vanished temple.

As they continued south he was beginning to sleep. He relished the '"always afternoon" sort of life'. The heat and laziness of *dahabieh* travel seem to massage away all cares. At El Kab they stopped to saunter round the old town with its 'thick crude mud walls' and see the graffiti-covered tombs cut into the cliffs. The heat was intense, and the surrounding hills were gradually lowering as the Nile became prettier. At Kom Ombo they visited the temple dedicated to the town's hawk and crocodile gods, and Huxley had a 'wonderful view of [the] desert from the top of the little hill on which the temple is placed'. Here he sat, pondering the fall of ancient worlds, 'very grateful to Old Nile for all that he has done to me – not least for a whole universe of new thoughts'.

Huxley's London lectures on race seemed a world away. On 1 March the Aswan bazaar showed them a real cultural crossroads. He stocked up with food, jostled by tall Abyssinians carrying bales, Nubians with lion skins and gun-toting Arabs. The next morning they visited the pretty temple of Isis at Philae, its columns still fresh with coloured depictions of Ptolemaic Egypt. Then the English Schamyl rode his camel to 'a point opposite Philae'. It seemed so remote, yet for all the spice and heat, they were never far from Britain. 'Sent letter IX [to Nettie] by Cooks steamer', he jotted.[8]

The return journey was even lazier, a dozen miles a day against hot headwinds. Each day brought more Ptolemaic temples, with their Greek and Roman influence, Edfu's, and then Esna's, with its relief of the Roman Emperor Decius. It was 'Exceedingly hot & close'; Huxley, his hair cropped short, brown skin and black beard, sat in the old *dahabieh*'s saloon scribbling notes: after a three-hour ride to Abydos to see the paintings on Seti's temple he jotted, 'Very hot, bad donkeys fatiguing'.[9] In truth, he was diverted but hardly better, whatever his protestations. On 16 March they reached Tel el Amarna. Huxley packed his paintings and books and left the old *dahabieh* at the railway terminus of Rodu.

The Nile brought time and tranquillity, but crumbling necropoli were no real cure for an obsessed mind. He left the cities of the dead as he stepped onto the Messina ferry on 19 March. Over the Mediterranean lay Sicily and then a more typical dash across Europe. He bounced from a hot past to an icy present. At Etna he found the 'old giant . . . half covered with snow'. But he had no heart to climb. On to Naples by train – he was there by the 27th, climbing the 160 steps to Anton Dohrn's mansion overlooking the beautiful bay. Fireworks heralded his arrival, with Vesuvius across the bay shooting molten rocks into the air. Dohrn was away, but Hal found his nimble 70-year-old father; and young Ray Lankester, his rooms looking like a marine laboratory, with the washbasins full of cuttle-fish larvae. More to the point he found the foundations of the Marine Station going in. Lankester and old Dohrn took Hal up to the north lip of the crater. The belching and 'blast furnace' explosions gave the Hell Gate a true Dantean image. At sunset the 'fiery stream found a lurid reflection in the slowly drifting steam cloud', while the exploding red-hot stones 'shone strangely beside the quiet stars in a moonless sky'.[10]

Through Rome and Turin he rushed, reaching Paris by 5 April. He got off the train in London the next day, a sunburnt face among the sombre throng. A waiting Nettie didn't recognize him,

> burnt to copper colour with beard moustache & short cropped hair! Jess & Mady were so disappointed at the change that they burst into tears when we got home! My great disapp^{nt} was to find him still suffering from dyspepsia & . . . little the better for his trip.[11]

Hal diagnosed himself fitter than Nettie did: 'I am back; brown, bearded, & brutal in health', he informed Hooker. But it was touch and go, and even Hal had 'a sort of impression that I had better be prudent'. Prudent meant that he 'took to mineral waters & horse exercises & gave up all private dinner parties'. With his regimen he must have felt like sickly Darwin. He must have looked like the venerable old naturalist too, with 'such a beard & moustache that you w^{d} hardly know him'.

But the hour's riding before work proved a bore, so he gave it up. And despite Foster's mineral-water cure Huxley still felt 'like a Holothuria' (a sea cucumber which squirted the contents of its stomach). In fact it was a time of relapses and depressions. He scared himself into taking life easy for a while. He published almost nothing for the year, and discarded and delegated where he could. Even looking back on the School Board wrangling sent a shiver, and 'I mean to keep clear of all that sort of semi-political work hereafter'.[12] But would the world let him?

He decelerated from the City of the Dead to the city of science, South Kensington. For a time life was unhurried, but the eternal afternoon did not last. How could it, with the Department of Science and Art conducting countrywide exams on a military scale? The number of students had increased fourfold in five years. 'Physical Geography' was the most popular subject, with Huxley's 'Animal Physiology' the fourth largest of the DSA's countrywide classes. Inspecting the 800 schools was itself a massive task, and 20 Royal Engineers were drafted in to police the students sitting Huxley's exams. From pacifying the Crimea to patrolling school halls, these uniformed invigilators completed the militarization of science. Huxley, a War Department examiner himself, thought the veterans perfect to mobilize the provincial irregulars.[13] A uniform gave science in the country its authority and national purpose. The *Pax Kensingtoniana* was ensured.

It was slow honing as he went back to the grindstone. 'I have just received a "missile" from My Lords', he told Foster in April 1872, 'to the effect that there will be about 5900 [exam] papers in Animal Physiology this year and that I shall therefore want 6 assistants'. So the General's own army expanded again, and down came Foster's Cambridge student, the 'young, energetic' Newell Martin. They were a socially cohesive group, and their lives intertwined at a family level. Foster even told Nettie of his engagement before his father, 'as the match is partly of your making'.[14]

They were a new breed of star demonstrators, Darwinians to the bone. Huxley's entrepreneurial flair for attracting Department grants paid their way. It was tough work for a man who had just broken down, but impossible to delegate. Behind the classes lay a vision. 'They are the commencement of a new system of teaching which if I mistake not will grow into a big thing', he told Tyndall, and for the present 'I am the necessary man to carry it out'.[15]

That loose cannon Ray Lankester joined him again. Edwin's son had a huge intellect and an irascibility to match. In the wake of the critical Commissions, Oxford's Exeter College had instituted a Natural Science Fellowship, and Huxley found himself examining his own demonstrator for it (Oxford was now routinely turning to Huxley for help). 'I should like to see him do well', Huxley admitted, 'but there is what we call "a screw loose" about him'. It showed. Ray got the post but turned round to roast the corruption 'and effete restrictions' of the place.[16] The Exeter post he dismissed as simply a sop to the science lobby in the wake of the Devonshire Commission.

With their different temperaments Huxley's men threw themselves differentially at Oxford and Cambridge. A reforming Cambridge had instituted the Natural Science Tripos in 1869. But while the affable Foster would attract a brilliant group here with his physiology practicals based on Huxley's pedagogical techniques, Lankester went off half-cocked. At Oxford he came up against the country gentlemen refining their morals and manners. Ray, another self-perceived 'poor' boy, damned this triumph of money and class over opportunity and merit, disdaining his cronies as 'flunkeys, snobs, spendthrifts and social bullies'.[17] Ray had found himself in a theological finishing school when he wanted a German science factory. He fell foul of Rolleston and was refused permission to teach in the museum. Latiny Oxford and obstinate Lankester saw science fail between them.

South Kensington's 'Science Schools' were to become the driving force of change. In June 1872 Huxley was ready to move. He finished his last Jermyn Street course, still a 'burnt sienna colour . . . and "bearded like the pard"'.[18] To the removals men he must have looked like a forensic boffin, as he spent his last days in Piccadilly picking at a macabre skeleton from King William's Sound, thought to be of one of Franklin's crew lost in the Arctic ice.

The hauliers carted truck-loads of apparatus through the unmacadamized Princes Gate in July. The experimentalists were moving in. Huxley would be joining with fellow X-man Edward Frankland with his relocated Royal College of Chemistry. 'The laboratory is a fine one', said Nettie, 'at the very top of a large building devoted to science. Below Hal's rooms are D^{r}. Frankland's for chemistry & beneath these D^{r}.Guthrie's for applied mechanics'.[19] Here Huxley would run his Summer crash course for the schoolmasters from the factory towns, required under the Education Act. His production-line turn-out would ultimately feed through, creating the need for science at the old Classics-based universities, underpinning his own profession and promoting scientific managers of industry. It was the vocational base of Huxley's dream of a liberal science college in South Kensington.

Older field naturalists spurned the laboratory for giving a distorted view of a dead, dismembered nature. And clerics celebrating the last Providential shreds of a happy contented Nature abominated it. But Huxley's new discipline of 'biology', created as a package that could be transmitted to the newly-built schools,[20] proclaimed the lab's privileged access to a deeper reality – a microscopic reality, comprehended by trained professionals. The laboratory, rather than the field, became the site for studying the new Nature. Indeed the 'field' was appropriated – Huxley not only brought Nature indoors, but put it under a cover slip, within the lens' 'field' of view. Here, deep down, one could see what the 'land is really like'.[21]

It was an irony that only in a congested city could real Nature be found. In the great age of burgeoning laboratories, designed to turn out hands-on schoolteachers wholesale, the microscope was portrayed as powerful and democratic, an open spyhole through to Nature's foundations. Really of course it offered no 'transparent' close-up. The tyros looking through an achromatic lens were baffled by the histological image. They had to learn the cognitive skills, learn to see and to stylize in diagrams, and it was a long regimented process. At South Kensington they first heard Huxley's morning lecture, where coloured blackboard drawings showed them what to expect (as, eventually, did giant papier-mâché models of sectioned snails and leeches, ears and brains). Then the students were expected to verify 'every material statement made in the lecture'. And yet, whatever was on the cover slide, the students tended to 'see' the picture drawn on the blackboard: they did 'not believe nature', Huxley admitted, they 'believed me'. The lab was as much a training ground for the demonstrators. Lankester, Foster, G. B. Howes and Thiselton-Dyer – the future professors – were 'generally up half the night rehearsing the demonstration for the following day', laying out Nature according to Huxley's Plan, rather than letting the students scramble it into chaos.[22]

The trainees' skills became instinctive through practice and exam reinforcement, when they too accepted the magnified image as obvious and 'natural'. Huxley was ruthless in his lighthearted way, and 'each visit inspired a certain amount of terror'. He would pause to look at a pupil's drawing, labelled 'sheep's liver' or whatever, and with that evil smile say, 'I am glad to know that is a liver; it reminds me as much of Cologne cathedral in a fog'.

He was teaching the teachers to see like him. They would sense Nature's iconoclastic strength. While older Classics dons objected to experimental studies because they encouraged students to question authority, Huxley actively turned the encounter with 'deep reality' into an attack on textbook tradition. He even relished it when advanced students questioned his own manuals: the wild-eyed Scot Patrick Geddes – the boy drawn from the Free Kirk to South Kensington by the *Lay Sermons* with their unimpeachable 'interpretation of existence' – teased apart a whelk's tongue and contradicted the master:

> 'Pon my word, you're right! You've got me! [Huxley told him] I was wrong! Capital! I must publish this for you!

His Nature became the new arbiter. Ultimately Huxley turned this virgin reality against a rival clerical authority – he used it against the priests in his attempt to claim territorial space, clearing out their supernature and usurping their authority to speak on the origin and meaning of life. Microscopic training became the academic's new credentials – his arcane entry card. A clergyman criticizing Darwin, and posting his articles to draw Huxley's fire, would receive the coded reply: 'Take a cockroach and dissect it!'[23] The cognoscenti saw 'truth' in those regions where only they were qualified to pursue it. It made microscopic training a perfect propaganda tool: Huxley was creating a legion of followers, looking at the world his way. The initiates were being taught the arcane skills of a new profession. The word 'biology' took root in the 1870s as the schoolmasters became the new authorities for Huxley's 'new Nature'. They had seen it for themselves.

Long-dead Edward Forbes had once thought that an 'educated youth ought, in a well-arranged museum, to be able to instruct himself'.[24] Twenty years on, Forbes' casual diorama experience was replaced by Huxley's experimental regime: a proper top-down training for students by State-paid professionals. The chaotic voluntarist aspect was waning. Nature ceased to be a spot of Sunday-afternoon recreation; an obligatory school science was being drilled into the nation.

That meant moving away from the crowded museum display. Laboratory logistics forced Huxley to minimize his exhibits. Where medical comparative anatomists like the old shabby-coated Lamarckian Robert Grant at University College had ploughed exhaustively through the animal kingdom – systematically following each organ system through the entire chain[25] – Huxley cut life up into a few exemplary 'types', and dealt with them as functioning wholes. And while at first he followed these old medical approaches by moving in a 'philosophical' way, from simple amoeba through to complex rats, that too would be reversed.

And still he overloaded his schoolmasters in the first years. In 1871 they had ten plant types, from yeast to conifers, and a dozen animals, from hydras to rabbits. There was a certain opportunism in his choice: his corpses had to be obtainable in quantity: amoebas, hydras and pond mussels were netted, frogs and rats caught in fields, and even the polyp *Cordylophora* was taken from Victoria docks.[26] But the skill required of novices to tackle minute yeast on their introduction to the microscope proved too much. So he reversed the order, starting them on the rat, and he cut the number of 'types' by a third. Expediency was at the birth of the modern biology practical.

No 'student of ordinary intelligence', one later said, 'could fail to see that the types were valuable, not for themselves, but simply as marking, so to speak, the chapters of a connected narrative'. But Huxley was teaching traditional morphology – the shape and structure of the basic 'types'; he kept one foot in the nineteenth-century morphological mainstream, which paid little heed to Darwin. And if there was any evolutionary 'narrative', it must have become hard to follow as he cut down the types and turned them around to start with the rat. In fact he first refused to 'mix up' evolution with his discrete types, fearing that it would 'throw Biology into confusion'.[27] He wanted his waters unmuddied and his types clear for the tyros. Ironically the need to simplify his school science left him looking less evolutionary than the old medical teachers.

He hurried daily out of South Kensington tube. Through the decorative arcade columns he marched up to his barren rooms, there to become engrossed in a cod dissection prior to his lectures. The fact that he started with no fittings at all forced him to requisition another £4,000 to furnish the natural history floor (which he wisely spent before the Treasury sanction was obtained).[28]

He tried to take life easily. He resolved 'to live scientifically & leave off politics which I suppose is, for me, the equivalent of "living cleanly & leaving off sack"'. His good intentions were for nought. Man was a born fighter, Carlyle said, but Huxley was a born general, ready to take on anybody's fight. For a year he had been trying to get Gladstone's bruising economizer Acton Smee Ayrton off Hooker's back. Ayrton was Hooker's Whitehall boss, and when he started pruning Kew Gardens, Huxley was on the garden gate. The 'idiotic mischief-making Ayrton' was sworn to cutting the public payroll. Kew to him was 'a semi-autonomous satrapy', rife with jobbers, and he sounded a threat to Hooker's independence. Huxley had rushed to 'make common cause and shew [Ayrton] that he has caught a Tartar in presuming to meddle with Science'.[29]

Thus began another debilitating fight to hold Science's territory. This time a hard one, for the case was about accountability. The professionals were using their claim to expertise to stand above the market-place. Now here was a new breed of populist cost-cutter who saw science as a tax drain. For years Huxley had been winning the Chancellor Robert Lowe over – wining him at the Royal, dining him at the X-Club, even escorting him on a pilgrimage to Downe. (He had met Lowe in Sydney with the future greats of Australian politics and knew him well.) Now he called in the chips, portraying Ayrton's action to Lowe as 'an affront to all the men of science'.[30] But others wondered if the scientific Establishment wasn't putting itself beyond parliamentary control. Like other professions science was setting its own standards and expecting a certain autonomy.

Huxley was dragged in by his camaraderie with Hooker. The lean Kew botanist had been his intellectual mainstay for 20 years. 'Like other good things you improve with age', Huxley told him: 'all but your handwriting which is horrid'. Kew Gardens had an international reputation: without it rubber would not have become established in the East Indies, nor cinchona (quinine) in Ceylon; and Hooker, famous for his work on Indian plants, shared in that reputation. Huxley hated to see him ground down by 'Ayrton the accursed (may jackasses sit upon his Grandmother's grave, as we say in the East)'.[31]

The Xs were turning science into a political force. It was not academic professionalism that bound them. After all, the group embraced philosophers and politicians and printers. But all saw science and industry as essential to the national health, and they supported an autonomous scientific civil service, based on specialist schooling and career opportunities. The group had the 'power of making ourselves unpleasant . . . and that is something the ministerial mind can appreciate'. They were 'wire-pullers', a critic said; and they proved it in every corridor. Tyndall waylaid Lord Derby at the Athenaeum and readied a petition against Ayrton for Parliament, which Huxley leaked to the press.[32] The story snowballed, and they made Hooker's hounding a national tragedy, even firing a debate in the Lords.

They had access to the Prime Minister through John Lubbock, himself in a rather invidious position as one of Gladstone's back-benchers. Not that it helped. Gladstone prevaricated, trying to avoid a Commons debate and a possible defeat. He preferred the preserves of Tradition to the pretensions of Science anyway. Huxley was infuriated by the PM's loquacious evasions: 'Some of these days he will turn himself inside out like a blessed Hydra, and I dare say he will talk just as well in that state . . . I never heard or read of any body with such a severely copious chronic glossorhea'.[33] It was the beginning of the Xs' growing disenchantment with Gladstone, and Gladstone's growing disenchantment with science. At best Hooker saw him as 'a craven bungler'; in time they would see him as something worse.

Old festering hatreds came to the fore when Ayrton had the haughty Richard Owen draw up a report on Kew to lay before Parliament: a report which reflected Owen's own imperial designs on Kew museum and accused Hooker of keeping an expensive herbarium for 'attaching barbarous binomials to dried foreign weeds'.[34] The Hookers of the world only knew about the law of science, Ayrton claimed in the House, while Ministers of the Crown were dwelling on the 'higher' science of law. He had a point but lost his seat at the General Election anyway. As *St James's Magazine* commented, a politician would henceforth 'as soon put his finger into a hornet's nest as treat a scientific man with contumely'. Corporate science emerged with its civil service ethos intact, in all its quasi-autonomous aspects.

Power continued accruing to the X-Clubbers. With four council seats in the Royal Society and the Secretary's chair, these senior statesmen oozed self-confidence. The next step, Huxley told Darwin in conspiratorial fashion, was to put Hooker in the President's chair. They managed it effortlessly and in 1873 Huxley was bidding Hooker, 'Oh King! come & reign over us'. With their man in front of the mace, the Xs could initiate their own Second Reform Bill. Hooker curtailed aristocratic privilege and – with the industrialists' money, £2,000 from Whitworth, £1,000 from the steel baron Sir William Armstrong – he set up a fund to subsidize poorer Fellows. As Huxley became the Biological Secretary in June 1872, the conservative Physical Secretary George Gabriel Stokes looked warily on the ginger group. He really 'dreads Huxley's being President', a fellow observed. Rather than cutting down work, Huxley cranked it up as he processed the Society's papers for publication. By now the Xs were divvying up posts almost by right. As Hirst informed Huxley of his election, Huxley was 'securing Hirst' – advising George Goschen (now Gladstone's First Sea Lord) over dinner to appoint Hirst Director of the Royal Naval College on its new Greenwich site.[35] And the Sea Lords were only too happy to install a physicist after the capsizing of HMS *Captain*. With George Busk settling in as President of the College of Surgeons (no worries here about having a gutsy wife), the Xs were becoming a sort of Institute of Scientific Directors.

Inside the *sanctum sanctorum*, they got things done. Huxley had the Royal Society's *Transactions* shipped off to Dohrn's marine station, that pan-European enterprise to unravel the embryology and evolution of life. And he liaised with Darwin to raise £500 from 'the land of fogs' to fund the Mediterranean enterprise. It was collected from 'each according to his ability': which meant that Darwin put in £75 while Huxley had 'no cash to spare'. But then Darwin was 'in all things, noble and generous', Huxley told Dohrn; 'one of those people who think it a privilege to let him help'.[36]

The new Secretary pushed open old creaky doors. No Royal Society paper had mentioned Darwinism (not even Huxley's). For ten years it had been shunned in the elite *Philosophical Transactions*, which remained factual, uncontroversial, anti-theoretical and aloof.[37] Evolution stayed on the literary fringes, in essays, press articles and reviews.

But the society's membership changes presaged new things. In came the academics and empire-builders, secular sons with their B.Sc.s, many echoing Tyndall's call for a new evolutionary imagination. Out went the marginalized clergymen (who dropped from 8 per cent to 5 per cent of the Fellowship in the 1870s).[38] Now the publication and grants committees gained a preponderance of Darwin sympathizers. But it still took a foreign revolutionary to break through the society's safe empirical confines. When the peripatetic Kovalevskii arrived in London to work on hippopotamus evolution, Huxley evidently persuaded him to submit his paper to the Royal. The revolutionary jumped at the idea, 'since "Phil. Trans." is a very stylish publication'.

Stylish or no, it still had a staid reputation. Huxley himself read the hippo paper at the society. But the Tory Anglican Stokes kicked up a kerfuffle at this first dazzling attempt at Darwinian palaeontology in England. He tried to cut out 'the objectionable passages', not wanting the society to sanction Kovalevskii's world of 'happy chances'. The Russian saw evolution in terms of chance modifications and changed terrains. But to Stokes this was 'flimsy to the last degree'. In his view, making speculative Darwinism as axiomatic as Newton's laws compromised the rock-like status of knowledge. How could a nihilist, known to Russia's secret police, be allowed to hail the 'complete revolution caused by Darwin's great work' in the *Phil. Trans.*? As befits Cambridge's Lucasian Professor of Mathematics, Stokes saw the 'continuous curve' joining the Creative

Acts as a piece of Divine Geometry. Life's course was planned. It was no 'Creation by Caprice'.[39] But Huxley pulled off the coup. He sent the paper out to sympathizers, who acted as referees, and they passed it. It was published intact to break the society's empirical impasse.

The high-pressure boiler whistled its warning again. Huxley teetered on the brink of a fragile recovery. He was unable to extricate himself from life, even its mundanities. Drink helped him to ease the pain, at least until Nettie hid the key to the cellar. The work piled up: during the June week that he posted the Ayrton petition, became the Royal Society Secretary, lobbied the Sea Lords for Hirst and started the teachers' practicals, he was trying to raise the cash for his house. He signed the contracts on 6 June 1872 and, with the extension costing over £4,000, he needed money. 'Brother John' came to his rescue: he placed £1,000 in Huxley's London & Westminster account. Unmarried and celebrated, Tyndall was 'perfectly secure' himself and could afford it.[40] It marked the start of a period of unprecedented help from Huxley's friends.

A year trying to move department, house and government alike left him complaining that his 'damnable bowels' were affecting his 'brains'. In August 1872 he migrated to a village outside Ilfracombe, on the rugged north Devon coast, to revise his *Lessons in Elementary Physiology*. He rented a house 'at the head of a ravine running down to the sea'; but there was no recuperation. The book simply kept the bustling world before him. Even reworking another textbook spoke of his dedication: while audiences were ready to fall at his feet at the sight of a blockbuster – a brilliant travelogue escorting them to an exotic Cretaceous age or Coal-swamp era – he was producing primers. And those in fast-moving fields. He knew that his *Physiology* might 'only stand for a year or two'.[41] He was sacrificing himself on the professional altar.

Sickness forced him back to London 'to recover from the effects of the country'! Crash diets followed; he left off 'meat, alcohol, & baccy' (to Nettie's pleasure) and improved for a while. 'I find that if I am to exist at all it must be on strictly ascetic principles', he told Tyndall, 'so there is hope of my dying in the odour of sanctity yet'.[42]

He was still discarding work where he could. In November he relinquished his Presidency of the Metaphysical Society 'with much joy'. He crawled to the end of the year trying to get the Marlborough Place house habitable, widening doors, worrying about the coal cellar, trying to fight his way into the wine cellar. They were kept out of the house until Christmas by the 'stupid delays of the workmen whom we had fairly to shove out'. It was hardly a pretty house, more a functional shrine to Victorian hard work and large litters, and big enough to accommodate visiting nieces or foreign dignitaries. The original white-painted cottage had become dwarfed by Huxley's uncompromising yellow-brick extension, the lot screened from the road by a row of ubiquitous Regent's Park lime trees.

It was Spring 1873 before the tiles were baked the right colour and they could move into the drawing room. On the walls went photos of friends and portraits presented by Royal Academy artists. Here the famous Sunday gatherings were to be held to the accompaniment of hymns from the Presbyterian church next door. Great men of science would sit with great poets. Robert Browning was a regular, as was the Shakespearean *grande dame* Helena Martin ('Helen Faucit'). Hal's study, the old dining room, was 'a mass of books – all round the walls, on the chairs and floor in heaps, everywhere'. Darwin sent Nettie a cheque to help with the furniture, but the rooms remained very simply furnished. The whole had a carefree cultured look, suggesting 'people of great refinement and with no pretensions'.[43]

Feeling 'such a dyspeptic hypochondriacal poor devil', the last thing Huxley wanted was a lawsuit. The builders had dug a well to improve the surface drainage and 'a knavish neighbour' claimed that it made his basement damp. The man was simply trying to swindle money out of Huxley, but it still went to court. 'Fancy finding myself a defendant in Chancery!' he wrote to Tyndall, on tour in America. The fees mounted as the case was put down to be heard before Vice-Chancellor Sir Richard Malins. James Knowles, his architect and *Contemporary* editor, heard about it all in each capacity. 'Macmillan wants another volume of essays of me', Huxley told him. 'I suppose you have no objection to my reprinting those I sent you for the Contemporary'?[44] Another compilation might at least help to defray the costs. He was set to call it prosaically *Critiques and Addresses*. It would still extol the moral and social force of science as he wove his way through the myriad tiny worlds of yeast, coal swamps or coral. But the new political tone was set by the opening pleas for State aid and State education.

On Thursday morning, 20 February 1873, Huxley won his case and was awarded £245 costs. It was a happier man who went off to the Royal Society that afternoon. 'You see that I have walloped my friend Mr Broad [the plaintiff]', he reported to Hooker. A huge weight was lifted; for an upright man, trying to disprove the myth that evolutionists inhabited a moral quagmire, the Court of Chancery was no place to be dragged over drains. But the euphoria ended when he found that 'the brute is impecunious & that I shall get nothing out of him. So I shall have had three months worry' and be left with court costs, though 'wholly & absolutely in the right'.[45]

Huxley was financially astute (even Matthew Arnold asked his advice about royalties on his poems). But money seemed to slip through his fingers. During the ordeal he tried to recoup with a new essay for the *Contemporary*. He jumped from hot water to the frozen deep. He did what he did best, act as science's salesman and glory in the first piece of 'Big Biology' sponsored by the State. The talk of technical decline and German competition had dented the national pride. Huxley now cheered as the government underwrote HMS *Challenger*'s voyage to sample the world's oceans. Science under the White Ensign could be rationalized as an assessment of global sea-bed resources, or sounding the depths for cable-laying. But in truth this was the first truly biological rather than Admiralty venture, and these were 'the best equipped voyagers who ever left the shores of England'. Later it would be heralded as the birth of modern oceanography.

The expedition under Captain George Nares would last four years and employ a host of civilian specialists. The 2,300-ton corvette set off with its cannon bays converted into labs. Criss-crossing the oceans, its dredge was hauled in from ever greater depths by the donkey engine. Up came bloated fishes from 1,000 fathoms, their eyes 'protruding like great globes from their heads'. The Victorians with their expanded evolutionary horizons were charting the last unknown. For Huxley it was a romantic trek: a quest in the unchanging depths for lost empires. Here might be living fossils, 'survivors of a world passed away', creatures from the dinosaurian Chalk Era. And why not? Wasn't the chalky *Globigerina* mud made up of microscopic shells like those in our Cretaceous rocks?[46] Might not other 'persistent types' lurk down there too? This hunt for past forms would become endlessly enmeshed in the science-fiction notion of prehistoric monsters dredged from the deep, but for a moment it seemed real.

The voyage cut to the heart of his own speculations. What of his primal-slime creature *Bathybius* (whose existence the Berlin protozoologist Christian Ehrenberg – revenging himself for Huxley's attacks? – had begun to doubt)?[47] Was the ocean floor carpeted by pulsating protoplasm as Huxley, Haeckel and almost everybody else now imagined? No secrets were to be left in the abyss.

The head of the *Challenger* staff was the rotund Charles Wyville Thomson (the new Professor of Natural History at Edinburgh). Interested in abyssal life, he had dredged with Carpenter as far as the Faroes and published *The Depths of the Sea*. He had sent Huxley armoured fossil fishes from Orkney's rocks and consulted him on the naturalists to take aboard. 'I rejoice that my friend Charlie has done so well', Huxley told Hooker, all thanks to 'the moral discipline he received from me'.[48] Now 'Charlie' was paid £1,000 a year on the *Challenger*, and he reported as faithfully to Huxley as to the Admiralty.

Others aboard the ship did too. The young German naturalist R. von Willemoës-Suhm sent reports from around the globe. He even had a talking parrot for Nettie, but neither of them reached port: Suhm died in the Pacific. With a chemist, artist, photographer and three naturalists aboard, every dredge sample was analysed and recorded. The records fell for life at the depths as tube worms came out of the peculiar red clay at 3,000 fathoms. The surprise was that there *was* a 'busy life which, contrary to all the beliefs of the naturalists of a past generation, blindly toils and moils in the darkness and cold'. These creatures of the abyss seemed to be continuous across all the oceans, but cut off from surface forms. It was as if, in Huxley and Thompson's view, the freezing uniform sea-bed had slowed evolution to leave a bizarre archaic population.

Huxley was the supreme publicist. But it was a case of two steps forward and one back. He sent the *Challenger* manuscript in April and received Knowles' contractor's bills by return. Knowles at least was relieved to find that Huxley's 'literary style is not badly affected by your blue devils – on the contrary one would swear from the print of your hoof that you were never stronger, more serviceable or more dangerous'. The *Review* reached the *Challenger* in Nova Scotia in May and was read by the naturalists 'with great satisfaction'.[49] Not so the ratings, evidently; they were unimpressed with the endless 'drudging' and five showed it by deserting.

But Huxley was unable to keep his head above water. Some £560 in contractor's bills were still outstanding and the money was due in late April 1873. Lady Lyell saw how 'harassed' he looked, and at her prompting the entire Darwinian–industrial complex paid its dues. She mooted starting a fund to Emma Darwin. Coincidentally Fanny Hooker too was proposing that the Xs cover Huxley's law expenses. The female household role was one of social support in the family, and the Darwinian brotherhood was a sort of extended intellectual family ('brother John', 'sister Nettie'). Clearly it was the women who were sensitive to Huxley's emotional state – and as the traditional givers of presents and philanthropy they were unabashed at the idea of a money gift. Yet the patriarch headed the family enterprise, whether intellectual or business, and the men now veiled the women off. The Huxleys visited the Downe hamlet on 8 March and probably gave the Darwins an account of the court case. Huxley clearly wasn't well. He was thin and haggard, and probably confessed (as he had to Foster) that he had 'to take the most absurd care of my eating & drinking – or I lapse from Grace'. He had a crushing feeling of 'everything having gone wrong in the world', Nettie confided to Lizzie, 'a profound melancholy' which made him wretched. Dr Clark had ordered him abroad for three months, and 'somehow it must be managed, tho' . . . money is not too plentiful'.[50]

Emma Darwin had Charles pass the plate around on 7 April. It piled high as it moved from X to X, and every deception was mooted for forcing the cash on Huxley. Darwin's brother Erasmus added £100, and so much enthusiasm had Darwin raising his own sub to £300. But he feared the female hand showing itself. Lady Lyell (the instigator) so disconcerted him by insisting on putting her own (rather than Sir Charles') money in that he resolved to 'keep her amount secret'.[51] This was to be a gift between 'brother' naturalists, and disguising Lady Lyell's role only emphasized the patriarchal prerogative. (And that was tragic because the day after Huxley received the money Lady Lyell died.)

Tyndall's 'magnificent success' with the ironmasters Sir William Armstrong and Sir Joseph Whitworth had the pot brimming with £1,700.[52] By the 11th Darwin was drafting a letter and quaking, but Tyndall thought that the 'brotherly spirit of the transaction' would win Huxley over.

On 23 April, £2,100 – two years' salary – was paid through Lubbock's bank into Huxley's account and Darwin posted 'the awful letter'. The 18 friends who subscribed refused to take 'no' for an answer; it was for his holiday and his health, and his acceptance would 'be a happiness to us to the last day of our lives'. The delicacy of it left them on tenterhooks. 'I tremble about his answer', Darwin told Tyndall, but 'it is a pleasure to think what a relief it will be to M^rs. H.'[53] 'I hope we may hear to-morrow', Darwin's daughter Etty wrote. 'It will be very awful'.

The sentiment overwhelmed Huxley that evening and turned his stern exterior to a shambles. After a sleepless night as he wondered 'what I have done to make my friends care so tenderly', he opened up groggily to Darwin in the morning:

> I accept the splendid gift . . . for the first time in my life I have been fairly beaten. I mean morally beaten. Through all sorts of troubles & difficulties poverty illness, bedevilments of all sorts have I steered these thirty years, and never lost heart or failed to buffet the waves as stoutly as they buffeted me . . . [But] I have for months been without energy & without hope & haunted by the constant presence of hypochondriacal apprehensions which my reason told me were absurd but which I c[d] not get rid of – for I was breaking down; sliding into the meanest of difficulties, the would be climber of heights, mired in a mere bog . . . Well I have poured out all this Jeremiad that you may understand what your . . . great gift will do for me . . .
>
> Have I said a word of appreciation for your own letter? I shall keep it for my children that their children may know what manner of man their father's friend was & why he loved him.[54]

It was 'so grand & sweet' that Darwin was quite affected.

There would have been more factory money. The Manchester mill owner Thomas Ashton's 'only regret' was that he missed joining 'with your old friends in their bank operation'. But even £2,100 would see Huxley proud, relieve his house and court debts, and it would prove to be the financial turning-point. 'I shall go & take a long holiday in the summer now without feeling that I am particularly guilty of fraud, and when the blue devil dances about me . . . I shall slap the cheque for £2100 at his head as Luther did the inkstand'.[55]

Spencer, rejoicing 'that our plot has succeeded so well', wanted Huxley to leave immediately. It was out of the question with 7,000 school papers to be marked. Anyway he was improving, and two new books would show that life was returning to 'the old dog'. The *Physiology* textbook had appeared in March, and he thanked his benefactors with copies of *Critiques and Addresses* in late April. That too was selling well, 'Bless the British Public', with booksellers taking half the stock on publication day.[56]

His 48th birthday was heralded by apple blossoms in the back garden. His new delight was to sit in the sun, smoking, a book open – perhaps Fitzjames Stephen's conservative *Liberty, Equality and Fraternity* with its 'world of muscular sense'. Or potter like Darwin; sowing beans and pulling up bracken, the 'type' plants of his practicals. 'I am steadily mending', he told his 'doctor of doctors' Andrew Clark. Clark was glad of it. He was now standing on Huxley's shoulders to reach the highest intellectual echelons. Through Huxley he made contact with Tyndall, and ultimately with Darwin, whom he subjected to an 'abominable diet'. But Huxley was doing well under Clark's regime: riding 15 miles a day or walking around Regent's Park, and in bed by 10 to sleep 'like a top'. 'The animal part of me is really getting into first rate order', he reported. '"Ape & Tiger" (as Tennyson has it) very much alive', even if the critical faculty 'has shut up shop'.[57]

Money in the bank, success in the bookshops and one of Clark's diets saw him off on holiday in fine mood. He celebrated the 'wifes birthday' on 1 July and then set out with Hooker. He left a 'Black mug!' still full-bearded. But the 'beauty & geological interest' of the volcanic Auvergne capped his recovery, not to mention an ice-age human that the 'happy-go-lucky pair' stumbled on in Le Puy museum. No longer the 'broken-down old fellow', he was so buoyant that in Baden-Baden he felt 'ashamed of loafing about when I might very well be at work' (he had skipped the 1873 schoolmasters' course). The beard now symbolized that 'dreary illness' and it came off as he turned the corner.[58] It was his 'old original phiz' that greeted Nettie and Len when they joined him in Cologne with a celebratory box of Jamaica cigars.

Nettie was full of news: the King of Sweden had awarded the Order of the North Star to the evangelical triumvirate, Huxley, Hooker and Tyndall. Even as that sank in there was more, the death of an older evangelical. He heard of Bishop Wilberforce's sad passing, thrown from his horse. Wilberforce had been as busy a professional on the other side of the fence, organizing his clergy, visiting parishes and demanding information and statistics. The anti-racist son of a great abolitionist, Wilberforce had made humans one moral community, and had refused to place blacks nearer to apes or countenance an immoral anti-Christian evolution. Huxley, who had traded insults with him at the BAAS and organized exhibits with him at the Zoological Society, saw only his Tory reaction. 'Poor dear Sammy! His end has been all too tragic for his life', he said. 'For once, reality & his brains came into contact & the result was fatal'.[59]

His death as Huxley was knighted showed the tenor of the times. Honours as a sign of privilege and place Huxley abhorred. But the Swedish award for scientific merit was 'a good honest acknowledgment of one's work' – assuming that an English civil servant could actually accept it.[60]

So Huxley finished a frightful year. The 'wretched despondency' had passed; 'he is as bright & merry, as ever', Nettie rejoiced, and the 'Years only knit us together in closer & tenderer love'.

The government allowed Huxley his North Star insignia. He had survived his worst mental crisis and come out 'safe, sound & flourishing' and sporting a scientific knighthood. 'I really am wonderfully better, more myself than I have been for these two years'.[61]

3

Automatons

NOTHING SEEMED IMPOSSIBLE in the world's leading industrial nation. History was made as Crookes worked on cathode rays and Bell perfected the telephone. Britain even felt safe enough to begin test borings for a Channel Tunnel. Science and technology were making news.

By 1874 the restructuring of science was under way. It was becoming State-managed, with curriculums tightly prescribed and classrooms tightly policed. From the regimented lab to the patrolled exam hall, the regime was in place. The South Kensington professors were turning out their 'Whitworth Scholars' to run machine shops or teach in school.

It was no coincidence that this restructuring occurred as the traumas over evolution graduated into new concerns. Darwinism was becoming endurable, even natural for the industrial few. The histrionics caused by the *Origin* and *Essays* had passed. *The Descent of Man* went into a half-price second edition without a murmur, even though the mild Darwin – who could hate with the best of them – added Huxley's scalping 'supplement' on the outcome of the ape-brain debate to spite 'the fiend, Owen'. 'Denuded of its controversial spice', even a Brobdingnagian fossil world began to lose its fashionable interest in the 1870s.[1]

But the new concerns allowed Hal to keep his capacity crowds. An industrial-age evolution was supported on deep piles, rarely seen and never doubted. These axiomatic foundations – like the immense underground piles Londoners saw going under the new tall buildings – were massive load-bearers: an undeviating uniformity of nature, the exact interchange of all forms of energy, and human thought as a function of the brain chemistry. This axiomatic undergirding legitimized Huxley's power brokers. Tyndall went further. In his pantheon this Trinity was flanked by pagan lesser gods – Determinism and Necessity. Huxley at first banned these house deities, but they kept returning to haunt him. For a while he too saw a mechanical 'higher design' in a self-developing universe, where 'the existing world lay, potentially, in the cosmic vapour'. If 'we could project ourselves back' into the primal gas-cloud, he said, 'and then look forward we would be seen drinking our gin and water'.

From this scientific temple the 'priesthood of science', as Holyoake dubbed them, made their pitch for cultural leadership. The evangelical appeal of Tyndall's poetically self-flowering universe inured an intellectual and street culture against all supernatural interference. Matter itself had become one great miracle. There was a flamboyant assurance to it, a beguiling romance to Tyndall's story which made Everyone a child of the Sun.[2]

Many felt it, some vicarages began to waver. Letter after letter dropped through Huxley's mailbox from vicars with problems, vicars with doubts, vicars who held him responsible. Perhaps he felt it. They told of disillusion and anguish. Revd W. H. Dalton, a year after his Cambridge MA, wrote:

> I have no other excuse for thus trespassing on your time than the fact that thus early in life (27) religious convictions similar to yours & that of Professor Tyndall have prompted me to take what I consider a true step & resign what is in Ecclesiastical Language called 'holy orders' . . . & what I want is some work as secretary or manager of some sort . . . Can you offer me such a position? or tell me to whom to apply, & what you would advise under the circumstances?

Then came the vicar of St Pancras, Revd Anthony Thorold (shortly to become the Bishop of Rochester). He tackled Huxley as 'a kind-hearted and truly considerate man' because his curate had 'run so completely off the rails' after reading Huxley's *Lay Sermons* and Tyndall's books, with their pious aura of cosmic inevitability and new rationales for existence. The poor man was 'drifting fast towards utter "materialism"'. 'You are his Pope', Thorold pleaded, 'he thinks there is no one in the world like you'. It said much of an age in change that the tolerant Thorold asked the agnostic Pope to chat to his drifting curate.

That curate was a Yorkshire squire's son 'at once rather intelligent & totally unintellectual'.[3] Perhaps with the Church a dumping-ground for so many directionless sons of the gentry, this was to be expected. Even the law began to reflect it. Not only were the sons of the cotton kings now admitted to Oxford and Cambridge, but a Clerical Disabilities Act at last allowed vicars to resign their orders (they had not been able to before). Still, Huxley – that sweet voice of scientific reason – was as much symptom as cause.

The material cosmos with its mystical molecular potential came into vogue in the 1870s, as the territorial clashes over education and health between Huxley's professionals and a pastoral clergy peaked. Huxley and Tyndall's new religion lay in duty and agnostic morality – acquiescence before the fact – rather than superstitious reverence. These were the credentials for the thrusting professionals jealous of the State-endowed Church. Science had to be State-endowed too. The campaign swayed leading Tories. Lord Salisbury agreed before the Devonshire Commission that, like parish toil, 'research is unremunerative' but 'highly desirable for the community'.[4] Weren't men of science improving the moral, educational and medical state of the nation as they raised its international prestige?

Temporal benefits were the prize as a sectarian science contrasted itself with the wealthy Church. Never had the Church been richer. With universities, palaces, Lord Bishops and deep coffers, it was 'the most socially powerful group of intellectuals in the nation'. Never had it seemed richer: new seminaries were graduating more clergymen for dozens of new urban parishes. That expansion only increased the territorial tensions. The new science was deliberately made to tell against the clergy's supernatural sanction. The urban dissenters saw no descending spiral of power passing from God through this State priesthood into a capricious Nature. Nor did they doubt that the Church had lost its divine spark and become a place of idolatry. In contrast, Tyndall and Huxley drew their power from the universal soul – Nature would back their claim to 'domination over the whole realm of the intellect'.[5]

The propaganda peaked in an infamous challenge. A surgery professor at University College Hospital mooted a 'Prayer Gauge', to test the power of prayer on the sick in the wards. It was a disturbingly simple sign of the intensifying border dispute over public health. Despite the great sanitation movement, national days of prayer to check plagues were on the increase. Nettie's Marylebone vicar Llewelyn Davies was almost alone in dismissing these cosmos-diverting responses as a 'mechanical prophylactic'. For the rest, the Prince of Wales' recovery from typhoid after a day of prayers seemed proof enough. The *Guardian* even called for more of this 'moral regenerating power' in place of impious science. The last straw was the medical profession's virtual exclusion from the thanksgiving in St Paul's Cathedral, which turned into a celebration of the Divine power of Church and Throne. The doctors responded with the prayer test, to be conducted in the medical schools, hotbeds of materialism and cynicism by repute. (Huxley's Dr Clark had him ask Tyndall for a lecture on the pointlessness of prayer at his own London Hospital.)[6] No such test took place. But had it, Francis Galton was certain that it would have vindicated the insurance brokers, who offered no discounts to the 'praying classes'.

The brutal polemicist hardly seemed so brutal at home. Here Huxley appeared to visitors 'as tender as a woman'. The corpulent cosmic philosopher John Fiske made Marlborough Place his Mecca. He came over from Harvard, carting his *Cosmic Philosophy* manuscript, desperate to experience this 'clean-cut mind'. Having been warned by a cockney expat in New York about the ''orrid hold hinfidel 'Uxley', Fiske expected a baby-eating ogre. But he found 'a very gentle old chap, for such a savage controversialist'. By the New Year 1874 Fiske was coming each Sunday to the Huxleys' 'Tall Teas'. His infectious humour matched Huxley's flair for the absurd. Whatever Huxley's eager burning intensity, 'he was nothing if not playful', and no scientific salon was so thick with puns. Even the damp walls now had Huxley joking about the 'fresh water lake under the basement'. ('I did not covenant for this valuable water property when the house was built'.) Nor, these being Sundays, did the agnostic see anything incongruous in standing Fiske by the piano to sing psalms.

In the little library, Huxley sat by the fire smoking a narrow brierwood pipe. He talked politics or theology with the same clinical precision as he discussed *Amphioxus* anatomy. He was 'alive in all directions', Fiske said – and peppy, judging by the pipe and 'noggin of Glenlivet'. Fiske's was a vibrant image of '*Patter*', learning Russian to read Kovalevskii, or burrowing into 'old Benedict' (Spinoza), his passion. (One corner was stuffed with crumbling old orthodox tomes, which he called the 'condemned cell'.) The heavens were overhauled in that room. Huxley found rest in change and devoured books rapaciously. Straight from South Kensington he would settle in to Spinoza in Latin or 'Sybil's French Revolution . . . until the witching hour'. Even novel-reading had the intensity of a dissection; still in love with strong women, he fell on George Sand's emotionally-soaked fiction as he would a new fish. ('She is bigger than George Eliot, more flexible, a more thorough artist'.) His encyclopedic recall and acerbic wit gave the common man an uncommon mind like 'Saladin's sword which cut through the cushion'. But Fiske's lasting impression, he told his wife on 15 January 1874, was of a 'lovely' man, even if the little 'Uxleys were used to seeing the chief cast as a 'cannibal'.[7]

The little Huxleys were not so little any more, even if '*Patter*' was still to be 'pulled about and tousled and kissed'. Len was already devouring Pater's and Tyndall's books. The girls were growing and life was sweet again. Jessie was turning 16. But it was Mady's contralto voice as she sang love songs that captivated Fiske. She was a delicate, sensitive girl. Privately her mental health left Hal and Nettie in 'constant terror', and each relapse caused Hal to 'collapse inwardly'. But to the world she was an artist with the mark of brilliance and she gave the exuberant Yankee a 'wonderful' painting of seven-year-old Ethel for his library. With their strong features the elder girls were already attracting admirers, chief among them the cheery illustrator Sam Waller and his architect brother Fred.[8] The Wallers, young Jim's distant cousins, were beginning to weave themselves into the family.

Spiritualism was all the rage in Britain. It had broken out of its confines among Pentecostalist plebeians and disillusioned socialists. Society swells now gave the manifestations a cachet. As religious authority outside the home declined, in darkened drawing rooms the spiritualist reaction to the materialism of the age intensified.[9] Wallace still awaited the spirit-delivered Millennium, but it was the conversion of William Crookes that really worried the professionals. Here was an elite chemist, Hofmann's one-time assistant, and the discoverer of the element thallium. Worse, he was a scrupulous experimenter.

Huxley was still fighting for the control of hearts and minds – still claiming cultural authority for his agnostic professionals. It required constant vigilance. Rival claimants to power ran from Scottish physicists with their unseen forces and romantic Owens with their Will-driven nature to these tricked-up table-turners. Agnosticism was a philosophic nicety and no threat to the wandering spirits manipulated by mediums. A more aggressive tack was needed to meet the new threat.

The mediums and their message had Huxley yawning. He could barely rouse himself to casual sarcasm; there was even a detectable ambivalence, for he had a 'sneaking admiration' for the real geniuses among the female fraudsters. Perhaps his problem was that so many mediums *were* women. When Ray Lankester did drag a psychic into court for a show trial on a charge of criminal fraud – duping the paying public – he made sure it was a man. (The original entrapment was set for the English medium Charles Williams, but the visiting American Henry Slade presented a bigger catch. He was sentenced to three months' hard labour, but got off on appeal.) Prosecuting a woman would have been inconceivable. But such a high-profile case belied the fact that spiritualism was a female preserve. In an age of sublimated sexual politics, when women's aspirations were high, when fathers and sons (judging by the Darwins and Huxleys, but it was probably true of much middle-class society) were agnostics while wives and daughters remained religious, mediumship became an autonomy-gaining, status-raising cottage industry which cashed in (literally) on the woman's traditional spiritual authority within the home.[10]

She was, in Tennyson's poetic stereotype,

> No angel, but a dearer being, all dipt
> In angel instincts, breathing Paradise,
> Interpreter between the Gods and men.[11]

The perfect medium.

Ghosts babbling like 'old women' did not appeal to Huxley. True, they argued eloquently against suicide. 'Better live a crossing-sweeper', he laughed, 'than die and be made to talk twaddle by a "medium" hired at a guinea' a time. He only attended the séance on 27 January 1874 after receiving the royal call. Darwin's son George was to hire Crookes' medium, Charles Williams – a psychic who had astonished Darwin's brother-in-law Hensleigh Wedgwood. They were to put Williams in a controlled situation at Wedgwood's house. As a rival experimentalist, Huxley had already learnt the black art: he could rap with his toes while his foot remained motionless. So he went incognito as 'Mr Henry'. He grasped Williams' hand in the dark and gauged the muscle strain as if he were testing a galvanized frog. Huxley's account of the trickery relieved Darwin. But Huxley's cover broke (he was spotted in the street), and all he got for his pains was Crookes' invitation to a six-week session with the psychic forces and a set of Wedgwood's best ghost photos.[12]

Public credulity showed how much further the New Reformation had to run. Always the educationalists wanted to sharpen Saladin's sword. Huxley was offered Playfair's Directorship of Science at the Department of Science and Art. But the Department had become byzantine in its complexity and impenetrable in its secrecy, and in 20 years Sir Henry Cole had turned from a 'bureaucratic reformer into a reformist bureaucrat'.[13] Besides, Huxley wanted to stay on the production side. So in civil service style Cole promoted a loyalist from within. Major Donnelly was upgraded with Huxley's blessing.

Huxley would have made a good organizer, but he was better spared for publicizing Nature's moral revelation. Not that anyone spared him. The Pope was expected to pontificate on every subject. The guardian of science had become Pythia's priest, with a status to match. From the sublime to the ridiculous, the requests rolled in. What did he think of free will and miracles, aquariums and *Amphioxus*? Would he go to the Lord Mayor's Dinner, or to the unveiling of Lord Derby's statue? What about an all-expenses-paid trip to India?[14] Would he review Mill's autobiography? Or write entries for the *Encyclopaedia Britannica*?

Huxley's illness had passed. Even so reports of his death were filtering across Europe, and he was being mourned by Kovalevskii in Russia. But his ghost was 'uncommonly lively',[15] and proved it by manifesting everywhere. He emerged at Aberdeen University to add a new post to his list. Here the Lord Rector was elected by the students and had real power in the Court. Huxley came in over a clansman, the Marquis of Huntley; and a Sassenach 'who stinketh in the nostrils of orthodoxy, beating a Scotch peer at his own gate . . . is a curious sign of the times'. Still, a dirty campaign had seen student intimidation and taunts, and the *Aberdeen Free Press* bewailed the 'deeper and darker blasphemies' which would creep north of the border with him. So much for abjuring the political arena. The students got what they wanted: a vigorous reformer rather than tartan title. And Huxley rang the changes – or tried to. 'I shall probably go down to posterity as the Rector who was always beaten', he prophesied to the students. Modernizing the medical curriculum was the least of it: 'I have been in Aberdeen fighting for the admission of Scotch dissenters to bursaries in my University & getting beaten', he told that English Dissenter Michael Foster, 'the parsons being too many for me. But we shall win yet'.[16]

A level playing field summed up his Rectorial Address. No religious or financial barriers; no Classics to the exclusion of Science and Art. The university had to be 'accessible to all comers'. Not that Aberdeen was a 'hot-bed of high-fed, hypercritical refinement', and he blessed its bursary system, which let poor boys trade their ploughshares for callipers. But the Rector was looking further afield. 'I have used the Aberdonians for the benefit of Oxford &

Cambridge', he told Foster, 'much as Tacitus drew the manners of the Germans for the benefit of the Romans'. The *Scotsman* called it wise and 'worth volumes of the emasculate stuff which the Lord Rector of Glasgow [Disraeli] recently' ventured. Still, said Huxley, 'I doubt if I shall be able to show my face in Oxford & Cambridge after it'.[17]

Huxley practised what he preached and returned to his workers' lectures. There was no wealth or rank test here; or rather there was, in reverse – only bona fide workers could get in. Occasionally students or reporters joined them, but, as Bernard Becker found on his survey of *Scientific London*, Huxley's theatre saw no '*Angot* caps and red opera cloaks'. It was crammed with real handicraftsmen. From the factory gates they trudged on Monday nights, not deterred by a 'Wild North-Easter', to hear his formidably titled 'On the Phenomena of Life as Motion and Consciousness'. Only in 1874 could such a penny-a-lecture series be a sell-out among such a class. Others tried to join them. His righteous science mated to social betterment had a stirring appeal. To young ordinands looking for a crusade it was irresistible. It wasn't only the freethinkers who infiltrated his lectures. One infatuated curate who spiced his sermons with science and knew the 'Physical Basis of Life' by heart begged a ticket, on the grounds that no man worked harder dashing around a parish of 17,000 souls.

The ease with which his lectures could be assimilated made them beguiling. Nettie said he had a sort of 'telepathic effect which enables you at once to perceive his meaning', or to think you do. There was no 'rustling, hushing, and settling down'. The artisans sat in deep silence as Huxley turned them into thinking automatons with an 'astounding bit of speculative philosophy'.[18]

But Huxley, becoming the solid middle-class professional, had a complex relationship with his factory hands. Some activists continued to cannibalize his science for their own co-operative ends. But he was a persuasive advocate; he made his labourers feel like a jury, and thus part of the process of scientific deliberation.[19] And many bearded workers tacitly accepted his lead and with it the hegemony of the Darwinian elite.

One can see why. By 1874 Huxley was becoming more the scientific determinist, making one's feeling of 'Free Will' simply an emotional warmth which accompanies some compunction. Yet only three years earlier, in 1871, his more cautious admission that the world was as likely to be the mental construct of a conscious mind as an objective material entity had brought jeers from the militant materialists on the street. They accused him of casting 'Idealistic dust in our eyes; seemingly to prevent the bigots calling him Materialist'.[20]

In 1874 Huxley's scientific dishes were spiced more to their taste. This March, he discussed Descartes' conception of brutes as self-adjusting machines. Epiphenomenal consciousness, reflex arcs, paraplegia: it seemed an unappetizing platter, but as always it came lightly served, and the factory hands had to like a lecturer who could moot the 'mechanical equivalent of consciousness'. Huxley was turning full-circle to his own back-street youth – to the radical Methodist Marshall Hall's reflex-arc concept at Sydenham College. After 30 years that Dissenting, alienating, Calvinistic concept had come to explain the very brain itself.[21] Huxley's automaton humans matched Tyndall's futuristic babies built from chemicals. And whatever Huxley's philosophic provisos, who among the godless unwashed would not have seen him throwing out free will and the threats and promises of an afterlife?[22]

America still beckoned. Tyndall had triumphantly toured from Boston to Baltimore. He had sold out \$5 seats and the star treatment ended in him joining Emerson and Longfellow in their 'galaxy of genius'. The takings reflected it, and he had left \$13,033 in trust, which would mature to endow Fellowships at Harvard, Columbia and Pennsylvania. Huxley organized the welcome-home party to hear about it. He was still a charity case himself: school fees, maids' salaries, meat bills and £150 cheques to drain the Marlborough Place 'lake' ate into his pay. Nettie could not even afford to go to the British Association with him. Huxley told Darwin that he had 'had an *awfully* tempting offer to go to Yankee-land', and 'two or three thousand pounds' was 'not to be sneezed at by a *père de famille*'. Rumour was rife in America: everyone thought that Harvard was about to make him a proposition. If they welcomed the 'raging infidel' Tyndall, Huxley's time had come.[23]

But where was the opportunity? He wanted Hooker to join him, but President and Secretary were held fast at the Royal Society. Every Thursday the senior statesmen did their duty. Hooker's lean figure could be seen swamped by the massive presidential chair, his worn face 'surmounted by a pair of those bushy eyebrows' which added gravity to his lean features. This was the imperial botanist who had just declined a knighthood as beneath the dignity of science. (Only Huxley approved, but, Hooker told Darwin, 'he *despises* Knighthood'.) Grave wasn't the word for the Secretary lounging in the armchair to his left, tweaking him that 'Sir Joseph looms in the future' so he had better practise kneeling in the bathroom mirror. The Royal was still a place of lords and commoners, but these two symbolized the careerists at the helm. And Huxley was for a continuing squeeze. As he said after one function: 'Noble Lords did not make good speeches. Plebeians, on the whole, distinguished themselves'.[24] He was in fine fettle again; and having done so much 'to gild the pill of science' he could afford to swank.

America was postponed for a year or so. Interminable lectures, 7,000 exam papers for school pupils and an oversubscribed course for their teachers required Olympian organization.[25] Huxley and Foster, the 'Best of Archangels', expanded their experimental work-force: the demonstrators now were of exceptional calibre – there was no team like it anywhere in the world. Rutherford had become the Professor of Physiology at Edinburgh; he brought his own pupil, the rising neurologist David Ferrier, already experimenting on the cerebral cortex for his book *The Functions of the Brain*. There was Martin, and the Gradgrinding Parker. More sons were co-opted. They were blooded young, and it was nothing for the 19-year-old Jeffrey Parker to be set marking the 'Elementary papers'. A corporate approach came with professionalization. Huxley began regimenting these research students, presenting each with an esoteric topic (the frog's larynx for young Parker) and coordinating the results.[26]

Huxley's heart was in London and his mind in the Black Country. An engineer he had wanted to be, and they were his men, with their frank, foundry-based, cause-and-effect universe. The family's industrial connections were being riveted tighter. In 1874 his niece Alice married the railway engineer Arthur Heath, who would go on to teach at Cooper's Hill (latterly the technological Brunel University). Steel towns welcomed Huxley: in 1874 he would speak as Governor of Owen's College in Manchester. Or he would take Nettie and the girls to his friend Sir William Armstrong, the munitions manufacturer, at his Gothic manor house Cragside, amid the wild heather-covered hills of Northumberland (in what would be the first of almost yearly Summer visits). And while the children rode and boated, Hal wheedled money out of Armstrong's steelworks for Dohrn's marine station.[27]

But the telling connection was with Birmingham. Birmingham – with its vast social-engineering projects centred on Civic Hall. This 'experimental, adventurous' city – once the most sickly, polluted and ghetto-infested in England – was proclaiming the new civic gospel. Here the old Radicalism had flowered into a spending municipal socialism thanks to one man, the Unitarian Mayor Joseph Chamberlain. Chamberlain's caucus, fired by the Nonconformist hatred of Establishment inequalities, had squashed private interests to clear the slums and clean the sewage-choked river. It had municipalized the gas and water companies and ploughed the profits into new buildings. Chamberlain was a Cromwellian to his teeth, a Roundhead in his political imagination; Huxley's sort of leader. And Huxley lauded the proud Midlands town as a 'political laboratory'.[28] It was a crucible of civic achievement where 'local self government' was honing the new professional politician.

Here Huxley had delivered his famous 'Duties of the State' address, as President of the Birmingham and Midland Institute late in 1871. No talk was better tailored to time and place: as Chamberlain's city was being swept clean, Huxley appeared as the well-fledged State interventionist. He challenged Herbert Spencer's hands-off and do-nothing demand of government (Huxley published his paper under the title 'Administrative Nihilism'). The 'plebeian' praised the Education Act – something Chamberlain's Radical and Nonconformist National Education League had pressured for. He had no qualms about government running the Post Office or telegraph services, and he saw the State's vaccination, sanitation and road-building programmes (like Birmingham's) lessen the misery which had fuelled the revolutionary movements across Europe.[29]

A proud city gave Huxley his closest brush with municipal socialism. But it brought a mail full of love and hate. From friendly snipes by Spencer to abusive postcards from 'John Bull' ('*mere rot*'), the criticism rained down. Then again, he never went far enough for the socialists, and Wallace was for nationalizing land and mineral wealth immediately. But the South Kensington militia was behind Huxley. Get the Birmingham speech reprinted, Cole said, 'I am good to buy a hundred copies at a shilling a piece'.[30]

In 1874 Birmingham hosted Huxley again. The radical caucus was erecting a statue of Joseph Priestley, making a hero of the long-dead chemist, philosopher and materialist Unitarian preacher (he was their sort of man). So Huxley came to praise Joseph Priestley, and the city fathers 'hung breathless on his words'. And obviously, because 'Satan whispered that it would be a good opportunity for a little ventilation of wickedness'. Of course, Huxley recalled that the Church-and-King bigots – 'with that love for the practical application of science which is the source of the greatness of Birmingham' – had set 'fire to [Priestley's] house with sparks from his own electrical machine'. Priestley's hounding became another plea for 'rational freedom'. Even back in town, frail old Lyell, who had been 'taught to honour' Priestley as a child, chortled at the *Daily News* report of Huxley's 'splendid address'.[31]

Real notoriety awaited Huxley at Belfast in 1874, during the British Association week. It was hot, crowds of holidaymakers turned up in trams to see the savants; the rooms in Queen's College should have provided shade, but the temperature increased with the speeches. Tyndall's election as President had topped even Huxley's for intrigue. The Irishman was loved and loathed for his fiery materialism. And the fact that he *was* Irish caused ripples in sectarian Ulster. A 'blundering idiot' of a Belfast mayor started a '"Home Rule" agitation' to mark the event, leaving the unionist Tyndall positively livid.[32]

No pantheistic Orangeman could arouse more feeling. For every Arnold who embraced his religious 'reformation', there was a Ruskin who scorned it. (In fact there could only be one Ruskin who expected a second Joshua to make the sun stand still.) Ruskin hated the lot of them: he dug at Huxley, thought Darwin showed an unhealthy interest in monkey behinds, and now launched a 'slanderous attack' on Tyndall. Ignore 'that lunatic', was Huxley's order. 'Men don't make war on either women or Eunuchs'. But Belfast was 'flooded . . . with Ruskin's diatribe' to raise the temperature more.[33]

So it was already hot when Tyndall was elected. And with him at the dispatch box of the 'Parliament of Science' the deterministic philosophy of industrial Britain peaked. Nature was presented as a great ironclad bound fast to Fate.

Hal sat in the hot August fields poring over his own speech. He thought of the last time he was a Belfast Ass, as a callow 22-year-old, and wrote home sweetly to Nettie that 'you were largely in my thoughts' then too. Twenty years told in the crowds that packed the anatomy hall to see Huxley in action. The press thought him more interesting than his subjects: the smart prose, the 'well-simulated . . . modesty' of a 'dogmatist' who 'thinks . . . upon his feet'. The earnest looks and clenched lips gave him the manner 'of the Puritan', the effect ruined only by his irreverent jokes.[34] He knew how to hold the bus-loads. Talks here had to grip 'those who know nothing (ie 9/10th of the audience)', and he did that. Even if he tried to 'dance between the eggs', the crowds willed him to step on a few. He turned down his notes and gave a spellbinding 90-minute metaphysical oration which was totally out of keeping with the venue. He talked on animals – and humans – as conscious automatons, without any 'free-will' to break the body's physiological sequences. If swimming decerebrated frogs act as automatons, perhaps brain-damaged war veterans in their somnambulistic trances do too? He nudged his audience into believing that even they were thinking machines. Their thoughts were simply the mental reflections that accompanied an action, without influencing it or altering the body's physico-chemical action. There was a rock-bottom logic to it, and Darwin heard his 'Automaton' paper called the 'magnum opus' of the meeting.[35] But Tyndall's related talk had already eclipsed the proceedings.

'Johnny's' Presidential call had carried feelings to a fever pitch. It was an echo of Huxley's 'Science and "Church Policy"' editorial a decade earlier, the same territorial demand by a profession clearing space, just as pointed but more public. In Tyndall's words, 'We claim, and we shall wrest from theology, the entire domain of cosmological theory'. There spoke a former £1-a-week surveyor in a position to raise his lot. The pulpits claimed it was 'an abuse of his office'.[36] What they really feared was it becoming the badge of his office. Science in the industrial age was being demarcated. Professional boundaries were moving, and the self-taught surveyors were implementing a new Enclosure Act.

Tyndall had composed his Presidential Address during a 'barbarous' cold snap in the Bel Alp. Secreted away, he had been chilled to the bone and surrounded by snow. Huxley had received the drafts and counselled caution, but the Alpine air had given them a spartan feel. In the bleak snowscape one felt helpless against the elemental forces, and an overpowering fatalism carried the address: 'its very well done', Huxley admitted, but 'I wish he had taken another line'. 'Lord knows what will be the effect'. The two prophets of the new reformation went to Ireland together, 'as Luther did to Worms' – Tyndall said – to meet 'all the devils in Hell there'. The talk thickened the sulphurous atmosphere, and generated occasional bursts of applause like the crackle of thunder. Nettie, too poor to come, heard of the 'theological thunder', which rumbled around Hal's speech as well. Tyndall, the Protestant Orangeman, who had cut away at Catholicism's idolatries, had carried on hacking to the bedrock of Matter. Here he was, at one with the bloodstained martyrs who had sustained his youth. There was an awe in his address, and it horrified the Presbyterian *Witness*. This was a hymn to the glories of cosmic progress, and in a city of 'virile Calvinism' where Man was still Falling. The rival pulpits saw him hastening mankind's 'ruin'.[37] One unappreciative listener even demanded his prosecution for blasphemy.

Tyndall's was an evocative vision of almost hallucinogenic perfection – the sort everyone had expected of Huxley four years earlier.

It meshed mechanistic science with humanistic values, unifying them in the cosmic process, which evolved molecules and emotions alike. Cosmic evolution was treated as an organic unfolding, like a flower unfurling, self-contained and mysterious. Old Lyell, losing his sight, his speech slurred, called it a 'manly and fearless out-speaking', meaning over-the-top. And local Presbyterians feared from its cosmological completeness and religious tone that it would 'quench every thirst'.[38] To sophisticates it looked like the triumph of Calvin over Carlyle, or was it Carlyle over Calvin? To simpler souls it spelled the fantastic success of Democritean atheism over two millennia of Christianity. The majority thought it mad materialism, but no one could quite define his crime.

Tyndall had welded Carlyle's romanticism to Dissent's steam-enginery. Man and machine bowed to the same unyielding necessity. In the ultimate attenuation of Enlightenment radicalism, Tyndall gave molecules 'the promise and potency of every form and quality of Life', making 'all our poetry, all our science, all our art – Plato, Shakespeare, Newton, and Raphael – . . . potential in the fires of the sun'.[39] Amid the avalanches of the unforgiving Alps, the brooding Tyndall had had a stark vision, and no one was sure whether he should be damned as a materialist, a pantheist or a mystic.

Deterministic science and radical Dissenting politics were surging through Morley's *Fortnightly* and Knowles' *Contemporary* reviews. Evolution was 'made the illuminating explanation of all things on earth' and placed in happy proximity to radical programmes of 'social and political renovation'. With Morley soliciting papers and Knowles 'going about like a Raptorial Bird seizing on contributions', Huxley was as 'spoiled as a maiden with many wooers'. He was sworn to Morley's rag, 'which is my old love, and the *Contemporary* which is my new', and he promised 'to remain as constant as a persistent bigamist'.[40]

The monthlies were Hal's bread and butter and he liked the company. They thrashed over Tyndall's deterministic universe with its convertible forces, where the equivalence of motion and heat and electromagnetic force spoke of unbreakable causal sequences. Friends saw Huxley's 'Automaton' paper in November's *Fortnightly* moving the same way. Weren't his conscious robots shackled to fate? They operated without any interposition of the will. His old ally Carpenter – whose medical thesis 35 years earlier had been on reflex arcs – balked at the extremism. Having contributed so much himself he pulled back. Pithed frogs actually sit motionless unless stimulated, that was the crux. So what naturally stimulates an unpithed frog? For him 'a conscious determination of the Ego' initiates the body's repertoire of reflexes.[41] The Ego did not directly control every muscle; it triggered the pre-programmed behaviours. This too was heresy, of a Unitarian sort. The ghost was operating the machine. But Huxley had exorcized the ghost. He had ejected the spiritual entity with its transcendent allegiance, to leave a mental physiology in line with his anti-supernatural strategy.

With the school-marms outperforming the masters, it was not surprising that Huxley had a woman demonstrator in physiology by 1874. As Miss McConnish lent over the men to dissect a frog's urinogenitalia the writing was on the wall. Career women were overcoming the odds. And overthrowing the aristocratic ideal of the 'perfect woman': that helpless ornament, stuck in the 'doll stage of evolution', 'cribbed, cabined, and confined' at home to become the conventional mental invalid.[42]

But the cult of masculinity drove deep into Victorian science. The antithesis of coy home-maker and battling breadwinner was set hard in *The Descent of Man*. Intimidated by intellectual women (rather than fascinated, as Huxley), Darwin scorned them as bores. His 'Sexual Selection' had males peaking in perfection through their fight to possess submissive females. Men's intelligence increased further as they struggled to provide for their families, while the woman's stagnated. Darwin's was an image of ineradicable sexual difference. His science turned the stereotypes into seeming hard knowledge. That served to reinforce the Anthropological Institute's exclusion order against the 'ladies', barring their access to knowledge.[43] And so the thing turned in a vicious circle. The 'Woman Question' was pooh-poohed and equality declared unnatural, and a little learning was deemed not so much dangerous as pointless.

Huxley subscribed to much of this – it was the cultural standard, defied only by Mill's *Subjection of Women* and the emancipating socialists. But with something approaching scientific *noblesse oblige*, he pulled culture away from nature (a tactic he would perfect in the 1880s) and refused to make women's biological 'limitations' the basis of a discriminatory educational policy. The paternalist was *granting* opportunities, not accepting inalienable rights. Even acknowledging the prejudicial yardstick of gendered 'strength', he wondered why careers 'open to the weakest and most foolish of the male sex should be forcibly closed to women of vigour and capacity'.[44]

With girls ceasing to be educated at their mother's knee, careers and higher education would inevitably follow. In a decade most would be at the new High Schools (doing the Huxleys' German governess Miss Matthaei out of her supplementary income).[45] And the High Schools in turn would create that 'bicycles, bangs, and bloomers' New Woman.

Already some were earning, saving and delaying babies. Jobs, whether for weavers, teachers, clerks or domestics (Hal and Nettie made sure the nieces could stand on their own feet as governesses), meant money and security. And with these – or rather with the articulate Frances Cobbe, questioning the values of a culture which lumps women with criminals and idiots, and denies wives a legal existence – came the 1870 Married Women's Property Act, giving three million working wives a right to their possessions.[46] The 'Woman Question' was being resolved by the women themselves: they were taking charge of their own finances, their schooling, their access to the professions and their destiny.

Not all felt the need. Nettie's gentrified acquaintances (in this case Lady Portsmouth) thought that 'forcing . . . the brain' of 'young growing girls' will end up 'addling' it.[47] But that wouldn't have gone down well with Miss McConnish, or the graduates coming to study under Huxley, such as the American Sarah Stevenson, who went on to take the Chair of Physiology at the Women's Hospital Medical College in Chicago.

'Work and independence!' exclaimed Sophia Jex-Blake as she became a teacher. She was 'one of the band' with Elizabeth Garrett and Emily Davies, and had already written a book on her travels to America to study women's education. But her move into a male profession, medicine, was to point up Huxley's conflicting interests. Women were a minority who happened to be in a majority, and Jex-Blake knew that they wanted their own women doctors. She had enrolled at Edinburgh University (even though Garrett did not think her particularly suited), taking advantage of new regulations which allowed women separate medical instruction. There was high-level support, but also virulent opposition from the closed-shop consultants, who feared that the influx of women would take away their clientele. Jex-Blake did nothing to allay fears that the women had a political agenda: in her Huxleyan way, she shunned the side-door approach. She wanted women's rights to be recognized, and she attracted a dedicated group of women students around her. One came top in chemistry, but was refused the prize scholarship, while others were denied certificates of attendance.[48]

When the professors disbarred the women's anatomy teacher,

Jex-Blake appealed to Huxley. And why not? Weren't professionals dispassionate dealers in a neutral medical science? Didn't they transcend petty feelings of 'delicacy'? Shouldn't women sit alongside the men? The tangle of issues left the patriarch performing his old balancing act. He deplored the placing of any but 'natural' obstacles in the women's way. They should be able to take 'degrees upon the same terms as men'. But the issue of mixed classes was prickly. He said that he had kept women out of his winter biology course, 'with rare exceptions', but it is clear that he had increasing numbers paying 'homage at the Shrine of Huxley'.[49] So while he endorsed single-sex classes, he declined to slap down a rival professorate.

One can see why. Professional protocols and professional friendships were involved. Jex-Blake's supporters had been bringing Huxley her natural history exam papers since 1872, which suggested that everyone saw her as a test case. But these papers were set by his old friend Wyville Thomson, and Huxley confirmed that they had been marked correctly.[50] 'Charlie' Thomson's involvement added the final complication. The fact that Huxley himself would be asked in November 1874 to be an Edinburgh professor – to deputize for Thomson in Summer 1875 while he was on the *Challenger* – shows the delicacy of his situation. Lyon Playfair and Edinburgh's Principal Sir Alexander Grant (both of whom had sided against Jex-Blake) were wining and dining Huxley. He officially accepted because 'the University ... has been civil to me'. Privately nothing but mercenary considerations would force him to 'expatiate myself to the howling wilderness around Arthur's Seat'. But the sums to be pocketed were irresistible. Edinburgh was still the academic Eldorado, even if Hooker called it suicide. 'What does your wife say?'[51] But Nettie too appreciated the pay.

The women ended up suing Edinburgh University. What with firework attacks on her house, sexual harassment and a lawsuit, Jex-Blake failed her exams. She called it discrimination. So it was the professors, this time, who sent her papers to Huxley, and he endorsed their decision. But he told the *Times* that women *should* graduate; and Jex-Blake still sought his support. An apartheid scheme was her only recourse. She realized that women had to take charge of their own bodies. And so, with Elizabeth Garrett and Huxley on the coordinating committee in 1874, Jex-Blake became a pupil in her own London School of Medicine for Women.

This same year, 1874, the women sitting London University classes petitioned to be allowed to take the degree, and shortly the Senate changed its Charter. Just as it had opened its doors to Jews and

Dissenters when Huxley was a boy, now London would lead the way in granting degrees to women.[52]

Long-suffering Nettie bore the babies, ran the house, organized the maids and governesses, administered the liniment and the religion, and in her exclusive domain – from which her workaholic husband stood aloof in befuddled admiration – she led a life 'not only of super-human, but of super-feminine, activity'. But she could never escape the home: research kept Hal from going mad, and she envied him the digression. Still, she was his hidden aide. She drew the diagrams, checked the manuscripts and translated the German (the Goethe quote closing his 'Automatons' talk was hers).[53] They travelled to functions together, 'Regina mea et Ego', when money allowed. His emotional dependence was obvious: he admitted that 'Few people appreciate her at her real value, or dream what part she has played in my life'. And Nettie's submergence belied her active role. A German Moravian schooling had given her an interest in higher education and she put all her daughters through the Slade School, while Rachel sat the Senior Girls' Cambridge Exam (a school-leaver's proficiency test).[54] Notes from Spencer or Dohrn, Foster or Playfair, would come addressed to her, their messages to be passed on in supplicatory style. She was a conduit to Hal in more special ways: women's groups went through her, wanting, and getting, his support for the National Society for the Improvement of Women's Education or the Girls' Public Day School Company (both set up by the emancipist Maria Grey).[55]

The stereotype of the 'angel in the house' – the redoubtable wife giving moral succour while remaining the repository of 'parsonese superstition' – was honed from chauvinistic images. True, Nettie trotted the children to Lisson Grove Church on a Sunday – in fact, the conventional Misses took themselves off to church.[56] Hal was happy to wave them goodbye, and the religious issue was surprisingly frictionless – perhaps because, on the key issue of agnosticism, Nettie preferred to miss his point.[57] But her influence on his social views is difficult to gauge. What did she think of him dining with the unmarried George Eliot and G. H. Lewes at North Bank? Hal had no qualms, but he went alone, whether to protect her or because she was censorious is not clear. Certainly he shared the excitement in the Athenaeum smoking room at George Eliot's *Middlemarch*.[58] But there is a cryptic hint that Huxley might have thought it unseemly for Nettie to visit Eliot and Lewes.[59]

While Huxley was restricting participation in science, the women's home circle was expanding it. Wallace's secretary Arabella Buckley would drop in to have tea with Nettie. She was soon to join the best children's science writers. They were transformers rather than interpreters, not disseminators but cultural reshapers. They parablized and packaged stories 'fraught with cosmic significance' for the mother–child market.[60] These unsung women popularizers were as important in their way for reshaping the culture. Just as Huxley's labourers actively sculpted their evolutionary edifice, so middle-class women, the traditional moral teachers, used their skills to tailor Nature to the nursery. They made it pregnant with moral meaning and sympathy: an ugly Darwinism became divinely inspiring. Buckley's mass-market *Fairyland of Science* turned the invisible forces into wonder-working fairies. Here and in *Winners in Life's Race* (note the upbeat Darwinian connotation) she imbued Nature with love, mutual help and life-guiding precepts. Her story-book science carried a growing generation from the Darwinian arena towards the agnostic City of God – or the socialist *fin de siècle.* In early Victorian times science had been retailed in the pub, the church hall and the mechanics' institute, but the laboratory doors had shut out the public now.[61] The academics were drawing in the boundaries of expertise, turning the vicars, the socialists and the dame-school matrons into marginalized amateurs. But Arabella Buckley shows how Darwinism was still being actively recreated, and nowhere more importantly than in the kindergarten.

Evolution was a stimulus, and it presented great new challenges for eager young anatomists. More than anything it sparked the search for intermediate life forms, particularly those bridging the great chasms, creatures the old teachers said had never existed. Which group – worms or starfish or insects – had transmuted into fishes to start the vertebrate explosion? And how on earth had they made the change? This was the great prize. Everyone was on the scent, Dohrn in his marine station on the Med, Haeckel in Germany, Huxley in London. But it was Kovalevskii's brother Alexander in Russia who took the laurel.[62] Huxley had sniffed close to the clues: off New Guinea the sailor had noted that the peculiar, sessile, sack-like tunicate or sea squirt had a free-swimming larva with a tadpole-like tail. And he had long held that the adult sea squirt's branchial region was equivalent to the fish's gill slits. And so it turned out. But Kovalevskii's coup was a decidedly Darwinian triumph: the young Kovalevskii was educated into German *Darwinismus* and had worked with Dohrn, who had committed his station to the study of marine embryos and evolutionary ancestries.

More and more of Huxley's research became part of the trend towards exploring links. In 1874 he and Lankester were sectioning that primitive sand-burrowing *Amphioxus*, another creature that had fascinated the sailor in his dredging days. It was fish-like but had no proper skull or brain or renal organs. Huxley's dissection showed that it did have an enlarged cranial development and antecedents of kidney tubes: in other words, rudiments of skull and brain, 'shut up like an opera-hat'. It was the sort of anatomical finding to 'take your breath away'.

His class heard it first. The tunicate larva's stiffened tail, with its dorsal nerve cord and muscles and fish-like development, had a 'fundamental resemblance ... [to] the Vertebrata'.[63] Sea squirts passed via an *Amphioxus*-like form to the jawless lampreys and hagfishes and ultimately all higher life. This was very satisfactory for Huxley. Behind it stood his original suggestion that the two body layers (ectoderm and endoderm) of the medusae and sea nettles were analogous to the cell layers in the vertebrate embryo, a point that Haeckel and Lankester were now busily working up.[64]

Darwinism was having the same impact on Huxley's fossil work. Despite the fact that for 15 years he had been harping on the prodigious time that crocodiles had persisted unchanged, continual study of that 16-foot Elgin *Stagonolepis* had him rethinking crocodiles. Now he saw them putting on a spurt in Mesozoic times. He traced their progressive acquisition of a secondary palate (the bony roof of the mouth that separates off the nasal passage). Quite whether it went with a modified lifestyle, or had something to do with the reptile being able to drown its newly-evolved mammalian prey without shipping water, Huxley wasn't sure. (Owen was far more adept at this sort of thinking.)[65]

In a sense, it was outside his jurisdiction. The *Origin of Species* had caught the medically-trained comparative anatomists on the hop. Its unusual ecological and population approach was quite alien to these dead-room men, interested in whole-body design. There was no study of the *Origin* in Huxley's class – that was something the students read at home, as they would a novel. The book simply stood outside the disciplinary norm. Ironically there was no space for it in a biology laboratory, no way that conventional anatomists could get to grips with its competition and geographical isolation. That would require a wholesale reorientation, and it would take Huxley years to integrate elements of an evolutionary view into his academic discipline.[66]

It certainly made little impact on his unsung work at the chalkface. He delivered some 120 stock lectures a year to students and masters. This is what the public didn't see: the weekly haul through the animal and plant kingdoms, starting with mould and ending with monkey brains. Then came the practicals, themselves a dash to prepare slides of bacteria, sections of ferns, demonstrations of bat anatomy (or, opportunely in 1874, dissections of a porpoise).[67] This was the business of biology, not Darwin's book.

True, Huxley emphasized the meeting point between plants and animals. Algae, unicellular animals and moulds preponderated in these lectures, partly because of Huxley's interest in the similarities of animal and plant cells. That was part of the synthetic tendency of the age, and went with Darwin's own interest in the almost animal-like activity of insectivorous sundews and flytraps. After this fundamental divergence, the plants had gone on to become 'the ideal *prolétaire* of the living world, the worker who produces; the animal, the ideal aristocrat, who mostly occupies himself in consuming'.[68] And Huxley saw his job as enumerating the types for the tyros.

In 1874 he was still telling them that 'all hypotheses [like Darwin's, were to be] . . . carefully kept in the back-ground, because theories on these matters are "excellent servants, but very bad masters"'.[69] This Jekyll and Hyde attitude to evolution – championing it outside, disdaining it in – confused many people. Darwinism was an ideological cannon to be fired in the street (at least until after his American trip, when one palaeontological big gun was hauled inside the walls). But for the moment Darwin's bulldog was content to confuse. There he was, shunning the 'bad master' in class, while defending Darwin in print.

So the students saw one Huxley, the 'neutral', tolerant professional, as Mivart's son Frederick testified. (He came home after his first day at South Kensington in October 1874 full of Huxley's kindness and carrying a note: 'Dear Mivart, – Wolves do not prey upon wolves, and I can accept no payment from you for your son's work with me'.)[70] But the public saw another: the ferocious carnivore in the evolutionary circus who, within eight weeks, would be savaging the boy's inept father.

Causes célèbres had a habit of seeking Huxley out. This one started with George Darwin. He was stomachy like his father, and like his father mending under 'D^r^. Andrew' (Huxley's doctor Clark). At a loose end while recuperating, he had written an article on cousin Galton's eugenics, to the disapproval of his prim sister Etty. His first *Contemporary* piece advocated divorce in cases of wife battering, sexual abuse or mental breakdown (to stop bad traits being passed on). St George Mivart, working in Germany from muddled notes, saw family values under attack and the sanctity of marriage succumbing to Darwinian bestiality. In a defamatory aside he even accused George of *encouraging* vice. What 'hideous sexual criminality of Pagan days' could not be defended 'by the school to which this writer belongs'? A stunned Charles Darwin made the *Quarterly* run George's rebuttal, but Mivart's 'apology' only rubbed salt in the wound. Darwin, unequal to the social fray, sought Huxley's advice on this 'Papist' matter. Remain aloof, counselled Huxley, 'like one of the blessed gods of Elysium, and let the inferior deities' stand in.[71] But a Victorian raw nerve was tingling. Talk of 'unrestrained licentiousness' transfixed a generation that dare not speak of sex.

Huxley emerged from his classes, read the reviews and found an old bogey: the Darwinians cast as evil corrupters. 'If anybody tries that on with my boy L. the wolf will show all the fangs he has left', he commiserated with Darwin. As it was, the wolf would savage any predator approaching the pack's cubs. So it was Huxley who promised not to 'leave a square inch of unwaled skin upon his idolatrous carcass'. To have 'slandered Darwin once' was disgraceful; to have repeated it 'in a more aggravated form' was unforgivable.[72]

Huxley had his pretext. 'Unless I err', he responded in print, Mivart includes 'me among the members of that school' which is to return us to the 'gross profligacy of Imperial Rome'. Forensic dissection was Huxley's forte, not that much was needed for this blundering breach of etiquette. A red-faced Mivart watched the issue turn to his perversion of the truth. And that pointed to something more vile than Nero's profligacy, namely 'the secret poisonings of the Papal Borgias'. 'Tremendous', cried Darwin, wallowing in the reproof, 'it is tremendous'. And George was proud to have Huxley take 'up the cudgels for me'. The clique acquired its identity and cohesion from this sort of posturing. The Mivarts and Bastians focused the party's gaze, and it watched spellbound as Huxley's lacerating tongue took off Mivart's hide. Glad to 'see that you haven't forgotten how to be 'orrid', crowed Fiske.[73]

Father Roberts, the priest who had coaxed Mivart from Darwin's explanation of ethics, was auditing Huxley's lectures at that moment. Roberts' ascetic life in a slum school appealed to Huxley. (As did his 'brain sharpener' cleverness, not to mention his unhappiness over Papal infallibility.)[74] And so through his favourite priest Huxley rid himself of a turbulent pupil: he severed all relations with Mivart. Darwin followed suit. Mivart's bitter regrets were to no avail. As

Father Roberts eventually left the Church of Rome, so Mivart was excommunicated from the Church of Science.

The Church Scientific was about to get its bible. The four years of experience with schoolmasters went into Huxley and Martin's book of '*practical dodges*' (Foster's apt description), the seminal 'how-to' lab manual, *A Course of Practical Instruction in Elementary Biology*. It was distilled by Huxley and his demonstrators from the Kensington course. They all had a hand in it, and Martin got his name on the title-page in 1875 through Foster's angelic intercession.[75] They knew it would increase his prospects of a job.

As dynasties changed the book became the standard. At University College the 80-year-old radical Robert Grant had died at his post. Innovative in his day, the only Lamarckian academic in England, he had become a deaf, dejected atheistic anachronism, his frayed French coat as funny as his archaic Restoration lectures.[76] One bull-headed professor replaced another, but the students noted the difference. The huge, domineering Ray Lankester swept in with Huxley's help. He was 'like those winged beasts from Nineveh', someone said. 'What you feel is just immense force'. The blustery, womanizing Lankester had hated Oxford, where 'life amidst old bachelor clergymen and a few cynical young classics is not normal'. He had been desperate for UCL. Once in, he refurbished the museum, introduced the latest embryological and morphological approaches and initiated practical work 'from 12 to 4½ twice a week', using Huxley's *Elementary Biology*.[77] He turned the department's fortunes around and put University College back at the forefront of evolutionary research in Britain.

With the rise of the new went the demise of the old. There was 'a regular clearing out of the old philosophers', as Hooker put it. Saturday 23 January 1875 was the day Charles Kingsley had awaited with 'reverent curiosity' all of his life. So passed the friend who had restored Hal after Noel's death. Not that their differences were ever resolved: 'You were one of the people he loved & honoured', Fanny Kingsley wrote to Hal, '& does still'. It made the point. Others were ready to smile down on Hal. Lyell's decrepitude had Huxley craving a 'speedy end whenever my time comes'. Huxley's soft spot showed as he loyally repeated his latest lecture on the *Challenger* at his old mentor's bedside. In a month he was bearing Lyell's body to the nave of Westminster Abbey. When Nettie saw the snowdrop-sprinkled coffin she felt an 'inexpressible pain' at Sir Charles' burial so far from his wife. But Lyell had to be enshrined here. His *Principles of*

Geology, with its grindingly-slow evolution of the earth's surface, might have troubled an older generation, but the Darwinians were securing its immortality. Huxley bore the old-world gent who had influenced and sustained him, equivocated and hesitated, and finally died believing that science must not 'disturb any man's faith, if it be a delusion which increases his happiness'.[78]

That was the concern of the age: the search for moral meaning. Were there transcendent truths freeing mankind from this cruelly-fatalistic cosmos? Huxley gave the unpalatable answer, pleasantly dressed up. An impenetrable net lay at the sensory extremity: there was no knowing beyond, and little point in hoping. Agnosticism provoked Christian fears that individual life would become purposeless. Was mankind at the end of an exotic evolutionary journey, or questing towards some future exotic end? With no object of veneration, no spark of divinity, and Huxley making a desert of the Unknowable, many despaired of a secular humanism.[79] The Positivists tried to put back the spark, Spencer tried to upgrade the Unknowable, but Huxley braved the task of giving a new meaning to morality itself, seeing virtue and worth in acquiescence to evidence. He too was trying to put the meaning back into life – it was the light shining from his *Lay Sermons* and *Critiques and Addresses*.

Lists of prospective books tumbled out of him, none to materialize: on 'Consciousness' for the International Scientific Series, on 'Ethnology', on the 'Classification of Birds', and (one Darwin wanted) a revamping of his workers' 'Lectures on the Origin of Species'. Too many; he hardly knew which way to turn. They were screaming for his *Introductory Science Primer*. The others in the series were appearing (Balfour Stewart's *Physics* had sold 7,000 copies in six months). Henry Roscoe urged him to finish because 'the Christian Knowledge Society & other Sinners' were pirating the idea, printing 'whitened sepulchre' imitations that were 'hideously bad'. The professional fortifications were still precarious in the 1870s and encroaching commercial and religious interests remained a hazard. Even shilling crammers for Huxley's exams were selling in 'enormous numbers & we ought to try to put them out'.[80]

Too many books and too much bureaucracy. Like Dick Swiveller in the chips, he would pay off an old debt only to run up two others. The Devonshire Commission was over: it had detailed the needs of a new scientific culture – university research, Oxbridge laboratories, a Natural History Museum, schoolteaching and the creation of jobs – and Huxley wrapped up its final report in 1875 with a call for public money to match.[81] 'Thank Heaven the Science Committee is over &

done with', he told the zoo's Philip Sclater. 'But it is one down & another to come on'. He was already sitting on the Royal Society's 'Polar-Committee' and poaching Sclater's zoologists for Captain Nares' voyage to the North Pole. February found Nares at Marlborough Place, planning. Bureaucracy was at least broadening Huxley's ecological outlook; he was taxing the ornithologists on Arctic birds to be observed, and Darwin on glacial phenomena to be noted.[82] But his real 'weary work' in 1875 was on a different committee, countering public hostility on the most divisive aspect of the new science.

Women were not only penetrating science, but intent on altering its practice. Frances Cobbe's anti-cruelty alliance was targeting live animal experiments and tearing at the nation's heartstrings. Her campaign was made for the moment: a new laboratory culture encouraged vivisections, and they were more tolerable to younger physiologists with the use of anaesthesia after 1870. Then there was a growing stratum of non-medical biologists, who experimented, not to alleviate human suffering, but to further knowledge. Cobbe 'would have gladly died' to save the suffering cats, and such martyrdom moved families. Sickly Etty Darwin signed Cobbe's petition; in Victorian semis where ailing was normal, hypochondriacal housewives were empathizing with the torture victims. Cobbe's Victoria Street Society for the Protection of Animals from Vivisection raised deep questions about the emerging profession: how accountable was it? And to whom? Should there be lay scrutiny, parliamentary control or self-regulation?

Cobbe would extend RSPCA surveillance from the cat-skinning hovel to South Kensington. Huxley had his own horror of experiments on *conscious* animals and forbade them. He always pithed or anaesthetized his frogs before showing teachers the blood flow or muscle action. But this wasn't a line Cobbe cared to draw; and even Huxley defended those who went further if they were intent on 'alleviating human suffering'.

Cobbe began drafting a banning Bill. But laws were for publicans and prostitutes, not the professional elite of the nation! The Darwinians called for pre-emptive action, 'or else these beggars will steal a march on us'. For Darwin the vivisectionist's gains were tangible, in medical care, humanitarian sympathy and pure science. But pamphleteers denied that animal sacrifice led to medical advance. And they denounced a 'Demoniacal Physiology' for its dehumanizing effect on students. Huxley wasn't squeamish, but 'the doctrine that men may suffer & knowledge stand still rather than dogs & rabbits should be made uncomfortable, makes me sick'.[83] As a non-medical teacher, he saw experiential learning – his fundamental track to true knowledge – threatened by Cobbe's 'fanatical following'.

Her broad alliance feared science's claim to cultural leadership. Many of her petition-signers were alienated, shut out as the lab doors closed, and horrified by the nihilistic implications of chance evolution and its moral vacuum. It showed in the vilification of the '*parvenu* profession'. The campaign was hurting. Huxley's State aid now brought State restrictions with it: an order rather pointedly banning vivisections in his lab. With Hutton's *Spectator* standing for Cobbe and Christianity, Huxley warned Foster not to do anything in the schoolmasters' course 'that could be laid hold of by Hutton & the "foolish fat scullion" '.[84]

Questions of pain and responsibility racked the nation. The Queen had a sermon preached on 'Vivisection, in which H.M. is *very* strongly interested'. And she had it sent to Huxley, who gave it the shortest shrift in the politest way. The women, so long lauded by the patrician Darwins and Huxleys for their moral superiority and concern with suffering, were turning this very aspect of femininity against an exclusive male profession.[85]

The socialists too became odd bedfellows, siding with the Crown and Church philanthropists against Darwin's Malthusian Nature progressing through cruelty and culling. Ironically the Darwinians, who embraced the kinship of all life, were justifying its mutilation, while Christians, given dominion over the animals, felt Methodism's sympathy for suffering creation. But Huxley the cat-lover left his sentiment at the lab door. He joined the squeamish dog-loving Darwin to propose a self-regulating system for licensing experimenters. They would make it part of the professionals' accrediting procedures.

Huxley went to Downe on 17 April 1875. Here he joined one of Foster's physiologists on his first visit, George John Romanes. This stuffshirt was a young Darwin, wealthy, a failed Cambridge ordinand subverted by Nature's creation. The evangelical had transferred the devotional power of his student essay *Christian Prayer and General Laws* to Darwin's altar (the book had taken the Burney Prize at Cambridge, its topic a response to the 'Prayer Gauge Debate'). Here was another whose home was a workshop where he could pick jellyfish apart. Darwin had asked them not to mention animal experiments in the 'presence of my ladies'.[86] But they mooted potential sponsors (Lubbock suggested Playfair), and Darwin sent their draft report to the Foreign Secretary, Lord Derby. Huxley knew that the fox-hunting MPs would rally to save their own skins.

The result was another Royal Commission, instigated by Disraeli at the Queen's suggestion, which seemed a further slight on the profession. But this one they turned to advantage. Huxley was adept at leading witnesses, and for once he was happy to be co-opted by the Home Secretary.[87]

Huxley was 'enlightening the Caledonians' by the time it convened. On 4 May 1875 he turned 50, one day into his Edinburgh lectures, standing in for that 'zoological Ulysses' Wyville Thomson. No longer the brooding romantic, Huxley was jolly and jowly, and as cleverly teasing as ever. He was away on his birthday for the first time, but what a present! The fame which had brought the autograph hunters – everybody from Millais to the charwomen – brought the students: 600 on his opening day. The Northern Athens was regaining its reputation, with a new zoology lab and new chairs of geology and engineering. He was among a staunch set of research-orientated professors. With no admissions tests the medical school alone attracted 900 students. It made Huxley's work pleasant, but 'still pleasanter was the pay'.

His star billing led the throng to expect a blast on Darwinism (his old friend Dyster's nephew among them). And for once he obliged, at least on his opening day. Dressed unfamiliarly in a gown, he gave them the icing from the cake first. He stroked Scottish vanities by holding up a single fossil as his emblem, the great Triassic 'crocodile' from the Elgin rocks. Then he conducted them through untold prehistoric aeons, as the crocodiles became more and more like those of the present day. He used it to explain the origin of birds, and to ask the fundamental question: how did this life transform? The audience was in his palm. Imagine, he said, a marsh – and there, suddenly, a crocodile springing

> into existence without anything to precede it – (laughter) – which was hard to believe, at least to an unimaginative person like himself. (Renewed laughter and applause.) Or . . . they might take what seemed to him the simple and natural explanation . . . that some primitive stock [like] . . . the crocodile of the trias, had in that long course of ages undergone those modifications which had converted it into the crocodile of the present day. (Great applause.)

The cheers showed the passing years. By 1875 the mood had changed. The students wanted to hear of life's variability and 'The production of Races in Nature & by Artificial condition'.[88]

Of course they had to eat the cake afterwards, 53 doses of 'dry facts'. But the parsons who mustered strong on the first day 'came to curse and didn't remain to pay'. Those who stayed were worked hard; 'panting' students found the daily pace 'awful' and crept out exhausted. But 353 stuck as the professor 'positively polished off the Animal Kingdom'. And had his talks been 'ten times as difficult', said one, they would still have been 'something glorious'.

Paying £4 each for the anaerobic exercise, they contributed substantially to a poor man's coffers. Huxley cleared about £1,000, a huge sum for a Summer course. He joked that it was 'one of the few examples known of a Southern coming north & pillaging the Scots'.[89]

Helping Thomson out, Huxley hardly expected the *Challenger* to torpedo him amidships. The corvette had left Cape York in sweltering north Queensland, a 'horrid place so close and muggy' that drained Thomson, as it had once Huxley. By June 1875 it had made Japan, and from Yeddo (Tokyo) Thomson sent the depressing news. The note was marked 'private'. 'None of us have ever been able to see a trace of *Bathybius*'. They had scrutinized every sea floor for three years, but without sight of Huxley's living gelatin, and they had lost faith that 'such a thing exists'.[90] So what was this enucleate jelly, christened by Huxley and considered by Haeckel to hold the key to the origin of life? The crew was perplexed until it was realized that *Bathybius haeckelii* only appeared when the ooze was bottled in alcohol. A precipitate!

Thomson's private note was to forewarn Huxley, to enable him to beat his breast before the news broke. And this he did, telling *Nature*'s Norman Lockyer that 'My poor dear *Bathybius* appears likely to turn out a "*Blunderibus*"'. *Nature* was more and more the professionals' mouthpiece, its success due to the judicious Lockyer (renowned himself now for studies of the sun's spectrum and discovery of helium). It was the place for a recantation. To stop enemies saying that '*Bathybius*' had been deliberately precipitated from his evil imagination 'I shall eat my leek handsomely'. And quickly. He published Thomson's letter and took responsibility for 'introducing this singular substance into the list of living things'.[91] And so perished a perfect fiction, a primal blob spontaneously generated by Huxley's sparks in the Victorian soup: a phantasm too easily seen during the 'protoplasmic' fever, when Haeckelian protozoology and Darwinian evolution conspired to make it real.

The 'Frau-widow' Nettie saw Hal twice during the Edinburgh Summer, as the penitent dashed back to Town for committee meetings. But Marlborough Place was like a university dorm – girls coming and going to University College soirées, and the Fosters living in, while Michael conducted the masters' course.[92]

He conducted it cagily while Cobbe's feathers were ruffled. Other feathers were looking equally dishevelled. Lord Arthur Russell, three-year-old Bertie's uncle, defended vivisection at the Metaphysical Society. As a good Deist and Darwinian, he believed that sacrificing 'the life of animals, for food or for knowledge . . . is the birthright of man in his struggle for existence'. Huxley had a preview of Lord Arthur's paper, and wrote to Knowles that it was

> refreshing to read his fair & manly statement after being wearied by the venomous sentimentality & inhuman tenderness of the members of the Society for the infliction of cruelty on Man, who are ready to let disease torture hecatombs of men as long as poodles are happy.
>
> Let Art & Science, Men & Women die
> But let no tear suffuse a lap dog's eye!

Wickedly, Knowles read out Huxley's letter after Lord Arthur's paper. Hutton flew into a 'white rage' and thought it 'ought to be "burnt by the common hangman"'. Of course it was aimed at him. Hutton, ordinarily a generous critic, was on his own diametric journey from Unitarianism to Anglo-Catholicism. It showed in the *Spectator*'s growing readership of 'gentle souls . . . declining gracefully', the doily set who 'looked askance at a Huxley travelling roughshod over their dearest orthodoxies' and awaited each Saturday when Hutton would put the world to rights. But vivisection was no party issue; in this rarefied atmosphere, Huxley had a degree of support that surprised even Knowles. Old enemies showed a friendly face. The Catholic Mivart rose to say 'how much & how far he agreed' with the letter's tone. And in the rumpus a sympathetic Gladstone in the Chair asked for it to be read again. Lord Arthur, said Knowles, 'is so much in love with it that he begged me hard to give it to him' as a 'certificate of character'.

> I have no doubt Hutton would like to see other productions of mine dealt with by some common or uncommon Hangman [Huxley replied]. Yet I know he has a kindness for me and when he looks down upon me from Abraham's bosom, he will beg the Cardinal [Manning, Catholic Archbishop of Westminster] hard to be allowed to fetch me a bottle of Apollinaris water out of the celestial cellar – if only to cool my tongue. But the Cardinal will see me — [damned] first.[93]

Huxley's friends would make matters worse. He was actually shot in the back by one witness before the Vivisection Committee. The bacteriologist Emanuel Klein was a Vienna MD who realized Hutton's nightmare. He should have been a safe expert, the co-author of the leading experimental physiology textbook. Klein had taken the name Edward on settling in London, but his pidgin English pointed up his Slav origins, and he showed a Viennese contempt for State interference. Huxley was absent when Klein provoked the committee and 'professed the most entire indifference to animal suffering'. He 'only gave anaesthetics to keep animals quiet!' Huxley snorted. 'I did not believe the man lived who was such an unmitigated cynical brute . . . I would willingly agree to any law which would send him to the treadmill'.

Commissioner Hutton stood shaken but vindicated. The ultimate horror – and the thing that should have made Klein a safe witness – was his job at London University. He was deputy director of its new philanthropically-endowed Brown Animal Sanatory Institute. He had the capital's horses and dogs in his care! His work on the sheep-pox virus here had been appreciated by Huxley. Now the man had 'done more mischief than all the fanatics put together'. Darwin was 'astonished & disgusted' and only 'glad he is a foreigner'. But it hit home: young Francis Darwin was actually working on his MD degree under Klein at the veterinary institute, and Darwin too had 'liked the man'.[94]

There was the solution. Nothing short of a voice from the Mount could sooth the Commission. Darwin was no authority on physiology, but he was an expert on life and death, and his word was sacrosanct. Encouraged by Huxley, he emerged from his country exile to testify. On 3 November 1875 Lord Cardwell greeted him like a duke and Huxley saw the craggy patrician to their largest seat. And from it the squeamish evolutionist talked nervously on the beneficent necessity of sacrifice. It worked.

4

The American Dream

'MY HEART DANCED WITHIN me', wrote Fiske at the news. Huxley was 'A1 copper bottomed' and set to sail for America in 1876. Nautical language was in the air again. In three decades he had swapped his surgeon's lowly rank for celebrity status. But he never forgot that day when, as a Naval hopeful, he had waved goodbye to his favourite sister, Lizzie. 'It is . . . thirty years since I left you at Antwerp, a boy beginning life', he wrote. 'Now I am a grey man looking towards the end of it . . . What ghosts we shall seem when we face one another!'

The 'whole nation is electrified', said an American banker. Fiske offered the Huxleys a drive through the 'glorious hill-country' of Massachusetts, where Fall brought 'the nearest approach I know to heaven'. The Huxleys, always interested to know what Heaven was like, accepted. Appleton began planning a press reception, and lectures. President Gilman of the new Johns Hopkins University, discussing Martin as the possible professor of biology, realized a coup and snatched Huxley to inaugurate a guest lecture series. As Huxley's plans firmed up, the 'flying visit' for a family reunion became a royal walkabout. Dickens and the literary greats had all toured, often with typical British hauteur. Even Prince Edward had crossed the Canadian border in 1860, but for some with long memories Huxley's was the eclipsing visit: 'We will make infinitely more of him than we did of the Prince of Wales, & his retinue of Lords & Dukes'.[1]

Preparations took place amid the usual turmoil. The 'hurry and worry of life' might increase 'with the square of your distance from youth', but even this formula looked simplistic by 1876, as new whirlwinds rose out of the steady turbulence.

The year had started off reasonably enough with a miracle and two fishes. Christmas found the family 'up to our necks in snow & over them in fog'. Huxley was locked in his study, revelling in Arnold's Spinozaist attack on the Philistines in *God and the Bible*, and contemplating the Catholic Wilfred Ward's challenge at the Metaphysical Society.[2] The rotund Ward, like a gentleman farmer pooh-poohing Biblical fads, had goaded doubters to forsake theory and grapple with a real miraculous fact. The austere agnostic was preparing to do just that. He drew gasps by taking up *the* miracle, the Resurrection.

But his widowed sister Ellen interrupted. She staggered in on Christmas Day and keeled over drunk. With her came the familiar stench of family decay. Boarding in West Brompton, the old crone had spent Hal's rent money on gin and run up a huge slate as 'Professor Huxley's sister'. Landlords, butchers, drapers and shopkeepers all collected from Huxley. 'Humiliating', Nettie called it, but even she was unprepared for the worst. Ellen's 35-year-old daughter Nelly had just had an illegitimate son by a Captain Seaton. Now Nelly and Ellen split the gin and pawned their clothes for more. In debt, in bare rooms, in an alcoholic stupor, they were tempting Nelly's teenage daughter Mabel into 'wickedness'. It was less a case of dead-drunk-for-tuppence than paralytic on Hal's £60. The iniquity was Ellen's taking a further 10*s* weekly from Huxley to 'educate' Mabel, and frittering it in a gin palace while Mabel minded the bastard.[3] Demoralized, he banned Ellen from the house. Here was the Professor, defining the new moral norm for a polite society, proving that agnosticism and depravity were not correlates, waiting for the sweaty hand to pull him back into the morass. Waiting for the scandal.

It was sickening. Nettie took to her bed ill and headachy for the rest of Christmas, only rising for New Year's dinner with Tyndall and Spencer. But there were stronger devils than Ellen to drive Hal. Knowles was impatiently awaiting to see Huxley's paper on Christ's alleged Resurrection, which threatened to do to Ward's Catholics what Klein had done to the Vivisection Commission. 'I have not written a line', Huxley apologized.

> Don't scream. I am subject to Demoniacal possession and the devil which came into me about ten days ago was a Fish – the most suggestive interesting brute that ever existed since the time of the old serpents. Like the latter my Fish is full of revolutionary ideas. I have been working twelve hours a day to get them into shape for a paper.[4]

Nature still took precedence. What diverted Huxley was a newly-discovered fish with lungs from Queensland. *Ceratodus*, with its ability to gulp air and walk on sturdy fins between drying pools, blotted out all other considerations. He had two corpses, 30 inches long, one from the Zoological Society and another especially procured by Sir George Macleay (the Speaker in the New South Wales House when Huxley was in Sydney, and W. S. Macleay's brother). Huxley noted *Ceratodus*' similarity to the two other surviving species of lungfish, while its skull-bones were like an amphibian's. Here was the interest. This was a very primitive lung-breather – so primitive that Haeckel's colleague Gegenbaur in Jena considered its lobe-fin as something like the first paired fin to evolve in the fishes. Behind all the excitement there was a sense that *Ceratodus* gave anatomists another lead on amphibian origins – pointing to the source of all higher vertebrates and mankind.

Huxley specialized in the shiny-scaled, fringe-finned (and, he guessed, lung-breathing) fishes from the Devonian period, that great age of fishes. But where before he had simply brought the relevant species together as 'Crossopterygeans', which he likened to the living lungfishes, now there was an evolutionary imperative to his studies.[5] He created the conditions for the later belief that the world's three remaining lungfish were relics of this Devonian group – living cousins of the stagnant-water air-gulpers which had evolved into the amphibians. As always, there was a chauvinistic excitement about it, a tingle, because this was the human line, *our* line.

It took precedence over the Resurrection. Through Christmas, through the Ellen fiasco, Huxley had his nose deep in the dismembered *Ceratoduses*, adding the stench of preserving spirits to the smell of family decay. 'I have been working tremendously hard', he told Sclater at the zoo, '& have been getting some good results'. On New Year's Eve he had mudfishes and primitive sharks sent from the zoo to South Kensington and the next morning was drawing the result. Len would collect shark foetuses from the British Museum to save time. As always Huxley could see past his scalpel and projected 'a series of papers', and as usual this was the first and last in the series. Even then he had to limit himself 'to the Brain & Skeleton' in order to have his paper ready for the Zoological Society on 4 January 1876.[6]

A week after one delicate dissection he was engaged in another. His forensic report on the alleged Resurrection was causing the squeamish to groan at the Metaphysical. Huxley, the genial chairman in 1876, kept his meetings at 'a high level of discursive analysis and witty repartee'. But if his geniality put everyone at ease, his topics made hairs stand on end. By now the Metaphysical had become a factional ecclesiastical court, adjudicating agnosticism and belief, spiritual interference and natural uniformity, experience and intuition. The very agenda was an epistemological sign of a industrializing culture thrown into professional turmoil.

Miracles were essential to Huxley's method. He always kept the onus on his rival's beliefs, never his own. And his rivals found his playful, mock-consensual rhetoric so easy and so hard to deal with. With Kant he pronounced nothing impossible and, as that Reverend heretic Moncure Conway laughed, he 'told the theologians that science had plenty of miracles, and would willingly add theirs, if proved'. But could they be? Could one seismic rupture at the fount of Christianity be verified? On 11 January 1876, vacating the Chair for Gladstone, he took to the floor to dissect the testimony of the Resurrection. He brought the most notorious test case in the Metaphysical's history. Old Father Newman – whose evangelical impulse had come from Huxley's Ealing school – was shocked that Manning had actually sat through it, wondering if it wasn't 'a ruse of the Cardinal to bring the Professor into the clutches of the Inquisition'.[7] Not that Manning had actually sat unaffected. It was 'pathetic' to see his 'ill-disguised amazement' as he 'listened to the ruthless and cold-blooded denials of what to him were self-evident and eternal truths'. For the first time a debate ran into the next meeting, and there was a detectable stiffening of attitudes. Huxley had gone too far.

Huxley returned to his High Chair to watch Gladstone, who was waging his own pamphlet war on Manning over Papal Infallibility. The raptorial anatomist peered down on the Grand Old Man's head. With a mortician's eye he sized up its 'curious breadth of parietals, & flatness', and imagined with undue phrenologicalness that its feline shape explained his 'eccentricities'.[8] These were intensifying yearly. Even now Gladstone was seeking some obscure link between Genesis and Homer's *Iliad*. He never understood the new science, nor the growing disenchantment with mankind's religious 'treasure'. Having dispensed with the Pope, Gladstone now invited the devil to one of his Thursday breakfasts. Huxley had to accept.

Huxley's Resurrection paper was too hot to handle. Even Morley declined such a 'deadly routing of the most sacred article in theology'. It was for scholars in conclave, not 'the profane crowd'. Morley had already burnt his fingers with the incorrigible William Kingdon

Clifford. This consumptive, Proudhon-reading, atheistic 30-year-old (for whom Nettie had a particular soft spot), was dabbling in the uncertainties of non-Euclidean geometry at University College and lambasting the certainties of Christian cosmogony in the *Fortnightly*. But the catcalls would be as nothing to the outrage if an idol like Huxley were to unstitch society's 'whole system of belief'. It would land 'the rotten egg and dead cat' on his doorstep.[9] It would enrage the Christian, said Morley, more aptly than he knew, as much as by calling his sister a slut. Huxley looked at Ellen and took the point.

Jessie was tall, striking, and 18 years old in February. Her dance was the 'brightest & pleasantest' anyone could remember. The dining room was turned out, and shimmering candlelight played on exotic blooms, sent specially from Kew. The party went on till 3.30, and even Nettie could not resist a waltz, although it was 'shocking' to be 'dancing at 50!' They looked at Jess in her mousseline-de-soie dress and realized that she had grown up. Not that it prepared them for the announcement of her engagement to Fred Waller. But Hal, forgetting his 'hatred of possible sons-in-law', was overjoyed (even if he did set his 'face against her marrying before she is Twenty'). Fred had a 'sterling character', Nettie said, and 'Hal & I both love him very much'.[10]

Nothing should have surprised them any more, but one thing did. At 55 Tyndall showed all the signs of confirmed bachelorhood: absent-mindedness, unnatural work-hours, a death-wish attitude to safety – in his speeches no less than his Alpine skirmishes. Huxley had received nothing but bottles of bacteria from him for months, so everything seemed normal. Tyndall was obsessively experimenting to prove that germs fill the air and were the cause of disease, and sending on the flasks. Huxley, his interest rekindled, at one point observed that *Penicillium* mould stopped bacterial growth. This would be the real medical moment for Fleming with his twentieth-century understanding of antibiosis and 'penicillin'-extraction techniques. But Huxley and Tyndall had their distinct nineteenth-century preoccupations. Huxley was concentrating on *Penicillium*'s life stages, and Tyndall was still consumed with the need to debunk the spontaneous generation of life. Obsession was driving the bachelor to live as an 'ascetic, to clear away this "Bastian fog"'.[11]

But an admirer sat weekly in Tyndall's audience, the imperturbable Louisa Hamilton. Through concerts and climbs the plain 30-year-old daughter of Lord Claud Hamilton pulled the abstemious Professor out of himself. Her parents bravely wafted aside their differences in age and class. The X thought she was dicing with death herself in trying to turn Tyndall into something approaching married normality. Nettie pondered the age gap, and 'considering what a radical & independent nature our brother John is, it is amusing that his wife is cousin to half the dukes in England'. Tyndall treated the wedding as rather a nuisance which got in among the germ experiments. 'After discussing the registrar, Moncure Conway & Gretna Green', he explained to Huxley, 'we turned . . . to Stanley'. The Dean's wife was dying, but it was her wish that he not 'lose sight of the men of science', and so he created an à la carte service almost tolerable to a freethinker.

The bells of Westminster Abbey pealed for the infidel who would seize the cosmos from theology. Clutching him was old Carlyle in a shabby black felt hat, nothing but a clean face and collar to suggest any preparation. There was no sign of Spencer. He had refused to soil his boots on hallowed ground. And the Dean's spirit was elsewhere (the wedding flowers would be on his wife's coffin the next day). It was a mercy to all that the service was shorn. Even so, Tyndall's ringing 'I will' contrasted with his sheepish 'Father, Son, and Holy Ghost'.[12] And so it was a card for 'D^r^. & M^rs^. Tyndall' to join Browning, Morley and Lord and Lady Arthur Russell at the next Marlborough Place dinner.

Nor was that the last surprise. America liked Huxley as the industrialists did. And as the factory bosses became powerful they showed their gratitude. 'God bless my soul', exclaimed Hal as £1,000 tumbled out of a letter on 21 March. It was a bequest from the Bolton cotton king Thomas Thomasson. He had been the retiring money-man behind the free-trade agitation. His coffers had kept Cobden afloat and the Anti-Corn Law League solvent, and in death the Quaker was keeping faith with the cause. Flush Dissenters put their trust in individual conscience rather than State-privileged Church, and their faith in a wheeze-and-snort world run by impartial law rather than miraculous whim. They understood *Lay Sermons* (it was Thomasson's favourite book). Around the Lord's table they praised Huxley's school drive and sought legitimacy in his democracy of knowledge. The cash, Thomasson's son said, was in 'appreciation of your services'. It 'was on account of Hal's religious opinions . . . & high moral nature', Nettie heard, 'that M^r^. Thomasson admired & esteemed him'.[13] The Dissenters were paying their dues.

With the cash in hand Hal and Nettie immediately bought tickets for America. It was time to do something for themselves. Huxley tied up loose ends. He gave addresses, accepted prizes,[14] dotted the i's and crossed the t's of his 600-page *Anatomy of Invertebrated Animals*, only 20 years late (his publisher John Churchill had died waiting). And as for 'that pietistic old malefactor, Shaftesbury', with his slur in the Lords that Huxley encouraged children to vivisect animals, Huxley made his 'Evangelical soul' shake with a thunderous rebuke in the *Times*. That was the last gasp of the vivisection debate before a compromise Cruelty to Animals Act was passed. In future only the licensed would be able to experiment, while their Lordships remained free to inflict more pain in a day's shooting than the physiologists did in a year's research. The Duke of Somerset had the temerity to say it, and Huxley thought him 'the only man who talked sense'.[15] That done, Huxley had only to deliver his Edinburgh course.

With Hal away, Nettie bore the brunt. She was of that powerful breed which carried Victorian families. She spent weeks organizing the troop, the Transatlantic trip and two months' wardrobe. What with the logistics and worrying about woollen shifts in the Southern sun, while seeing to adolescent daughters during the London Season, she 'had a very hard time' of it. In a year of betrothals the last word came just before she left: from the widower Hooker, about *his* engagement to Lady Jardine, an ornithologist's widow and bred-in-the-bone naturalist. The X-Club patriarchs undertook marriage with professional detachment: Tyndall wanted a domestic lab assistant, Hooker a replacement mother and scientific secretary, and the ladies obligingly jettisoned their titles to join the intellectual aristocracy. With that news, plain Mrs Huxley trundled off in a 'huge omnibus, with luggage piled to the top, & a cab besides', marshalling a governess, three servants and five children (the elder girls having gone ahead) to meet Hal at Armstrong's Northumberland estate.

Sir William and Lady Armstrong had no children, and his enormous engineering works on the Tyne, ever experimenting with breech-loaders and iron-clad cruisers, had left the industrial baronetcy in luxury. They could afford to lavish care on the hard-pressed Huxleys. With the children settled, Hal and Nettie set off for the New World. Nettie – her 'seven darlings' lined up at Rothbury station to be kissed in turn – hated leaving them, and the emotional Mady as always 'sobbed bitterly'.[16] They were leaving the children for the first time. But in a year of marriages they were due their own second honeymoon.

On 27 July 1876 they were at Queenstown, in Co. Cork, settling into their berths on the *Germanic*. It 'must be a delightful trip nowadays, such splendid ships', an expectant Lizzie wrote, recalling her own seven-week ordeal on a tramp sailing ship. Indeed £63 tickets bought them a bit of gracious living. The liner ploughed through the Atlantic waves at an unprecedented 13 knots. Nettie was seasick but the old sailor relished the salt air. The huge funnels belched smoke from the furnaces, the foghorns blasting every few minutes through the first night. The next morning Hal and Nettie woke to the sight of icebergs, a reminder of the Atlantic's hazards.[17] But the weather calmed and warmed and after a week of deck reading they sighted Manhattan.

America lay waiting, wondering. English intellectuals had a reputation for airs and graces, but would the new moralist be grave and the philosopher high-falutin? American culture had itself become scientific and exciting. No longer was English fiction the staple. The post-Civil War years had a new way of rationalizing the hope and progress of reconstruction. 'Now it is English science. Herbert Spencer, John Stuart Mill, Huxley, Darwin, Tyndall, have usurped the places of Tennyson and Browning, and Matthew Arnold and Dickens'. Appleton's red-cloth books had carried the Word, and the archangel Edward Youmans had heralded the Coming. As a result Huxley's democratic depiction of knowledge and his musings on the pain of existence were acclaimed by Californian miners and Kentuckian bankers; his worldly piety fired Boston intellectuals and New York businessmen; his profane Calvinism explaining man's hard relation to Nature could discipline a new industrial workforce. The Gilded Age welcomed this 'monumental embodiment of rational energy'. They had read him to find American values, and they had done so through Spencerian spectacles. The New World was riding the evolutionary torrent 'onward and upward to ever higher and better manifestations'.[18] They had taken what they wanted; they had taken it aplenty and now they prepared a handsome reception.

He reciprocated in his rational admiration. Catching his first sight of the Manhattan skyline on 5 August he asked about the two conspicuous towers. Told they were the *Tribune* and Western Union Telegraph buildings, 'Ah,' he replied, 'that is American. In the Old World the first things you see as you approach a great city are steeples; here you see . . . centres of intelligence'. He had endeared himself before he put a foot ashore. And more than he knew: the new *Tribune* tower had been inaugurated amid speeches by Darwinians exalting the new scientific progress. No wonder the hacks had forgotten the Prince of Wales and were awaiting Huxley's royal progress.

The couple were whisked from the sultry quayside to the Appletons' 'beautiful place on the Hudson'. In an exceptionally hot Centennial Summer their country estate was cooler, and it gave the Huxleys a glimpse of the 'wild scenery'. After a night's sleep they braved the 'broiling' city. It was sticky and bustling, 97° on the sidewalk, a crush of carriages and people, with looming telegraph poles sending the eye up the tall, flagstrewn buildings. He fought his way to Appleton's office on Broadway. Like a good publisher Appleton had lined up the press, and the newsmen were as surprised by the philosopher as he was moved by the razzmatazz. The *World* found him of the 'commercial' class, and not 'highfalutin' at all. He was proud of that. 'We may be rich yet', he laughed to Nettie. Reports said he was 'good-humoured, and exceedingly unpretentious', and it showed in the squibs about Professor Protoplasm and skits about the discoverer of the 'life principle' ('Anything to do with insurance?').[19] In New York science came with a pinch of salt, but wisecrackers still made a meal of it.

Now there was 'nothing but solid railwayable ground' separating him from Lizzie. Seeing her was a 30-year dream, but his schedule was packing out impossibly. He was reduced to a lightning visit; and even then, 'to economise time', he asked her to meet him in Nashville. The fact that he could only spare her four days in six weeks showed how much more the tour had become. Proselytizing now ruled his 3,000-mile itinerary. And Hal's diary totting showed the money to be pocketed. Offers still came in: would he lecture in St Louis for $1,000? Nettie, watching the purse, knew from Appleton that they could have gone 'home with £10,000 in the Spring'.[20]

Huxley hurried along with the New Yorkers, listening to the paperboys shout of the latest banking scandals. Urban America was vibrant, its technology entrepreneurial. Here venture capital was set to illuminate the modern world. Edison was already in his private laboratory over in New Jersey, perfecting the phonograph and light bulb, and ensuring the boom for consumer gadgetry. Trains were furbished for businessmen in a hurry. Huxley saw the future as he tried the new-fangled 'drawing room car' on his way to New Haven.

Yale gave him the best week of his trip. The Peabody's fossils alone were 'worth all the journey across'. Othniel C. Marsh, the 'magician' in charge, had the robust looks of a Western explorer, and he could produce any number of exquisite fossils from his frontier forays. But it was one in particular that Huxley had come to see.

Marsh was the solid product of Peabody money. He had been installed at Yale as America's first professor of palaeontology by his tycoon uncle George Peabody, and the millionaire's money had paid for five expeditions to the parched Badlands. The steadfast fellow was surprisingly 'full of stories about his Western adventures', Huxley regaled Nettie. Marsh was a new breed of palaeontological robber baron, whose plunder Huxley had come to see. He held Huxley captive with talk of his trek with Pawnee scouts, Buffalo Bill and cavalry troop into the Rockies in 1870, and again to the Smokey river in western Kansas in 1871. He had scoured Dakota like a frontiersman, slaughtering buffalo indiscriminately in Oglala Sioux territory. But his meeting with Red Cloud in 1874 and discovery of the scale of the swindling and treachery by traders and agents had turned him into a passionate campaigner for the Indian nations. They had shown him the 'thunder beasts' (huge fossil titanothere skulls washed out of Badland rocks) – creatures of legend which roamed the plains during storms – and he had been adopted into the Oglala tribe as 'the man who chops out bones'. Marsh's hectoring of President Grant over their plight was to little avail (although he did get the Secretary of the Interior fired). Even as he was telling Huxley, the news was of Custer's massacre two weeks earlier. The Sioux' fury had been unleashed after the invasion of gold miners into their sacred Black Hills.

Huxley experienced a little of the Peabody hospitality. Marsh installed him in Uncle George's apartment, lavish enough for Connecticut's Governor to pay court. Most evenings Huxley dined in Marsh's mansion and sashayed along the elm-lined avenues afterwards. But from 9 to 6 it was business.

While roaming the Smokey in 1871 Marsh had found the fossil that had brought Huxley so far. It was an extraordinary Cretaceous bird, still with teeth, but only a stumpy tail. The six-foot *Hesperornis* had vestigial wings but powerful legs, and the fact that Marsh called it a 'carnivorous swimming ostrich' piqued Huxley's interest.[21] It fitted his evolutionary genealogy – from strutting bipedal dinosaurs to struthious flightless birds. Marsh, custodian of the key evolutionary link, prided himself on agreeing.

Links were in their mind as they travelled 60 miles to Springfield on 14 August. Huxley had used the Connecticut fossil footprints for years as proof of the ostrich-like gait of many dinosaurs. Now he walked with them; along the sandstone bank of the Connecticut river, beside the primeval three-toed tracks. Here Triassic dinosaurs had once trotted.[22] It was grist to the mill and he would grind it well for American consumption.

The West was putting American palaeontology on the map. Huxley was set to extol evolution in his US lectures. He had started writing one, on elephants, almost nostalgically: he reminisced about sleepy Ealing and the Summer fairs of his boyhood, full of 'red-faced & top-booted farmers' and lads charging past 'canvas booths stocked with gilt gingerbread'. He recalled a Wild Beast show, with its awesome hoardings of pythons devouring oxen. He looked on himself as an inquisitive stripling, armed with 'nuts & buns', beckoned into a dark foreboding tent by the unearthly 'roars & grunts' to see his first towering elephant. That was the way to start a lecture.

Marsh interrupted the day-dream. He cantered out his fossil horses. Box after box of bones, real fossil gold from the Nebraska hills. Huxley's elephants vanished like his reverie. Marsh seemed to have everything, from yesterday's pony-like *Pliohippus* with a single toe, down to the sheep-sized *Miohippus* with three toes, and ultimately the four-toed, fox-sized *Orohippus*. The collection was 'the most wonderful thing I ever saw'. It overhauled the horse's supposed European ancestry; indeed 'The more I think of it the more clear it is that your great work is the settlement of the pedigree of the horse'. Marsh's horses came from progressively older rocks. *Orohippus*, the oldest, went back to Eocene times. But Marsh thought that an even older five-toed ancestor might have lived in the shadow of the dinosaurs. To cap his conversion Huxley dashed off a cartoon of this conjectural pygmy '*Eohippus*', and added a conjectural rider, a pygmy '*Eohomo*'.[23]

He pored over the fossils. He would call for a *Protohippus* hoof or a *Miohippus* molar. Line up Marsh's 30 species and it made Kovalevskii's point: tiny browsers had changed with the Miocene grassy plains into swift grazers, their molars enlarging and faces lengthening to deal with the tough meadow grass. 'I believe you are a magician', Huxley told his host, 'whatever I want, you just conjure it up'. Marsh's was a pedigree in the truest sense, an American bloodline for a noble thoroughbred. He had jettisoned the confusing variants to leave a neat image. From a tiny forest dweller to today's high-stepping sprinter: the horses had stretched their legs, fused the lower limb bones, evolved the single tip-toe and grown tall on the high plains. In the Centennial year American palaeontology was proving its independence. With Marsh proclaiming Wyoming and Nebraska the 'true home of the Horse', Huxley could puff America and Darwin in the same breath.[24] He had the perfect lectures for a continent that was being conquered in the saddle.

His rounds continued with the sea-urchin expert and mining entrepreneur Alexander Agassiz, a troubled man torn between Darwin's evolution and his father's memory. The late, dynamic Louis Agassiz, founder and general factotum of Harvard's Museum of Comparative Zoology, had given the world Ice Ages, but it wasn't the cold his son feared. Old Louis had died within a week of Alex's wife, and in an act of self-immolation Alexander had thrown himself into managing the museum. He was 'a driven man', he told Huxley, 'trying to keep all [of his father's] irons hot'.

Then came a *de rigueur* meeting with the botanist Asa Gray at Harvard. Gray had done sterling service selling an insipid theological version of Darwinism to waverers. He had even visited Downe, still looking to pump a little Design into Darwin, only to find the *Origin* commandeered and smothered by infidel connotations by the 'Huxley set'. Still, the fogeyish Darwin was attached to the fogeyish Gray, and that was enough for the visiting diplomat. There was more wholesome enjoyment among Fiske's 'sweet-scented pine-woods' of northern Massachusetts on 21 August, and ne'er a word on infidelism: Fiske knew that there was more real religion in Huxley's 'honest scepticism' than in any 'timorous assent to a half-understood creed'. The jovial cosmic philosopher, the most corpulent in America, laid on a gourmet feast to repay all those convivial high teas, before giving Huxley a taste of 'primitive New England life'.[25]

And so to Buffalo, where the British Ass saw how the American Asses advanced their science. His renown preceded him. So did Marsh, who was to be his rugged chaperon for much of the trip. The ambitious Marsh could see off the unwelcome attention of rivals (the race for dinosaurs was deteriorating into a range war against his erratic foe E. D. Cope). Marsh needed Huxley's imprimatur as Huxley needed Marsh's bones. Having given Huxley his theme, Marsh was on hand for the plaudits. Huxley's remarks at the American Association for the Advancement of Science came off-the-cuff. He moved from New York's preternatural press corps to America's revelation in the wilderness. The high plains had turned evolution from informed speculation into 'matter of fact'. To reassure their guest at Buffalo, Louis Agassiz's old students admitted that they were all now for Darwin. The euphoria lingered in Buffalo after the delegates had packed and gone, at least until the revivalists Moody and Sankey arrived to sanitize the city with battle-hymn and harmonium.

Like all second honeymooners Hal and Nettie stayed at nearby Niagara. They lay low for a week, Hal writing his lectures, trying not to create the sort of stir associated with the dare-devil tightrope walkers at the Falls. The couple braced themselves in the 'roaring of the winds & waters & tempestuous spray'. Ahead lay a gruelling

30-hour train journey via Cincinnati to Nashville, and the moment of reunion.

The damage of time showed in both brother and sister. Lizzie's 'thin grave face' told of a struggle in the carpetbagging South: 'there's nothing young about me', she had warned Tom, 'but love and sympathy'. She was 62, with bad eyes; Scott's death in 1872 had ended a tragic era and left her dependent on the children. Yet time had not erased her 'old motherly feelings towards you'. There was apprehension on both sides. Never mind that 'he is grey, and 50', Nettie wrote ahead from Niagara, 'your hearts will bridge across the years'.[26]

They did. At dusk on Monday 4 September the New Orleans Lightning Express pulled into Nashville. England still provided cultural leadership, even in the South, and the visit of a British Great was an occasion for a turn-out. Among the waiting crowd at the Church Street depot, Lizzie was instantly recognizable by her jet-black eyes. It was a poignant moment. Lizzie clasped her brother and in the lantern light saw 'the most lovable . . . face in the world'.

He had last seen her on that fateful day 30 years before, as they fled across the Channel carrying two-year-old Flory and new-born Edith. Now the girls were Southern Belles. Tears probably clouded the family's journey to Edith's South Vine Street house. But it had the warmth of home, with English books, the 'racket' of three small children, and now laughter and singing (although Lizzie's voice – so evocative for Tom – had gone). Edith's husband, the urbane and humorous Albert Roberts, ran the city's cosmopolitan *Daily American*. As 'John Happy' Captain Roberts had been the rebs' rousing pamphleteer. The veteran of Shiloh was now the great conservative campaigner for a new industrial South.[27] His training and investment schemes, and schooling and health-care campaigns, put him squarely behind Hal, whose speeches he had reprinted. For a moment Hal could have been in any developing city. But this was Nashville, the 'buckle on the Bible belt', heartland of the 'Lost Cause': his nieces had grown into Presbyterian churchwomen, and Roberts' vision had a dark underbelly. The jobs and education were for whites – and when his ethnically-cleansed Tennessee was mooted the air must have chilled.

All was newspaper talk. Flory's own husband Robert Roberts was the *American*'s business manager – the sisters had married brothers and ran their lives according to deadlines. Lizzie's son Tom, working on the Mobile and Montgomery Railroad, was there to meet his uncle and namesake. But it was Lizzie whom Huxley had come so far to see. These two, always so close, were the polished mahogany flotsam washed up from the wreck of a family. There was no one else now. 'George, poor fellow, is dead. William I have not seen for twenty years. Jim is as near mad as a sane man can be' and Ellen was lost in 'drink quarrels debt & vice'. Lizzie told of her own heavy-hearted years and the hopes for her sons. And she still worried over the golden boy, knowing that 'all the world watches what you do'.[28]

Despite having only four days with Lizzie, Tom's time wasn't his own. Trying to keep his visit low key had proved futile, for the Governor requested his pleasure the next morning. Governor Porter, up for re-election on a better-schooling ticket, saw no votes lost in hobnobbing with Huxley. And so the visiting dignitary was honoured by a state tour, covering everything from the Federal Courts to Fisk, the South's new black university (built with money raised by the Jubilee Singers, who had entertained Britain with their Negro Spirituals in 1874). On Wednesday the widowed Mrs Scott saw nothing for it but to join the entourage. They all walked a bit taller after coming face to face with a bust of Tom at the new Vanderbilt University. And this, Lizzie must have noted, in a Methodist school under Bishop McTyeire's Board! They visited the European-style science departments. Then hearty theology professors showed Huxley where they beat the rhythm of old-time religion, and 'where we should be glad to have the opportunity of beating a little into you'. 'Ah, sir', said their guest, 'if I were here I should give you novel theology'. He slapped backs at Fogg High School for its physics and chemistry classes, claiming that Tennesseans could show the backwoods British a thing or two. He was so courteous. Lizzie was lost in admiration, desperately pleased that her baby brother was not the 'pugilistic Boanerges he had been painted'. If only 'old Vanderbilt would leave Hal a couple of his superfluous millions'.

Tom was unable to shake his civic tail. It had taken him 30 years to reach Lizzie's doorstep, only to be whisked away. A deputation dragged the 'Great Scientist' off for another appearance. The good folks, equally sceptical of his son-of-thunder notoriety, wanted his 'view from his own lips'. Whether Huxley acquitted himself in the 700-seater Masonic Hall is debatable. Still, the South's lushest theatre outside of New Orleans resonated to his 'Sermon in Stone'. Bewhiskered preachers and professors in kid gloves sat amid scarlet drapery; judges strained to hear from their gold boxes; Southern beauties fanned themselves; and an Ealing Englishman showed them the real rock of ages: a little Lyell, a little Darwin and a lacing of local geology. Look at the aeons that Niagara has been cutting its gorge, and the ages since mastodons roamed the region – look beneath Nashville to the Pharaonic dynasties of life. In half an hour he had covered the history of the world. Then suddenly realizing his place, he apologized for appearing 'a sort of fanatic in these matters'.[29] Tennessee forgot itself too and cheered at evolution, led on by the *American* – but then Edith's husband was editor.

Too soon, the next morning, he was gone. His motherly sister had lived to see him praised by the God-fearing South as the 'great apostle of modern science' and the 'whole-souled' missionary of education. She hoped they would meet again, but both seem to have doubted it. The parting opened Lizzie's old wounds as she returned to Alabama and reflected on 'the sins that drew down on me the discipline of being banished from the land I love'. She could never quite close 'that page of my inner life'. Tom too was lost as the 'wild wooded scenery' of Kentucky flashed past his carriage window.

He awoke to the vastness of the continent. Having spent long hours behind great locomotives, with their kerosene headlamps and balloon smokestacks bellowing out black clouds, it was fitting that he should be met by President Garrett of the Baltimore & Ohio Railway on 9 September. Marsh joined Hal and Nettie in Garrett's 'Montebello' mansion in Baltimore. Adjoining their grounds was the Hopkins estate, another product of railroad money. The Baltimore & Ohio had been the first passenger line in America, and opening up the Midwest farm belt had made Johns Hopkins a fortune. Some $3.5 million of it were now building the new university. The money had come across as railway shares. In America real steam was being turned into real intellect.

The Huxleys were in a Quaker community of liberal emancipists. Their hostess, Mrs Garrett, let them know 'that all women sh^{d} get better educated'.[30] The university was itself an experiment. It was no architecturally-resplendent mausoleum, but a vital think-tank. Boom money was bouncing Baltimore into the vanguard of American higher education. Johns Hopkins' President Gilman projected an advanced graduate school to staunch the flow of students to Europe, a Ph.D. factory to meet the nation's needs. Behind his thinking lay the strange concept of organized research, and he cited Huxley's biological workshop as a prime example. Hopkins professors were to be paid to research and, with the largest bequest in US history, paid well. The Trustees saw friend Huxley as their man.

He was to open the guest lecture series on 12 September, on the eve of the first enrolment. With his awe of science, Gilman would make Hopkins a 'shrine for her worship'. And who better to stamp his assent than the agnostic Pope? Gilman had seen Huxley perform in London, where Huxley's deliverance from grace was only matched by 'the grace of his delivery'. Gilman also knew of the standard sectarian problems with universities. So Johns Hopkins would have no 'sectional bias'. Gilman the lapsed Congregationalist had learned from his ally President White, frustrated with the sectarian sniping at Cornell. White's myth-making *Warfare of Science* in 1876 reflected his anger at all this religious bickering. It was a book, and a programme, Huxley could endorse.

But friend Huxley was flagging; more than that, for the first time he was flummoxed. Gilman escorted him onto the Hopkins stage at 11 o'clock, trailing the Governor, Mayor, state and federal officials, a Japanese Minister and university presidents, who tailed away to sit in the orchestra pit. Gilman, already praised and abused for his celebrity choice, promptly exacerbated matters by opening the proceedings without the rudiments of a religious blessing. Go-ahead Quakers had seen no need of a prayer, and even critics perceived the giant incompatibility. 'It was bad enough to invite Huxley', one snorted. 'It were better to have asked God to be present. It would have been absurd to ask them both'.[31] Instead Gilman quoted the Quaker poet on America's Saxon debts, and Huxley stepped forth. His benedictions were famous for soothing the wrinkled brow. Then he looked at his notes.

He had made a stupid mistake. To get an accurate transcription into the papers, he had summoned up heroic strengths and dictated it to an Associated Press stenographer the day before. But the fair copy arrived too late, on flimsy paper; standing before the 2,000 he couldn't read a word of it. And he couldn't improvise with his speech being *reported* across the land. Stymied, he tried to recall his dictated words, so as not to deviate from the printed version. Even the unostentatious Quaker ladies thought the result was too, well, unostentatious. It 'had no glow', said a puzzled Gilman.

Glow or no, it was quintessential Huxley: the poor man praising a brains before bricks policy (Hopkins' money was going into research, not a fabulous façade); the intellectual commending America's steel barons for founding secular academies. If it wasn't the 'vigorous & exhaustive' triumph that the loyal Nettie claimed, it was redeemed by his 'noble & touching conclusion'. In the last minutes the golden touch returned, the prophetic glint. The voyager had seen eight states, and with 30 more (Colorado was the new 38th state) he sensed an awakening giant. But size and territory do not a nation make: 'The great issue, about which hangs a true sublimity, and the terror of overhanging fate, is what are you going to do with all these things?' He had a touching faith that America was a Greater Britain bent on 'a novel experiment in politics'. So what of the 200 millions he predicted by the bicentenary of 1976? Would they hold together under 'a republic, and the despotic reality of universal suffrage'? As the cities burgeon 'and the pressure of want is felt, the gaunt spectre of pauperism will stalk among you, and communism and socialism will claim to be heard'. A deathly hush crept over the audience at the prospect of a Communist America. No, of course; with 'fortresses ... of the nation' like the Hopkins providing inspiration 'America has a great future before her'. And may the university's Renaissance freedom draw students 'from all parts of the earth, as of old they sought Bologna, or Paris, or Oxford'.[32] With that he sat down. Nettie gave him kiss and was quietly proud.

As so often at home, his old demonstrator H. N. Martin was in the audience. Or rather Professor Martin. The young, dedicated Martin had come over to head up the Hopkins Biology Department and adapt the Kensington laboratory technique 'in usum studiosum Yankietatis'.[33] Huxley was leaving him in charge, a sturdier reminder of the way things were done in London.

The next day they took Gilman's private railway carriage for four hours of sightseeing in Washington. After the 'magnificent' domed Capitol building there was the Smithsonian Institution, and they still fitted in the 'very theatre where poor Lincoln was shot'. The exhaustion was showing by the 14th as they took in more anatomical theatres in Philadelphia. Here were American fossil mastodons and sloths, and the doyen himself, Joseph Leidy, to show Hal around the museum of the Academy of Natural Sciences. Old Leidy was a dry anatomist, but he had seen the light: for him, the *Origin of Species* was 'a meteor [that] flashed upon the skies'. Huxley was in seventh heaven himself: here the prize exhibit was a 25-foot dinosaur skeleton, the *Hadrosaurus*, which had been cast standing on its hind legs by Huxley's book engraver and friend Benjamin Waterhouse Hawkins, the first such mount in the world. It had proved so great a crowd-puller that another had been made for the Centennial Exposition in Fairmount Park. Hal and Nettie were escorted there too, to see the new-age wonders, including Bell's patented talking telephone. The Californian exhibitors, tickled that Huxley should stop to talk to them, told of 'how the miners read his books & by their fires talked over his deepest problems'.[34] Perhaps they really did.

The 15th saw them in New York's Westminster Hotel. Nettie was now 'tired & stupefied' by the constant 'sightseeing & travelling'.

But the stream of visitors only increased, and the requests. The Professor was taxed on the sublime and the ridiculous: would he comment on the evolution of the heavens? And on chimney ventilation? Would he discuss Biblical exegesis and fossil fish? A bevy of 'Fannies' and 'Lucys' besieged him for autographs, and august bodies besieged him for lectures. Finally Nettie mounted guard in the sitting room, barring all entry, and for five hours on Sunday the 17th Hal shut himself away in the dressing room to finish his lectures.[35]

He needed to. Horace Greeley's progressive *Tribune* was zealously trailing Hal's appearance. The newspapers had reported each speech and raised expectations of his three New York lectures. The *Herald* proclaimed him one of the world's great exponents of science. Even as the letters pages countered with thoughts on Genesis, the *Times* prided itself that Huxley would find no English-style prejudice in this secular, ticker-tape city. To prove it a preacher at the Church of the Strangers refused to call him an atheist. These 'scientists' 'are nothing of the kind', he conceded. 'They have a religion of their own'.[36] They did, and the crowd was baying for it. The evangelism of science was beginning to produce its own Great Awakening. Appleton felt the rush for the $5 tickets at his Broadway office, and astutely brought out Asa Gray's theistic *Darwiniana* to cash in on Huxley-mania.

Chickering Hall, on 5th Avenue and 18th, was packed to capacity the next night. The entrance was thronged with top hats and feather bonnets. Here were 'New-York's best', the 'familiar faces' of the Social Register set. It was a 'highly respectable crush'. Tactically adept (some said inept), Huxley had only to walk out holding Milton's *Paradise Lost* (with its epic depiction of Creation) to make the next day's headlines: 'The Gauntlet Thrown Down by Modern Science' screamed the *Herald*. It made good copy. The *Herald* assumed that Milton was a 'courteous' cover, to save Huxley mentioning Moses, and even then warned him that Milton-lovers would not stand by and 'see him cuffed over the ears to make a scientific lecturer's holiday'.[37] If he meant the Good Book, why didn't he say the Good Book? The story grew in the telling, until the *Daily Graphic* capped it with a full-cover cartoon of 'Huxley Eikonoklastes' battering a statue of Moses with Milton's bust.

Huxley talked quietly, gravely, and listeners found it difficult to get his measure. These weren't his working clods, whose colloquialisms he could capture, or his West End toffs ready for buttering. He lacked the American stump-style perfected by hellfire preachers. He seemed reserved, English, 'unimpassioned and deliberate'. His incisive hits came understated, his humour had an unaccustomed irony. There was drama in there, in his seemingly common-sense demands for an orderly universe undisturbed by 'external agencies'.[38] And in his theatrical juxtaposition – setting this off against *Paradise Lost*'s earth-shaking Sixth Day of Creation: 'out of the ground up rose' each beast, 'The tawny lion, pawing to get free . . . ' He gave science its moral solemnity, where the press was expecting histrionics. It was clever, but confusing. Wasn't he an 'intellectual athlete who is shaking the old beliefs'? How to report his subtleties, where a sardonic glance doubled for a wild flourish? He seemed measured, but surely he wasn't. The *Times* came closest to unravelling his rhetoric, his 'Ciceronian way of saying that he will not denounce such and such an hypothesis', while damning it by his very denial.[39] At breakfast New Yorkers read of the brouhaha about Darwin's vicar and Milton's idolatry. It ensured a packed second night.

On Wednesday the 20th came the 'favourable' evidence for evolution. Not for Darwin's mechanism, but for the belief that life was a connected whole. For once Huxley did not overplay his 'persistent types'. The fact that American scorpions had not altered since coal-swamp times simply showed that change was not inevitable. But change there had been elsewhere, spectacular change – tails shortened, teeth lost, scales turned into feathers. This was his sensational bird ancestry. Behind him were pictures of the chicken-sized dinosaur *Compsognathus* and the Connecticut footprints, and America's fossil toothed birds. Marsh had blown them up, and Marsh and America collected the kudos as Huxley showed how Nebraska's toothed divers could have evolved from free-armed dinosaurs. And what of that unique feature, feathers? Whether the delicate dinosaur *Compsognathus* 'had them we don't know', he admitted, but merely to moot the possibility of a feathered dinosaur made an avian descent seem so plausible.

He talked cagily of the famous *Archaeopteryx* with its bony tail and three wing-fingers. Later in print he still expressed doubts that *Archaeopteryx* was on the direct route to birds. It was a cousin, the royal line having already run from the 'bird-leg' dinosaurs to ostrich-like birds.[40] It was one more piece of circumstantial evidence that this real bloodline had existed.

Only a direct sequence of fossils could provide the 'Demonstrative Evidence of Evolution', and that he saved for Friday's finale. The socialites escaped from New York's 'threatening skies' to the prairies of Nebraska. Past them cantered the horses from Marsh's palaeontological stable – first high-stepping modern thoroughbreds, then tapir-toed proto-ponies, and bringing up the rear the miniature

Orohippus. What would be found next? An older Eocene forerunner with a fifth toe? The prediction gave the *Herald* its headline: 'Horses with Fingers and Toes Discovered in America. The Last Toe Wanting'. Even that caught the serious side. Huxley was applauding the United States for providing the real palaeontological proof of evolution, important during the centenary as the nation counted its achievements. Marsh, emboldened by Huxley's talk of 'Demonstrative Evidence', would henceforth tell Americans that 'to doubt evolution . . . is to doubt science'.[41]

At the finish Huxley apologized for his gravity. These were not issues, he said, digging at his critics, to be 'dealt with by rhetorical flourishes'. The shoe was now on the other foot: the man of science had emerged as the true Puritan in a nation proud of its heritage. The alienated, Dissent-backed activist clawing power in his own fragmenting Anglican culture had emerged in Manhattan as the true voice of Nature. Here the press had a word to match the incarnation: in America he was first called a 'scientist'.[42]

It was 'splendid', said Nettie, 'he was in great form'. Notes of congratulation poured in, talking of the 'profound impression' he had made. Everyone migrated back to the hotel '& drank our health in champagne'. There was the indefatigable Youmans, conniving with Marsh to get Huxley's lectures into book form with the Yale illustrations. The Appletons, too, were relishing a rise in sales as the pulpiteers declared 'war against Hal'. But the patriotic Nettie was sanguine, 'they cannot crush facts'.[43]

A 10¢ commemorative issue of the *Tribune* containing all of Huxley's speeches was on the streets at 8.30 the next morning, Saturday 23 September. The couple were already on board the liner *Celtic*, saying goodbye to Youmans and Appleton, and Professors Marsh and Martin. Thirty minutes later the great ship slipped its moorings.

Their spirits were dampened by a cold, cheerless, 12-day voyage home. For three of them Hal lay in bed 'wrapped in linseed & mustard poultices'. Exhausted, and always 'rebellious ab[t] overcoats', he had walked the stormy decks and caught a chill. But the mulligrubs passed on sighting land. And the ledger looked good: £915 *8s 6d* for Hal's cut of the profits, minus £300 expenses, 'Say £600 profit on the whole Transaction'. And by the time he got home he pronounced the 'Wife younger by ten years'.

'Never did I so love, or so appreciate the quiet loveliness of England' said Nettie of the green fields.[44] The Pope too, glad to see his 'dear native mud again', figuratively kissed the ground.

5

A Touch of the Whip

IN MARCH 1877 the eagle-eyed raptor nodded off on his Secretary's perch and slept through Frank Darwin's paper on teasel plants. The Royal Society was rather astonished. It wasn't the Huxley of old. 'I am not quite happy about Hal', Nettie told Lizzie as the inner man sagged, 'but don't say so beyond y^{r} home'.[1] Others saw his candle burning down fast.

Huxley was a glutton for punishing work, with endless opportunity to indulge himself. Thursday, his last free night, was finally sacrificed when Stanley started his meet-the-eminent evenings for young clerks and shop assistants at Westminster Deanery. Nettie was furious. Even the Professor was finding 'that as I get older doing more than two or three things at once becomes somewhat troublesome' – or so he told the Quekett Microscopical Club (of which of course he took the Presidency). And the 'Government never gives Hal any peace'. It co-opted him now onto his eighth Royal Commission, to look into the Scottish universities. Thus began more trips to Edinburgh and 'much work & no pay'. Even then the Treasury had the gall to query his expenses. But he had to get aboard to push through his reforms, and take 'up the case of you troublesome women', as he told the wife, 'who want admission into the University (very rightly too I think)'.[2]

Nettie sat at home awaiting the daily numbered letter. A genteel circle came to her aid: Lord Arthur Russell would arrange a ducal box at Covent Garden, or she would accompany the older girls to the Season's soirées. By day the younger, boisterous Nettie and brother Len would 'chase & battle' about the house. 'The rushing, the screams . . . ' and their mother laughing too much to be able to stop them. And the youngest of all, Harry, 12 in 1877, was 'wonderfully affectionate'. His father thought that 'women will play the devil with him, & he with them'.[3]

Overextension was a lifelong problem. In Huxley's study papers lay part-finished, like 'full many a flower, born to blush unseen'. Among them was his *Lessons in Elementary Psychology*, umpteen years old,and each year reduced the chance of him catching up. Work was 'a debt which whatever payments you may make grows continually vaster'. He began to lay a dead hand on precious specimens, like a secret collector with a priceless painting. With that modern *Argo*, the *Challenger*, back in port, and Thomson dubbed Sir Wyville by the Queen, Huxley had his pick of the prizes. The hold was loaded: 6,257 casks and jars full of the world's sea-bed treasures, enough to keep Europe's biologists busy for a generation and fill 50 volumes of reports. From the 4,000 new species Huxley picked a tentacled cephalopod, a cuttlefish relative with a flesh-covered coiled shell, *Spirula*. In 69,000 nautical miles they had found only one, and Huxley had another from the Governor of the Windward Islands. These smelly, preserved specimens lay dissected on his desk through 1879, a 53-page manuscript almost complete, plates engraved. But somehow the last heroic effort seemed to elude him.[4] Always there was some new challenge, some hidden hand beckoning him away.

Nor was it surprising, given the work he *did* wrap up in '77. Book after book came out, generating review after review. In May his 'wonderfully clear and rich' *American Addresses* brought 'the doctrine of evolution to the house'. Marsh's diagrams were fuller; and it was the first British book to make the fossil case for evolution. Marsh's archaic toothed birds reinforced Huxley's dramatic avian ancestry (which, joked J. A. Froude, resolved the chicken-and-egg question). A month later Huxley was putting the preface to his technical *Anatomy of Invertebrated Animals*: two decades on the desk, that one! Then there was that 'priceless gem', as sister Lizzie called it; the best of the crop, in Nettie's words: the *Physiography*, the book that spoke to the little ones, a mere seven years late. To stretched parents that spotter's guide to the land, the rocks, the weather and the world was 'worth silver and gold'. And that was what Huxley received for it, with tills ringing up 3,386 sales in six weeks. It was a bedtime book that turned from tiny everyday observations to gigantic prehistoric explanations. Radical in its conception, the *Physiography* set the trend for post-Darwinian geography. It took children from their parish to the outer reaches of the solar system. Huxley stood the old geography on its head: making local events the launch point was revolutionary, even if his strategy was to subordinate a distant

Jewish geography on the school syllabus. In line with this, the book looked to the causal connection of things rather than their Divine harmony. Morley's stepson couldn't be prised from it: Oh no, he would say, offered a novel in exchange, 'I'm at an awfully interesting part, and I can't leave off'. Morley saw it as 'a real service to the human race'. By Christmas there was a second printing and *American Addresses* had sold out. So, said Hal, 'I hope to tap Macmillan pretty freely'.[5]

Nettie gave thanks, and she chose a new shrine. Lisson Grove was too long a walk and she switched to St Mark's Church in the next road. The big spire promised wealthy pews for the socially mobile St John's Wood set. It was an upmarket move. The Revd Robinson Duckworth was the Queen's Chaplain, and fresh from his trip to India with the Prince of Wales. (They had long known Canon Duckworth; he was Ethel's godfather.) Not that Nettie's observance here was so fulfilling, or so central any more. Hal saluted the Sunday troop off. He had been open about his doubts, but he thought 'self-righteousness . . . worse than any wrong religious beliefs', and he knew that 'Their mother has a sneaking love for the old story'. St Mark's never fostered it. The church was uninspiring, so was Duckworth. And on sunny days Nettie could admit that

> I get more good out of Nature than, by going to church & hearing things put in such a way that they are simply irritating – or hearing things that to my mind are untrue & heathenish.[6]

Hal found his own Kingdom of Heaven in the New World. The prophecy was fulfilled. Seven weeks after waving goodbye in New York, Youmans announced Marsh's discovery of his five-toed 'dawn horse' *Eohippus*. In fact, Marsh had it all the time:

> I had him 'corralled' in the basement of our Museum when you were there, but he was so covered with Eocene mud that I did not know him from *Orohippus*. I promise you his grandfather in time for your next Horse Lecture if you will give me proper notice.[7]

If Huxley had any faith, it was in 'the inexhaustibility of the contents of those boxes', he told Marsh. So it was back to the circuit, with more talks on American horses and American birds with teeth. The Badlands horses changed Huxley's understanding of evolutionary timing yet again. Watching their growth from dog-sized ancestors to today's thoroughbreds, he began to contemplate a parallel series of human fossils. No talk now of Silurian men, or lost pre-Cambrian ancestors. After the Pliocene, Miocene and Eocene horses he could suggest that 'when we obtain the remains of Pliocene, Miocene, and Eocene *Anthropidae*, they will present us with the like series of gradations'.[8] He joined Wallace and Darwin to await the discovery of apemen.

'So far as animals are concerned I am quite satisfied that Evolution is a historical fact', he now said, adding cryptically, 'What causes brought it about is another matter'.[9] There was the rub. While Hooker – or rather Sir Joseph, for he had caved in and accepted the Star of India, recommended by Lord Salisbury for his monumental work on the Himalayan flora – got to grips with Natural Selection in his Presidential Address to the Royal Society, his Secretary was distancing the fact of evolution from putative 'physiological' causes. It showed in the first-ever article on 'Evolution', which Huxley wrote for the *Encyclopaedia Britannica*. Darwin was nonplussed to find himself the culmination of Cartesian philosophy and biological discovery. His contingent and chancy Natural Selection was mentioned once, only to be neutered by talk of some innate tendency for organisms to vary.[10] Huxley had managed to portray 'Evolution', not only without 'Natural Selection', but without any 'Natural History' either.

But for better or worse Pope Huxley was Darwin's representative on Earth. When an admiring solicitor Anthony Rich offered to leave Darwin his fortune, it was Huxley who went to Worthing to check on the donor's respectability. Back went a report to the Darwins on the odd gent's bachelor house with its fine-lawned two acres:

> Well he is an alert, bright-eyed little man with a long beard & croaky voice – very frank & straightforward and with a sort of abrupt courtesy & kindness, that's rather taking . . . He seems to have had a loose ended sort of life – spending many years in Italy & studying art – and is about as pronounced a heretic, theologically morally & politically as I have yet met with – which you will allow is saying a good deal for him. But the man is a gentleman in the best sense of the word [this was Darwin's main worry, having spent a life trying to avoid being tarred with the disreputables].[11]

Huxley's report on the 'man who had strayed so eccentrically into the path of wisdom' gave the Darwins 'a real good laugh'. Huxley, seeing the rich get richer, 'had half a mind to try & cut you out', a joke with an edge that would come back to haunt him.[12]

When Darwin and Huxley were put up in opposition for the Académie Française in 1877 – with Huxley offered the better odds 'as being more orthodox!' (as George Darwin laughed, another joke with an edge) – Huxley quietly withdrew.[13] The world had a habit of genuflecting and withdrawing before Darwin. Even Gladstone, spending the weekend at John Lubbock's High Elms estate with those other Liberal deities Playfair and Morley, and descending on Darwin's hamlet on Saturday 10 March 1877, was chaperoned by Huxley to ensure proper etiquette in a superior deity's presence.[14]

New forums were opening up. Knowles' monthly, the *Nineteenth Century*, which he established in March 1877 after falling out with his old publisher, was an instant success. Tennyson plotted its course in his opening poem, where Huxley was one of those 'wilder comrades, sworn to seek'

> If any golden harbour be for men
> In seas of Death and sunless gulfs of Doubt,[15]

while its opening symposium on 'The Influence upon Morality of a Decline in Religious Belief' caught the anxieties of the 1870s. And of course it had Huxley throwing his agnostic spanner into the works, suggesting as ever that 'Religion is the affair of the affections, theology of the intellect' – meaning it was the latter that was declining as real religion reflected the awe of modern science.[16]

So Huxley the persistent bigamist switched one of his partners and spread his favours liberally. From now on Morley's *Fortnightly* and the *Nineteenth Century* were to 'occupy the best place (for every body but parsons & country squires) in England'. Morley and Knowles were still rending contributors in twain like 'ravening lions'. If Knowles had the bigger mane, Morley had the radical cunning. 'Why should Knowles – with all his flocks and hens, some of them uncommonly bovine and ovine – grudge me my one ewe lamb?' Morley asked Huxley: 'Were you ever mistaken for so gentle a beast before?'[17] So Huxley sent Morley his contribution to the tercentenary of William Harvey's birth. Harvey's discovery of the circulation of the blood became another platform for Huxley's justification of vivisection and the right method of doing science, vindicating not only Harvey, but implicitly Darwin as well.[18]

More justification for 'torturing' angered the *Spectator*. But Huxley declared with a twinkle that 'Controversy is as abhorrent to me as gin to a reclaimed drunkard'.

The abstemious pugilist prepared more screeds for Morley. Nettie was a scientific widow: Hal's dinners, meetings and lectures kept him out till all hours. The ewe wrote on the hoof. His 'Technical Education' was finished on the morning of 1 December 1877 and read at teatime at the Working Men's Club. That paper too fitted Morley's radical design. It made the mechanic one with the anatomist, who dissected with the finesse of a monocled watchmaker. Vocational training was as necessary for the lab as the workbench, and in both the 'empyreal' mists of speculation were wafted up the ventilation shaft. 'Mother Nature is serenely obdurate to honeyed words', he said; she respects only the craftsman's 'tangible facts'. He made it his licence to speak to the workers.[19]

The wealthy City livery companies had prompted his talk. The Clothworkers Guild was now investing in the Yorkshire College of Science (to become the University of Leeds). The Grocers Company was awarding science scholarships. But they sought their own vocational college, and they had Huxley do a feasibility study. He knew the needs of heavy industry. Yearly the family stayed with the steel magnate Sir William Armstrong. And if Huxley was partly responsible for the theoretical – rather than hands-on – bent of technical education, the big guns were behind him on that too. Armstrong, shown Huxley's report, was even more adamant on the need for pure science, and more 'competent teachers' to teach it.

This *theoretical* bent was part of the professional scientists' strategy. They were equating science's moral training with the Classics' character-forming ability. It was their pitch for power. Pure science was escaping its sordid image, hitching itself to traditional values. And so a theory-based education for mechanics and managers became the norm. Huxley's men were elevating the mind, rather than teaching 'fingers to earn money'.[20]

If Huxley's industrial ties haven't been noted before it is because his family hasn't been set in the foreground. Armstrong's ballistics expert Captain Noble – the man to put modern breech-loading cannon onto Her Majesty's warships – had Huxley's eldest son Len to stay with his boys. And when the family were with Armstrong Mady and Jess would go to Newcastle balls in mob caps with Noble's daughter Lily. The Huxleys kept close to Pater's Coventry roots, even to his old factory mentor George May (the ribbon-master with whom he had pondered the divine government). Len, at University College School with May's boy, was sweet on 16-year-old Margery May. He would bicycle 120 miles in a day, and on iron wheels! setting off from London before sunrise, passing through Coventry, to stay with her.[21] Professional welding and family rivets locked these industrial connections tight. Huxley was a unique institution: a sort of cultural Telford bridge between the old steel Dissent and new professionals.

University College seemed the natural home for Huxley's son. Mady was there, studying art at the Slade School. She had grown more talented, judging by the prizes, and more stunning, judging by the stupefied men. The governess was appalled to see one in the street 'literally stopped with his mouth partially open' as she passed. The skittish beauty dangled suitors. It was unseemly for a Victorian Miss to have had three proposals of marriage by 19, and Nettie foresaw 'trouble . . . with her & her admirers'. Mady's work caused the same flutter. In 1877 she took the composition prize for her *Death of Socrates*, and another for etching the following year. At the 'Tall Teas' there was admiration for her sketch of her father, ironically because it gave him the 'look of the Bp. of Oxford'.[22] (There was a resemblance: Huxley had actually been mistaken for Wilberforce's son shortly after the 1860 fracas.)

Len was 'a good steady worker'. But he was aimless, and his mother wished 'he had a decided turn for some one thing'. Professor Huxley was the exponent of exams as the gates to professional excellence, and London University had the stiffest in Britain. Len passed the 15 hours of tests in 1877, despite an attack of mumps that left him feeling 'as if the back of his head were coming off'.[23] But he would not join the professionals' sons in godless Gower Street. The boy had been rather shepherded; he clearly had no scientific bent, and he was using the exam to gain a diploma of school achievement – common practice in London. His parents were left wondering what to do with him.

The solution came from Huxley's broadest of Broad Church admirers, Revd Benjamin Jowett. Such was the liberal ascent that the Greek professor who had been accused of heresy for analysing the Bible historically was the Master of Balliol now. He was still trying to inject science into the Oxford degree (and still being opposed by his own science dons, 'on the ground that it will lower the character of [science] studies'). What better than to have the son of Britain's most famous scientist under him? Jowett advised two terms at St Andrews in Scotland, which was cheap and small 'so that the pupils get more careful grinding'. It was a preparing school where Len could work for a Scholarship to Balliol. Jowett accordingly arranged tutors in Classics and mathematics. And so, instead of walking across Regent's Park, Len travelled to the North. But he remained his father's son and complained that the Rector's opening address 'contained a lie on Evolution'.[24]

If there was a feeling that this was second best, there was also an awareness that the old dames of Isis and Cam were changing their clothes. Huxley the Devonshire Commissioner had helped to pay the costumier. Science, seen on all sides as an authority-questioning upstart, was rudely pushing beneath the spires. The £120,000 belatedly pumped by Oxford's fat colleges into laboratories would surely have an effect – notwithstanding the physics professor's feeling that it was 'not etiquette' to enter a dirty lab. No one had yet said 'to punish a scientific man ... appoint him to an Oxford professorship'.[25] Perhaps science could prosper here, as at Cambridge.

Darwin's Alma Mater signalled the changes by awarding him an honorary doctorate in November 1877. Cambridge was committing herself to the future. The traffic between Kensington and Cam said as much. Foster's eager students came down yearly to help run Huxley's courses, and Cambridge got that 'sharp fellow' Patrick Geddes in return. (The wild-eyed son of the Kirk had left his Positivist Church in Chapel Street, but Cambridge seemed dismal without Huxley's moral light and he moved on, ultimately to transfer Huxley's physiographical analysis to urban development and develop an unlikely career in town planning.)[26]

Foster's team was happy to see Darwin invested. At exam times they were taxing students on the struggle for existence (which was more than Huxley was doing), and Darwin's crown legitimated their claim on the new biological laboratory being built on Downing Street.[27] There was home-grown talent too, it wasn't all coming up from London. One student stood out, Frank Balfour. Such was the brilliance of Balfour's Trinity College Fellowship exam that Foster told Huxley (an examiner) not to bother coming up for the *viva*. Balfour was a man after Huxley's heart. And Nettie's: she saw in his 'dash and verve' Hal in his *Rattlesnake* days, and Foster noticed it too. The brilliant Balfour had an 'old head on his young shoulders'.[28] He had been to the Naples station to study marine larvae, and he was now lecturing on animal relationships as revealed by their embryological development.

They all watched Darwin's crowning in a packed Senate House. Rowdy undergrads perched irreverently on statues and raised a monkey-puppet to roars. An embarrassed Darwin was lauded in Latin for works that the wrinkled dons had once damned as 'grievously mischievous'. If the Public Orator could not quite relate Moral Man to 'the unlovely tribe of apes', the anatomy professor George Humphry could. He claimed that 'the University has by todays proceedings committed itself to the doctrine of evolution'. It was a 'great step for Cambridge', said Huxley, 'though it may not seem much in itself!'[29]

But Huxley could not resist the snipe that would never have occurred to the affable squire. He 'chaffed the dons so sweetly':

> M[r] Darwins work had fully earned [the] distinction you have today conferred upon him four & twenty years ago . . . [With 'wise foresight', instead] of offering her honours when they ran a chance of being crushed beneath the accumulated marks of approbation of the whole civilized world[,] the University has waited until the trophy was finished & has crowned the edifice with the delicate wreath of academic appreciation.

It was a mere 'touch of the whip', which 'was so tied round with ribbons that it took them some time to find out where the flick had hit'. But the sight of pink hides had Frank Darwin 'boiling over with enthusiasm' and his father bubbling about his 'generous friend'.[30]

Yet Huxley's own haggling over evolution continued to confound. He had broken his *Spirula* work to make the gesture at Cambridge. But what was he doing with the tentacled molluscs? He had moved on to the related belemnites, those rod-like cuttle-bones from the blue-lias cliffs. The shirt-sleeved prof, relishing a Bohemian seaside existence, had taken the family to the Esplanade at Whitby for their holidays, close to the cliffs, where presumably he had picked up the Jurassic fossils. Before he knew it he was sucked into an encompassing history of all the nautiluses and ammonites. Sea-slug shipments arrived from Naples, and he set in for the duration, devising a novel combination microscope, a simple lens for gross dissections with a compound lens that could be swung on top for detailed work. The result, in class, was the sober Dr Jekyll, still damning the 'growing tendency to mix up [evolutionary] speculations with morphological generalizations'. But madly, brilliantly and privately he fleshed out evolutionary trees.[31] He depicted ancestral snail-like molluscs differentially curling their shells like *Nautilus* or *Spirula* or uncurling them like certain ammonites or even straightening them like cuttlefish and belemnites. And this wild Mr Hyde then escaped the theatre and burst onto the London Institution stage to talk on the 'Probable Causes of Evolution'. Dr Jekyll seemed the strange *alter ego* of the flamboyant Mr Hyde of these populist moments.[32]

The *doppelgänger* confused Darwin, as it did later historians, who saw only Huxley's monographs (no evolution) and popular essays (championing evolution). Yet buried away was the link: his private research notes were littered with phylogenetic tree trunks: every mammal group was followed to the flowering branches of its existence, so were reptiles and amphibians, and the sudden efflorescence as birds evolved out of reptiles – these evolutionary diagrams came to dominate his notes. They were the heuristic link. The evolutionary trees underwrote, perhaps even drove, much of his work from the later 1870s, but they left barely a trace in his class lectures or his stripped-down descriptive papers. So much of each pedigree was informed guesswork, as it had to be. Such genealogies were ephemeral, liable to change – simply lightning sketches to investigate possibilities. Made public, they would imperil the public image of the solid bedrock of biological knowledge. So they remained hidden.

Nothing could be allowed to jeopardize the new professionals' claims. Dr Jekyll's solid image of science matched his new face of bronze. Thomas Woolner had fixed on Hal's stern lines for immortalization. Who better to sculpt him than one of the original Pre-Raphaelite Brethren? Long before, Hal had seen Nettie's mournful look in their ethereal paintings, now his own bust would go on show at the Royal Academy. With art fastened to anatomy, and the artists fastened to Mady's skirt-tails, Marlborough Place was every bit the fashionable salon. The Victorian Masters of the languid graced Nettie's table – Lawrence Alma-Tadema, with his eye for a classically-draped figure, and her favourite neighbour Briton Riviere, whose scenes of ill children moved an infirm nation. William Roden slipped from Gladstone's lopsided head to Huxley's setjawed features (slyly hoping to sell a few reproduction paintings on the side). In an age when Science – not Art – was daring, Huxley was the darling of Academy dinners. Here he exhibited the Great and Good to his New World friends. 'When I was in America, you showed me every extinct animal', he told that 'large hearted' blood brother of the Sioux, Prof. Marsh. 'Now, if there is a single living lion in all Great Britain that you wish to see, I will show him to you in five minutes'.[33]

Sundays' 'Tall Teas' could still be a refuge for an alienated world. Leslie Stephen, lonely now after the death of his wife Harriet (Thackeray's daughter), became a regular.[34] And in the late seventies as the elite correspondents sat in – George Smalley (*New York Tribune*), Archibald Forbes (*Daily News*), that old Africa hand Henry Morton Stanley, and J. R. Young (*New York Herald*) – the cigar talk became more expansive.

With a maimed British lion savaging the Zulus, and the British in Kabul under siege, it dissolved into imperial deliberation. 'Catch me discussing the Afghan question with you you little pepper pot', Pater would declaim to Jess, before holding forth on the Khyber Pass tribes as 'a pack of disorderly treacherous blood-thirsty thieves'. The Tories had discovered jingoism, and so, it seemed, had Huxley. But Nettie could only 'wish that we had never had a Clive in our History'. The exotic Disraeli was making the Empire central to Toryism, but he was hard pressed to keep that minor jewel, the mountain stronghold of Kabul, in the crown. And by flattering the Queen as Empress of India he even turned discussions to the monarchy itself. Huxley buttressed the palace so backhandedly in his flippant sexist way that guests wondered if he wasn't a republican at heart. 'So long as the throne is held by the present Royal family, in which the intellect is entirely confined to the females', he said, 'the monarchy is quite safe'.[35]

Ten thousand feathered Zulus slaughtered in defence of their 'hearths and homes' brought Gladstone alive. The groans of the dying evoked during his Midlothian campaign helped to sweep him back into power. Huxley too found Sir Bartle Frere's invasion of Zululand unacceptably genocidal and pulled out of an association backing him. But he shared the nation's conceit about its civilizing influence, even if moral duty meant a heavy hand. The '"family" declare I am becoming a Jingo!' he exclaimed, surprised that the minors could show the Huxley bent for independence. With the *Daily News* war correspondent Archibald Forbes besotted by Mady and enticing the girls to his campaign briefings, the cadets put up spirited resistance to the General. At times Midlothian sentiments positively swept the ranks to insubordination. 'Pater is becoming quite a conservative', said Mady. 'Fancy, Prof Huxley a "true blue"!'[36]

That was qualification enough to put him on the Eton governing board. Actually what put him there was the Public Schools Act. It allocated one seat to a Royal Society nominee in an attempt to force changes on Eton. But Huxley might well have stumbled into a Zulu kraal, considering the resistance he met. With Rorke's Drift fortitude he overcame the odds to get a science block built, imagining that this would breed sweet reason into the twentieth century's generals. They were out there, on the playing fields.

'I think I commenced to become respectable when I was elected a Governor of Eton College', he later confirmed. He had followed a line of Deans and Divines, who found the devil rather a charming chap, and he too could not help thinking them 'nice fellows'. The girls feared the worst. The outsider was now in the heart of the Establishment. But it was not easy to convince uncomprehending Churchmen, who saw the Classics as the mark of culture, that

Science added anything to the national character. Some schools prevaricated, notably Westminster, which insisted that the Royal Society nominee be an Anglican.[37] But Huxley shrugged them off. Politics was now against the older monopolies, and with him.

Whatever his unbecoming hue, Hal still took royal hob-nobbing a mite less seriously than Nettie. Her family letters were beginning to ooze stately acquaintance. He endured invitations to dine with the Crown Prince and Princess, or attend M'Lady's reception, or call on the 'Rootle-Tootles', who, he was astonished to learn, 'have a bigger drawing-room than ours' ('perhaps', he asked Jess, 'you will tell them to have it made smaller before I visit them'). One confidence trickster even used him to prey on passing countesses.[38] The 'Comte de Veysey' got close by offering to translate one of his books into Russian, but niggling doubts sent Huxley to Chief Superintendent Williamson at Scotland Yard where he saw the arrest warrants.

The con men at least had begun to appreciate his new standing.

6

A Person of Respectability

HUXLEY'S SCIENTIFIC BROTHERHOOD gathered on a warm sunny Saturday 4 May 1878 – Hal's 53rd birthday – for Jess's wedding to her young architect Fred Waller. Only an unwell Tyndall was missing, but Louisa carried his blessing, which was 'as good as the parson's'. Hooker sent 'heaps of lovely flowers from Kew' and the bride wore the Darwins' gift, a ruby and diamond star. 'It is the first break in our family', Huxley told Haeckel, and he felt it. He 'was grey in colour from the suppressed emotion' as he walked Jess towards Canon Duckworth. Naturally this 'ecclesiastical part' was 'quite out of the question' for the blimpish Spencer, but he deigned to attend the 'social part' afterwards in his 'passive' way.[1] He milled with the barons of science and industry. And at least one Right Honourable artist, John Collier, 'Jack' to everybody, son of a former Attorney-General and a constant presence in the lives of the arty girls.

'Married & done for' pronounced a footloose Mady, dangling her bevy of men. But the footsteps of fortune are slippery. Days later the marriage was overshadowed as the children came down with diphtheria, Mady dangerously so. Her throat was an agony. She was gasping and feverish. Her blood poisoned, she 'lost her sight her speech, & lastly the use of her legs'. Clark and the family doctor stood by helpless. By 17 May Nettie was fraught and 'worn out with nursing'. By the 20th she herself had not had an hour's undisturbed sleep for a week. Hal's face showed the desperation as he watched Mady 'for several days hovering between life & death'. 'I never saw a man more crushed', said his lab technician Jeffrey Parker.[2]

The day Mady began fighting for her life Huxley tore himself from her bedside to deliver the first of his Davis Lectures at the Zoological Society. He started to talk on the common crayfish as a key to the relationship of the crustaceans, but he was close to breaking down, and his mellifluous voice choked. The gallery listeners, not realizing, pressed him to 'speak a little *louder*'. But by the time he came to give a workers' lecture on 20 May (everything was now crustaceans) the worst was over. Four hours later he returned home to 'find a wonderful & blessed change'.[3] Mady would still have three weeks of excruciating pain, but she had turned the corner. As Huxley went back to crayfish he was also chairing a public meeting to discover the cause of the diphtheria ravaging St John's Wood (he tracked its source in the contaminated milk coming from a Kilburn farm).

Crayfish were the 'hidden hand' which drew him from *Spirula*. He veered off, lured by a new promise and would never finish the tentacled molluscs.[4] Crayfish acquired their own momentum and for an instant invertebrates again took over his life. His absorption was evident. Devotees approached seeking enlightenment on some backboned animal only to be outrageously deflated: 'Codfish?' he mumbled at Parker, 'that's a vertebrate, isn't it?'

By the time he had finished his five-week working men's course on crayfish he had two weeks of his concurrent Davis Lectures to run. Mady was still paralysed but recovering as he topped his work off. He had started from the commonplace, the dinner-table familiar, the edible crayfish bought from a French vendor. These had two rudimentary filaments, one-tenth of an inch long, next to the gills. He moved to the exotic, looking at primitive Australian crayfish to see perfectly developed gills in these slots. Then he cast his net wider, to lobsters and marine crays. At the zoo he used these varying gill plumes to investigate the 'Morphological relation of all the forms', and to draw a full 'Phylogeny' – as he had done with the coiling shells of *Spirula*'s relatives. It was a logical pedigree or Haeckelian family tree. 'I need hardly say that the bearing of all this upon the theory of evolution from a common type was very important'.[5] He might say it, but when he came to summarize his conclusions on gills and classification on 4 June 1878 in a paper to be published in the Zoological Society's *Proceedings* he remained his usual factual self. By and large, evolution was reserved for a public canvas.

The Crayfish might not sound like a stimulating book. But it was destined for the International Scientific Series. The ISS now stretched from physics to psychology and beyond. It outdid the evangelical presses in pumping out rationalist books for Everyman. A huge force for deterministic and social evolution, it mixed modernity and notoriety to sell titles through umpteen editions. Science was becoming 'mightier and forever mightier' and flaunting its celebrities. Here was

1. T.H. Huxley in Birmingham. He was the darling of the city's slum-clearing Unitarian fathers. Like the mayor Joseph Chamberlain, Huxley was a Cromwellian to his teeth.

2. Huxley on London's pace-setting School Board. He made science part of a modern curriculum, and had a touching faith that the Bible might be read in class for its poetry and selected ethics. 'He had a vision of heretical Huxleys instructing innumerable little Huxleys'.

3. (*Top*) The medieval gloom in Huxley's painting of Tangier's berbers reflected his despondency following a nervous breakdown in 1872.

4. (*Above*) The skies brightened as his houseboat passed the Meidum Pyramid on the fashionable Nile, 15 February 1872.

5. (*Above*) Shouting science's importance. The solid 'Science Schools Building' in South Kensington, finished in 1871. The discipline of 'Biology' was forged in Huxley's laboratory on the top floor.

6. (*Opposite, above*) The lab, with its regimented practical classes.

Huxley's reluctance to moot evolution in class belied his private pedigree-chasing in the 1870s. These family trees in his notebooks are typical.

7. (*Opposite, below, left*) A Haeckelian lineage for mammals.

8. (*Right*) The ancestral snail-like mollusc differentially curling its shell to produce a *Nautilus* or *Spirula* or straightening it to evolve a belemnite.

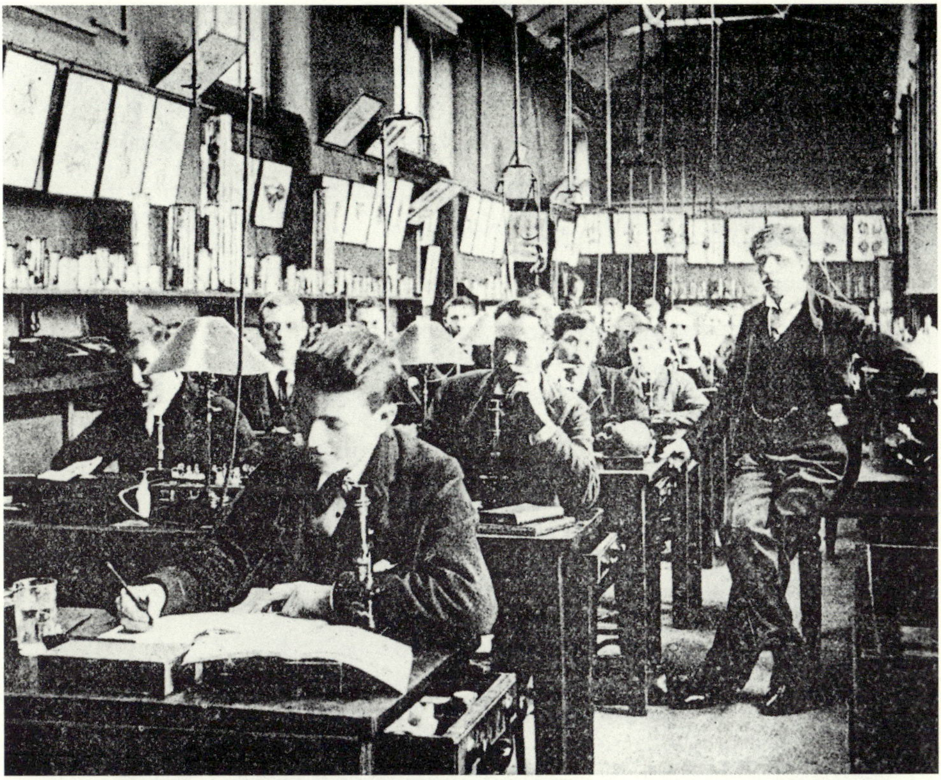

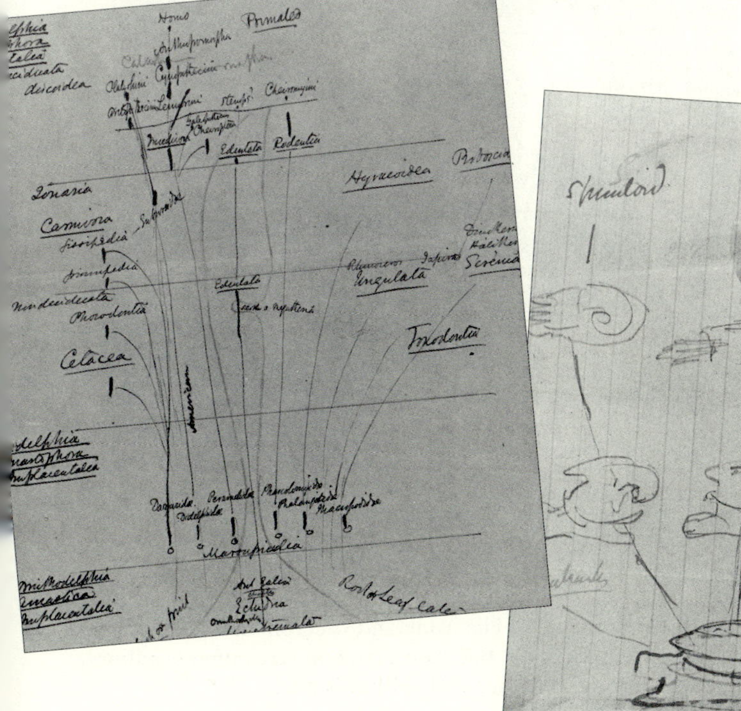

Homo
Primates
Edentata
Rodentia
Hyracoidea
Carnivora
Ungulata
Edentata
Cetacea
Toxodontia
Marsupialia

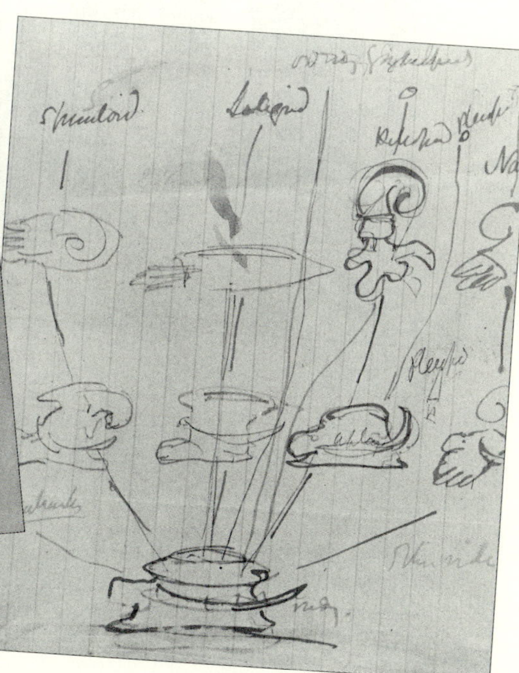

THE DAILY GRAPHIC

AN ILLUSTRATED EVENING NEWSPAPER.

39 & 41 PARK PLACE.

VOL. XI. | All the News, Four Editions Daily. | NEW YORK, WEDNESDAY, SEPTEMBER 27, 1876. | $12 Per Year in Advance. Single Copies, Five Cents | NO. 1104.

Th Wust

HUXLEY EIKONOKLASTES.

Grand in the light the sacred records throw
Old Moses stands, a hero of all time—
Lawgiver, prophet, on his form sublime
Wrought with his art great Michael Angelo
And Milton, whose blind eyes with clearer ray
Grand visions saw, and fixed with mighty pen,
Unwielded yet by hands of newer men,
The vision of Creation's primal day—
Stands ever, and shall stand while Time shall be
A shadow of that God of whom he spake
Not thou, O Huxley! though thy frame should break
Can'st harm these giants, hew thou mightily
Hold off! hold off! and go thy chosen way
Nor Moses with thy fictious Milton seek to slay

9. Huxley Eikonoklastes in New York, 1876. His irony and Ciceronian understatement confused Americans used to a Hell-fire style. But they gave him screaming headlines. Here he is battering at Moses with Milton's bust.

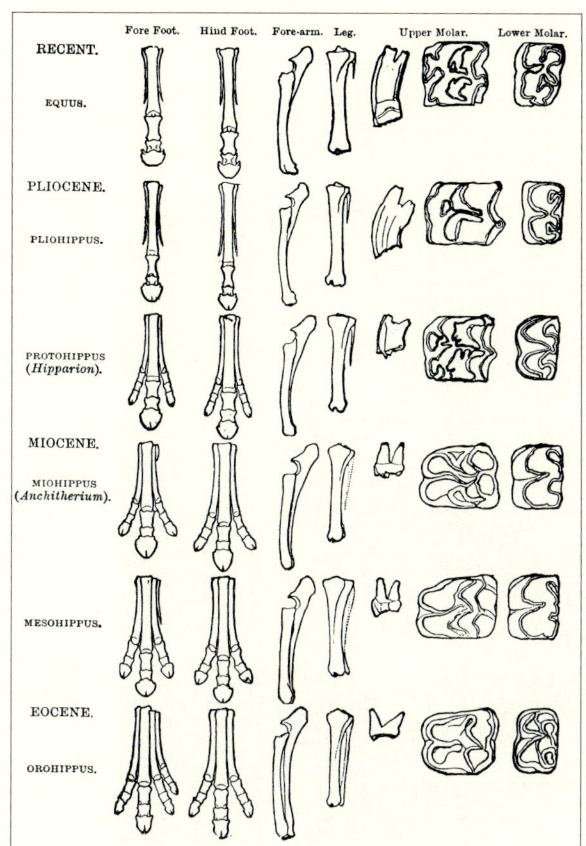

10. Huxley found his palaeontological proof of evolution at Yale. O.C. Marsh drew up this table of his fossil horses to accompany Huxley's lectures. The oldest horse is at the bottom with four toes and low-crowned teeth, the latest, tip-toeing plains-runner at the top.

11. Projecting backwards to an even older five-toed ancestor, Huxley dashed off this sketch of the anticipated '*Eohippus*', with a suitable rider, '*Eohomo*'. Ironically, the dog-sized *Eohippus* was already in Yale's basement, waiting to be unpacked. Marsh's horses forced Huxley to reconsider the timing of human evolution.

12. A print capturing the sectarian turmoil in the Church-dominated 1870s. Note that the political atheists stand fenced in at the bottom right. By contrast, Huxley, the monkey Darwin, and flag-waving Tyndall appear top left on the side of Dissent, here seen pulling the chocks away from the State-supported Church.

Spencer's influential *Study of Sociology*, Bagehot's *Physics and Politics*, Bain's *Mind and Body*, Tyndall's *Forms of Water*. And the most successful, by a Methodist, University College-trained, Yankee emigrant, John Draper – a bullish mood-catcher, a warmongering account of 'contending powers' to rival his own *History of the American Civil War*. A book to cap the professionalizing, dissenting militancy against Rome. This was Draper's *History of the Conflict Between Religion and Science*.

These were Huxley's people with their own provocative encyclicals. He started *The Crayfish* after the Summer holidays in 1878, giving his own text an alluring evolutionary gloss. He intended it as the beginning of his own series.[6] He would take readers from the 'insignificant' and common-or-garden into the profound depths. The crab-stall was the portal into an exotic invertebrate kingdom. Next would come the fireside *Dog*,[7] an open sesame into the world of vertebrates, and *Man* would complete the trio. It was another forlorn hope, for he only ever prepared the *Crayfish* hors-d'œuvre. Although the starved customers found that so tasty that they came back for seven editions.

If the evolutionary agnostics were rewriting the times, they were rewriting history to match. Huxley's long dalliance with the sceptical philosopher David Hume would become a stronger engagement with Morley's bribe: £150 if he would add *Hume* to his new *English Men of Letters* series. Morley, who had made the *Fortnightly* the most discussed and doctrinaire organ of literary radicalism, was adding saltpetre to sulphur. Hume was an 'easy, sensible, compatible . . . sort of man', and with Huxley a model of rational lucidity, he had the mix. Huxley's homily-clad style would put the final torch to Hume's powder-dry rationalism for the 'ordinary person'. Would Huxley plebeianize Hume's logical remonstrance against miracles? and ready the manuscript for the 1878 Christmas rush? 'It would be a seasonable book for that holy time'.[8]

Huxley's eyes were bigger than his mouth. Nothing could be done on the *Crayfish* until *Hume* had been finished. So a few weeks later he packed his family and himself off to North Wales at Penmaenmawr, Gladstone's favourite village, squeezed between mountain and sea. The holiday was a furious excuse to fill 200 sheets in a bid to subdue Hume into Victorian respectability.

There was to be no holiday for Len. He was dispatched to Herr Professor Haeckel to 'to pick up your noble vernacular'. In Jena the 'German Darwin' was firing students with his declamatory style; not that everyone wanted a 'Darwin' in Deutschland, and one critic considered his *Evolution of Man* a 'fleck of shame on the escutcheon of Germany'. It was Haeckel's new *Freedom in Science and Teaching* that absorbed Pater back home. *Darwinismus* in the classroom had acquired political overtones in Germany, and in his preface to the English translation Huxley, for the first time, defended the principle of teaching evolution in school. (Although in practice he knew that children needed nature lessons before answering more ineffable questions, making his *Physiography* – now in its third printing – the essential grounding.) In a famous speech, reported in the *Times*, the steadfast Rudolf Virchow, Professor of Pathology at Berlin, wanted *Darwinismus* proscribed, ostensibly because of its degree of uncertainty. And yet, countered Huxley in his introduction, dropping his School Board moderation, how much greater the uncertainties about 'the linguistic accomplishments of Balaam's ass' that Christianity subjects schoolchildren to![9]

Huxley's *Hume* was to cut the ground from these 'preposterous fables'. His Hume was a mental anatomist, whose epistemological dissections would legitimize 'the laboratory [as] . . . the fore-court of the temple of philosophy'. It did not take Nettie to see that the book had 'as much of Huxley's as of Hume's' philosophy. On holiday mornings he made Hume's scepticism 'police . . . the whole world of thought'.[10] Then a pause for inspiration on a brisk walk into the mountains. Under this regime a modern Hume emerged whose behaviourist arguments for animal thought were given physiological grounding; a Hume who sounded like Huxley demanding evidence for miracles; and a Huxley who saw like Hume that good religion should be devoid of bad theology.

For a week Huxley drew breath. He crossed the Irish Sea, to be heralded by a Public Orator in formidable Latin as an Honorary Doctorate was bestowed by Dublin University. Then it was on to the British Association stage in the university, to talk a little evolution in Ireland as President of the Anthropology Section. His eyes still burned, even if the silvery sideburns aged him: 'See there is Huxley', said a gent behind Nettie; 'there is such a fascination in his face I cannot keep my eyes off him'. But oh! replied a lady. 'He looks faded'.

With that, the family's deflation of his proud headship began. The girls ribbed him as 'fascinating but faded'. The cockerel's coxcomb drooped. (In an easy house, he 'loved to imagine that he was entirely ruled by his family', observed a student, horrified into disbelief, 'and spoke of himself as chicken pecked as well as hen-pecked'.) Back in Wales he continued to boil 'at high pressure'. By day he made *Hume* a paragon of Victorian sense, but at night the safety valves blew in his sleep as the pressure left him 'grinding his teeth, or scratching his head!'[11]

Middle-aged, post-Mill, post-*Descent of Man*, Huxley was an uncomfortable utilitarian. He had no 'great respect for . . . mere knowing as such', he said. Knowledge had to pay, less in 'pudding or praise', in its fight against germs or farm pests, as in laying a foundation for life. David Hume had made social and personal benefit the utilitarian explanation of morality. *Hume* inched Huxley closer to Darwin, who had made the utilitarian moral instincts evolutionary products.[12] But primarily *Hume* celebrated the Victorian sense of the material world. It put out of mind what was 'out of reach'. Morley had his tract for the times. The contemporary frock-coat made 'the old sage' into 'a new figure'. That was 'capital'.[13]

As the troop decamped for home the potboiler lacked only one detail, the Life. And Huxley, sympathizing with the struggling man, while the fêted 'David . . . begins rather to bore me', added that peremptorily. Morley was staggered at the turnaround. 'I'm a pretty rapid worker myself', but he confessed 'to some amazement' at this.

Advance copies were in hand by Christmas Day. Old Darwin uttered dire prognostications: philosophy left him cold and, apart from the 'interspersed flashes of wit', he saw nothing to suggest a sale. How wrong. Morley capitalized on the Christmas sale with a 5,000 print-run, and Huxley declared the book 'a measure of what the public will stand in frank speaking'. For the Twelve Days of Christmas *Hume* went 'with a fine rush'.[14] By 26 January 1879 4,400 copies had crossed the counter and it was still selling 50 a day, with a reprint in hand. (Ten thousand sold over the next 18 months, making the sceptical philosopher more famous than in his own lifetime.)

The book sold on Huxley's name, but the figures also suggest that it caught the mood of moralizing materialism of the mid-Victorian public. Critics praised its jargon-free tone, if not its dogmatism. 'Twenty years ago I should have been posted for it', said Huxley, yearning for the old martyrdom. 'Now, respectability itself pats me on the back'. 'There must be something wrong somewhere'. Copies went out to the literary elite, the Arnolds and Stephens, who found it a bit short on actual biography. More were dispatched as printed replies to troublesome pamphleteers. George Stokes, sending his *Conditional Immortality* (which admitted that there was no *natural* evidence for the soul), got *Hume* by return. But the book itself leached through these literary strata to petit-bourgeois levels. Blue-collar staff debated its sceptical sanctity, and the poor chemist's assistant 'w^{d} cheerfully pay three times the price of "Hume" for a book even half as good'.[15] This wide constituency confirmed that Huxley's impact extended much deeper than ever Arnold's or Stephen's.

Morley's success even had Huxley mooting a profile-raising 'English Men of Science' series in imitation. He fancied himself editing 'à la Knowles', and collecting a 5 per cent royalty à la Morley.[16] Such a series would have reinforced his ascendant cultural tradition. But Huxley's potential contributors despaired at seeing him knock off *Hume* in a month, and they quickly killed the project.

No matter, *Hume* itself did the promotional job. Hume's powder-puff wig and knee-breeches had been whipped off and the philosopher who died in the year of the American Revolution had become the voice of Victorian scientific agnosticism. It was another pitch for Huxley's specialists, who were to patrol the outer limits of legitimate knowledge. Huxley still distinguished his pure agnosticism from rival products. He scorned the religious observance of Positivism, with its vacuous Host, abhorred Bradlaugh's atheists hammering on the Establishment door and eyed socialism warily. When the social missionary and father of secularism George Holyoake went blind, Huxley was invited to join a fund-raising committee. The distant cordiality between Huxley and Holyoake could be touching; Holyoake would giftwrap his *History of Co-operation*, and Huxley wished him 'with all my heart a speedy return to the visible world, which is on the whole a pleasant spectacle'. But while Huxley contributed for the man 'who has so long & so faithfully served the cause of Free thought', he knew that a committee seat would send the wrong signal.[17]

The signals were important. In Germany Virchow, taunted by the Social Democrats, was making *Darwinismus* look like a terrorists' manual. Evolutionary godlessness had led to the Commune, and it pointed to the apocalypse now that 'Socialism has established a sympathy with it'. At home an unctuous Tory *Quarterly* rebroadcast the message to scientists 'playing with edged tools'. Huxley froze at this scare-mongering. It was scurrilous 'to frighten sober people by the suggestion that evolutionary speculations generate revolutionary schemes in Socialist brains'. Having sanitized evolution for the scullery and study, he wasn't about to be made 'answerable for the horrors of the Paris Commune'.[18]

Nettie rather sweetly wanted him to encapsulate his own philosophy in a book. Arabella Buckley did too, an exploration of his agnostic world. 'No one w^{d} make a greater mark', Nettie said patriotically, but 'he laughs & asks how he is to get time'. Still, he was 'sowing good seeds', which was 'greater work' than 'writing a system of philosophy'. She saw the seeds germinating in a rounded scientific humanism; and even Hal accepted that 'freethought' would ultimately 'organise itself into a coherent system embracing human life & the world as one harmonious whole'.[19]

But how? Huxley's base was never the secular networks or radical chapels. His was a cerebral freethought suited to the agnostic literati – to an elite sub-class, not to the streets. There were attempts to cast the net wider. Moncure Conway founded an Association of Liberal Thinkers in June 1878, grandly calling it 'the first effort ever made to unite persons interested in the religious sentiment and the moral welfare of mankind on a plan absolutely free from considerations of dogma, race, names, or shibboleths'.[20] In an emancipating, imperial Britain, the socialists and humanitarians led the way towards racial and sexual tolerance, and a steering committee of deists and Jews, Unitarians and secularists, a Hindu, a Parsee and four ladies invited Huxley to be president. But he shared the doubts of Morley, Stephen and Tyndall (a Vice-President). When the council met in Nettie's dining room on 25 January 1879 it was clear they had no common vision, and the mere attempt at a mission statement saw the association fly apart. Huxley's 100-day 'Ministry' collapsed and he resigned. This, the shortest Presidency of his life, illustrated the difficulty of organizing a 'coherent' humanism across classes, races and religions.

It was an Honorary Doctorate from Cambridge a few months later that really rang the social changes. Huxley's men were in place, part of the new hegemony. The modernizing university had been willing to use him, now it was willing to honour him. Huxley, splendid in red gown, hereafter looked 'to be treated as a PERSON OF RESPECTABILITY. I have tried to avoid that misfortune, but it's of no use'.[21] And having honoured him, they made use of him, wanting his views on the abolition of compulsory Greek for entrants to Honours courses.

Pater's choice of Oxford for Len said even more about the tide of change. The status-conscious mandarins of science were renouncing their outsider origins and recolonizing the old seminaries. The Lankesters, Fosters and Carpenters, those sons of Dissent, were seeking legitimation at Oxford and Cambridge. Where once the 'monks of Oxford' were 'sunk in prejudice and port', now Jowett's tipple was Biblical criticism and science. And his 'experiment' with Len worked. Not even the Paternal embodiment of Science, or the more declamatory reasoning of Herr Haeckel, could steer Len from his course. With further Classics-cramming under Jowett's appointed tutor Len gained an Exhibition – a fee-paying scholarship – which would 'lighten Pater's cares'. What was an odd turnabout for the world turned out to be a coup for Jowett, who was 'very much pleased to have a son of Professor Huxley's at Balliol'.[22]

Huxley and Society met in a liberal confluence, and marriage mixed the rivers into a mighty torrent. The artist Jack Collier came with the radical flow. Forty years earlier, in the great parliamentary debates on Church monopolies and Dissent's disabilities, his grandfather had voted to exclude bishops from the Lords. Jack happily suffered in the family tradition. Jack's proposal to the daughter of the MP Joseph Hardcastle had her outraged father scalding this 'half playwright half art set' Bohemian 'who has the contemptible conceit to profess himself an unbeliever'.[23] No gruff Hardcastle protestations from Hal, of course. He found Jack a 'right good fellow'. Collier had long been a brotherly presence around the Slade girls, and there was no greater 'friend of the house'.

No one would forget his kindness in taking Clifford to Madeira on the mathematician's last journey. The consumptive Clifford, at 33 the most cynically brilliant and playful Spinozaist, had set off with Jack, chloroform bottle in hand to ease the pain: 'you always were goodness itself', Clifford had told 'moo'. (Nettie was *Moo* to her brood and becoming a universal mother to the materialist brotherhood.) From Clifford's 'lung mischief' Huxley feared the worst. 'It is a thousand pities, for . . . time would have ripened him into something very considerable'.[24] The group paid Clifford's fare to the dry air of the Mediterranean, where Jack had watched over the dying man.

Secretly Moo was pleased to see the teasing Miss Mady tied down – never mind being bound in such splendour. Jack's father was building a luxury house in Chelsea where they would join the family, with their own maid and footman and fine studio.[25] The Colliers were even further past the wig-maker stage on their own evolutionary journey towards the woolsack. Wasn't Jack's father Sir Robert a former Attorney-General and now a judge of the Court of Appeal? The small, fair, bespectacled, stuttering artist was made for the tall, striking Mady. The Victorian marriage of art and radicalism took place on 30 June 1879.

Hal felt the loss of Mady and Jess, and the next day asked for the flowers to be taken away. A holiday in Devon only confirmed that they were getting old. Nettie was laid up with swollen ankles, and that kept Hal in the house. So he taught himself Greek. 'It is quite wonderful the freshness & directness with which Hal goes into a new thing!' she said, still astonished after all the years.[26] He wanted to find out at first hand why Aristotle apparently saw only three chambers in the human heart. Of course what started in Teignmouth as background to his paper on William Harvey and the blood circulation took on a life of its own and pushed him into Aristotelian studies.

He ploughed on to finish his long-overdue *Introductory Science Primer*. Finally the children's series would have its opener, written expressly to retain control of the dissemination of elite knowledge and preempt the motherly vulgarizations and Christian manipulations.[27] Technology was visible, telephones were a novelty, Siemens' electrical trams were experimental, electric companies were the rage. Even the stodgy *Quarterly Review* saw the need for primers now that science has 'ceased to exist only for the few'. But exponents should fire the 'popular imagination', not abuse it by debasing 'the highest problems of life'. The shire Tories were still twitchy about science as subversion, still apprehensive as Huxley and Tyndall spoke in the industrial Midlands. They feared the baseness of Tyndall's man 'bound fast in fate'. They hated the new scientist whose own 'soul is not above the level of a laboratory'.[28] Huxley was in the black belt again in 1879, visiting the steel town of Sheffield as Vice-President of the BAAS. Nettie stayed with young Jim the industrial chemist and his wife Gaite. The shock of finding Jim already balding only reinforced her autumnal view of life. Amid the threatening smokestacks of chemical factories, she blamed his unhealthy workplace.

The Tory critics of the new science need hardly have worried. If Darwinism had moved from the radical fringe towards the central stage by 1880, it was because of its anodyne social presentation. In popular books and lectures evolution was talked up positively, as a history of meritorious promotion: 'we who are now "foremost in the files of time" had come to the front through almost endless stages of promotion from lower to higher forms of life', as Tyndall phrased it.[29] Benignity had replaced Darwin's bloody struggle; optimism and merited progress suited a striving middle-class audience. The sanitization came with a soothing social message.

The image was even more enthusiastically played up in America's Gilded Age, where evolution promised an onward-and-upward sweep. And reinforcement came with the fossils streaming into Yale and Philadelphia from the West. In 1877 a buckskinned Marsh had opened up the Morrison formation in Colorado with its mountainous dinosaurs: first *Titanosaurus*, with foot-long vertebrae, eight-foot thigh-bones – the largest land animal ever known at 60 feet.[30] Then came the first *Stegosaurus* with plates down its back. The rush was on for the fantastic wealth of the Rocky Mountain states. These extraordinary Jurassic finds turned the rivalry between Marsh's and Cope's quarry gangs into bone warfare. Pot-shots, bribes and desertions on the sites were only matched by dirty tricks in the press as the priority-grabbing Cope and Marsh traded insults. Then came the Como Bluff site in Wyoming and *Brontosaurus*; indeed, in a few years, a hundred sites were being strip mined for their prestigious fossils.

The Como Bluff bonanza threw up tiny intruders in 1878 – the first American Jurassic mammals.[31] As the news came in, Huxley was lecturing on that most primitive mammal, the egg-producing platypus, and thinking on its origin. What had that waddling, duck-billed enigma, marooned in Australia, actually evolved from? Like a biological Occam he flashed his pen across the page on 29 January 1879, sketching the logical family tree. He visualized twin branches, one passing from the amphibians through reptiles to birds (his 'Sauropsida'). The other from amphibians via 'some unknown "promammalian" group' (Haeckel's term) to the platypus.[32] It was eminently logical – all sauropsid skulls had a single condyle (or ball articulating with the first vertebra), all the mammals had a double condyle. And the aortic arches leading from the heart are so different in birds and mammals that the split must have occurred in extremely ancient stock. The solution was neat and tidy – and totally avoided fossils.

And this from a biologist who had insisted that evolutionists had to back their claims with 'title-deeds', fossils. In truth Huxley was trying to scotch Richard Owen's rival image: the festering hatreds after the ape-brain debate had never healed, and Huxley held Owen high in his demonic pantheon. Owen at the British Museum had endless mammal-like reptiles from the Cape – by 1876 a whole *Illustrated Catalogue* full of *Lycosauruses* ('wolf-reptiles') and *Tigrisuchuses* ('tiger-crocodiles'). Some were formidable predators: *Cynodraco* was a reptilian 'big cat', the size of a lion, with a sabre-tooth's canines and a flexible paw for lacerating flesh. He spotlighted them in a new order – the Theriodontia ('beast tooth') – and took a bow at the Geological Society for showing the 'great gains' Triassic reptiles had made towards the mammalian constitution. And he kept the supply of fossil skulls coming from South Africa by having the Treasury fund ox-cart expeditions onto the parched Karroo plateau.[33] Imperial science was marching with the Redcoat's rifle to bring home bones to order.

Huxley had the logic, but Owen had the fossils. Actually Owen's image was much fuzzier. He believed that the erect-standing dinosaurs approached the mammalian grade too, and used his mammal-like reptiles as more proof. As always Huxley's coterie kept their intellectual distance from Owen; indeed, they kept their physical distance: in 1879 Hooker was only elected to 'The Club' (London's ultimate club, founded by Dr Johnson, so exclusive it could shut its door on a Lord Chancellor) after Tyndall gave the all-clear that 'Owen rarely appears'. Huxley waited to join until Owen was all but gone.[34]

Logic is dicey where the exigencies of life are concerned. Owen, told of the impossibility of reptilian forebears, merely had to walk to his drawer of *Cynodracos*.[35] Huxley's was Tweedledee logic, as it turned out: 'If it was so, it might be . . . but as it isn't, it aint'. The fossil past was a Wonderland where one independent reptile group could grow skulls and hearts like mammals. In 1878 Cope found even older (Permian) mammal-like reptiles from Texas, typified by that great sail-backed predator *Dimetrodon*. Clearly the mammal-ancestors were a well-marked fossil lineage. As an idealistic Harry Seeley said (and it took an archetypal realist to say it), reptiles were a *grade*, and while some filled the 'morphological interval between Amphibians and Mammals', others appeared between amphibians and birds.[36]

Huxley had trouble with Platonic grades of existence. Cope appreciated his rival logic, but he took Huxley's clever Penelope's web and rewove it. He envisaged two streams: one from archaic armoured amphibians through mammal-like reptiles to the platypus, and the other via small dinosaurs to the birds. As the evidence tumbled about him Huxley began to waver.[37] Evidently two great empires of unrelated fossil reptiles *had* once thrived, the dinosaur bird-ancestors, and Cope's *Dimetrodons* on their way to the furry mammals.

As the past expanded the present world contracted. Space and distance were collapsing. Only in 1878 had University College students packed a room to see a telephone working. Two years later there was an exchange operating in London. How much more could the planet shrink? Once the forlorn sailor had waited eight months for his fiancée's replies from Australia, now the 'phone promised 'to bring the whole world within speaking distance'. The 60-year-old physicist George Stokes, Huxley's fellow Secretary at the Royal Society, was already practising on his newfangled typewriter. But Huxley retained his drunken-crayfish approach to creative calligraphy. At 55 he was burning out faster than most. He had worn out more professors' caps and Commissioners' chairs and pumped out more memoirs and essays than any five rivals. He reckoned he had but 'ten years of activity left'.[38]

With the *Science Primer* published and his school regime sinking in, he began to brush off posterity. Over 19,000 *Primers* sold at the turn of 1880, and a generation of schoolchildren were setting in.[39] He told a trade-unionist that 'if I am to be remembered at all, I would rather it should be as a "man who did his best to help the people" '. He had helped. His carrot and stick goading on technical education had shifted the sluggish beast. He was already liaising with the government and City Guilds on blueprints for a Central Institution for Technical Education (the 'City and Guilds'). It wasn't going to be an apprentice-shop – he was adamant that industrial skills should be taught close to the engineering plants. His idea was a red-brick tech to turn out teachers in applied physics and mechanics. Locating this college up the road in salubrious South Kensington might breed sneers about 'Art and Science among the roses', and have the *Electrician* pondering the heroic efforts of handicraftsmen to reach it, but it would keep the professionals in control of the educational infrastructure. Huxley still had his territorial ambitions. In the event his 'pet institution', the City and Guilds Institution, built by Alfred Waterhouse close to his Natural History Museum, ended up turning out industrial managers. Even then, Huxley said, it might nurture 'another Faraday or Whitworth or Armstrong'.[40]

Always he left others to finish the building. So much was rubble, and around it the 'ghosts of unfinished work flitter threateningly': tentacled molluscs, lungfishes, educational books, 'English Men of Science', more promises unfulfilled. The spirit was so willing and the flesh growing so weak. His sharp features in portraits were starting to acquire that resigned sadness. An equally sad Foster listened to his papers on mammal ancestry. They were so 'full of suggestive thought' and yet the master seemed 'to suggest that others, and not he himself, were to carry out the ideas'. The intimations of mortality were creeping in.

> It is a curious thing [Huxley told Morley] that I find my dislike to the thought of extinction increasing as I get older and nearer the goal.
>
> It flashes across me at all sorts of times with a sort of horror that in 1900 I shall probably know no more of what is going on than I did in 1800. I had sooner be in hell . . . at any rate in one of the upper circles, where the climate and company are not too trying.[41]

7

The Scientific Woolsack

HELL HAD TO WAIT while there was a flicker of 'life in the old dog'.[1] He was a Janus-faced sentinel now, guarding the professional portal. In the 1880s he watched his legions march out to meet sacrilegious agnostics on one side and pious Prime Ministers on the other. He looked to the future as the ethical implications of Evolution and Socialism became pressing concerns, and then back again to the beginning of the Darwinian era.

Huxley himself had become part of history, and the passing years showed. Jessie's baby Oriana, born on 11 February 1880, made them grandparents at last. Hal felt a grandfatherly creakiness. He was 'very tired & worn out', and with Nettie suffering from bronchitis, the couple took off for the Surrey countryside early in April 1880. Here he devised a surprise blessing for Darwin. Excruciating toothache ruined his break and a local dentist had to extract two teeth. Inflamed gums or not, he dressed in evening costume to come up to the Royal Institution on the 9th. The perk of power was munificence, and he showered it in his Darwinian benediction. Huxley called his talk 'The Coming of Age of the "Origin of Species"'.

Darwin was at first perplexed, '& then . . . the meaning of your words flashed on me!' It had been 21 years since Murray had chanced his arm on that royal green 15*s* *Origin*. Huxley was giving Darwin the key to Science's door. It was a political gesture, suggesting Darwinian maturity; a celebration of the 'prodigious change in opinion' which had left many 'worshipping that which they burned, and burning that which they worshipped'. The 'Coming of Age' masqueraded as history. It had the *Origin* sweeping away antique notions in 1859, of 'Great and sudden physical revolutions' causing global extinctions, and equally sudden and supernatural reCreations. But had it? Rewriting history was one of the spoils of victory, and Huxley's reinvention of geology showed how false his memory played him. When the *Origin* appeared in 1859 no Londoner was still clinging to a 'catastrophic' past. Foreign extremists such as Louis Agassiz, who had indeed sent ice-sheets sweeping across the planet 'like a sharp sword' to sever past and present life – using his Ice Age to entomb the planet and kill off all prehistoric life prior to God's next Act of Creation – had long been declared 'glacier-mad', a lunatic doting on 'moonshine'.[2] The mighty Owen was already talking of life's spreading tree, growing slowly and continuously, like a stately old oak.

Huxley was relocating the extremists on centre stage to give the old squire a dramatic cast. This wasn't history; it was propaganda which turned the past to advantage. But it started the trend for reducing the pre-Darwinian era to 'fragmentary' debris in order to highlight the 'simple, unified and comprehensive cosmos' of the 1880s.[3] From the moment Huxley opened his talk, picturing himself as the 'under-nurse' at the *Origin*'s birth, viewing the 'pretty turmoil about its cradle', his whimsy released the tension. Ape-ancestry embarrassed, titillated and shocked the tight-laced matrons, but Huxley's pantomime performance caught them offguard. In the stalls they laughed at the baby's 'naughtiness', the *Standard* said. He had them in the palm of his hand. It was a confidence-building trick, a way of smuggling in the new evolutionary certainties. He was meeting an emotional need as the old standbys vanished: making Darwin a new Rock. And yet in private he was more circumspect. Guests at his High Teas still heard that the *Origin* had been 'difficult to understand. When it first came out, H. said "This will take me about seven years' fighting", & so it did'.[4] Huxley was coming up from behind, reinventing himself as Evolution's midwife.

With no room for equivocation he made no mention of Natural Selection in 'Coming of Age'. The neurotic Darwin still feared Huxley was 'giving it up'. But he was simply making evolution indispensable, telling old war stories lest a new generation forget, knowing – as he put it in one of those enduring aphorisms – that the 'customary fate of new truths' is 'to begin as heresies and to end as superstitions'. Some already saw a new superstition in the making. For years Froude had been wondering if Huxley could 'elevate Evolution into a theory which will satisfy the eagerness of the imagination' while making it an ethical foundation for life. If so, 'then science has the world in its hands. If not, I cannot shake off the fear that we may have another era of . . . superstition before us'.[5]

And so the *Origin* had come of age. Evolution, the word and the deed, was accepted. As partial proof of it, the Metaphysical Society wound itself up. Huxley said that its top-heavy protagonists had embraced one another to death and 'died of too much love'.[6] But 'voluntary euthanasia' was the only course with the revolution complete. The issues they had thrashed out had become clear-cut and the protagonists stalemated. The painful birth pangs of the first industrial revolution were over; Dissent was emancipated; the 'Scientist' was established. The social changes that carried Darwinism were complete.

The issue now was less the fact of evolution than Darwin's originality. That was the point scored by Samuel Butler. His *Evolution Old and New* made Darwin steal the credit from his evolutionary forebears by an 'intellectual sleight of hand' and then insult them with his mindless universe. Butler liked a row. A gifted writer who craved Rome's 'conservative stronghold' (and only wished the Pope would give up miracles), a Pantheistic Lamarckian who enjoyed Mivart's put-down of the *Origin* as 'puerile', he had Huxley's sort of incendiarism. 'Has Mivart bitten him and given him Darwinophobia?' asked Huxley. 'Its a horrid disease and I would kill any son of a [*drawing of bitch*] I found running loose with it without mercy'. Not that Huxley would let Darwin do the culling. He was too protective of his untarnished image. 'If I say a savage thing, it is only "pretty Fanny's way"', Huxley once told him, 'if you do, it is not likely to be forgotten'. But they thought Butler was craving notoriety and refused to rise. It angered Butler even more to be ignored like his pre-Darwinian evolutionists. And for Huxley 'the best thing that could happen is that he should get madder'.[7] Butler never knew that Huxley was behind the boycott, but he did know that the bishops posed no threat: 'Men like Huxley and Tyndall are my natural enemies'.

With evolution commonplace, it was also time for Huxley to remake his own discipline – palaeontology. He remade it as the inductive foundation of evolution. The *Times* editor, Thomas Chenery (another dinner guest), recruiting the best pens to broaden the paper's political base, had him show what he meant – show how our spyholes on to the past had enlarged, to reveal the cavalcade of life in its true evolutionary light. Huxley peered through, to see the tapirs, rhinos and horses converge in the past, the lungfish and coelacanths close ranks, the birds merge with the gracile dinosaurs – like the branches of a tree traced to the stem. It was so obvious that 'if the doctrine of Evolution had not existed' the modern 'palaeontologist would have had to invent it'.

This planetary lifeline provided a secure anchorage for an uncertain age. Huxley's Church Scientific, with its canonizations and demonizations, invited a sublimated form of worship. He talked in parables. At the Working Men's College, he retailed Voltaire's legend of the Babylonian Zadig, who predicted the sex, size and stance of missing royal pets from their tracks (which left the 'magi with the desire to burn' him, seeing their ruin in his 'carnal common sense'). In the same way Huxley's own caste of Zadigs had told of five-toed horses browsing the Eocene foliage before a single bone had been seen. Science's 'retrospective prophecies' showed that its mundane powers could appear magical.[8] Huxley gave no sense of the long training required before a tyro could actually understand fossil bones in an evolutionary way. His rhetoric played up the self-evident, the transcendence of common sense. Evolution was the Victorian revelation, its prophets the new magi.

'Huxley is the king of men!' Darwin told Marsh, *Eohippus*' stable keeper. Huxley relished his role as Darwin's Protector, and the students recognized it, even if none had ever seen Darwin. Each day the Professor briskly entered his class (about 90-strong now), with an oppressive expression, starting the lecture before he reached his chair. Then one day all changed. He ambled in with a bearded stranger, Huxley leading, chatting, pointing out the new apparatus. 'Darwin was instantly recognized by the class . . . and sent a thrill of curiosity down the room, for no one present had ever seen him before'. Darwin's blue eyes were beaming, emitting a saintly 'benevolence', recalled a student, and Huxley's 'piercing black eyes . . . were full of admiration, and at the same time protection of his older friend'.[9]

It wasn't only the *Origin* Huxley was celebrating, but his own silver wedding. He liked anniversaries, he told Darwin, 'being always minded to drink my cup of life to the bottom'. He didn't need excuses. A steady stream of politicians, littérateurs, artists and scientists graced his 'Tall Teas'. There might be the Tyndalls to talk Physics, Alma-Tademas to talk Art; the US Ambassador James Lowell to hammer out a Transatlantic copyright agreement, and Henry James, agreeing to make it known to American authors.[10] The intimate circles of 30 years had become a galactic spiral, and among the risen stars Huxley interspersed the small asteroids – perhaps his 'clever' American lab worker Emily Munn, or the 'pleasant . . . & well informed' Henry Fairfield Osborn, who would take the 'Huxley method' back to Princeton to create the future nucleus of a distant galaxy.[11]

By contrast, the relatives were walking embarrassments and segregated to their own parties. Those that could walk, that is. The 'enormously stout & very emotional' Polly, brother George's widow, was flying high, disgusting Hal and engrossing the children with her pie-eyed antics (woozy on her three daily bottles of the morphine-based sedative 'chlorodyne' – an addict, clearly[12]). Ellen had crashed: the latest policeman to evict her after she had 'neglected & beaten' her grandchild '& pawned every thing' found her 'tipsey in bed'.[13] The boy eventually died and she begged more money to bury him. Not even Nettie's secret cheques could now save the 69-year-old from starving in a coffee-house.

The children remained Huxley's strength. Rachel at 17 was about to join her sisters at the Slade when Mady made the break. Her lot was 'easy & pleasant' in Chelsea, working on a painting already acclaimed by Alma-Tadema. The highly-strung Mady was Huxley's real heir. 'She was not only beautiful, with a strong likeness to her father', said the *Illustrated London News*, 'but she had genius'. And devilment. This picture, 'The Sins of the Father', was hung at the Academy as she turned 21 and sold before it went on public show.[14] To her father's horror, for it showed Nettie and 14-year-old Ethel gambling with cards. And 'the father' a good evangelical who held betting in abhorrence! Later, Mady's nude lying lasciviously on a beach had one outraged lady at the Grosvenor Gallery exhorting the subject, 'Get up you slut, and dress yourself'.[15] Artistic licence and Huxley latitude had combined to breed a sensation-loving New Woman, the sort who raised eyebrows by riding atop the open buses.

The loss of four more teeth under laughing gas left Darwin's bulldog a toothless old hound. A new set of false teeth saw Hal off on holiday to south Devon in August. The more the old man craved escape from the 'workaday harness', the more he succumbed to the 'exquisite views of hill & dale & sea under the louchest of cloud flecked blue skies'. He would walk for miles with Nettie and then lie on top of the red cliffs in the evening sun. It seemed symbolic of their autumn years. But he could never escape the work, and interminable dissections of Cape lobsters were interrupted by endless Home Office or India Office calls to discuss compulsory vaccination or ways of improving Indian agriculture.[16]

As Huxley slowed, the age seemed to rush past. His had once been a hectic life driven by steam. Others saw the new technology as symptomatic of an age out of control, overridden by great impersonal forces. Every August saw the awful crashes, after the summer heat buckled rails; and they were topped in 1879 by the terrible Tay

Bridge disaster, when a train careered off the track during a storm, killing everyone in a 'mighty crush of iron & humanity'.[17] Instead of the carnage being Providential, deaths were becoming statistical, insurance problems, part of the randomness of a Darwinian order.

The big institutions were already installing Siemens dynamos. Spottiswoode had two to light the Royal Society, but then Siemens was a Fellow. The rich were fitting them at home, despite the danger here too. Mrs Spottiswoode fell and dislocated her shoulder while showing off her electric lights to Huxley.[18] Technology was impinging on life. It was exciting, frightening, new. Huxley wasn't asserting science's cultural hegemony against Theology and the Humanities alone. His harping on the integrity of pure science in education was as much a reaction to the overpowering threat of technology, precisely because it was so successful. Of the two, only science could enable us to evaluate life and its problems, to usher in the moral reformation, to criticize beliefs – in short to challenge Classics as the stamp of the cultured man.

'Science and Culture' was his theme at the opening of Josiah Mason's Science College in Birmingham on 1 October 1880. Birmingham, that national showpiece of social engineering: 'parked, paved, assized, marketed, gas-and-watered and *improved*'. Chamberlain's city cried out for Huxley's scientific legitimation. And how alike were Chamberlain and Huxley, as became apparent when the politician turned up at Marlborough Place for tea – frank, with that ironic look and cynical turn of Scriptural phraseology, mated to a Church-disestablishing sense and attention to public duty.[19] Chamberlain had demanded a liberating education to unite the classes, and Josiah Mason was realizing it, putting up £180,000 for the new science college.

Mason had come up the hard way. Starting on Kidderminster's streets selling cakes, he had ended with a factory producing four million steel-nibbed pens a week. His wealth was financing a Dissenting 'guerilla force' in applied science, according to Huxley. The Birmingham faithful gave Huxley a podium to justify Science's enlightening role against the Oxbridge Classicists, those 'Levites in charge of the ark of culture'. His success in breaking the Classical mould – in pitting hands-on experience against Latin learning – was finally being reflected in curriculums from Clifton to Eton. Indeed, Matthew Arnold, so supportive for so long, was beginning to sense an all-devouring monster and to reassert literature's humanizing aspect. But the industrial Midlands was standing up for itself. Granting that 'culture' gave us the means to criticize life and society,

Huxley wondered whether Greek and Judaic literature did the job. Wasn't an expansive science, with its anti-authoritarian spirit, its child's innocence before the 'fact' and its ethical obligations towards free expression, the supreme critic? And didn't it provide a devastating critique of this ancient literature itself? That was intellectual manna to Mason's Trust, which had excluded 'mere literary education' from its college.

Huxley was in his constituency, among Unitarian factory bosses and social engineers. He spoke to them all. The manufacturer was told that the learned 'seek for truth not among words but among things'; rational Dissent was reassured that science shuns the dogmatic Word and makes a democratic appeal to Nature. Huxley was in his muddy boots, moving the centre of the world, making the dead Oxbridge outer planets revolve round the solar furnace of the Black Country. And where better to harmonize class relations, to teach 'the capitalist and the operative' that the 'common principles of social action' were an 'expression of natural laws'?[20] Never would he give Nature such a social spine again. Even now, the socialist clouds were gathering.

The first spots of rain could be felt. Within weeks he was helping Darwin arrange a pension for Alfred Wallace. They all worried about the implacable old chap's spiritualism, which had to be concealed.[21] While his socialism was unmentionable even among themselves. Wallace, the rank outsider, the President of the Land Nationalization Society, was already touting the American Henry George's *Progress and Poverty* as the most 'original book of the last twenty years', with its cure for chronic poverty in the common ownership of land. Not for him Darwin's Malthusian defence of property as the honing stone of social fitness.[22] It would be a few years before scientific socialism flowered in Britain, but Wallace was already looking forward to the operatives harvesting the full crop.

Huxley was thinking more of the fish harvest as he did his own bit for the sluggish economy. He was at home during Christmas 1880, supposedly working on shrews, but contemplating the expense as the water pipes froze. With the door blocked by a snowdrift, he took to his desk, trying to earn more, writing on education for the *Times*,[23] putting his essays into a new volume, *Science and Culture*. Hack work was still a necessity with his lecturer's pay seeping through the vast pyramid of dependent relatives.

Two days before Christmas the Government stepped in. Gladstone's radical Home Secretary, Sir William Harcourt, was for positive discrimination, securing jobs for the scientists. He offered Huxley the Inspectorship of Fisheries, and then fought the Treasury for £700 a year and lightened his duties to make the offer attractive. After all the unpaid seats on Royal Commissions Huxley was at last offered a decent supplementary income. *Punch* saw the radicals finding jobs for the boys in its skit on the oilskinned 'Professor Huxley, LL.D., F.R.S., £.s.d.' The *Athenaeum*'s, too, was a 'carping' announcement. But, he explained to Darwin,

> whereas for the last twenty years I have been obliged to make as much again as my official income in order to live decently & do justice to my children – the new appointment . . . will about do that business & relieve me from the necessity of bread-making.[24]

'So three cheers for Harcourt'. Nettie rejoiced at the end of the scrounging 'to make up enough', little realizing how much work the new job would entail. Thus Huxley settled part-time in another set of rooms with a prestigious Whitehall frontage. Afternoons would be spent at the Home Office, listening to fisheries deputations and Billingsgate fishmongers, followed by weeks on the rivers and coasts, investigating pollution and dwindling stocks. The job might have been created under the Salmon Fisheries Act of 1861 but he told his son that 'you are not to expect salmon to be much cheaper just yet'.[25] And in late 1880 Huxley's remit was much wider.

The post was given him by a Government hopelessly bogged down on the Irish question. As Irish peasants starved and 10,000 tenant farmers were evicted during a year of plummeting agricultural prices, Fenian terrorism increased. Gladstone had failed to pass a Coercion Bill compelling landlords to compensate evicted tenants, and was even now alienating back-bench Liberals (no less than Huxley[26]) by drafting a new Land Bill. Britain needed to increase yields during the Depression, including fish, and part of Huxley's job was to study fish diseases and increase North Sea catches. He had no time for those who feared the depletion of stocks from over-fishing (although he did extend in-shore restrictions, because too many lobsters and crabs were clearly being taken).

No sooner was the Inspector's job secure than there was more money in the offing. The old solicitor Anthony Rich was so taken with Darwin's emissary that he added a codicil to his will bequeathing Huxley his house on the Worthing coast, as a base 'for your Fishery work'. The canny Darwin, a wealthy absentee landlord, reckoned that Huxley could realize £3,000 on the lot. But it was the generosity which struck Huxley. 'If all the sea & fresh water fishes together had tumbled on to my head I could not have been more astonished'. Nettie was over the moon, even if Hal saw this particularly 'tough old gentleman . . . outliving his legatee'.[27]

It seemed likely given Huxley's tearing lifestyle. Added to his other work, he was dissecting herrings and pilchards, taking shipments of diseased salmon (and taking abuse from fishermen for being too 'scientific' and un-practical), studying the Black Country's river pollution or standing at exhibitions 'until my back is broken'.[28] Everything had to be fitted around fish. Robert Browning persuaded him to let the realist painter Alphonse Legros paint his portrait, but time permitted only a single sitting. Squeezing more hours for the inevitable Boehm bust was as hard. Edgar Boehm's self-confident statues dominated imperial London, and everyone tried to slow Huxley to a speed the sculptor could capture. It took a year and still did not do him justice. But then it had to be fitted around research, Home Office bureaucracy, and dashes to seaside inns to listen to rancorous old fisherfolk.[29] Every family jaunt – to Worthing to the delight of the lonely old bachelor Mr Rich, or a day return from Waterloo with Herbert Spencer – had to be wrung out of a tight schedule.

Huxley never knew his limits. The archetypal scientific civil servant found that Commissions were endemic in his constitution. The word from Lord Spencer that they wanted him on yet another – to examine the medical qualifications offered by Britain's 19 licensing bodies and establish a uniform licensing control by the State – gave him more work and no pay and chopped up his holiday on Lake Windermere still further.[30] As the State encroached more on every aspect of life, the scientist was penetrating deeper into the byzantine bureaucracy of the State.

By the time he got back to Windermere after delivering the last day's lecture to the Seventh International Medical Congress, Nettie threw up her hands: 'Poor darling! he looked so worn & tired'. Holidays were now patchy affairs, but Nettie knew that even a few days in the 'peaceful beauty & sweet air will do him good'. It also gave him time to catch up with Len. Despite Jowett's goading essay topics on the origin of morality in the individual and the race – giving the Professor's son his evolutionary rope[31] – there was no hanging a young Huxley. Len had gone over totally to the Classics. Each term Jowett had pronounced him better, and at Windermere came the news that he had got his First at Oxford. He had gone over to the enemy in another way. From Windermere he was cycling to nearby Rydal, where he was sweet on Matthew Arnold's niece Julia.

By contrast, the old seminaries were trying to tilt towards science. They were struggling to come to grips with an alien culture. Cambridge succeeded, and Huxley designed Trinity College's Fellowship exam, building an unprecedented three days of practicals into it to ensure 'that the College shall have either a good man or none'. With science came a new rigour. Struggling was the operative word for Oxford. But he had allies in place. The Broadest of Churchmen Revd George Bradley – like Stanley, a good intellectual friend (Huxley had put him up for the Athenaeum) – also took his advice on Science Fellowships. With these clergymen the broad and agnostic churches developed an ecumenical spirit. It showed in the Huxleys' 'great grief' at Stanley's funeral in 1881. 'No one can replace him', said Nettie, 'not one'.[32] But one man could. Another of his ilk would keep Westminster Abbey's door open to the agnostic scientists: George Bradley.

The *Essays and Reviews* set – that gifted group of rationalist clergy – were now powerful and making overtures. When the Linacre Professor George Rolleston died word was flashed to the Huxleys. Mrs Rolleston was 'out of her mind' from the trauma, making the funeral 'one of the most tragic scenes' Huxley had ever witnessed. 'We have been so mixed up in this woe', explained Nettie (Rolleston's daughter Rosie had recently been staying at Marlborough Place). Jowett doubted that the plummy Rolleston had ever really had 'the spirit of a Scientific man' – but he knew who was its living incarnation. The day after the death the Oxford liberals offered Huxley the chair. Having lured Len to Oxford, Jowett thought his father's acceptance would be the 'very best thing that could happen to the University'. There would be no sniff of '"odium theologicum": Nous avons change tout cela'. But they appreciated the impudence of asking a London intellectual to deign to grace Oxford – let alone be assessed for an anatomy chair by the Archbishop of Canterbury![33] Huxley was a Londoner through and through: the modern Babylon had the vibrancy, the science, arts, the clubs; it was the revolving hub of the Empire. The dank seminarian surroundings would never have suited. Of course he politely declined.

The maudlin Nettie was lapping on the edges of agnosticism herself now, only ebbing away at the thought of extinction. 'The old question', she mused on Rolleston's death, 'Wherefore this world, its creatures?' Do we all just 'shrivel up'? Does destiny lie 'in some sun', '& what is the good of it all . . . if we with all our aspirations are to perish for evermore, only living on through the race . . . And yet in spite of all these feelings, I have faith that all is wisely planned, however inexorable its details'. And the Victorian grand matriarch threw up her hands in Christian exclamation, '& any way I have my work to do, part of which is submission, the hardest part of all'.[34] In duty she could agree with her husband.

With the offers coming in, South Kensington opportunely increased the incentive for their own man. The next month, August 1881, 'after 9 years of shilly shally on the part of Gov^{t}.' the 'Science Schools' was renamed 'The Normal School of Science' (Huxley's idea, after the French *École Normale*). It became independent of the Geological Survey, all fees went to the government and the professors were put on fixed salaries. Huxley officially became the 'Professor of Biology' and Dean of the School. It was a dignified title which simply meant more work, but he milked it for all of its ecclesiastic worth. Don't you know, he told Donnelly, 'that a letter to a Dean ought to be addressed "The Very Revd."'? The school was shaping up. It wasn't training 'scientists', but creating the middle-class infrastructure upon which corporate science could develop. The *Prospectus* saw its clientele as the future science teachers and industrial managers.[35] Hal's son Harry with his mechanical bent would join them for a few terms, before switching to surgery as a career.

The bribes increased. Would Huxley like the cushy Mastership of University College, Oxford (£1,200 tax free, a house and 'no fixed duties'), made vacant when Bradley left for Westminster Abbey? That said it all. The Masters, usually clergymen, corruptly sinecured as many saw it, had done little to manage their colleges. Gripped by reaction, seized by an anti-science movement as Depression and radicalism racked the country, the University had dropped 'behind the general current of thought', and reformers implored Huxley to drag it towards the twentieth century. But his name wasn't for sale. Nor could he swap the 'inestimable freedom' of London for a cloistered existence. 'I do not think I am cut out to be a Don nor your mother for a Donness', he explained to Len. Still, his astonishment was unfeigned, 'and I begin to think I may yet be a Bishop'. Astronomic sums, pulled out of hats, failed to shift him. Agassiz at Harvard supposed it was no use offering 'say $10,000 a year for the benefit of your presence'.[36]

'I find I am regarded by the outside world as a sort of King-Maker', he said. Certainly the eternal acolyte Michael Foster – in 1883 elected as Cambridge's first Professor of Physiology – was ready to 'follow your bidding'. As Huxley tried to clear some of the decks by resigning from his Working Men's College and his office at the Royal Society, Foster was ready to keep the Secretary's cushion warm.[37] But still Huxley had more livings than was good for a man. As he let the chair go in 1881, the Fisheries Inspector had to set off for a cold Christmas in the Welsh valleys. It was like the old days, marching along riverbanks, except for 16-year-old Harry in tow. The man famous for his elegant essays was a very muscular littérateur: with an epidemic of salmon disease, father and son walked 'ten miles between 3 pm & 5.30' each day, examining infected fish. He discovered the fungal cause of the sores, and the growing culture in his lab led to his prediction that he would soon be able 'to furnish Salmon Disease wholesale, retail, or for exportation'.[38]

The kingmaker considered others too hot-headed for a crown. Or, in Lankester's case, with screws so loose that they left the upper regions unstable. Having impetuously thrown over University College London for the lucrative Edinburgh Chair at Christmas 1881, despite Huxley's caution, the fickle Lankester about-faced before his induction, declared the University not to his taste, and returned south. Lord Rosebery at the Home Office had been wary of arming this loose cannon, and probably only appointed Lankester on Huxley's word that he was 'far & away the best man'. The fiasco left Huxley with egg on his face and Hooker reassessing their credibility as government advisers. The kingmaker penned an apologetic letter to the *Scotsman* and exonerated Rosebery. The throne had been made a laughing-stock, and the mad Regent's attempt to 'cut his own throat' did nothing for the scientists' carefully cultivated image.[39]

The new Dean was slitting more exotic throats. He had to run a school now, as well as his classes, and cram his research and his rivers in between. In February 1882 he was dismembering assorted sauropsids from tortoises to ostrich chicks, searching for the common features of bird and reptile lungs.[40] A new intake of scientific sappers was anatomizing this huge vertebrate group, while the General dissected a kiwi's lungs to refute Owen's claim that New Zealand's furry-feathered bird could be a link to the mammals.

He was ageing badly. 'I see it', said Nettie, '& it goes to my heart'. The work was overpowering him. The passing time was registered by a second grandchild. Jess named him Noel 'after our lost darling' (even now Nettie could barely 'bring my lips to utter the name'). And even more by an old messmate's painting of the donkey frigate *Rattlesnake*, recalling that 'peculiar kind of life' on the high seas. The days of self-taught warship scientists were long gone. Huxley had only to look around at his students dissecting in rows. A pump-and-grind drilling of graduates was breeding a new civil service. The memories made him feel 'confoundedly old – 150 at least, and I talk seriously of putting up the shutters, as it becomes a double bundled Grandfather to do'.[41]

As 72-year-old Darwin, the great evolutionary theorist, confounded the world with his *Formation of Vegetable Mould, Through the Action of Worms*, the redoubtable Emma came up for Noel's christening. She joined John Tyndall to renounce the devil. Jessie, like her mother, swore by this inoculation against sin, and Emma endorsed such preventive spiritual medicine. A heart attack at Christmas had left Darwin invalided into her care. Her home remained a sanatorium, where she ministered to her old husband, wretched with angina pains and fainting fits. His life was emptying of experiments, and he 'looked forward to Down graveyard as the sweetest place on earth'. Huxley sent his latest collection, *Science and Culture*, with its plea for technical education and celebration of the *Origin*'s Twenty-First. But it was the *tour de force* on 'Automatism' that bucked the old man up. He saw his disciple going on 'ad infinitum to the joy & instruction of the world'.[42] But his own day was done.

A seizure on the Sandwalk in March 1882 had Darwin lurching into the house to collapse in Emma's arms. Morphia eased the pain, but the attacks left him decrepit and frightened. Huxley tried to be cheery as he advised on the cleverest young doctors. As always your words are the 'real cordial to me', Darwin wrote on 27 March. 'I wish to God there were more automata in the world like you'.[43] Those were the last words to his disciple of 30 years.

The letter dropped through Huxley's door on Thursday afternoon, 20 April 1882. Frank Darwin concealed his grief in the clinical details:

> He died yesterday afternoon about 4 o'clock; he was not unconscious except for the last ¼ hr. He had an attack in the middle of Tuesday night in which he had some pain which was continuous but not severe. He fainted and soon regained consciousness and remained in a condition of terrible faintness and suffered very much from overpowering nausea interrupted by retchings. He more than once said 'if I could but die'.

Trauma had left Emma 'very calm'. Frank, trying to give Huxley that desperate reassurance he needed, added, 'how often I have heard him express his affectionate regard for you. We all feel your friendship was an unvarying cause of real happiness to my father'.[44]

Darwin was dead. It had been almost 40 years since he had confessed his 'murder' – his belief in evolution – to that other sea-dog Joseph Hooker. The years had firmed their friendship into something immutable, and the shock left Hooker 'utterly unhinged'. He was incapable even of penning a few words for *Nature*. As Hooker collapsed at the thought, Huxley buried his grief in action. The consummate politician, he went into conclave with Darwin's cousin Francis Galton, agreeing on the cultural import of a public burial for this 'royal character', as Galton had it – for the man who had delivered up a new Nature for the new priesthood. He had died, fêted abroad but unrecognized at home; even now his body lay in a rough oak coffin ready for interment in Downe churchyard. As Huxley said, '50 or 100 years hence it would seem absolutely incredible to people that the state had in no way recognised his transcendent services to Science'. On Friday night Huxley sought to remedy this. At the Athenaeum he and Spottiswoode talked to Canon Farrar of Westminster Abbey (Huxley's old supporter on scientific schooling) about the ultimate recognition. Meanwhile Lubbock, another of Downe's great folks and now MP for London University, whipped up Liberal support in the Commons. The night-time plotters brought off a coup to deposit the agnostic in the Abbey. The alliance of Broad Church and liberal science sealed 'the Westminster Abbey business', Huxley informed Hooker.[45] Dean Bradley, who had tapped Huxley's brains and tipped him as his Oxford successor, gave his blessing.

Grand pall-bearers were summoned: the Dukes of Argyll and Devonshire (head of Huxley's influential Commission) and Lord Derby. 'I have written to Lowell [Huxley's friend, the American Ambassador] & Sir JH telegraphs consent', George Darwin told Huxley. He added embarrassingly: 'It has suddenly flashed across me that Wallace is a man whom it w^{d} be gracious to ask to be a pall-bearer. What do you think. The only objection that I know of is that H. Spencer might think it more his place'.[46] Huxley knew that it would be hard to lure Spencer into the Abbey, let alone to the altar. And so Wallace, that perennial afterthought in the Darwin story, prepared to bear the body. The bells pealed in Darwin's praise, and the *Times* declared the Wilberforce clash in 1860 so much ancient history. While sermons up and down the country talked of Natural Selection fulfilling Divine Destiny, Huxley dashed off a chivalrous leader for *Nature*, mourning the saintly naturalist who had captured the heart of Christendom

And so the rough box gave way to a magnificent coffin. On Wednesday 26 April the X-Club, Huxley, Hooker, Spottiswoode and

Lubbock, bore it in solemn procession, arms locked with the Church (Farrar) and their Lords. Past a black-draped Nettie and her boys – Leonard was Darwin's godson – and on in sombre procession to the north-east corner of the nave, beneath Sir Isaac Newton's monument. The aristocracies of birth, spirit and intellect were proclaiming their faith in evolution as a preserver of the social order and a provider of future glory. Perhaps, the *Times* surmised, the 'Abbey needed it more than it needed the Abbey'. In the canonization they had snatched the body from the heretics: the Moncure Conways, the old Chartist leaders, all there, in the back rows, radicals who might have appropriated it for more subversive ends.

Canon Farrar invited Huxley to his 7 pm. service that Sunday to hear the final benediction. The ascent of the liberal clergy gave science its spiritual recognition. As the religious press praised Darwin's exemplary character, they linked conventional mores and social stability to his Malthusian gospel. That gospel of struggle and reward had become the sacred book of the liberal meritocracy. Darwin's thought reappeared 'under a hundred disguises in works on law and history, in political speeches and religious discourses', said Morley. 'If we try to think ourselves away from it we must think ourselves entirely away from our age'.[47] Darwin's clever, competitive, uncharitable Whig-workhouse motor for moving life forward summed up the century.

In the will there was £1,000 for Huxley, and the day after hearing of this tax-free legacy he started repaying. Iron Dukes had their imperial monuments as the conquerors of nations; why not one to the fallen hero for his 'conquests over the realm of Nature'? Huxley primed the pump with 10 guineas and even Spencer managed £2. The fund overflowed as word spread world-wide: 2,300 subscriptions came from Sweden alone and the Finns raised £94. Within a year they had £3,300,[48] enough for a marble statue by Boehm, who made the old recluse a commanding public figure, something he never was in life.

With deification, the very scraps that Darwin hoarded became prized. In life he had been George Romanes' father confessor, absolving the desperate sceptic, whose godless cosmos had lost 'its soul of loveliness'. Romanes craved the evangelical comfort of evolutionary certainty. It showed in his anguished *Candid Examination of Theism*, a book that became the talking point at Huxley's 'Tall Teas'. It showed in the way he brought morality firmly under the yoke of selection. He probed the minds of savages and the insane to prove that 'man and brute have much more in common . . . morally, than is dreamt of'. Darwin's death shattered the adulatory Romanes. His was 'the sorrow of a heart broken as it never has been before'. Not even his own father's passing had left 'a desolation so terrible'. In his blinded state he planned his own memorial. Darwin had passed on the 'Instinct' chapter from his manuscript *Natural Selection*. Romanes now planned to publish it. Huxley, invited to a reading at the Linnean Society, thought this a 'crude & unfinished piece' which would do Darwin an injustice.[49] 'Colossal', Romanes had called Darwin's intellect; every snippet carried the mark of genius. But the years had given Huxley a fuller understanding. A 'clear rapid intelligence', yes – but 'tenacious industry' backed by a 'passionate honesty' had been Darwin's strength. The probing Socrates, disdaining the clouds, had humbly ploughed the earth to find 'a great truth trodden underfoot'. Darwin's published works were his epitaph.

Darwin's death set a sombre tone for events at home. Mady had been the highly-strung daughter, the one 'painfully attached' to Nettie, clinging and crying if she were sent to Downe or the Armstrongs. The insecure daughter with the knife-edged emotions: she shared her father's brilliance and she suffered his psychology. In the Spring she collapsed: 'first she lost her sight, & for three months, c^{d} not . . . read or write & even had her food cut up for her'. Then came stomach problems, and the 'racking headaches'.[50] No one at first appreciated the danger for the girl with the Pre-Raphaelite looks.

Huxley ploughed on with the Darwin Memorial as she regained her sight. Poignantly, her old Pre-Raphaelite mentor John Everett Millais had him preside over the Artists Benevolent Institution dinner. Here struggling Science sympathized with struggling Art, and Huxley's growing anti-Darwinian belief that 'blood is thicker than water, but sympathy is thicker than blood' netted £1,600 for the orphans.[51] But from now on Mady's tightrope walk would transfix him as he widened the divide between a harsh Darwinian Nature and benign human ethics.

It was a sad Huxley who gave his Summer course in 1882. Among the 31 teachers dissecting rabbit capillaries was the chameleon-like Annie Besant, a 35-year-old who had left her parson husband to become an atheist missionary. Science had always seemed liberating to staff writers on the *National Reformer* like Besant. Huxley found her a 'well-conducted lady-like person', and 'very hard-working'.[52] But Tory MPs took exception to her penny blasts on republicanism, atheism, female emancipation and worse, and prevented her from receiving her teacher's pay, even though qualified from the Science and Art Department. It was a sign of the sharpening antagonisms of the 1880s.

The day Huxley's lab course finished Frank Balfour was killed in an Alpine fall. It seemed a bleak end to a bleak Summer. Seven weeks earlier Balfour had been given a special Chair of Animal Morphology at Cambridge and with his death Pope Huxley saw the demise of his Cardinal successor. And so his short life passed from rumour to legend in a brilliant flash. Nettie had asked Balfour as he set off to be especially careful. 'To me he was very dear', she said, 'as well as to Hal'.[53] Huxley, bogged down in interminable Fisheries work, could not get the image of Balfour's frozen body out of his mind.

The bleakness was affecting. He moved towards his own bitter Winter probing diseased oysters. For a time it was fish with everything, lectures on eels for the workers, herring for his students, oysters for the Royal Society. He managed to write on the smelt's oviducts, but growing paperwork ruled out any more scientific memoirs for four years. The fisheries were taking over his life. Free days would see him dissecting his way from primitive sturgeons to modern salmons; Christmas caught him in a sou'wester gazing from a desolate Cromer hotel onto the 'wintry sea'.[54] And then his briny face would reappear in class for lectures on fish anatomy.

Work was his anaesthetic, but he kept awakening to think of Mady. She had regained some strength and had become pregnant, giving hope that motherhood would soothe her spirit. But losing the baby only heightened her hysteria. Nettie, whose nightly thoughts were of her own Noel, watched in 'sickening anxiety' as Mady's 'nerves began to give way'. She would get 'despairing' notes from Jack and rush to Chelsea to find her 'grown darling sobbing bitterly, very frightened at the constant palpitations she suffers from'.[55] Nights camped by her bedside were wearing Nettie down.

Huxley's world had forged closer to Mady's. On Royal Academy nights the eminent would pinch his sleeve to enquire of her. Jack, in between arranging country convalescences and live-in nurses, was painting the definitive portrait of the battered patriarch, skull in hand, shadows disguising his worried eyes. As Hal's old sparkle vanished, one ontologically-confused artist 'remarked that it was a better likeness of me than I was'.[56] So close was the scientist now to the Academy professors that he even sat for group portraits.

Jack's painting was hanging behind him as he talked at the Academy banquet on 5 May 1883. It was part of his continuing engagement with Matthew Arnold over the nation's education. That engagement had a literal aspect now: Len had continued to manoeuvre adroitly around his intimidating father. His betrothal to Julia, the daughter of fellow Balliol man Thomas Arnold – Matthew's brother – rather shocked them. He was too young, too aimless, and they made him promise a long engagement. But it was his filial way of making Matthew Arnold's point. Jowett had encouraged him to become a master at a public school, so Len took a post unannounced at Charterhouse.[57] He too was escaping a domineering Science. The oddity of Professor Huxley's eldest son becoming a Classics master to the upper classes was striking, but Pater never gave any signs of disappointment.

Arnold at a former banquet had looked sceptically on Science, as it barged forward to rival Art and Literature 'in the pursuit of the eternal and unseizable shadow, beauty'. But Huxley continued to soothe the spirit. Science was no 'monster rising' to devour 'the Andromeda of Art'. Or, if a monster, it was 'a very *débonaire* and gentle monster'. Nor was he among the 'scientific Goths and Vandals' who would desecrate other forms of culture. The real vandals were those Classical seminaries at Oxford and Cambridge, which still shunned modern English studies. That gents could be turned out 'epopt and perfect', and ignorant of the past three centuries of literature or history, was 'a fraud practised upon letters'.[58]

Huxley would have science deep inside One Culture, not suzerain of a breakaway province. Evolution was secure by the 1880s, so there was no fearing a *rapprochement*. Indeed it was becoming necessary as Huxley pulled ethics out of Nature and offered it to the humanities. But with Arnold reasserting Art's role in a technocratic age, and the fight for educational resources during the Depression fuelling the Classical reaction of 'Young Oxford',[59] the cultural split only increased.

Spottiswoode died of typhoid in June 1883, the first member of the X to break ranks. Headstrong old men now, his X-colleagues rampaged like 'rogue elephants' around the body. Spottiswoode was one of 'us', and he died as President of the Royal Society. Busk was for social recognition in an Abbey burial, but Hooker hated 'touting for the Abbey graves' and was for saving 'poor Spottiswoode's bones', while the old bull Spencer simply gave an anti-clerical bellow. They reflected the nation's confusion. What was the Abbey, a State Pantheon or a Christian Shrine, the social Establishment or the Church Established? The two were no longer one, and the divorce was disorientating. In the end Spottiswoode, the Queen's Printer and stolid mathematician, was rather bizarrely buried there, but it threatened to 'smash the x completely'.

There would be no communal elephants' graveyard for the remaining rogues as they ambled off to their retirement homes. At 66 Hooker was waiting to 'throw off the trammels of official life' and retire from Kew. Darwin's £1,000 enabled him to plan a bigger house in six acres of Scots-pine country at Sunningdale in Berkshire, and to pay Huxley's son-in-law Fred Waller to build it. The Tyndalls' house too was 'going on prosperously' at Hindhead, atop the plummeting Devil's Punchbowl of the North Downs, and they too dreamt of 'escaping from London'.[60]

Spottiswoode's accolade said so much about these erstwhile dinner-conspirators. More *anciens honorables* than *enfants terribles* now. It was hard to believe that they were ever agitprop activists, looking at Princess Louise's screen embellished with their photo-silhouettes (courtesy of Mrs Spottiswoode). It was even harder to imagine it on looking at Mrs Huxley, making satin heliotrope dresses for her Court presentation. And at the Palace she found the new royals more *au fait* than the old Queen, with the Princess of Wales immersed in *Science and Culture*.[61] Few appreciated how much scientific agnosticism was being cut into the Establishment cloth. The *Times*, unable to credit it, misheard Bradley's funeral eulogy to say that Spottiswoode 'regarded Science as the "handmaid of religion"', where the Dean had really said that Spottiswoode 'never followed science in the spirit of that "often misused phrase"'![62]

And for a Dean to say it showed the temper of the times. But agnosticism was being sanctioned in the highest courts.

The Huxleys were still straddling worlds in 1883. Just how short the distance from the Royal court to the law court was shown by the letters in the post: would the agnostic champion raise his voice against 'cruel and barbarous sentence' – a year in Holloway jail – imposed on G. W. Foote for the blasphemous cartoons in his penny *Freethinker*? (He did, quietly, petition the Home Secretary with Leslie Stephen, Spencer and Llewelyn Davies on its severity, but he deplored Foote's own 'coarsely & brutally insulting' behaviour and gave the begging writers short shrift.)[63]

This was the Foote who lambasted the 'ghoul-like . . . twaddle of the clergy over Darwin's tomb', who made evolution the shell in the atheist's breech-loader – and who quoted the writings of Huxley and other 'high-class heretics' in his defence. But exactly why Huxley snubbed Foote's henchmen was revealed in the landmark ruling following the case. The Old Etonian Chief Justice Coleridge for the first time agreed that Christianity was *not* 'part of the law of the land'. Simply disavowing it was no longer an offence. How could it be with Jews and Unitarians having civil equality? He talked instead of the *manner* rather than the substance constituting a blasphemous libel. And since scurrility had always been abhorrent to Huxley, he could agree with the judiciary on Foote's offensiveness. While the bench would reciprocate by de-privileging Christianity. The Judge actually contrasted 'the great writers alive' who show

> a grave, an earnest, a reverent, I am almost tempted to say, a religious tone in the very attacks on Christianity itself, that shows that what is aimed at is not insult to the opinions of the majority of Christians, but a real, quiet, honest pursuit of truth. If the truth at which these writers have arrived is not the truth we have been taught . . . they are not to be exposed to a criminal indictment.[64]

Huxley's professional strategy was being sanctioned by the law. His tomes were legitimized, while the political atheism of the penny trash was outlawed. Foote seethed that 'respectable Agnosticism' got away scot free because it 'is more cultured'. Lord Coleridge was living up to his reputation. He had piloted the Bill abolishing the Anglican monopoly at Oxbridge and had succeeded Collier's father as Gladstone's Attorney-General. He was an FRS, inducted into the Royal Society by Huxley himself; more, he was a friend who relished Huxley's complimentary books.[65] Through this suave old boy, high society was throwing a protective cloak around its agnostic elite. It was redrawing the red line, redefining the class divide. It was permitting its aristocrats of intellect to question Christianity, while threatening rougher working-class attacks. The pact was sealed.

'The law's a hass', as Mrs Bumble said, but it was now Huxley's 'hass'. Never mind that his moral vision was leaving a trail of unemployable ex-clergymen – men who had seen it destroy their cosmic theodicy.[66] That might have lengthened the welfare queues, but it never threatened the social fabric. Quite the reverse, he was aligning agnosticism with conventional family pieties. Sixteen months before securing Darwin's place in the Abbey he had refused to press for George Eliot's plot in Poets' Corner. On that occasion he told Spencer that the Abbey was 'a Christian Church & not a Pantheon' and that her life was 'in notorious antagonism [to] Christian practice in regard to marriage'. Propriety before greatness. Sanctification would invite public muck-raking about her cohabitation with Lewes.

Such was old Dean Stanley's liberality that he would have taken her on Huxley's say-so. But Huxley refused to ask Stanley to read words she considered lies, and for which he would 'be violently assailed'. If 'peace & honour' were to 'attend George Eliot to her grave', hers should be the unconsecrated infidel plot in Highgate.[67] And that is where he stood over her coffin, one snowy December's day, this woman whose perceptions had long pierced his own armour. After 30 years he was still trying to unhitch freethought from free love, still trying to decontaminate agnosticism.

The realignment was accelerated by the militant upsurge on the streets. Huxley found himself outflanked by a wave of young agnostics led by the rationalist publisher Charles A. Watts. Watts & Co. had moved away from the *Freethinker*'s Bible-bashing to trade on agnosticism's respectability. It promised intellectual upward mobility; it was proven to penetrate the Establishment, and it was ripe for exploitation. Piracy was still part of street publishing: Watts canvassed Huxley's views and coolly printed his reply without leave in the first *Agnostic Annual* in November 1883. Huxley, outraged at the way 'that free thinkers "make free"', found himself 'paraded . . . as a "contributor" among as queer a crew as Jack Falstaffs'. But his imprimatur looked genuine: Watts had the man who had coined the word to dignify our ignorance about matters on 'which Metaphysicians & Theologians both orthodox & heterodox dogmatise'. The letter appeared on the *Annual*'s title-page. As Huxley had said, 'I have a sort of patent right in Agnosticism – it is my "trade mark"',[68] and with his seeming endorsement the logo was passing to Watts' populist press.

Falstaff's crew had a flair for retailing science. They turned 'agnostic' into a buzz-word. Huxley lost control as the monthly *Agnostic* in 1885 preceded a spate of books capitalizing on the need for agnostic texts, all following *The Creed of a Modern Agnostic* by a blacksmith's son with a London B.Sc., Richard Bithell. The *Secular Review* became the *Agnostic Journal* and 'Saladin' (Watts' satirical side-kick W. S. Ross) produced his apologetic *Why I am an Agnostic*. This was entrepreneurial agnosticism, given mass appeal by its rich blend with Spencer's synthetic evolution, itself the determinant of life, religion and ethics. Huxley's ascetic method lumbered under continuing accretions. The movement turned religious, with exhortations to worship the wondrous 'Unknowable'. Disciples even began plans for an Agnostic Temple in Brixton, where incantations on Nirvana as the evolutionary goal might be chanted. Watts '*must* be a lineal descendant of Watts' Hymns', Huxley steamed, 'nobody could be such a knave without pietistic blood in him'. For Huxley agnosticism wasn't a creed. It was 'the essence of Science', the sensual veil, the correlate of a knowledge-seeking method – making it a tenuous host for an Agnostic Temple. But he recognized the public thirst and knew that 'If there were a General Council of the Church Agnostic, very likely I should be condemned as a heretic'.[69] The revolution was consuming its leaders.

Watts' search for respectability had been a reaction to the atheist Charles Bradlaugh – the reviled street hero, the *National Reformer*'s founder, the former Dragoon Guard whose tactics were splitting the movement. Malevolent papers portrayed Bradlaugh as an 'Alpine bandit'; in fact he was a self-immolating, sad-eyed martyr to the cause, the evangelist of confrontation who invited howls of 'Kill the Infidel'.[70] He was still grabbing headlines, still in and out of court (a former solicitor's clerk, he knew all the tricks). As Northampton's new MP, he would be the first open atheist in Parliament. But not yet; the Sergeant-at-Arms was still barring his way, and inviting Tory MPs to throw him into the street.

Bradlaugh's was political atheism, a frontal assault on the privileges of Church and Throne. Huxley wearily restated his opposition to 'Bradlaugh & Co – For whom & all their ways & works I have a peculiar abhorrence'. Telling Watts that agnosticism undermines 'not only the greater part of popular theology but also the greater part of popular antitheology', he was fingering Bradlaugh. But philosophy meant nothing in the slums, and it was here that Bradlaugh had his impact. The atheists had about-faced on one pivotal issue: after a century of abusing the 'revolting' Malthus, they now accepted that population outran food supply. It explained Mrs Besant's horrifying statistic that a third of the children were dying in Britain's worst ghettos. The population had risen 3.4 million in a decade. London was growing at 1,000 a week and the East End was at crisis point. Exposés like *The Bitter Cry of Outcast London* in 1883 were shocking, but not as much as Bradlaugh's solution. If his 'Neo-Malthusians' now accepted Darwin's analysis of struggle and destruction, they deplored his assumption of its continuing necessity. If mouths outstripped food supply, decrease the mouths. 'Neo-Malthusian' became a euphemism for birth control – 'Bradlaugh & Co' were advocates of contraception to break the poverty trap. Besant's *6d* worth of sexual advice and adverts for intimate appliances, *The Law of Population*, made the *Origin of Species* an argument for birth control.[71] For a few pence the atheists would supply 'one pound weight of Malthusian Leaflets', in an effort to end the perpetual-pregnancy condition of womenkind and raise the quality of life.

Darwin, the cocooned, wealthy patriarch, had feared that birth control would 'spread to unmarried women & would destroy chastity'. So did a genteel nation, which considered six months in jail quite fair for Bradlaugh and Besant. They received it for reprinting an old birth-control pamphlet *Fruits of Philosophy*, described on the Old Bailey charge sheet as 'indecent, lewd, filthy, bawdy and obscene', and Besant lost custody of her daughter. But the convicts never lost faith in rational science as a route to liberation. Besant had passed the first part of her London B.Sc. exams, taking honours in botany. Now, refused entry into the Botanic Gardens in Regent's Park for her practicals because of the 'opinions attributed to me', she begged Hooker let her come to Kew.[72] The fallout from the case was still being felt in May 1883 when even University College forgot its godlessness and banned Besant and Bradlaugh's daughter from its botany classes 'without reason'. Huxley signed a protest petition and summoned an extraordinary council meeting, on the pretext that this was an infringement of religious liberties. But privately he admitted that

> freedom of thought should be carefully distinguished from laxity in morals. Freethinking does not mean Free love . . . [and if the banned *Fruits*, which he had never read, undermined] the safeguards of sexual intercourse among unmarried people . . . we are out of the region of speculation and into that of practice – and I have no objection to her exclusion.[73]

Huxley was tying Darwinian agnosticism to middle-class values. It was a genteel stand, something he could luxuriate in, not a problem of agonizing death in the ghetto. He had to manoeuvre adroitly to champion 'philosophical freedom, without giving other people a hold for saying that I have identified with Bradlaugh'.[74] The Darwinians ensured the undefiled purity of Malthusian views, dreading Bradlaugh's sexual contagion which would rot the respectable evolutionary edifice.

Upholding the social conventions gave Huxley an air of moderation. He perfected the rhetoric of neutrality and balance. He said he had witnessed 'every form of human society from the uncivilised savage of Australia and the civilised savage of the slums' and still saw nothing to commend the 'somewhat over-civilised members of our upper ten thousand'. But in truth his professionals were becoming central to the Establishment's reforms, based on education and competition. He was functioning among the 10,000, but only the context shows how well. Wasn't his talk to the Eton boys on Nile geology early in 1883 innocence itself? Not if one looks at the radicals' condemnation of General Wolseley's recent defeat of the Egyptian nationalists. They slated this 'war of aggression' in Britain's Suez interests. By contrast Huxley was celebrating victory with a briefing to the future generals in the Eton Volunteer Corps, passing, in his slick 'physiographic' way, from the strategic history of the Nile to the geological explanation of its topography. Every General his own scientist, it was a simple message if Britain was to win 'the terrible [and ultra-Darwinian] game of war'.[75]

By tightening his grip on the Establishment he changed part of its nature. That was true of his own Presidential period. The Royal Society mace was beginning to look like the X's mascot. Huxley had heard the whispers, that 'Some time or other you ought yourself to be President'.[76] On Spottiswoode's death Huxley slid easily onto the throne as caretaker President. And so, at 58, he sat on the woolsack of the Scientific 'Lords', guardian of the *sacred penetralia*, staring at the mace in front of his massive Presidential chair. Oddly it was an anticlimactic moment, one Nettie almost feared.

And 'like Johnny Gilpin', Tom Huxley had 'little thought when he set out (some forty years ago) of running such a rig'. The rig had been run hard along a stony track. The last of his old Christian Socialist comrades, Frederick Dyster, guessed 'that a certain Lady is prouder of "Hal" . . . (if that be possible) than she was when I found her up to the elbows in a Devil fish' (on their honeymoon). Proud or no, Nettie was still 'dead against it'. Her worries over the extra work and financial strain gave Huxley 'a cold fit', even if the world's support was '"grateful & comforting" like Epp's Cocao'.

Science paralleled Parliament, whose Members were expected to finance themselves. This had always tipped the scales in favour of the grandees, who considered trusteeship of the nation's moral and material treasures part of their public calling. Noble Presidents could spend time and money, entertain lavishly and liaise with ministers. But just as more commoners took government posts, so the Royal Society was finishing with 'Lord Presidents'. The workers in the intellectual factory wanted 'to keep out [the rich] traders on the one hand and mere noblemen on the other'. Science needed no social sanction, nor should it dignify wealthy dilettantes. Huxley's term would be proof 'that a poor man – who does not mean either to entertain . . . one whit more than before – can hold the post'. The nobility of poverty was a nice principle, but it left a drooping Nettie wishing 'we were rich' with a budget for outside caterers.[77]

The press announcement on 6 July 1883 brought a note from Jim, not so mad that he couldn't congratulate Tom on the woolsack. 'The family is ennobled', he mumbled, as if in sad compensation for the drugs and drink: the unworldly son's science had provided a moral purity, just as in olden days the seminary boy had been the family beacon. 'You have now the highest scientific distinctions and will sit where Newton sat'. Huxley's control of the Upper House of Science was supported by 'all the younger & working' Fellows. The rumour that G. G. Stokes – dubbed 'Gabriel' for his angelic heralding of Christian conservatism – might run in the November elections, backed 'by the "goodies" to keep such a d—d infidel . . . out'[78] – had the backbenchers raising such a 'howl' that Hal's interim period was made permanent. Nettie wailed the more.

Not without cause. The Chair automatically entailed new duties, including Trusteeship of the British Museum. But it also gave Huxley the ear of Prime Ministers and Privy Councillors. And he used it to see scientists honoured, not for great science – that came from 'the verdict of their peers' – but for public sacrifice. He plumed the hats of those who gave 'their knowledge energy time & money to the service of the country'. Roscoe became 'Sr'enery' for a life's work in Manchester, and, with Owen retired, Huxley slipped the courtly Flower into the Director's office at the Natural History Museum and recommended a title to match.[79] He had the gall of a cultural politician. With Owen out and Flower in, Huxley sensed the ultimate conquest. He was in charge of the Darwin Fund, with a Committee that included the Xs, 61 FRSs, five MPs, the legally-compliant Lord Coleridge and the theologically-acquiescent Dean Bradley. Thumbing his nose at Owen's statue of Adam, guarding the portal to this gothic Cathedral of Science, he suggested Darwin's shiny white statue take central place in the nave. And that piece of Darwinolatry concluded Evolution's institutional conquest of London.

The knights of science were taking their place alongside the great statesmen and military figures. But the man who had sacrificed most health and time to make the New Nature serviceable to the new State was Huxley, and the press continually announced his own honours. 'I think we will be "Markishes"', he laughed at the latest rumour, 'the lower grades are getting common'.[80] The jest oozed an uneasy contempt.

Nor would he succumb to Palace pressure to put Court favourites into the Royal Society. Rather, he tried to open the gates wider to careerists. His was an easy, open regime. The cold meeting room put on a friendlier face. Above his Chair in Burlington House Newton still gazed sternly, and the weary-looking Robert Boyle glared down in full-bottomed wig. But no bigwig solemnity for the new President. The young bloods were encouraged to turn the committee chamber into a smoking room and open the library in the evenings (this reflected a changing social composition, with fewer FRSs joining the London clubs). Foster brought in cosy chairs for 'Free & Easy' nights 'where they may do what they d— please'.[81] Stiff upper lips quivered. Huxley even tried the ultimate reform – to abolish fees altogether to level the field for the poorer Fellows. Armstrong offered £7,000 to start a fund, but matching it proved too hard and the scheme collapsed.

With his poor-toiler ethos Huxley invited Chamberlain to the anniversary dinner on 30 November. The railer against the idle rich who, 'like the lillies of the field . . . toil not', was putting his principles to work nationally as President of the Board of Trade. There was no more charismatic leader of the radicals. Chamberlain's National Liberal Federation lured many away from Gladstone. Morley was with them. He had left the *Fortnightly* and been elected by Armstrong's factory workers as Newcastle's MP. He was one of the affirmative-action intellectuals who called for religious liberty, free schools and land for the poor. Chamberlain's contempt for the G.O.M.'s tepid reforms rivalled Huxley's for his torpid piety. Huxley, 'who vies with the Tories in hating Gladstone', was ready to put 'Science . . . in league with the Radicals'.[82]

Chamberlain had once produced cheers for declaring a republic inevitable. With Morley sharing this republican strain, Liberal Federation thought infected the X. President Huxley sat in judgment on the immortal status of minor associations. The Meteorological Society wanted the *Royal* prefix, but Huxley's caucus thought that they should be 'content to worship in a Republican form'. This 'multiplication of "Royal" Societies is an evil', Hooker said; 'give us decent weather' and he would 'consider their claims not only to Royalty, but to Divine honours'.[83]

Quality of life was at the core of the new civic pride, and Huxley's school campaigns and fisheries work, combined with his suite of unremembered chairs, from economic entomology – looking at food pests – to the London Sanitary Protection Association – looking into drains – made the rational scientist the civic darling. For his own technocratic principles he was made a Freeman of the City of London in 1883, sponsored by the Salters Company. And while he took the freedom of the City, future cities were exercising a certain freedom in taking his name. Pioneers had carried it West; maps of the newest state, Dakota, showed a frontier town called 'Huxley'. Be thankful, joked Fiske, that it 'escaped the everlasting Yankee final syllable' and wasn't called 'Huxleyville'.[84]

The Summer produced posts like administrative plums, too juicy to turn down. Satiated, and still offered a seat on London University's Senate, he pushed it away because he would rarely be able to attend. But the Chancellor, that tactful old Whig Lord Granville, called his bluff:

> Clay the great whist player once made a mistake and said to his partner 'My brain is softening' the latter answered 'never mind, I will give you 10,000£ down for it, just as it is'.[85]

And on that principle they co-opted him. The University was leading the rolling revolution in higher education. This was Huxley's moment. The Senate had just started Graduate Teaching Diplomas, and a new D.Sc. by research thesis, and passed out its first woman in medicine. 'Haul down your flag', *Punch* told the men, as women took 10 per cent of the B.Sc. degrees – a fact which would liberalize the curriculums of the girls' schools. Huxley joined the other liberal patriarchs trying to cope.

By the time he faced the first woman D.Sc. in 1884 his stomach ached from all the plums. The Fisheries were drudgeries: paperwork, conferences, speeches and exhibitions left him 'dog-tired'. The man organizing D.Sc.s in his off-moments had drifted from his own research. Was this how he would end a 'misspent life'? How could it be 'frittered away in all this drivel'? As his automaton body ground to a halt from 'the awful friction' the epiphenomenal nightmare began.[86] He had become a 'yes' man; even as he sank in the Summer 1884 his gluttony led to more punishment.

Lankester's bulldozering agitation for a Marine Laboratory, similar to the Naples one, was paying off. He was summarily conscripting lords of the manor, scientists, the Fishmongers Company and anybody with money into a Marine Biological Association. Obviously he installed his father-in-science as President.[87] A sinking Huxley joked that he would do as little as possible to deserve the honour, but he stayed at the helm trying frantically to collect £10,000 to build a Marine Station at Plymouth.

'Huxley looks fagged', Hirst noted in his diary. Not even the Fenian bomb attacks in Pall Mall and Scotland Yard could shake

Huxley in his Home Office rooms. Exhaustion had got the better of him. 'I don't like to see him working like this', Nettie sighed as she watched him trudge between Commissions, Senates, Whitehall, the Royal Society, the Normal School and the Fisheries, while juggling 'tens & tens of letters' daily with their demands or their damnations; 'oh how I wish he c^d^ give up this rush'. Everything was suffering: the students only saw him in the lab once a week and he was beginning to lose contact. A cab would dash him from Whitehall to Kensington at night, where he would try to snatch half an hour for dissecting before staggering home at midnight. But depression left his scalpel hand leaden.

Trapped by a 'thousand and one entanglements', all he could think of was Mady. The birth of baby Joyce had left her in a 'deplorable state', nervous, her sight failing again as 'the old hysteria' returned: 'her mind is affected', admitted Nettie. She was 'a prey to gloom & horrors', and it left her father an emotional cripple. London became 'a perfect loathing' to him. He yearned for flight, escape, the old cathartic smell of wood-smoke. Nettie arranged continual trips to the Downs, or to country farms. Hal even hankered to buy one. 'How I long to live in the country', she said after each pick-me-up, '& so does Hal'. September was spent on Surrey's sandy heaths discussing his quitting work on his 60th birthday.

He had his last four teeth extracted, and the bulldog who had cut them on clerical opposition was reduced to mushy puddings. The mirror each morning revealed a sunken-jawed depressive. The Fisheries was a quagmire of 'Jackass' poachers and squabbling squires. He tried to rationalize the feeling of wastage and void, to subdue them by that famous scientific mind, but the thought of Mady's frailty brought nihilistic waves. Swamped, he saw the coming term's work as 'the death of me'. On 19 September he left for the Devon fisheries, to see if he could cast the blue devils into 'a herd of Cornish swine'. But he returned in 'terrible anxiety' about the girl. 'It is a pain eating into our hearts', Nettie admitted.[88] A few days later, on 1 October, he tried to start his lectures.

1885–1895

The Old Lion

8

Polishing off the G.O.M.

HUXLEY'S BREAKDOWNS were peculiar. A mental lethargy left him unable to face the world. He had no 'positive complaint', just a 'deadness that hangs about me'. His haggard looks had Matthew Arnold in tears after a chance meeting. The 'great anguish about Mady' had immobilized Hal again. And yet, ordered off to sunny climes, and told by his adoring superiors to '*at once* act upon Sir A Clarke's [sic] advice', he had the will to work his way to Venice. He should have been fighting through the snarled-up traffic to his office. Instead mid-October found him sitting in a gondola.[1]

Nettie remained, left with her own burden of organizing Rachel's wedding. She never forgot 'the agony of that time, Hal away, in torture of mind & weak in body', as she too 'lost hope'. A bleak telegram told them of Mady's total mental collapse, turning Hal into a silent 'wounded beast'. He slunk back for the wedding on 6 November. Rachel was marrying a blue-eyed civil engineer Alfred Eckersley, on a contract to build a railroad across southern Spain. But the wedding was a tortured dream: a flounce of feather-hatted bridesmaids, the shower of rice vexing the bride, Nettie in her Court dress trying to seat 90 to breakfast. By 3 o'clock it was all over and Rachel on her way to Spain. The worry returned as Nettie looked at Hal. 'Between him & Mady, my soul has been torn'. Like a typical depressive, Huxley was unable to cope with it in his daughter. The *Times* reported his flight, leaving the Fisheries men flummoxed. But Gladstone's Ministers agreed on the need for a 'Coercion Bill first in his case'.[2] Not that it proved hard to evict him from Britain.

The couple returned to Italy as Britain froze. They left Foster editing a new edition of the *Lessons in Elementary Physiology* and looking after affairs. He dropped in to Marlborough Place to find

Miss Nettie the 'mistress of the House doing accounts on the drawing room table'. And he took Sir Andrew's note to the Home Office and with Donnelly got Huxley's 'banishment . . . prolonged till April'.[3] And so two months' leave turned into six, giving the Lotus-Eaters time to roam.

Roam they did. From Locarno they took a steamer up Lake Maggiore to a chilly Pallanza. On they pressed, to the picturesque Verona, with its tombs of La Scala and monument to Dante.[4] And on, to find Milan freezing, Bologna too cold, Ravenna too snowy. They rarely stopped a day or two until Clark's pills and the autobiography of 'that delightful sinner', the courtly Renaissance artist Benvenuto Cellini, carried them to Naples.

A thousand miles away South Kensington woke up to its loss. Huxley had left announcing his intended resignation. But 'what the devil shall we do for a Biology Professor'? Donnelly asked. Huxley left a well-oiled machine at the Royal Society. His ally Sir John Evans, a pulp-mill manager and expert on coins and *Archaeopteryx*, 'seemed to enjoy sitting in the big chair'. He told Huxley 'on no account to hurry back'.[5]

They escaped Naples' filthy backstreets by sightseeing in Dohrn's steam launch. Huxley's ups and downs were hitched to the telegrams about Mady, and when they reached that city frozen in pumice, Pompeii, Nettie was 'terribly anxious' about him. Even Huxley thought 'he was sinking'. The dead sentinels of Pompeii seemed to shriek of mortality, and Nettie looked on a world without health as 'tasteless ashes'. Hal joked about the expense of bringing him home in a box. But it wasn't needed, a local quinine pick-me-up 'worked wonders':[6] whether it cured any organic disorder or not, the stimulant brought him back to life.

Their drug-raised spirits entered Rome, and Hal's gravitated to the 'gruesome' catacombs. He claimed that the pagan crypts protected his Puritan soul. In reality he relished the Papal appeal to his prejudices on the streets above. These returned to their healthy level as strychnine supplements toned up his system. Nettie marvelled at the faun of the Vatican, while he mocked the festival of St Peter's Chair with its 'devout adorations addressed to that venerable article of furniture'.[7] And no morally-indignant Protestant could pass the Vatican without reassuring himself that the wispy-haired Galileo had suffered that the Inquisitors' Earth might stand still.

While Huxley pored over skulls in Roman museums, England was stunned into 'mourning, humiliation and rage' at the news of the Gordon massacre at Khartoum. 'I wonder if he has entered upon the "larger sphere of action" which he told me was reserved for him in case of such a trifling accident as death', Huxley mused. Huxley had known Major-General Gordon as Donnelly's friend. He was another Royal Engineer, and 'a great soul . . . sacrificed' by Gladstone's dithering. The mystic with the cold blue eyes 'filled with the beauty of holiness' became an imperial martyr, praised for his fights against the slave trade and searches of the Holy Land. Idiosyncrasy only coloured the legend. He once sent Huxley a photo of the 'Forbidden Fruit' from Mauritius, which he had settled as the site of Eden. It was typical that, of the two men, Gordon and Darwin, who struck Huxley as having 'something bigger than ordinary humanity . . . a sublime unselfishness' and sense of purpose, one was a Christian General in the field.[8] Donnelly, the Crimea veteran who would soon retire himself with the rank of Major-General, saw another comparison: he had his boy christened 'Gordon Huxley'.

The Huxleys left Rome after the Carnival with a trunkload of Italian books on neolithic artifacts. Through the hills of Tuscany they returned, and a few days in Florence saw them 'with minds enlarged and backs broken' as they took in the art treasures. Hal was degenerating again. The train journeys, flat out at 'fully twenty-five miles an hour' – and 'very few donkeys could have gone faster' – were excruciating. When they landed in Folkestone on 8 April after a four-day trip, he was barely able to dress himself. Clark, reading of a new drug, put him on coca extract – 'the plant of which the S Amer Indians chew the leaves'. Cocaine fortified him for his last set of lectures.[9]

They had returned a week before Len's wedding. There was a discernible sense of disappointment about the boy. He had a 'lack of ambition', noted their Fabian friend Beatrice Webb. But marriage to a dynamic Julia Arnold, who was well educated, 'clever & possesses a strong character' would provide a compensating spur.[10] Huxley could not wish a better match than Matthew Arnold's niece.

Then Professor Huxley dragged himself into his final biology course. It would be the last time for those unique lectures which had become the template worldwide.[11] He was drugged and fighting despondency. It showed in H. G. Wells' portrayal of a 'yellow-faced' teacher fastidiously dusting the chalk from his hands. Even so Wells was in awe of the old man, clubbing with his friends to buy each *Nineteenth Century* with a Huxley broadside; and he became 'excessively agitated with pride' the first time he spotted Huxley's 'drab spatterdashes' next to his own table. Huxley's strict morphological course taught him 'coherence and consistency', while the Dean's liberating articles revealed the prehistoric panorama of an ocean bed or flayed a decaying culture from behind the cloak of biblical criticism. But most of all Wells was moved by Huxley's new ethos, which saw research – unlike Oxbridge textual criticism – as an open-ended voyage of discovery, full of unpredictable possibilities. For the 'fragile, unkempt' trainee teacher, these few weeks under Huxley in Spring 1885 were themselves liberating; it became, 'beyond all question, the most educational year of my life'.[12] And to remember it, he had himself photographed laconically apeing Huxley's lecturing style, arm around a gorilla.

Pater was more touchingly captured by daughter Nettie, another aspiring artist at the Slade. She sketched pigs in the zoo and her father snoring in a chair. Her fast friends breathed the new decadence, that self-obsessed hedonism soon to break. The girl was 'mad with restless vanity', public singing and partying; a 'handful' for her father, and outside the family ménage now, another reason Beatrice Webb noted for Huxley's 'wearing anxiety'. The art-set returned with her one night. In came Oscar Wilde, that blasé presage of the naughty nineties, although not, presumably, in his plum velveteen suit. Into the house of propriety, with his risqué quips; a house reacting to the drink and drugs outside; an upright house, as it had to be, headed by a Darwinian agnostic who spoke for the new morality. And Wilde, at 30, a homosexual who projected all the 'petulances and flippancies of the decadence, the febrile self-assertion, the voluptuousness, the perversity' of the new Hedonism. In slouched the epitome of reaction to two decades of Puritan naturalness, who would make his exotic Art a celebration of Nature's death. An incongruous meeting, surely, verging on the absurd, something confirmed by Huxley's order: 'That man never enters my house again'.[13]

At 30 a brash Tom Huxley had talked of the rarity of any 'enduring work after the age of threescore'. It were better that scientists be throttled at 60. 'So the "day of Strangulation" has arrived', wrote the irreverent Foster on 4 May 1885. He implored 'your Sixty-ship' to keep the Presidency of the Royal Society but give up the Fisheries and the 'Black Board at S.K.' But the General lived up to his word. On 11 May he penned the awful letters. He resigned as professor at the Normal School of Science, and as Inspector of Fisheries, and warned the Royal Society that he would resign there too.

> I would rather step down from the chair than dribble out of it. Even the devil is in the habit of departing with a 'melodious twang,' and I like the precedent.[14]

Oxford's announcement that it was conferring on him a Doctorate of Civil Laws was 'a sort of apotheosis coincident with my official death'. 'In fact I am dead already', he added, 'only the Treasury Charon has not yet settled the conditions upon which I am to be ferried over to the other side'. Whitehall was working on his pension, responding to the roar from all sides for the man who had forced science and modernism on a backward British culture. Donnelly reminded them that Huxley had steered ten Commissions, made economies in the Fisheries Department, driven the School Board, taught publicly for 30 years, and put science at the heart of the imperial nation. The Treasury was chivvied, and the outgoing Gladstone – shamed by Khartoum, failing to get local Home Rule in Ireland and defeated on his budget – bowed to the clamour with £1,200-a-year. Not to be outdone, the Tories came in and Sir Stafford Northcote – now Lord Iddesleigh – dropped a note from 10 Downing Street asking if Huxley would accept a further £300 Civil List Pension for 'distinguished services'. The Civil List had always been for indigent gents who were eminent, worthy and acceptable, and an *enragé* who could savage Gladstone was quite acceptable. Of course it cut deeper. The cosmic evolutionary world that Huxley had 'opened up' was beginning to seem universal, non-partisan, as attractive to blue-chip Tories as blue-collar radicals.[15]

He had made his sectarian world-view seem neutral and unproblematic. What had been damnable for 30 years appeared natural now. His philosophy looked positively inoffensive. After all, science could say nothing about ultimate Matter or ultimate Spirit; the argument for a deterministic universe stood exactly where it had in Thomas Aquinas' day, morality lay in acquiescence to evidence, and the agnostic's lips were sealed where that writ ran out. Phrased like that, 'Radicals and Conservatives alike agreed in praising it'.[16] It was agnosticism for the floating voter.

Their Excellencies were waylaid in official corridors. The British had been shamed by bestowing no honour on Darwin during his life, Donnelly told Lord Spencer. Now Huxley 'holds a position scarcely inferior to Darwin'. They knew Huxley's abhorrence of bits of ribbon and 'CB ships & KCB ships', but he had once joked that

> the only kind of honour I should care about as a man of science – for there is not the *slightest fear* of its ever being offered me – . . . is a Privy Councillorship. There is a possible appropriateness in that, a kind of fiction that one was called to the Councils of the State on behalf of Science.

Donnelly reported this verbatim to the government.[17] Shouldn't Science, the new Baron of culture, be summoned to the inner sanctum to advise the Crown? Ought it not sit where the old Norman squires sat, at the highest council table? Linking a Privy Council seat to Huxley's services to science – something inconceivable a generation earlier – might make it the ancient order he *could* accept. And what less for the man who had scientifically stiffened the nation's spine?

The General left a modern command structure in South Kensington, with proliferating ranks of assistant professors and demonstrators.[18] The modern university was taking shape: a labyrinth of labs and theatres, and modern offices where 'Providence & the Telephone was agin' you. He said goodbye to South Kensington as the axis of the Victorian scientific empire: where his 'pet institution', the City and Guilds Institution, was about to open, and a £390,000 budget was already earmarked for a twentieth-century Science Museum. Not quite goodbye. As Honorary Dean he still kept a room in the Normal School 'with all appliances about him'.[19] But his day was over.

The last act was to defile Owen's Temple of Nature. Through the Natural History Museum's gothic arch he trooped on 9 June 1885, four days after his last lecture. Owen had gone, but even he might have admired Huxley's retinue of three earls, even more lords, the Archbishop of Canterbury and Prince of Wales. They heard Huxley eulogize Darwin for irrevocably changing the way men thought.[20] He handed over Boehm's statue of the minor squire who had presented the new professionals with their new sanction. And thus, in the nave, the marble Charles Darwin sat, the host in Owen's Cathedral.

Then the Huxleys beat a retreat to the south coast – to Bournemouth, 'the "English Naples"'. There the husk of a man could be seen sitting by the sea. Not even cocaine could keep him upright now. He passed his days dissecting 'Tusk Shells', tapering white-shelled molluscs, while wishing he were a sea cucumber 'and could get on without my viscera'. They tried to put the thought of Mady's dreadful decline 'away from us as much as we can & live on from day to day', but it was stirring the pit of his stomach. Even here, on the far side of the Styx, or as near as a geriatric could get, he still guarded the evolutionary portals. He muted Mivart's proofs where they criticized Darwin. But, looking back now, he admitted that in protecting Darwin he had perhaps struck 'much harder at his adversaries' than he should have done.[21]

Huxley had been ferried away to the wails of the Royal Society radicals. He resigned the woolsack on 30 November with one last act, getting Ray Lankester the Royal Medal. Lankester's touching response was faintly echoed by so many: 'Since the day when I brought to you 25 years ago the jaw of Stereognathus [one of the first Jurassic mammals] you have been the chief actor in every event which has seemed to me of importance in the chronicle of my life'. In his valedictory address Huxley looked back twice as far, to his own youth when 'there was no such thing as a physical, chemical, biological, or geological laboratory' in Britain[22] – when aspiring chemists looked to Giessen, and Tyndall's physicists travelled to Marburg. Now a laboratory made the school and pure research was a driven activity. The university was becoming 'a factory of new knowledge' in the urbanized, labour-intensive 1880s. Knowledge had become a commodity, to be brokered by the State. Lankester talked of '*creating new knowledge*' as if it were production-line goods. Yet the research factory was an industrial metaphor utterly alien to an old Oxbridge generation, which had prided itself on creating the perfect drawing-room ornament.[23] Dissent's industrial ideology cast the very soul of corporate man.

The relief as he shed jobs was immense. With Mady stabilizing again he began 'to feel thoughts rushing through his mind as they used to'. The grandparents wintered in Bournemouth, where they were joined by Jess and Fred and their three children, including little Noel or 'Buzzer', a 'regular pickle', and already at kindergarten. 'It is 25 years yesterday 15th Sep.', Nettie wrote, looking at the little chap with twinkling eyes, 'since our sweet Noel was taken away from us – & still the memory of that day is keen & bitter'. The thought turned her mind to Mady with a shudder. Jack's mother brought down Mady's baby Joyce, blue-eyed and with that 'determined Huxleyan mouth'. Bournemouth and babies were an escape, and Hal would have been happy 'to remain buried here' far from all responsibility.[24]

The best of the Xs had dispersed, ending an era. The old men were breaking the 'thraldom of official life', and Hooker's advice was to '*soak* in that freedom, get it well into your capillaries and lymphatics'. Hooker had left Kew one of the capital's great attractions, with over a million visitors each year. A restless Tyndall, taking drugs to help him sleep, escaped to the devil's punchbowl wilderness at Hindhead. 'Wicked people have spread the report that "a colony of heathens" is being established' here, he laughed, inviting Huxley down. 'Your presence . . . would complete the evidence'. He bade farewell to the Royal Institution, and at a glittering farewell looked back at his own climb 'from the modest Irish roof under which I was born' to the top of the world. Friends dropped away, although the 'sad & cruel' manner of Carpenter's passing stunned them all. (The lively 72-year-old kicked over the burning gallipot under his vapour bath and died enveloped in flames.)[25] But he had lived to see his deterministic Unitarian universe become the scientific norm and his modern London University curriculum set the Empire's standard.

Huxley was anticipating a tranquil pasturage. It should have been a quiet time to contemplate fossil insects for their own sake. But once more it was controversy that drove him to it. Gladstone, 76, out of office himself, sat dejected in the shadow of Khartoum. Isolated, the Grand Old Man toyed with Home Rule for the spiritual advance of Ireland, while relieving his frustration by torturing God's Word. England's first statesman made the Genesis verses on the creation of fishes, fowl, cattle and creeping things so many 'astonishing anticipations' of Victorian palaeontology. Here was proof that the Good Book was 'God-given'. Gladstone was putting down the theologian Albert Réville's *Prolégomènes de l'Histoire des Religions*, which made Genesis 'a venerable fragment' to be surrendered to Science. Many saw him putting down modernity itself. 'Even I saw his gross errors', said Nettie, but Hal! 'It roused Hal to fury'. He went 'blaspheming about the house with the first healthy expression of wrath known for a couple of years'. Gladstone's

> ignorance of the present attitude of Natural Science in this matter is as the Yankees say phenomenal [Huxley told Oxford's expert on Oriental mythology Max Müller, who had brought Réville out in English] – and his grand argument about the 'fourfold order' is utter bosh. I really cannot use respectful language about this intrusion of an utter ignoramus into scientific questions.[26]

And that was the gist. A Statesman had presumed to talk for Science with 'magisterial gravity'. Added to this mortal sin the venial contraventions of a Home Ruler, anathematized by the Unionist intelligentsia, a man who had turned the 'stupendous' ignorance of the upper classes into a force to break up the United Kingdom, and Huxley sensed the political payoff in pinning out this 'copious shuffler'.

Max Müller knew that the religious portions of Gladstone's 'brain are petrified; hard as rock', rendering any factual 'Dynamite . . . useless'. But he encouraged Huxley's Fenian exercise. Huxley was adept at scientific terrorism. In December's *Nineteenth Century* he pointed out that the 'fowl' – the Jurassic first bird, *Archaeopteryx* – appeared after every manner of 'creeping thing', from Silurian 'scorpions' to Triassic mammals, and not before.[27] He lampooned Gladstone's morality of elastic interpretation – and the audacity of Classicists who reduce the complex, tree-like branching of hundreds of thousands of evolving, retrogressing, adapting fossil dynasties to a banal axiom. The professional hauteur was obvious in his discussion of the latest Silurian scorpions; and in the gusto with which he announced that the origin of birds from terrestrial reptiles was in every tyro's textbook. It was a show of moral authority. The solid geological column was the new totem. It gave no leeway for shaky exegetics, even from shaky PMs.

The battle 'stirred his bile as to set his liver right'. Gladstone provided the cure that quinine and cocaine couldn't. The New Luther lived for the moment of nailing his proclamation. As energetically as Gladstone threw himself into textual contortions, Huxley threw himself into fossil scorpions. The toothless bulldog could still leave a mark. He too sublimated his existential worries into an exuberant theological warfare. Knowles was exultant over Huxley's 'Interpreters of Genesis and the Interpreters of Nature'. 'It is as if all the fire which has been kept in so long & smothered in uncongenial work, had at length burst out again'.[28]

The fee of £25 seemed cheap for an article which pushed Britain's thinking monthly into a second edition and spawned a debate in the *Times* on the meaning of 'creeping things'. Spencer never understood Huxley's 'appetite for . . . fairy stories [Christian myths]', but he too 'chuckled' over Huxley's ridiculing of Gladstone's literalism. A surprising assortment of people did: the old Kirk preacher who would substitute Huxley's religion of love for Gladstone's ritual incantation, the Broad Churchman who relished his higher criticism, the Catholic Mivart who was blinded by his brilliance[29] – where was the enemy for a cold warrior in 1886?

'Alas for Gladstone!' Armstrong wrote. 'You have extinguished him in first rate style'. Privately, Gladstone admitted his haste and turned for help. Where else could one extinguished Grand Old Man go but to another? The retired Sir Richard Owen – Vice-President of Richmond Liberal Association – was newly knighted by Gladstone. He was a sad octogenarian in a skullcap whose only child would shortly commit suicide. Surely help was on hand from Sir Richard, whose new armorial crest proclaimed '*Scientia et Pietate*'? It would have been invaluable support, too. Owen was still Britain's premier palaeontologist. Into the 1880s, while Huxley vainly hunted for his hypothetical 'protomammals', Owen was etching out a new fossil 'Cat Reptile', *Aelurosaurus felinus* from the Cape, which fitted the bill. He had the ancestor of the mammals. But only a greater deference distinguished Owen's response to Gladstone from Huxley's. Triassic mammals *had* emerged before the Jurassic *Archaeopteryx*, reversing the sacred order. And what of the oldest unicellular fossils, which appeared 'ere the distinction of animal and vegetal'? For Owen the flow of life pointed to a continuous Presence rather than an Old Jehovah. The Bible was a moral guide for the masses, 'intelligible to the age it addressed'.[30] But palaeontology's precise findings should not be muddled with it. Gladstone never received a politer hands-off notice.

But Gladstone was on his own moral crusade. He inserted a rather squirming paragraph and posted off his unrepentant 'Proem to Genesis' after receiving Owen's last letter. An astute Knowles slipped Huxley an early copy to ensure the monthly parry. Another furious turnaround: on 31 December Huxley had the 'Proem', and a week later his rejoinder was typeset. Part smart parody of a demagogue, part forensic dissection of a wheedler, it oozed mock bewilderment that the Grand Old Man should pin the truth of revelation on a palaeontological howler. 'Mr. Gladstone & Genesis', Knowles called the piece, which even he considered '"pulverizing" & final'. But too earnest. This was, after all, Gladstone. Would Huxley 'be a little less fierce' in his 'vivisection'? Huxley 'tamed his wild cat', but he still played the infuriating heckler with his trick questions: if Gladstone now saw Genesis as a sermon, not a lecture, does he mean that the latter, 'so far as it deals with matters of fact, may be taken seriously . . . while a sermon may not'?[31] He was impugning the integrity of the nation's leader-in-waiting.

The General Election in January 1886 ended the fray. The vote was a plebiscite on Gladstone's Irish Home Rule and, if it hadn't been for the science-grant-slashing Randolph Churchill, Huxley would have voted Tory for the first time in his life. As it was he abstained. Gladstone re-entered No 10, leaving the wild cat with his bloodlust up. Knowles' suggestion of a more general article resulted in such a manuscript on 'The Evolution of Theology' – the longest Huxley had ever written for him: '40 pages long! double my maximum' – that it had to be split across the March and April issues of the *Nineteenth Century*. It was a palaeontological peep into someone else's *sacred penetralia*. In white coat, Huxley hammered at the rich 'fossiliferous strata' of the eleventh- to twelfth-century BC Books of Judges and Samuel. He reconstructed the ancient genus of Elohim ghosts of the polytheistic Israelites of the land of Goshen – making them a sort of child-sacrificing Tongan race of antiquity. (A fundamentally pre-Darwinian concept, based on the premiss that all peoples passed through the same 'grades of social organization'.)[32] He left unsaid that one superior species of deified ancestral ghost, Jahvah, evolved under cultural pressure into the Israelites' supreme deity and Christianity's sole god.

He planned to say it. He would begin chiselling away at Christendom's ancient strata in a 34-chapter book, 'The Natural History of Christianity'. It would show the religion becoming associated with society's ethical code – show this Elohim ghost-deity, 'thoroughly human' in its feelings, policing moral behaviour with promises of rewards and threats of unearthly torment. He drew on the Book of the Dead (the indefatigable Amelia Edwards was already signing him up to her Egypt Exploration Fund) and his voluminous readings in the Valley of the Kings, to suggest that the moral code itself, if not a number of Commandments, came to Moses from his 19th Dynasty Pharaonic foster-parents. Here was the first reformation, when Moses refined the Book of the Dead into the Book of the Covenant, and the Egyptian ethics into the Jewish social code – just as Calvin 'built up a puritanic social organisation' from the remains 'of the ethics and theology of the Roman Church'. Such parables made Huxley's sermons comprehensible and uplifting. It was Whig history writ large: the Victorian age was the culmination of a succession of reformations. History was read backwards: the eighth-century BC prophets Isaiah and Jeremiah had tried 'to free the moral ideal from the stifling' old idolatry. They

> pour scorn upon the whole sacrificial system . . . To them there is no atonement save the offering of a contrite spirit . . . They ignore the priest; & have no manner of respect for decorative theology – neither for incense, nor for music . . . Their sole guide is the inner light of reason & conscience . . . The prophets of Israel are the earliest & the extremist of Protestants.[33]

Refleshing the sacred fossils – making Isaiah as Victorian a cultural construct as Owen's rhino-like dinosaurs – the modern patriarch was preparing the way to detach the ethics and destabilize the theology for the final revolt: the 'New Reformation'. With this the Positivist strategy of the age peaked. The 'Evolution of Theology' was 'thin & pretentious' in Gladstone's view. But Huxley's homespun higher criticism, Knowles enthused, had the 'invincible strength of common sense'.[34]

It was a chilling Winter. Around him frustration was turning to rage as 1886 scooped a deep trough in the Great Depression. In a freezing

February, the coldest for 30 years, Carpenter's widow Louisa was helping to feed 8,500 ragamuffins in a Leeds soup kitchen. The mood turned ugly as begging gave way to rioting, and the wrench opened up the Darwinian divide. After the evictions in Ireland the socialist Wallace had founded his Land Nationalisation Society. Huxley shuddered. He saw 'the "earth hunger" of the many' as a 'plea for the spoliation of the landowning few'. He feared the false millennium, 'when the "Have-nots," whether they lack land, or house, or money, or capacity, or morals, will have parted among themselves all the belongings of the "Haves" – save the last two'. Socialism's head was above the parapet now. The Fabians were appealing to the genteel classes, while Wallace's *Bad Times* attacked speculators and millionaires. Huxley was suddenly in unfriendly terrain. And he felt the power of the Marxist-led Social Democratic Federation.

On an icy 8 February 1886, 'Black Monday', the emeritus professor tore himself from the revises of 'The Evolution of Theology'. He was busing through the West End as it fell to the mob. Already stiffening against demagogues and ultra-democracy, he was caught as the starving East End rampaged West. A bad tip-off had sent the police to protect Buckingham Palace, but the crowd ransacked Piccadilly instead. The Social Democratic Federation lost control. Omnibuses were overturned, people robbed, the gentlemen's clubs attacked in London's worst riot for 50 years. He 'escaped unhurt from the wanton outrage' on his bus. But he sensed an ominous force as thousands smashed and looted.[35] He retreated from the war zone to salubrious Bournemouth.

Socialism was drawing sustenance from secularism. The usual suspects went over. Aveling – already translating Marx's *Kapital* – was in the crowd. Annie Besant was singing duets with George Bernard Shaw at Fabian meetings. 'Why I am a Socialist' was her latest pamphlet – and the answer was '*because I am a believer in Evolution*'. But her sort of 'Evolution' pushed on from Darwin's bestial world of 'individualistic anarchy' to produce a more efficient State organism. Huxley was mulling over his contribution on 'The Progress of Science 1837–1887', just commissioned for the jubilee volume, *The Reign of Queen Victoria*. How had the agitators missed the point? Hadn't the 'new Nature begotten by science' given Victorian England its social and technological 'revolution'? And 'worked miracles', breaking the bounds of time and space – a revolution that could put men 12,000 miles apart in instant touch, and through steam-print 'destroy the effect of inequalities in wealth among learning men'? Education would liberate people to rise, according to their ability, and no artificial redistribution was needed. This age which could detect a new planet, or the chemistry of stars, or equate magnetism and motion, or look to its evolutionary history – it still hadn't learnt that the common 'gifts of science are aids in the process of levelling up',

> of removing the ignorant and baneful prejudices of nation against nation, class against class; of assuring that social order which is the foundation of progress . . . and against which one is glad to think that those who, in our time, are employing themselves in fanning the embers of ancient wrong, in setting class against class . . . are undertaking a futile struggle.[36]

But the Great Depression had dampened the public's faith. Few saw material progress promise a political New Jerusalem any more. Or science offer a chimerical stabilizing equation. And without jobs, what hope that technology could satisfy the workers' material demands?

Meanwhile a broad alliance was forming against Gladstone's Home Rule Bill. For X-Clubbers the final reformation sat ill with idolatrous Papists in an Irish Parliament. One fanatical Unionist told the *Times* that, 'sooner than hand over the Loyalists of Ireland to the tender mercies of the priests and Nationalists I would shoulder my rifle among the Orangemen'.[37] That was Tyndall, and like Huxley he was arming.

Huxley thought the destruction of the Union a 'cowardly wickedness'. Breakaway Liberal Unionists regrouped around Joseph Chamberlain, who wanted social reform in an Ireland that remained part of the State. They contacted Huxley. Would he help in 'fighting the enemies of the Union'? His word meant so much in America, where sympathizers were funding the Irish Nationalists. Could he 'get behind their supplies & cut them off'? Huxley loathed that 'profligate old demagogue' Gladstone, and if democracy meant an Irish Parliament then it showed that 'government by average opinion is merely a circuitous method of going to the devil'. They elicited such a bilious lament that his letter was passed around the Liberal Unionist MPs.[38] No sooner had Gladstone introduced his Home Rule Bill on 8 April 1886 than they placed it in the *Standard* (itself founded 50 years earlier to thwart Catholic Emancipation). From there it was waved alongside the Union Jack in every paper through to the *Monthly Record of the Protestant Evangelical Mission.*

In an extremist age it seemed 'the quintessence of the political wisdom of today', an antidote to 'outrage & Dynamite'. But it showed the same hysterics that he deplored in the *enragés*. For two months the country went mad. Pro-Union speeches in the House even had 'the unimpassioned Lubbock waving his hat above his head'. To a nation reclining with pride as its searchlight swept the world, Gladstone was a fanatic breaking up the Empire: 'Have you read Gladstone's *Genesis*?' ran the joke; 'No, I'm waiting for his *Exodus*!'[39] They didn't have to wait long.

Huxley's view of Irish aspirations was coloured by the pervasive anti-Catholic prejudice. The butt of his perennial Paddy quips, the navvies had come to sum up a menial, superstitious culture. The 'careless, squalid, unaspiring Irishman' was the '*less* favoured race' of Darwin's *Descent of Man*. And although Huxley avoided talking of an Irish 'race' or 'Celtic blood'[40] (that was the Nationalists' warrant for a separate state), the stereotype still allowed him to damn the Parnellites as a pack of 'ingrained liars'. But not their Protestant, Cambridge-educated leader. Charles Stewart Parnell was cold and mesmerizing. Democracy and riots had left a reactionary nation looking again for heroes. Huxley was no different. He sympathized with strong intellects, and despite the anger caused by the Fenian assassinations (he knew Lord Cavendish, who had been stabbed to death in Dublin in 1882), he recognized Parnell's 'great qualities'. It was a back-hander, but he conceded that at last 'the Irish malcontents have a leader who is . . . honest'.[41]

The X had regrouped behind Chamberlain. Tyndall wanted them to draw up 'a scientific declaration' for the Union. His signatories would be the 'unbiased sons of science', true men who championed 'true liberty of thought'. Dispassionate science was to denounce Gladstone's 'tyranny'.[42] No such damning sectarian document ever went off. It was scuppered by a more realistic Huxley, who knew the groundswell of Separatist feeling among the younger FRSs.

The X was 'going to smithereens', said Huxley amid the Fenian blasts. There never had been any new members admitted, and attendances by the old rogues were spasmodic now, although none could 'bear to think of its extinction'. The odd Thursday saw a 'doleful' meeting of Dad's Scientists. Half stayed out at pasture. The 66-year-old Tyndall looked 'very worn' amid the Hindhead gorse. And Hooker in Sunningdale was trying to finish his *Flora of British India* and get a life devoted to imperial botany rewarded by a decent pension. (Considering the £40,000 and untold lives he saved the Bengal Government yearly by transplanting quinine-producing cinchona from South America to India, along with the rubber, it should have been easy, but it was not.) While a blimpish Spencer was going about Brighton in a bath chair, threatening to write his autobiography. At one point he tried to inveigle Huxley onto a yacht for a therapeutic two-month sail. 'Just fancy' being cooped up 'with H.S. in a yacht', exclaimed Hooker: 'I should go before the mast, & stay there'. Once the X could have staffed a scientific university, now their aches and pains could complete a clinician's manual. They were decrepit and, for each of them, Death had a stalking-horse. Tyndall's bosom friend Hirst was emaciated, 14 pounds down in seven months. Busk would be dead by the summer, 'Poor dear old Busk', that shoulder Hal had once leant on.[43] They prepared another notice for the *Times*.

Over summer 1886 the X took the airs in their codgerly ways. Switzerland was now the playground of Thomas Cook's tourists. Columns of them could be seen snaking over the glaciers. Even the old mountain goat Tyndall, who had built a chalet on the breathtaking Lusgen Alp, now felt grateful to Cook's agents for helping him along. The Huxleys made their own snake on 2 August. They came up 18 miles and 2,000 feet in a caravan – 'four mules & five bipeds' – from Evolena to Arolla, off the Rhône valley. Here, 'at the tail of a glacier in the midst of a splendid amphitheatre of 11–12000 feet snow heights' they settled. It 'suits us to a T', he told Tyndall. If religion could not supply a religious experience, the Alps could. This was the sublime 'dream region', Leslie Stephen's 'sacred place' which evoked pure unrefined emotion. Here faithless Victorians could worship the indomitable force of Nature.

Amid the splendour the old man sat among the purple flowers sketching. He took 'a sudden mania' for the trumpet-shaped gentians, Alpine herbs whose tubular flowers show different adaptations to insect pollinators. 'I have become great on the varieties of Gentiana purpurea', he told Tyndall. 'Satan doth not find my hands idle'. Life near the snowline left him in fine fettle; the world seemed brighter, the reports of Mady were better; and he had to look in the mirror at 'the increasing snow cap on the summit of my Tête noire (as it once was), to convince myself I am not twenty years younger'.

We 'shall catch you with the spade before long', said Foster on his return. True, Huxley was soon planting specimens from Kew. Nettie was happy to see him 'madly working at botany' if it kept him 'free from his "blues"'. The pottering turned serious of course. 'I am amazed at your taking to Botany in your old age', Hooker wrote, as Huxley plundered his library and recaptured the botanical infatuation of his long-haired days. Being 'unanointed and unannealed' in the ways of plant systematics, he swept past the experts to assemble the flowers into morphological groups. The Linnean gents were nonplussed to see him draw a tree-like chart showing the gentians' increasing differentiation. It was all à la Haeckel, down to the extrapolation of a hypothetical 'ancestral' herb.[44]

Gentians gave way to reflections. Frank Darwin's *Life and Letters of Charles Darwin* would start the public glorification of the 1860 Oxford confrontation. Huxley's chapter on the 'Reception of the Origin of Species' made it a moral 'victory' to be proud of, so important in an age of imperial defeat, with Gordon fresh in the memory. The General was elegant and heroic as he backslapped old friends and crushed old enemies and moved salt cellars around the table. But a mite too indignant; even Frank thought him a bit 'hard upon the "Quarterly Article"'. But Wilberforce's 25-year-old review was still 'absolutely scandalous' to Huxley's mind. With Huxley's 'Reception' Whig history was issuing a caution: it would apprise the 'villifiers of the present day . . . that they may yet hang in chains'.[45]

The Alps put a spring in his step. His tripping-up of Cardinal Newman's advocate W. S. Lilly in November's *Nineteenth Century* reminded Spencer 'of the way a good-tempered Newfoundland knocks over & tumbles about an impertinent puppy'. Lilly joined a long line of Catholics to portray Huxley as immoral. 'With whatever rhetorical ornaments he may gild it', Huxley's agnosticism was plain materialism, and to see what that meant Lilly looked to Revolutionary France: a country whose godless excesses ran to placing 'natural children' on 'a footing of almost complete equality with children born in wedlock'. It was the old bogey, materialism sapping the strength of establishment ritual, and it had some foundation. Huxley responded with his own *Apologia*, 'Science and Morals'. It was the last act of that divine comedy which began with the Wilberforce drama, when a powerful theology with its eyes to heaven met a carnal science sifting through the 'mole's earthheap'. The sublime and ridiculous, angels and apes, were Huxley's trademark, and his undercutting sense of moral authority gripped a nation. The boy from the back-street school made a comic absurdity of scholastic authority. Huxley's morality plays portrayed the winning ways of innocence. The young waif Science eyed her old sisters, Theology and Philosophy.

> Cinderella . . . lights the fire, sweeps the house, and provides the dinner; and is rewarded by being told that she is a base creature, devoted to low and material interests. But in her garret she has fairy visions out of the ken of the

> pair of shrews who are quarrelling downstairs. She sees the order which pervades the seeming disorder of the world; the great drama of evolution, with its full share of pity and terror, but also with abundant goodness and beauty . . . ; and she learns . . . that the foundation of morality is to have done, once and for all, with lying; to give up pretending to believe that for which there is no evidence.[46]

Cinders, ground down in menial reality, slaving for others, had her visions of beauty and truth, and Society's Prince Charming would make her the Princess.

'I have painted that Lilly:' he crowed to Tyndall, ' – with nitrate of silver'. Of all people, it was Mivart who admired Huxley's caustic ink. Never had he read a Huxley critique 'with more relish'. But Catholicism's liberal son was under siege himself. He was feeling the chills in an increasingly inquisitorial climate. This 'Pontificate of Pius IX' was 'calamitous', he told Newman.[47] Mivart would be excommunicated by Rome for liberalizing Hell as he had been by the Darwinians for liberating the soul. Huxley's 'constant reader' would die in no man's land, in defiance of any authority. He was more an heir than either of them would admit.

'I know only too well *I* have made mistakes', Mivart confessed, '& life is short'. Others were feeling it. On 25 November an envelope popped though the door bearing a strange hand. Inside, it began 'My Brother'. It was from Tom's long-lost brother William. Ostensibly it was a request to have a friend's Geological Society certificate signed; in fact William at 67 knew that his 'sands of life are running low' and he was making overtures after 40 years.[48] And so the two brothers spoke again for the first time since 1845.

The calls on Huxley's time had scarcely diminished. On 12 January 1887, the Prince of Wales had him speak at the Mansion House in the City on a new pet project for South Kensington. The Prince's new complex would celebrate the Jubilee, and herald science, industry and empire in an 'Imperial Institute'. It was a Scientific Age, Huxley agreed, and such an Institute would 'mark the Victorian epoch in history' as the Parthenon had marked the ancient world. Huxley's was 'the most interesting speech', according the *Pall Mall Gazette*. But then his Darwinian diatribe blew away all the dreary talks. He depicted the industrial competition with Germany and America as international 'warfare', with starvation befalling the losers. The 'Imperial Institute' was to help Britain win the industrial 'war'. It was a line which appalled socialist economists.[49]

There was the 'war' again. Huxley's Nonconformist generation had written competition large on the world. It had made technical education the *sine qua non* of imperial success. The boy had not been born with a silver spoon in his mouth, but the Salters Company in the City presented him with a pair to mark the Jubilee.[50] Even if the socialists shunned his science as a deceptive panacea (a fact that would push Huxley more and more into politics itself), the Liberals echoed his industrial 'war' cry. Lord Hartington, Gladstone's Minister of War before his defection to the Unionists, talked of 'famine, indigence, and starvation' as the price of economic defeat. And the Chancellor, Goschen, waded in to deplore the prevailing Oxbridge manorial mentality which regarded business as a necessary evil. *Nature* applauded Huxley's application of 'Darwin's great theory to commercial competition'. While the *Times* advocated 'spending freely [on science] to protect ourselves from [economic] aggression'. They understood Huxley's image of the Imperial Institute as 'the drill-grounds of the army of industry'.[51]

The General had turned Dissent's competitive ethic into the military image of the day. Darwin had blooded it with his 'concealed war of nature'. The age had seen South Kensington being built by Crimea vets and patrolled by Royal Engineers. It had tingled at Huxley's Total War with Theology, itself awash with Church Armies and Salvation Armies marching as to war.[52] The uncontrolled – or rather conscripted – metaphors had taken on a life of their own in this propaganda-saturated environment.

Huxley's only scruple was about the Prince's proposed site for the Imperial Institute – in South Kensington. Huxley backed big business, which wanted it in 'the heart of our . . . mercantile organism – the City of London'. The City had expanded enormously, sucking in provincial banks and foreign financiers to become the centre of the world's money markets, and here the trade guilds were solidly based. Over in leafy South Kensington the City & Guilds 'Tech – 'so portly outside and . . . so . . . starved within' – was struggling. The *Times* thundered its backing for Huxley, but he was in bad 'odour at Court'. Pledges of £10,000 'at a packed meeting of stockjobbers' saw the Imperial Institute founded on Exhibition Road despite him. (This 'industrial University'[53] – the Imperial Institute – would ultimately amalgamate with Huxley's Normal School and the City and Guilds Institute as Imperial College.)

Huxley seemed a solid presence at the Mansion House. But he was collapsing inwards: those around him were becoming 'all shadows', ghosts receding into the twilight. He was dropping 'back into the unreal world he lives in'. 'The old lion is broken down', Beatrice Webb noted after a meeting in May, 'he has only the remains of greatness'. Alternately animated and depressed, he opened a little in her presence. He seemed to scream failure, as he did during his depressions; 'melancholy has haunted his whole life', she said, and with skewed insight blamed his 'indifferently dutiful' and 'dull' children for lacking any understanding of their father. Twenty-three-year-old Nettie had 'taken without a care to public singing'. (She had impulsively – and expensively – apprenticed herself to the London Symphony Concert's founder George Henschel, and accompanied him to Boston in Spring 1887. Henschel had been the first conductor of the Boston Symphony Orchestra, and the Agassizes, who funded it, helped her settle, only to find Oscar Wilde's *amie* making herself the belle of Boston's balls.) Another, 'his brilliant and gifted child has sunk into hysterical imbecility'. There was the real reason. Huxley was crushed by worry. He 'dreams strange things', noted Webb, 'carries on lengthy conversations between unknown persons living within his brain. There is a strain of madness in him'.[54] There was at this moment.

The dreamer could still pick at a fossil reptile skull.[55] But mostly he lost himself in metascientific thought on fate and determinism. Still, anyone who tried to beard the broken old lion in his philosophical den 'got his reward'. The Duke of Argyll declared that a Darwinian 'Reign of Terror' was stifling creative science. The Duke had borne Darwin's body into the Abbey, but he stood on the Ministerial fringe of science. In fact His Grace was the noblest of Owen's supporters, and he disparaged the *Origin* as 'a guess which includes a few *bits* of the truth'. The Duke was 'a clever man', growled Huxley, 'who thinks he is much cleverer than he is'.[56] The ageing lion was 'out of patience with his meddling' and 'not exactly sorry for the provocation he offered'. It was an excuse to unsheathe his feline claws.

Birth was no longer an open sesame into science, and the Duke's Totalitarian accusation came as the professionals shut the laboratory door. Against these experts Argyll offered a nobler vision which reinforced an older order. Evolutionary change reflected a Decree from On High, rather than any self-development. His Grace's 'natural law' was the Will of God, whose Writ still ran from the great dome of St Paul's to Inverary Castle. As Canon Liddon affirmed, God's was the highest Law, the illimitable Royal Edict. It could suspend 'lower' ones, and in the case of Lot's wife turn living tissue into chemical residue. It could guide evolution, or stop it at Armageddon.

This conservative mannikin view of God and his creation had been laughed out of court by radical Dissenters in the 1830s. Nor had they viewed Owen's Law-as-Divine-Fiat more sympathetically. Argyll was restaging the Romantic fight with radical Dissent's cold, determined universe. And just as the Unitarians had considered old S. T. Coleridge 'half-crazed' for his aristocratic Willed Nature, so Huxley was predisposed to think His Grace no saner. Providential Evolution seemed, after 40 years, 'rather flabby'.[57]

It was so much 'Pseudo-Scientific Realism'. Argyll's own pot-boiling *Reign of Law*, written while the Duke was juggling Reform Bills 20 years earlier, described the descent of power from God down through Nature. His Grace was making 'Natural Laws' the instruments of Divine legislation and evolution the 'fulfilment of Creative Purpose'.

Huxley had not bothered with the book before. And he only waded in now on being fingered as a new Danton. His response was radical Dissent's: to laugh at a marionette Nature, capriciously manipulated from above. The idea of laws tugging and pulling one another seemed the 'acme of absurdity'. The Royal Laws were like so many 'Eastern despots' who 'descend in wrath among the middle-class and plebeian laws, which have hitherto done the drudgery of the world's work'. Laws *cause* nothing, neither the fall of apples nor the descent of men. They are 'a mere record of experience', a sign of the constant conjunction of events, a symbol of universal order.[58] The professional was snatching the passionless cosmos away from the reconciler who has not 'undergone the discipline' necessary to understand it.

There was a certain cachet in being 'abused by a Duke'. As usual Huxley felt 'wonderfully better' for it. So good, he told old comrade Holyoake, that 'I may yet serve the good cause by something better than chastening impatient Dukes'. Radical evolutionism was corroding the aristocratic foundations of science, just as the democratic acids were etching away at old political privileges.

In this area too Huxley was clapped by the old comrades. He chaired a public meeting to collect £20,000 for a free Public Library in his borough of St Marylebone. It was vintage Huxley as he persuaded the council to put a halfpenny on the rates to run it. It was the old Nonconformist ethic: free education, helping the best to bob up to the surface. There was to be a leavening of talent in the Duke's top-heavy society. Huxley did not

> believe that if 100 men were picked out of the highest aristocracy in the land and 100 out of the lowest class, there would be any difference of capacity among them. (Cheers.) Men of mark and capacity were rare animals. Perhaps one in ten thousand . . . and if all the cost of the Education Act and all the money spent on free libraries enabled them to catch two of such men a year . . . the thing would be dirt cheap. (Cheers and laughter.)[59]

'She was a brilliant creature', he said of 28-year-old Mady. The world saw her as his gifted heir. What more could a patrician father admit? She was a woman with 'a career before her'. Once, with the Chelsea art-set, life had 'smiled on her from all sides'. But the sun faded with the suffering, and in 1887 she plunged 'down hill'. Nettie was terribly shocked that for a time 'she did not know me'. Hal privately feared 'the worst of all ends – dementia'. Mady knew that 'she was going mad and I knew it too by her look of melancholia'.[60]

In desperation they contacted the great neurologist and specialist in 'hysteria', Jean-Martin Charcot. It was Charcot who had dignified it as a serious mental illness, characterized by the blindness and loss of voice that Mady suffered. Freud, studying hysteria under Charcot, stood in awe. He watched Charcot hypnotize his female 'hysterics' to reveal the powerful mental processes hidden from consciousness. Despite the hundreds flocking to him, Charcot came to England to examine Professor Huxley's daughter. He invited Mady to Paris, where he planned to use hypnotic suggestion to remove the emotional 'conflicts' causing her brain disorder.

Mady hardly knew her three-year-old Joyce, the tot who had 'wound herself about' Nettie's heart. The grandchildren gave the family ballast. (Julia and Leonard, in their rose-clad cottage close to his Charterhouse school, had Julian in 1887.) They needed the ballast with so many buffeting relations. Polly, deranged by her second husband's death, became wild on morphia and brandy and punched Hal, screaming, 'No wonder you drove Mady mad!' It hurt. Such was the end of George's wife, the scamp who had fussed over him after the *Rattlesnake* voyage. He continued to pay a doctor £20 a year to look after her, but 'I don't think Hal will ever go near her again'.[61] Hal's cash was still a featherbed, and illness was still their lot. His own fight against pleurisy this summer portended difficulties, and Nettie was growing apprehensive about her own bladder operation.

Some invitations couldn't be shirked. Industrial Manchester too was raising taxes to fund local technical education, and Huxley had agreed to inaugurate the scheme. On 13 November Sir Henry Roscoe was preparing his room. Jack had taken Mady and two nurses to Charcot's Salpêtrière Hospital, a huge 40-building medical complex devoted to women's diseases. 'It was a forlorn hope', sighed her father. The telegram arrived a week later, on the morning of 20 November. Run down, she had died from pneumonia before Charcot had even managed to see her.

'Oh Lizzie', cried Nettie, 'I know that it is for the best – her sufferings are ended – but I want her so'. Her father, bitterly stoical, knew that she was 'spared that most miserable of endings', madness. But he was ashen-faced, and lost. Mady had passed 'beyond his veil', Knowles said, feelingly. Nettie gave an inner scream; she desperately wanted to believe in 'another happier world that shall make up for all the cruelties of this'.[62]

The black-edged envelope brought a touching response from 'brother' John. Being childless, he had always suffered 'with your sufferings', and 'I have been drawn towards you, in feeling and affection, more than you are aware of'. So it would be 'to the end'.[63] With Mady were buried rare gifts, and many of Huxley's hopes. The blow symbolized the loss of all the optimism born in that year of her birth, the Victorian *annus mirabilis* 1859. But there would be reminders. In one of the kindest acts, the owner returned Mady's painting 'The Sins of the Father'. It would now be hung over the big fireplace in the drawing room.

Everything was cancelled, Nettie put back her operation to get over the funeral. Nobody expected Huxley in Manchester on the 29th. Yet he felt honour bound, having fired them up – and he was incapable 'of chalking up "no popery" and running away'. Nettie, finding no distraction, watched him scribbling grief-stained lecture notes and could only 'envy him his work'. But the bitterness exploded in his spattered image of nature's butchery. Mady's death blackened his soul; and the more he was politicized by the Depression, the more he damned Nature's violence. Was it Huxley or Darwin who depicted the deceptive calm masking the massacre of the innocents?

> You see a meadow rich in flower & foliage and your memory rests upon it as an image of peaceful beauty. It is a delusion . . . Not a bird that twitters but is either slayer or [slain and] . . . not a moment passes in that a holocaust, in every hedge & every copse battle murder & sudden death are the order of the day.[64]

It was Huxley in a riot-torn 1887, but it could have been Darwin in a Dickensian 1837. The two men were mirror-image dancing, one in his storm-tossed morning before the sunny Victorian Noon and the other with the coming dark night. Malthusianism was back in contention in the socialist 1880s. But Huxley saw continual overpopulation as a spanner in the co-operative works, forcing unending competition which defied any egalitarian socialist solution. Bloodthirsty Darwinian struggle was inevitable in Nature: Huxley was swearing to the 'primacy of Satan in this world' where once he had faced a calm angel.[65] But the bloodier he made Nature, the more it forced him to fortify a pure human ethics. His Darwinian world was peeling apart. Nature was losing its moral spine.

It was torn out in the scrum of overpopulation, competition and culling. Where Huxley had been loath to mention natural selection in an evolutionary context, politics and personal tragedy had him thrusting it into a social context. With increasing Atlantic and European rivalry it was a case of retooling and retraining or die, he said. This was the 'fatal necessity' of business existence. His theme returned with a vengeance: industrial competition was war by another name. Darwin, cocooned with his £¼ million, had welcomed the human struggle, but for Huxley to embrace a 'humanity doomed forever to be at war' was an act of cynical desperation. And utopian promises of

> The improvement of morals, the advances of science, the universality of that Liberty Equality & Fraternity to which many look as to a new Heaven & new Earth will do nothing for us here.[66]

He had hoped to make Nettie's 'later days peaceful & happy – but such plans are folly'. Cynicism carried him to Manchester. The fury of it – 'I travelled 400 miles and made a speech of fifty minutes in a hot, crowded room, all in about twelve hours' – tinged his words.[67] The Town Hall meeting, hosted by the Mayor and trades leaders, was exposed to an apocalyptic justification for technical education.

Grief gave his tendency to distance human ethics from Nature's carnage a dramatic wrench. The toned-down essay, published in February's *Nineteenth Century*, and retitled 'The Struggle for Existence in Human Society',[68] still evoked the strife-torn side of Nature. His world of brooding malevolence damned 'the optimistic dogma, that this is the best of all possible worlds'. By cursing Nature for the Darwinian carnage and Mady's death, Huxley was *having* to detach his own ethics, wherein rested the beauty of a flower or the goodness of a young girl.

This was deep in the Great Depression. The streets swarmed with the starving. Growing numbers of socialists were besieging science and society demanding co-operation and redistribution. Huxley was using a competitive biology to police and pacify the crowds – the rioters who had attacked his omnibus. But he could only defend the capitalist war in nature and industry by dubbing it, as Kingsley had once done, a 'gladiator's show'. He bowed to its brutal Darwinian necessity as he detached his ethical sorrow for its dead victims. Kingsley's moral duty was to a Beneficent Deity promising rewards. But Huxley recognized the indiscriminate meddlings of a different divinity: the Babylonian goddess of war and lustful mother of renewed life, Ishtar. To her were the first-born sacrificed. To her we owe the deafening shrieks as she ravaged the land. Their million wails crescendoed above every field. Darwin had taken bleak consolation in the struggle honing a better-specialized descendant. But to the cynic 'it is not clear what compensation the *Eohippus* gets for his sorrows in the fact that, some millions of years afterwards, one of his descendants wins the Derby'. Darwin had looked to the species, Huxley looked to the individual. And what does it profit a species anyway? With the globe ultimately heading for an ice death, life will devolve and degenerate in a final 'universal winter' and end in the meanest of Hooker's Antarctic diatoms. A death shroud descended over Huxley's philosophy.

'Huxley looked upon creation and saw that it was bad'. There was no compensation, even in a favoured imperial nation. Ishtar added a new mouth every hundred seconds and demanded her sacrifice accordingly. And increasing the output to keep up meant an 'internecine struggle' with other nations for markets. Moral man abhorred it, but Ishtar dictated it. No 'fiddle-faddling with the distribution of wealth' would help. Population drove the war on. The speed of technological change, which was already breaking the traditional apprenticeship system, demanded greater technical mobilization. The government was right to allow the manufacturing districts to raise new rates to pay for new training. Manchester's, he said, was a sort of 'war tax . . . for purposes of defence'.

He was rationalizing pain in an industrial nation and policing the masses with Malthusian biology. It was too much. Reviews of 'The Struggle for Existence in Human Society' were crushing from Right to Left, from the Christian anti-protectionists to the socialist co-operators. 'Since Elisha prescribed for the leprosy of Naaman never was a simpler remedy offered for a terrible disorder', moaned the *Standard*. It was a calumny that 'evolution has nothing better to offer'.[69]

But his own mind would revolt against it too. Overpopulation might have demanded a continuing evolutionary struggle, leading to the survival of the Darwinian Elect. But he was beginning to eschew this Biological Calvinism, and to think that all men might be saved. As he mellowed he would have ethical man reject Ishtar's savagery. Moral *Homo sapiens* was trying 'to escape from his place in the animal kingdom', as Huxley was trying to escape the pain. Nature's Darwinian outrage had hurt him, and he was beginning to look inward.

But for now there was grief. A day or so later Nettie had her tumour removed. As she went 'icy cold' under the ether her last word was 'Mady'.[70]

9

Christ Was No Christian

HEART TROUBLE CONDEMNED old Huxley 'to the life of a prize pig': 'corporeal stuffing with meat and drink' and 'as few manifestations of intelligence as possible'. In 1888 he was at last forced to take it easy. That January came another warning, a second dose of pleurisy, which left him gasping and as 'melancholy as a pelican in the wilderness'. 'Bellows very creaky', he reported to Hooker.[1] His doctor, George Hames, ordered him out of London's smog to Bournemouth, and thus began the great cosmopolite's final exile.

They were all fleeing in their own ways. Jack left for Egypt, supported by Fred Waller and Harry, where he was to sublimate his grief in temple sketches for his painting of 'The Death of Cleopatra'. Nettie pored over Mady's childhood letters, retreating into the past, where she was 'quite happy'. Torn from the Good and Great, a croaky Hal vowed to attend no more banquets. He resigned his last posts – the governorships of those diametric bulwarks of his educational empire, Eton and University College. In maudlin mood he would 'jog along the declining path of life'. He hardly needed Nettie's confirmation that 'Old age is not exhilarating'.[2]

He remained the figurehead President of the Marine Biological Association long enough to see a fine Marine Laboratory built on Citadel Hill overlooking Plymouth Sound.[3] That too took him back to old Plymouth and his *Rattlesnake* adventure. London officialdom was now like the outback's snagging vines; having cut them with a machete chop, he was free to roam as a cultural ambassador for science.

When he could roam, that is. He was confined to his seaside digs through the Spring, coughing, the 'dreadful oppression' of his lungs lifting only slowly. The 'hermit life' depressed him, away from the clubs and gaiety of home. He survived the days of tight-chested pain by writing a long Royal Society obituary of the man who had scientized the liberal struggle, Charles Darwin. A little every day got him through. He read the '"Origin" for the sixth or seventh time', grumbling at Darwin's higgledy-piggledy ways to the truth 'as dark as those of the Heathen Chinee'. He dug into the book daily, laying out the bare bones of the argument. The Royal Society had never honoured Darwin for his *Origin of Species*, and so Huxley was deliberately giving the dead hero the society's imprimatur.[4] He was officially gazetting the book after the society's years of cavilling.

Darwin was cast in the heroic mould. It was a life for the times. Darwin's had been a paradigm struggle to overcome a stunting Classical education. The youngster had forced his way through the extra-academical byways at school and Edinburgh, via that peculiar apprenticeship on HMS *Beagle*, to a career in science. As Huxley was writing, word from one of Darwin's midshipmen, Huxley's friend from his outback days, Philip King, reached him from Australia. For '4 years we occupied opposite corners of the Beagles poop', King recalled. 'He at his microscope and books and I making charts'. But that was an ancient world. Philip's brother Robert, who had gazed at tropical horizons from the *Rattlesnake*'s stern, was 'now a full blown archdeacon with breeches and gaiters'. Huxley found it hard to look back on the scuttle-bucket without the sensation of 'studying a fly in amber'. Outside the resin preserve the ageing Professor saw his own extinction. He wanted Hooker's reassurance that the obituary was sound. 'I am getting nervous over possible senility', he explained on 4 May 1888, '63 today & nothing of your Evergreen ways about me'.[5]

Huxley's 'Struggle for Existence' had met a resounding response from Right and Left. It had been one thing for Darwin to advocate the human struggle in the stable, affluent, Victorian Noon, that Age of Equipoise, but quite another for Huxley as the Depression crushed spirits in the mid-1880s. Right-wing individualists and left-wing anarchists railed hard. He knew Spencer would be 'in a white rage' at any talk of State-sponsored technical training, 'but he knows I think he has been doing mischief this long time' with own hands-off call to government.[6] Spencer was exiled to Brighton for his health (travelling back and forth to his guest house in a 'hammock slung diagonally in an invalid carriage'). He hated the corporatist, State-spending solution of Huxley the Chamberlainite. But there were more interesting exiles to the salubrious suburbs.

Britain now hosted one of the most famous revolutionary refugees, Peter Kropotkin. The amiable red-bearded Kropotkin – looking, said George Bernard Shaw, like a 'shepherd from the Delectable Mountains' – was responding to the deepening crisis with his *Conquest of Bread*. This was the first full-blown exposition of anarchist communism, in which fair distribution by local communes was to replace wages and property. Russia's revolutionary Prince and Ealing's rational Pope came from different worlds.

The Prince, once the personal page of Tsar Alexander II, had seen the world in exile. He had started in the gulag-wastes of Siberia, where he had become revolutionized by the rotting human flesh of the labour camps (and where his 50,000-miles study of tundra life from the Steppes to the Far East had made his reputation). He had travelled an equal intellectual distance towards a mutual-aid anarchism with a biological base. He was the propagandist, not of treason and terror, but of humanity's fraternal growth. Nurtured in a Darwinian age, familiar with Huxley's works (the *Science Primers* were even now being sought for Russian schools),[7] Kropotkin saw revolution as accelerated evolution, speeding us towards a benign Kingdom of Man. He projected benevolence onto Nature, as Darwin had projected bloodletting.

From Clairvaux prison in France (convicted of being a member of the International) he had written for Knowles' *Nineteenth Century*. Pardoned after an international outcry he moved to England in 1886. No sooner settled than Huxley's 'Struggle for Existence' had him planning a reply and putting the biological base to his anarchism. Kropotkin's 'Mutual Aid among Animals' in the *Nineteenth*, Knowles told Huxley, was 'one of the most refreshing & reviving aspects of Nature that ever I came across'. It was the first of a series of articles which would become the classic *Mutual Aid*.

Huxley portrayed primal man's savagery as a 'gladiator's show', a 'continual free fight'.[8] Darwin had seen morality develop from the social instincts, but for Huxley the instincts were antisocial, an amoral vestige to be repressed, the primeval lusts. Moral man was trying to escape them, trying to escape to his new kingdom.

For a Russian anarchist it was so different. His 'primitive' living tribes had always been bonded by customs into co-operative groups. So it was for many other species. The underpopulated tundra had shown the cossack a different nature, where mutual support among ants or yaks helped them in a hostile terrain. Sociability was the driving force, something played down by the English Malthusians. It destroyed Huxley's divide between savage and civilized man. Social cohesion was rooted in our biological past and the sanction of our future ethics. Instinct and morality were one, on a continuum, not on a war footing.[9] Man wasn't trying to *escape* his place in nature. He was trying to re-establish the primal balance destroyed by the capitalists who had caused mass starvation in Huxley's industrial 'war'. Overpopulation and starvation weren't the necessary correlates of progress, but a hideous corruption of an unjust technological society.

Huxley's writings started Kropotkin's search for a new moral philosophy based on a co-operative Nature. The two men showed how malleable Nature was, as easily appropriated by capitalist as anarchist. The age of extremes was nearing now; indeed, having over-elaborated the struggle in the days after Mady's death, Huxley with his meliorative tendencies and Chamberlainite sympathies was never that unsympathetic: Kropotkin was wrong, but his work was 'very interesting and important'.[10]

Switzerland was a familiar destination in Summer 1888. Huxley's life was now a perennial holiday in search of mountain sun. Away with Jack and Ethel, he had the physiological job of exercising one ventricle in the high dry air. He got his legs back, eventually 'going up 1500 or 2000 ft & walking 12–14 miles a day!' He swept back home to pick up the 'two or three cwt. of letters', only to be engulfed in the London fog. The black sooty vapour might have been the sublime canopy of the World City, but it belched from Hell's grate to kill the old. Everything beyond the front door disappeared and the suffocating stuff 'got down into the house & choked us'. It fouled Huxley's lungs and Hames ordered him out again. So they tried coastal Eastbourne for the Winter. 'I shall not have been home a month all the year', he told Hooker, but it was paying off. He went down 'weak, silent & depressed but gradually he became merry'. Striding out from his clifftop guest house over the Downs or up to Beachy Head saw him returning to normal.[11] The Mady crisis was finally over.

The Royal Society's troop of emancipated Huxleyites (or 'scientists' as they called themselves, although Huxley avoided the word) paid its parting respects in November 1888. The Copley Medal was its prestigious crown, the laurel of high rank. It was a sign that 'the scientific *orbis terranum*' now encircled the Huxleyan Sun. The medal would fill the gap on the mantelpiece where the nugget-like Royal Medal had stood before George's death. This one the old man would not have to hock. Hooker had taken the Copley in '87, and Huxley relished their 'niches in the Pantheon' together.[12] Sir Joseph was himself an aged idol turned to bronze and oil. He too could be seen on the Royal Academy walls, wedged between the nudes, incongruously wrapped in Lyell's old fur coat (a legacy) in Herkomer's portrait. The old sea dogs, whose 40-year masonic bond came from being salted on creaking ships, were the last of their Senior Service generation.

Deafness was forcing Huxley to fight shy of society, and he ceased public speaking. 'It irritates me not to hear – it irritates me still more to be spoken to as if I were deaf – & the absurdity of being irritated on the last ground irritates me still more'. But, for all the indignities, the spirit was kicking, and 'age hath not cooled the Douglas blood'. He proved it on front pages and letters pages, remaining a pillar of disbelief in the absurd. The cynic was incapable of letting the ludicrous pass. There were epistles to split sides: 1889 opened with him showing *Pall Mall Gazette* readers how to employ the tendons of the big toe like 'delicate Ariels' to produce spirit raps. There were rants in the *Times* on the 'cock and bull' about steam trawlers depleting fish stocks. And he snapped his fingers at the evangelical mythmakers. He squashed the rumours of Darwin's death-bed conversion, only to face American reports that he himself 'had been at Lourdes', seen the light, and was about to enter the 'Catholic Church!'[13]

The barbarians were on his borders, pressing at his own Hadrian's Wall. The agnostic populists shunned his scientific sackcloth-and-ashes approach. They arraigned Huxley for sticking to 'phenomenal evidence'. On Huxley's cleared ground they were busy erecting an Agnostic Temple to Spencer's 'Great Unknown' – the Thing on the far side of the sensory veil. The 'Jewish tribal God' might be dead, but in this temple 'our best feelings, such as love, hope, conscience, and reverence' might 'find reflections of themselves in the Unseen World'.[14] This urge for a 'super-phenomenal' Something to satisfy the emotions led to new catechisms from the new Saladins, even a graft of Zoroastrianism from the agnostic chairman of the London and Brighton Railway Samuel Laing. It was a mockery, a new idolatry, as the rationalist priests made 'metaphysical teraphim out of the Absolute, the Unknowable, the Unconscious'.

This perversion of agnosticism heated him to 'boiling pitch', and 'I really can't keep the lid down any longer'. The Puritan lashed the market traders from the Temple, furious at the pagan idols. He met them with a rambling exegesis of 'Agnosticism' in 1889, surprisingly his first. He romanticized his own search for a new authority, and told how, coming out of the trap of youth like the fox shorn of its tail, he had invented the term *agnostic* 'to show that I, too, had a tail'.

(He had coined the word privately, at the Metaphysical Society in 1869, but until this moment not even his X-Club friend Hirst had realized that it was Huxley's neologism.) Boiling away happily, Huxley almost vaporized the concept. Agnosticism was 'not a creed', he said, 'but a method'.[15] It was a Socratic questioning, the 'axiom' of science, a holding fast only to what is good, the 'foundation of the Reformation', a demand that every man 'give a reason for the faith that is in him'. And in keeping this faith 'a man . . . shall not be ashamed to look the universe in the face'.

His blunderbuss shot peppered the fat Church Congress on one side and faddist Church Agnostic on the other. The Positivists were hit by the ricochet. (As Huxley dug at them: 'Charles the Second told his brother, "They will not kill me, James, to make you king"'. Nor was science 'destroying the historical foundations of the noblest ideal of humanity [Christianity]', to put Positivism's 'incongruous mixture of bad science with eviscerated papistry' in its place.) The 'Agnosticism' article was pure Huxley, so full of 'tender devotedness', said Knowles, that he would 'win souls' 'even from Baptists'.[16] It was 'about the very finest article you ever wrote'.

The ascetic sceptic was thoroughly ashamed of the pleasure he took. The more so because Dr Wace at the 1888 Church Congress had had the temerity to call him an 'infidel', a sorry 'unbeliever' in Biblical authority. That gave Huxley the excuse to shift the article onto Biblical ground to attack that rival authority. Through the years of Mady's madness he had buried himself in ancient demonology, studying that 'preposterous and immoral' story of the devils cast by Jesus into the Gadarene Swine. In 'Agnosticism' he made Jesus just another orthodox Jewish teacher, a product of his culture with a contemporary faith in unclean spirits. Indeed, for holding that Gentile converts had to obey the Jewish Law, Christ was portrayed as another 'infidel' himself in Wace's book. As possessed pigs became the nation's dinner talk, Huxley separated Jesus' Nazarene beliefs from the later Christianity fashioned by Paul.[17] Here was the leitmotif of his 'Natural History of Christianity', if he could write it.

In the 1880s no elite scientist accepted a literal Day of Creation or a Deluge that left a geological trace.[18] (Sounded out by No 10, Huxley called the President of Canada's McGill University, William Dawson, the colonies' last 'Mosaic Geologist'. Thereupon Gladstone promptly knighted Dawson, but not before echoing his claim that palaeontology proved the Divine inspiration of the Pentateuch.) If the Bishop of Oxford had tried to revive exorcism in the 1850s,[19] Jowett's *Essays and Reviews* had buried it. By the 1880s Huxley was simply exploiting miracles and demons to market his rival agnostic product. His technique was to make contemporary religious testimony tell against venerable traditions – testimony retrieved by the historical and scientific expert.

These clever digressions into first-century events were a sign of science's new cultural authority. Scientific naturalism had been part of urban industrialism's assault on the old landed interest, but now the new professionals claimed to speak on the country's behalf. By contrast, the Church of England was portrayed as a party organ, 'not the Church of a nation but of a class'. This class aspect was complicated as the situation blackened in the 1880s. In the Depression, bread rioters and socialist agitators menaced the Establishment from below. The theological spine noticeably stiffened, and there were concerted efforts to discredit Huxley's rival naturalistic morality. Lilly saw the moral bud blighted in the theological darkness, and the 'Baal of Dead Mechanism' degrade children and ruin women. For Mallock 'the miserable [moral] rags . . . [with] which [Huxley] attempts to cover the life which he professes to have stripped naked of superstition are part and parcel of that very superstition'. Morality and social safety were impossible without a supernatural sanction. From the Godhead a descensive spiral of power passed through his Church – indeed the 'whole structure of society is pervaded by the will and power of God'.[20] His presence is revealed in a sequence of miracles from the Creation to the Resurrection.

Huxley was kicking away the supernatural props of a rival profession. It was a social response, a ratification of a new cultural order. The Church had used its supernatural sanction against socialism; now Huxley would be forced to find new arguments. Having tarred the theological despots who ruled through the 'terror of possible damnation', he would have to make Nature rule against the revolutionaries too.

Agnosticism's weak freedoms had been hard won: freedom to follow the evidence, a freedom sanctioned by the Protestant appeal to private conscience.[21] Vigilance was wanted to protect them. Jowett, 'a coward of a man of peace', marvelled at Huxley's martial attitude. 'What a tremendous controversialist he is!' 'Such smashing blows!'[22] He took it as a sign of renewed health, and he was right. Huxley considered it almost indecent to have gone through so much and still be 'above ground'.

He was 'wonderfully well'. Just as Kingsley had revived him after Noel's death, so 'Agnosticism' was balm for his weak joints. According to Nettie, the paper 'seemed to run from the end of his pen &

gave him inexpressible pleasure'.[23] In late January 1889, Hal sat by the wintry sea, wallowing in an infernal Dantean world. He was dutifully discrediting medieval witnesses to the miraculous when the family news completed the spring in his step. Having doubted Church authority, Pater now found himself in and out of Church. Ethel, their youngest, not yet 23, had been Jack's companion in the dark days after Mady's death. She had shared his love of painting and taken over Mady's toddler Joyce. They became engaged.

It was a 'noble thing' to take charge of Joyce, said Ethel's godmother, Lady Armstrong. (Sir William had capped the industrialists' rise with a peerage.) Ethel was 'undoubtedly the proper person'. Proper or not, it was still illegal. Jack was her brother-in-law. Marrying him was against the law. The Deceased Wife's Sister Bill sought to change all that, but it was still before the Lords and being resisted ferociously. The law was 'an ageing iniquity', said Hooker, but it was the law.[24] The bishops would uphold it on a reading of Leviticus, although their real concern was for that Victorian custom of chaste girls keeping house for their married sisters. Their Lordships were removing temptation.

Huxley found the 'Bishops and their aristocratic *clientèle*' patronizing. Might not the sister be the best stepmother, making the arrangement 'eminently beneficial'? Friends rallied round. Hooker took Collier's devotion to the family as 'a strengthening of an old undying love'. Jack had 'been tried by fire, & come out pure gold', said Nettie, happy to see him accompany Ethel 'in life's journey'. And unlike Mady, Ethel was 'absolutely fearless'. She was prepared for the snubs of parsons' wives.[25] There was no better match.

Pater had hardly got back to impugning the saints when the impulsive Nettie became engaged to a mining engineer. The rugged Harold Roller had done well in America, and he was on a private income. He was introduced at dinner on 23 January. During the dreaded 'mauvais quatre [sic] d'heure' in Professor Huxley's study, Roller found the paterfamilias 'completely patched up – seams caulked and made seaworthy'. The terror of Mady's madness was receding, even if they thought of her 'every moment of the day'.[26]

But the old ship was still docked in the Thames fog. Now, with the last girls engaged, and Harry preparing to go into practice with Dr Hames, they could search for a seaside mooring.

The sea had its attractions. Huxley still dreamed about those New Guinea palms. Amid the din of a glittering reception, he would see himself 'waking up on the flat plank . . . in the bright dawn of a tropical morning . . . when every noise was hushed except the lap lap of the waves'. But no Mauritian paradise for them – it would have to be the Channel coast at Eastbourne. Beachy Head would provide a continuity with those gale-tossed days on Caldy cliffs. And if the rolling Downs did not quite evoke the Alps, they served to blow away the same London ills. The mountaineer was a little stooped now, and comical as he trailed a pack of sheepdogs over the hills, attracted by his undressed wool coat. With his aching ears protected by huge cap flaps, he looked a bit 'doggy' himself.[27]

The chicks had fledged. Some were flying. Rachel was accompanying Alfred to Mexico on rail construction business. Len was about to start a school in New York. Jess, sharing her mother's Moravian interest in education, was writing an article for the *Nineteenth Century* on the moral training of children. With the last engagements announced, Huxley bought a plot high above Eastbourne near Beachy Head, and Fred Waller drew up the plans for a house. Huxley would call it 'Hodeslea' (the archaic name for 'Huxley', he supposed). Although one of the first men to know his ancestry back to Devonian days, he did not know where he came from. The man from nowhere was inventing a somewhere. He was pushing down ersatz roots. Hodeslea – 'temp. Henry IV' – was a last-minute legitimation, even though he could trace no farther back than his innkeeping grandfather. Nettie was no different. She knew now that she was illegitimate and was scouring the imperial fringes for her forebears. With Lizzie's son sailing to the Caribbean, she asked him to make enquiries about her mother, 'a Miss Thomas', born in Antigua, and her grandmother, three times married in the colony.[28]

People wanted to know about Huxley. But he had to be 'bothered . . . out of my life' before he would supply the most perfunctory autobiography to accompany a published portrait. And then the few pages were curiously truncated – as lamentably short-breathed as Spencer's was laughably long-winded. What passed as an autobiography was a pastiche of anecdotes and smokescreens through which he remained invisible. Nothing was given away. He felt like Dr Johnson, ready 'to take Boswell's life' on hearing of any biography. The autobiography fizzled out even before Darwin's début. The pages were published without his knowledge in an obscure 'who's who' and reprinted in the Normal School's own magazine, greedy for crumbs from the Dean's table.[29] But the students were none the wiser.

'Agnosticism' had pushed the *Nineteenth Century* through four editions. Everyone had been reading it: at Windsor Castle M'Ladies had been astonished, and Knowles goaded Huxley to lash the bishops and get Wace into the 'witness-box' again to convict himself on 'all that herd of swine' stuff. And so 'Agnosticism: A Rejoinder' was set going in February. Knowles rubbed his hands. Others saw what was happening. Hooker wasn't alone in his dismal view of 'Editors, who feed like maggots on controversial articles'. The confrontations were stage-managed. Knowles even hung pictures of his participants on the wall, and now added a new sketch of Huxley bought at Christie's. Given a lull in the fighting, he would drop in Mrs Humphry Ward's article on the 'New Reformation', using Len's sister-in-law (herself under a cloud at the Church Congress for her loss-of-faith novel *Robert Elsmere*) to start a second front. The frisson increased his circulation. And Huxley loved every moment. 'You can't think how I enjoy writing now'. One last 'little shove to the "New Reformation" ' and 'I shall think the fag-end of my life well spent'.[30]

It was a case of consecutive articles and marriages. In the buoyant mood he sailed through Nettie's wedding on Shrove Tuesday, 5 March. It was the last time they would see Marlborough Place decked out in palms and flowers. Nettie, tall and gangly, wafted down the aisle waving her bouquet, looking, a friend said, 'like some handsome giraffe'. The wedding gifts were laid out in the front room, and with the rising crime rate in the Depression they were watched over by a detective.[31] With 200 guests, it doubled as a farewell party for their London friends. The next day Huxley 'bolted' back to Eastbourne to finish his 'Rejoinder'.

Knowles had it four days later, and his £44 cheque paid the wedding bills. To his joy he found it more 'A Rejoinder' and less 'Agnosticism'. Huxley was now camped so securely in the first century – making Christ's Nazarene sect so many more 'infidels' – that it was doubtful if he would ever escape back to the real world of Devonian swamps. Christ no Christian! 'The Church founded by Jesus . . . became extinct in the country of its birth'! No wonder the April *Nineteenth Century* shot through two editions in days. Biblical criticism became Huxley's *cheval de bataille*, revealing him for the old stump orator he was. The Pauline religion which 'coalesced with the State in the 4th century . . . is Alexandrian Judaism and Neoplatonic mystigogy', mixed with 'much of the old idolatry', and its success owed little to 'the truth or falsity of the story of Jesus'. By now Huxley, the pure popularizer, was muscling in on the assyriologists' work – using it to pound the historical authority of a rival profession. He was exploiting esoteric German sources to score points against Wace and Gladstone. His was still a Manichaean world of 'us' and 'them', and on the question of who was 'to have the confidence of the general public',[32] the *arriviste* agnostic made sure it was 'us'.

Knowles dubbed it Huxley's 'Gospel of Common Sense'. But it wasn't a gospel. There were no rival articles of faith; nothing on that holy trinity of scientific naturalism: physical causation, the uniform order of nature, and an objective world. And wisely so, given his pitch to the public. For Huxley had the same faith that 'order is lord of all' that Wace had in Our Lord as the cause of order. It was simply an axiom underpinning his deconsecrated cosmos. It 'cannot be proved', as he knew, even if deductions from it 'are always verified by experience', and so his onus remained on discrediting witnesses who claimed to find any miraculous deviation. But Knowles was right in using Huxley's favourite term, 'Common Sense'. This was how he struck the gadget-marvelling Victorian public. He made them feel that 'the whole edifice of practical life is built upon our faith' in an unbroken chain of causation.[33]

There were fewer clergy to face now. With no chance of passing the Deceased Wife's Sister Bill – and the English 'fanatics' getting even 'the Swiss Gov. to forbid such marriages' – Jack and Ethel sailed to Norway on 29 March to marry. A frail Nettie was unhappy at not making the North Sea crossing, but Hal, who sailed with them to Christiania, thought it 'quite unfitting for her to go'. He got back to watch Joe Chamberlain fight the 'bigotry & opposition' against this 'much needed social reform'.[34] Huxley put pressure on the Liberal Unionist Lord Hartington to get Lord Salisbury to allow a free vote, but the Bill was defeated on 9 May.

With his fourth article in five months the critical response began to pall. 'Agnosticism and Christianity' appeared in June's *Nineteenth Century*. Leslie Stephen had alerted him to one of Newman's old Tracts, and the Cardinal's denial that 'evidence [was] the test of [religious] truth' served to hang every ecclesiastical iniquity. But the relentless impeachment of faith was wearing thin. Hooker really thought 'you have exhausted the subject, & completely vindicated our position'. Tyndall saw him 'hacking a dead horse'. The high-flyers of the fifties had become the old fogies of the eighties. Gone were the glory days of Darwin and Lyell, Colenso and *Essays*, when the miraculous base of the powerful State Church was eroded by radical Nonconformists, when the boom economy allowed new professionals the luxury of looking for a New Reformation. The interminable Depression had coincided with a specialist age, as young Gradgrind scientists put their heads down and looked to their pay packets. 'They shut their eyes to the obstacles which clericalism raises', Huxley moaned.[35] They were not following him.

Huxley's age was passing: the Dissenters' meritocracy was yesterday's victory. In the gloomy Depression many who had sought scientific redemption turned to the new politics, to socialism, suffrage, the New Woman. Those 'dirty Radicals', Hooker seethed to Tyndall. 'It makes one weary of life to see the spread of democracy and socialism'. The world was sweeping past the old cronies. Socialism was questioning the Malthusian core of Darwin's eternally struggling Nature. Technology at its finest hour, as the great boring machines worked under the sea (the Channel Tunnel was already a mile long), was failing to feed the masses.

The literati were getting blasé about Huxley's onslaughts. The new *Review of Reviews* abstracted his explanation of Biblical miracles in one word: 'lies'.[36] He was stymied by his own success. He had made doubting a middle-class virtue. Even as he denounced sweeping devils into the Gadarene swine as a violation of Victorian property rights, he was being cited as a 'well-behaved blasphemer' by MPs trying to extend legal protection to non-Christian faiths after Lord Coleridge's judgment.[37]

A divisive politics was even shaking Huxley's social group. The X-Club was 'almost in xtremis'. Two or three would struggle in to St George's Hotel, down the road from the Royal Institution; sometimes Hooker would 'sit-alone at table'. Hirst, 'shrunk to a skeleton', hardly presented a corporeal presence.[38] But the old rogues would still clash tusks over politics. By November the ivory giants, Spencer and Huxley, were locked in their death-throes. The sexagenarians were fractious, sensitive to the slightest lapse of protocol (Huxley even stopped reading Spencer's proof 'Autobiography' in October after it arrived second-hand from a daughter of one of Spencer's friends!). High dudgeon became high drama in November as Huxley waded into a *Times* dispute over land socialism with a series of letters which cuffed Spencer's *a priorism* in politics and science. They made Spencer 'treat cholera by deductions from physiological principles'. A smarting Spencer took it as a public slap, thinking that Huxley was 'making me look like a fool to a hundred thousand readers'.[39] An extremist age had simply exposed the political gulf. The two old friends had diverged. From a common reaction to a strangling Church monopoly, Spencer had gone on to make his Nonconformist fair-competition ethic a total government hands-off call: no State favouritism, no State spending, no endowments, whether of Church or Science. But Huxley the government scientist, the State Commissioner, clawing professional power, wanted a State-paid education, a 'ha'pny' on the rates for libraries, spending on science, on schools, on the modern State Secretariat.

It 'abruptly ended' a 35-year friendship. Spencer's letter of resignation from the X sent the others into a spin. Intellectually ponderous, he was unequal to his nimble antagonist, and Hooker thought it incumbent on Huxley to say something 'soothing'. Spencer was a sensitive anachronism in a growing social democracy. Do not further 'aid in his downfall', they pleaded. Be 'merciful as you are strong'.[40]

But Huxley wondered how he had put up for so long with that boorish 'long winded . . . pedant', who had 'about as much tact as a hippopotamus'.[41] He, of course, was tact itself.

Knowles wormed his way in, sniffing controversial carrion. Already in November he had convinced Huxley to follow up his *Times* letters on the 'New Radicalism', upping the ante to £3 a page. It led to a set of essays that had Huxley applying the brake to socialism's demands. Henry George's land-nationalizing *Progress and Poverty* 'has had an *immense* effect', agreed Knowles, and Huxley could see no 'more damneder nonsense'.

George's *Progress* was an attack on property, competition and Malthus: the whole Darwinian establishment. It was being touted by none other than Alfred Russel Wallace, the co-inventor of natural selection, now a pensioner living in Dorset. Wallace was an outsider to the end. A renegade on Human Darwinism, he remained true to socialism and spiritualism, which he used to redress the political balance. To him they were all of a piece: the spirit powers made economic competition redundant by guiding society. He even saw the economically free woman as the way ahead, the sexual selector, the chooser, not the feeble chosen of Darwin's *Descent of Man*. Wallace had always been interested in the political goal of human existence. Ever the propagandist, he had posted Huxley books (the latest was Arthur Bell's *Why Does Man Exist?*). Though never daunted by Darwin, he had 'never got over a feeling of awe for Huxley'. Now the outsider was in Huxley's sights – or rather his egalitarian ideal.

This was the world to play for. Huxley's manuscript, said Knowles, receiving it on 13 December, 'makes a final end . . . of the tom-foolery'. But the title, 'Rousseau & rousseauism'! Knowles saw his profits dribbling away, and since 'I especially want working men to read the paper' he turned it into a blatant 'On the Natural Inequality of Men'.[42] There was no disguising their intent.

Never once was *Progress and Poverty* mentioned, but he made it fall with 'Rousseau's blether'. Huxley set into noble savagery, ancient communes, free-born men and dreams of primeval equality. Rousseau *was* George, a 'stalking horse' for the revolutionized masses maddened by hunger, the dreamer who 'clothed passion in the garb of philosophy' and would end injustice by the 'perpetration of further injustice'. Huxley's 'savage' was a slave to inheritance and circumstance, a gritty survivor in a primevally privatized world, never the egalitarian of Wallace's 'land socialists' or Kropotkin's 'primitive communism'. Society had to be ruled by 'sound judgment', not the 'despotism of a majority'. The 'cook and the loblolly boys' could no more countermand the Captain's orders on a man-o'-war than the ship of state – and so saying Huxley echoed the top brass which had damned his own shipmates' demands 45 years earlier. He was accused by the Left of latter-day hero-worshipping,[43] but Huxley really had in mind a latter-day Benthamism: rule by a technical elite.

The phrase 'Social Darwinism' was just coming into use – first in France, whence it spread to England (the French translated 'The Natural Inequality of Men' specifically to meet their own labour unrest).[44] Until this time 'Darwinism' had subsumed the social dimension; the Darwinians had never doubted that animals and society were to be explained in the same biological terms. Huxley was ripe for translation as the expanding Continental industries tried to pacify their own labour forces; his papers had honed the political edge of Darwinism – and 'Social Darwinism' carried a new anti-socialist intent.

For him overpopulation was the serpent in the Socialist Eden. For a Darwinian, the unprecedentedly high growth rates of the 1870s[45] confirmed the Malthusian prediction. Peace and plenty in a socialist arcadia would only increase the number of births and start the struggle for resources all over again. Huxley had no faith that even a 'despotic government' could control population by a eugenics programme. (Nor would it be desirable: coming from a family having its share of failures, he knew how minuscule a change could turn the 'unfit' into successes.)[46] Birth control with its threat to chastity was no option. Yet it was becoming one for the younger generation, even for his own civic-reforming pupils. Patrick Geddes, a maverick professor who looked like a Greek Orthodox bishop, had become Besant's friend and Kropotkin's host, and he was considering it in *The Evolution of Sex*.[47] Ultimately Huxley, like Darwin before him, was asserting mid-Victorian, male-governing, family values.

Knowles was engineering events furiously. He was running Kropotkin's papers on co-operation in animal communities, and urging them on Huxley as the most uplifting articles on Nature that he had ever read. Then he had Spencer fire salvoes from the other side. Spencer's own elephant's memory went back two decades to Huxley's attack in 'Administrative Nihilism'. Relations were at a low ebb now; 'for a man who goes whining about that I have killed him', noted Huxley, Spencer could still summon up an 'allowance of spite'.[48] Too many years of benign indifference towards Spencer's epistemological shortcomings turned to contempt for his *a priori* ethics and politics.

Others saw the futility of the two men bickering when the nation 'seems ready to thrust itself into the arms of the Socialist'. Huxley's politics were unmasked now. Some asked his views on socialism, or the Southampton dock strike. Others didn't any more. For them his materialistic science remained a potent force, spreading 'the common particles of Light', but it was becoming 'a gigantic Mrs. Pardiggle . . . assuming the airs of a social censor'. Malthus and Darwin had canonized the struggle for resources, restraining the altruists who would wade into the 'social swamp' to save the drowning. But this uncharitable Malthusianism was under attack; Darwin was under attack. Huxley, having struggled himself to accept Darwin's desperate Malthusianism, ironically found himself under attack. His own Darwinian diktat had the Left grieving 'that the religion of Science, hailed by all of us as the birth of a new day, is fossilising already into a religion of despair'. What 'sadder sight' than

> Professor Huxley fighting for the *status quo* in Politics . . . the man who argues in favour of Force as a proof of ownership, and of a statute of limitations in matters of secular wrongdoing, will one day have to cast in his lot with Ecclesiasticism and the Bishops . . . for Church and State stand or fall together.[49]

The glint of truth shone from those menacing words. The professionals were defending their hard-won stake in society. Had the rioters peered through the smashed windows of the Pall Mall clubs, they would have seen the liberal scientists hobnobbing with the liberal clergy.

Deep in the 'Class *v.* Mass' debate, Huxley was revealing the politics that lay behind his supposedly 'neutral' science. Knowles cleverly corralled him with the 'Classes'. The editor ignored the response of the Social Democratic Federation's Henry Hyndman, a former City gent converted by Marx's *Kapital*, and a 'poor fool' in his view; he ran instead a poorer fool's reply – a pastry-cook's. Huxley had dared to damn land nationalization in the people's interest, dared to speak 'for them, of them, and at them'. Huxley and 'his bosom friend the Duke of Argyll' were simply 'too high up in the social scale' to see why 'millions of thoughtful working men' saw hope in Henry George's doctrine of the 'natural rights of man'. From the jam-puff shop he was just another of the 'dukes, earls, professors, ministers, lawyers, soldiers' who 'produce next to nothing' and yet 'are all well housed, clothed, and fed'.

Huxley was horrified. Knowles had printed the pastry-maker's 'passionate prejudices' to expose the 'mind of his masses'. But impassioned prejudice could look like a passionate plea. 'It is very easy for well-fed dukes and professors to philosophise', seethed the cook. Just give them

> 20*s*. per week of sixty or seventy hours' hard labour, and give them a wife and four or five children to provide for out of this magnificent income. Just give them five years of this life – as a very interesting experiment, you know

and when they are screaming for justice quote them Huxley's high-sounding words. The scientist had 'got out of his groove in taking up politics'. Pleas from the gut always touched Huxley. Now an extremist age had marked him as the oppressor whose highfalutin tongue justified 'bâtons, bayonets, bullets, and battering rams to keep the power to rob'.[50] Knowles had turned the tables, throwing a bolshy cook into the plush-leather heart of the Establishment to draw *Huxley* out.

Wasn't he the popular champion, wafting away priestly hobgoblins, levelling the vaunted aristocracy, twitting the bishops, welcoming a secular State? The workers did not realize that he was clearing a professional space, making a middle-class revolution. False expectations led to fierce denunciations: from the anarchists' *Commonweal*, which saw equality and suffrage, 'the Professor's bugbears', as the driving 'forces in the evolution of modern society', to 'the servant gal's' *Daily Telegraph*, where Henry George's friends berated him as the 'specialist transformed into the dilettante'.[51] Sitting at Beachy Head, the old chap in the shaggy wool coat watched society drift past with equanimity.

Another blast, 'Natural Rights and Political Rights', would blow the misty vapours from 'men's eyes – even the "Socialists"', said Knowles. Huxley was left defending the 'might and right' of an amoral Darwinian nature to undermine the dream. But the more he stressed inequality and struggle, the more he had to salvage human ethics. It was the relentless pressure of socialism with its assumption about *natural* rights that made him drive the wedge deeper between

Darwin's 'ceaseless and pitiless' civil war, as the *natural* state of things, and the civilized curbing of these 'anti-social and anarchic tendencies'. By 1890 a bloody Darwinism and buffeting socialism had pushed him into the ethical realm. No longer could a cut-throat Nature provide the rules of ethical conduct. He was still intent on stabilizing society, but Nature would henceforth play a vastly different role in his lay sermons. The question became how far *moral* rights should infringe on a natural 'unmitigated selfishness'.[52]

Huxley could not even sail off to Madeira in early April without revises of 'Government: Anarchy or Regimentation' chasing him to Plymouth. The trip was to give 25-year-old Harry a holiday in the sun before he started in medical practice. It was a far cry from 1846 when bishops blessed creaking wooden ships and Anglicans ruled the waves. In Plymouth the latest shrine to science was suitably hewn from Devonian coral limestone. He paid a visit to the new Marine Station on Citadel Hill, with its labs and aquariums, his last as President of the Marine Biological Association.[53]

Luxury liners were also a far cry from donkey frigates. But Hal could show his son up on the four-day run: 'head wind all the way', he reported home, 'and enough rolling to make Harry take to his berth'. No swabbing decks, no sick-room muster, but deckchairs and sea air, and the luxury of poring over botany books and putting the finishing licks to his paper. On deck he tore at both Spencer's deregulation – no taxes, no State aid, no State education – and socialism's 'despotism of the "general will"'.[54] So what was *his* solution to social regeneration, critics asked. It was the sum of all he had stood for: an open, competitive meritocracy, overseen by a strong progressive government counselled by experts. His technocracy was Chamberlain's, the stuff of public libraries, compulsory education, Council water and lighting. Perhaps it was the way of the future, between the extremes.

The beginning and end of life were spent sailing from political turmoil. Now a queasy son joined him at the rails as the ship steamed into Funchal on 3 May. 'The last time I saw the place was in December 1846. All my life lies between the two visits. I was then $21\frac{1}{4}$ & I shall be 65 tomorrow'. The sleepy town was a bit bigger now, with a few English villas dotting the hills. Otherwise half a century hardly told. Wheeled carriages were still unknown, and the daily pace was dictated by the plodding oxen. It was a last nostalgic look back. The memory gave him a sprightly air. The 65-year-old proved it on his cob mare, as he took Harry for a five-hour

> ride up to the Great Curral . . . – about 10 miles . . . & 3500f^{t}. up. We started at 11. the weather looking very doubtful and heavy clouds overhanging the mountain top. We passed the little Curral up to which I, and a party of mad middies rode 44 years ago – (I wonder we did not all break our necks) and then rode on & on, through fine forests.

The staid Harry already had the makings of a 'worthy but dull' doctor. By comparison Huxley felt 'the youngest man of the family'. 'When you & I were five and twenty, my pet, there was a sort of go in both of us', he wrote to Nettie, 'which I do not observe in any of our children'. Harry was no mad middy, but he had the Huxley independence. The casual mention of his engagement to a nurse before he left elicited his father's wry promise 'to be the young lady's slave . . . By the way, you might mention her name; it is a miserable detail, I know, but would be interesting'. This last fling took them both over breakneck passes. Harry, seeing his father's burnt sienna face and flashing eye, must have sensed his exotic past. Atop the volcanic crater with its deep ravines a puff of 'wind cleared the clouds away and the whole basin . . . – the bottom 1500 f^{t}. below us & the top of its great wall 2000 f^{t}. above us – was revealed. It was a wonderful sight'.[55] A religious scene of subtropical splendour: Huxley had the 21-year-old's fire in his belly again.

The zest showed in his 'itch to be fighting'. That was 'always a safe & good sign', agreed Knowles. The cold warrior returned to trot out more £70 articles. The editor kept putting up 'targets', showing how routine the pot-shots were becoming, making him a mill for cranking out controversy. How about that shocker in the *Essays and Reviews* mould, *Lux Mundi*? Here was a collection by Church progressives who treated miraculous Floods and Daily Creations as allegorical. Revd Aubrey Moore, the Oxford Reformation historian and fearless Darwinian, was among them. He could happily follow Huxley in tracing our image of Creation to Milton's poetry. Moore's God worked within Darwin's nature. But for Huxley, at the end of his life, the real issue was the critical approach to sacred texts. That is what made the 'antagonism between Science & Theology' so complete.[56] The *Lux Mundi* progressives had 'distilled away every inconvenient matter', wafted aside the salty 'transubstantiation' of Lot's Wife, dismissed Jonah's 'submarine navigation', made the Deluge a bogey used by Jesus as a moral tale, and yet they 'continue to pay divine honours to the residue'.[57]

Huxley stiffened with every year of controversy. Even his last-ditch Unitarian belief – that Jesus' personality had been cause of Christianity's departure from Judaism – melted away. Christ's Nazarenes were just another unoriginal Jewish sect.[58] Huxley's hardening showed as he started funding secular societies. He put money into the ailing *Agnostic Journal* to keep it afloat. (Given his standoffish nature, the editors were 'surprised to notice how accurate was his knowledge of the work we belligerent Agnostics were carrying on'.) And he was projecting a 'strict secularity in State education' – no more Bibles.[59] He was harder, cynical still, and older by far. That is how Jack Collier painted him in 1890, as a subject fitting his own anti-clerical themes, to be followed appropriately by his painting of 'The Inquisition: Waiting for the Accused'.

He was an old Ironsides – the solid Puritan with a 'military bearing', wanting only the clunking metal. There was no need to run his pike through *Lux Mundi*; Canon Liddon in his fine 'silvery voice' did the job at St Paul's, insisting that Jesus wasn't 'accommodating' himself to a rude age. The 'trustworthiness of the Old Testament is', insisted Liddon, 'inseparable from the trustworthiness of our Lord Jesus Christ'. Huxley liked self-immolating deductions. It was his warrant to turn Noah's Flood into a 'Bowdlerised version' of an older Babylonian fable and hang Christian theology. It was slick and sensible and it caused as much fright as popping a balloon: and yet '30 years ago no decent magazine would have dared to publish such articles'. By now a scientific world-view had become the *de rigueur* perception for all things. He was a victim of his own success. One acolyte saw him as the 'High Priest of the New Religion' whose sermons grew slicker and more predictable by the day.[60] 'The Lights of the Church and the Lights of Science' passed without a stir in July's *Nineteenth Century*.

The decadent nineties hardly noticed. The new Hedonism was already flushing out his old Puritanism. Society was lost in *fin de siècle* abandonment. People wanted fun. Freak and perversity were the order of the day. Oscar Wilde was outraging London. Beardsley returned the exotic to Art. The Gadarene devil reappeared in *The Picture of Dorian Gray*; and, said Dorian in his topper, 'Life is a great disappointment'.[61] Nothing shocked the Upper Classes.

But old men are serious and this one wandered off to Stonehenge. He stood alone, between the megaliths on a wind-swept Salisbury Plain, far from any gaiety. Perhaps he was thinking of his deep ancestry, of a distant migration of peoples from the East. He was striking out in a last ethnological paper. With the young Oxbridge anthropologists disappointingly looking on anthropology as a background to the Classics, Huxley held to a multi-factored evolutionary method. He drew wide – prehistoric climates and archaeology, ethnology and philology, Ice Age glacial boundaries and Mediterranean changes – to pinpoint the cradle of the Aryans just west of the Urals.[62] Like a giant Gulliver, he watched swarms of men, the ants of neolithic history, migrating, diverging in peripheral pockets, evolving proto-languages, discovering copper. The detail blurred into his profoundly secular image of the immense human journey since the emergence of Europe's beetle-browed Neanderthals (then definitely known, from two skeletons found in Belgium in 1886, to be palaeolithic hunters of extinct mammoths).

He had an evolutionary belief that other modes of thought – like older forms of life – had existed in the past and persist as living fossils into the present. His positivist justification for wiping out these religious relics – born of Dissent's mid-century campaign against entrenched Anglican power – made prehistory more an ammunition dump to be mined than the basis for a proper sociology of religion.[63]

Knowles called him 'one of my chiefest pillars', and considering that his *Nineteenth Century* stable ran from Oscar Wilde to Bram Stoker, and Gladstone to Kropotkin, that was saying something. Seven articles in 1890 gave Huxley £500 to plough into his Eastbourne garden. He poured it into levelling land, building conservatories and paths, and planting shrubs from Kew. The house was planned with the large rooms at the back looking onto the South Downs, and with an attic playroom for Joyce. Nettie scooted around in a bath chair choosing tiles and placing electric 'burners', tickled by the novelty of the new touch-of-a-switch lighting. But the delays in finishing: 'fitters, paperers, and polishers are like bugs or cockroaches, you may easily get 'em in, but getting 'em out is the deuce'. The couple had to live out of suitcases in the Grand Hotel until November. Hal swore that this was his last move, 'except to a still smaller residence of a subterranean character!'[64]

London was no place any more. The city had lost its sobriety and charm and honesty; it was a city in search of the bizarre and exotic, its dandy shallowness a reaction to two decades of staid Puritanism. It were better to be in Eastbourne. Leaving Marlborough Place distanced them further from the Mady tragedy. It would still break Nettie's heart: 'every room is brim full of memories', of daughters and sons traipsing off to school, Hal coming home full of news, Mr Darwin popping around on Sunday morning. That world was gone. And its finality was confirmed at Christmas when sister Ellen and George's widow Polly died within days of one another. Naturally, the 'details were ghastly', the one scrounging money to die drunk, the other 'morbidly hysterical' and reeking of drugs.[65] But that cut the millstones from Hal's neck, the financial weight and worry dropped and he sprang back.

Death brought a clarity to times past. The Puritan's cosmos was blackening as sun after sun went cold. The endless losses, 'One feels them awfully on wakening every morning', said Hooker. And as Hal stood over the grave of Ellen Busk, his Egyptian priestess, the loss was 'grievously painful'.[66]

Gladstone's accusatory finger in *The Impregnable Rock of Holy Scripture* had Huxley making a rival gesture. He relished the G.O.M.'s 'rough coming on'. He was morose without a crusade, and delivered thanks to Providence for sending Gladstone to keep ''ome 'appy for me'. Again he would rubbish Gladstone's first-century beliefs – delivering theological right hooks and political lefts. Gladstone was being 'spread eagled' as much for his Irish politics; he sensed it, he saw his character being 'besmirched'. Tyndall's cheers accompanied the pounding of the Home Ruler. '*Hit this man*', he shouted from the ringside, seeing each punch lead to his political weakening.[67] And so it was Gadarene pigs again, or rather a Galilean foreigner's legality in sending them over a cliff (which was justified by Gladstone). Huxley made it a comment on the Home Ruler's cavalier attitude to the law of the land.

Huxley was a heathen foreigner himself in Eastbourne and the nosey locals kept an eye on him. The Professor had arrived fighting the greatest statesman of the century. This was the gossipy sticks, not the anonymous metropolis, and the *Sussex Daily News*, having witnessed the unholy onslaughts on Noah and Jonah, was reassured to see Huxley's daughters in church. Still the yokels thought these Grand Old Men could be better occupied than fighting over swine.

But Huxley could not 'give up tormenting ces drôles'.[68]

10

Combating the Cosmos

OF COURSE THE HATE MAIL started arriving. He was 'the Infidel and enemy of mankind' whose depraved writings 'are of the devil'.[1] And the Salvation Army was marching out to meet him.

The Army was led by another General. 'General' Booth's Army had a massive military field structure by 1890, with 9,400 officers commanding 1,375 corps and three-quarters of a million recruits. Having spent his later life studying the origins of sects, Huxley found one springing up under his nose: 'a new Ranter-Socialist sect', whose spine-tingling trombone parades and hymn-singing corybantism was so much 'sanctified buffoonery'. The two autocratic Generals, sharing so much and so little, prepared to do battle for the imperial spoils of the hinterland, the souls of the dispossessed. Their armies stood poised, their rival flags of Spiritual Democracy and Technocratic Professionalism fluttering, the one with its street carnivals, the other with its Darwinian promises. It was horribly uneven, for 'not even a Salvation Army of Huxleys' could stop the simpletons singing along with Booth.[2]

General Booth was four years younger. When Tom was in his back-street anatomy school run by that democratic New Connexion Methodist Marshall Hall, the working-class Booth was living up to Hall's democratic 'Methodist Jacobinism'; he too had joined the New Connexion; he too was a Chartist supporter. Like Tom, the evangelist was a prey to despondency and sought regeneration in a crusade. His Methodists denied the Anglicans' providentially happy world teeming with 'delighted existence'; for them, 'the whole creation travaileth and groaneth'. In his war cry, *Darkest England*, Booth could speak with Darwinian vigour of the weakest going 'to the wall'. But he was another whose radical religious duty was to aid this suffering creation. *In Darkest England and the Way Out* was an affirmation that all life could be redeemed. Booth's image of a tormented Creation was little different from Huxley's. But he demanded something more than Darwin's struggle and Huxley's Calvinist resignation. The fittest were not the Elect. For Booth, 'Everybody might be saved'.[3]

Booth had begun his East End social work in the 1860s as Huxley (20 years out of Rotherhithe himself) was preaching scientific salvation. And as Huxley had shouldered his rifle in the Volunteers, so this mobilization became Booth's inspiration, and he renamed his mission the 'Salvation Army'. This other shilling sergeant recruited to the razzmatazz of military bands. With mass unemployment and the socialists marching, Booth's Jacobinism emerged as 'social salvationism'. Day centres and hospices were set up. Hand-outs to striking dockers' families gained socialist sympathy. Shelters for battered women brought suffragette approval. (*Darkest England* even envisaged vigilantes to hunt rapists and force them to pay maintenance.)[4] The East End's no-go ghettos were 'as unexplored as Timbuctoo'. But the Army's revivalism was a sort of 'moral coca', giving it the strength to march into *Darkest England* as Stanley had penetrated 'Darkest Africa'. Had this been an educational or sanitational reclamation Huxley would have cheered – but he saw it as a soul-saving militia parading with socialist regimentation, and he was horrified.

In Darkest England was published on 20 October 1890. Booth's name was on the title-page, but many doubted his primary authorship. Beside him stood the former *Pall Mall Gazette* editor with the literary know-how, W. T. Stead – the founder of the *Review of Reviews* (which had infuriated Huxley by abstracting his articles on miracles under the rubric 'lies'). Stead the spiritualist stood on the other side of 'a gulf'. The 'filthy ex-convict' was loathed by Knowles for dealing in 'stolen goods', pirated abstracts in his *Review*. *Darkest England*, Knowles tipped off Huxley, 'was written & boomed by that most accursed of all Iscariots'. His 'hoof-prints are on every page'. Certainly two days after publication Stead had sent Huxley a copy, explaining that he 'had some hand in licking it into shape'.[5] Whatever the truth, Knowles cranked up the antagonism, adding a literary dimension to the political and religious friction.

Booth's campaign plan was to feed and reclaim the under-class in 'City Colonies', send them to the depopulated countryside for moral and agricultural training, and finally – under the influence of Stead's social imperialism – ship them out to the real colonies (and hadn't Huxley on the *Rattlesnake* seen the potential for new Indian empires started by the hungry millions from home?)[6] The scheme, said a rival missionary, was 'sensational through its very *audacity*'. Talk of shuffling off the rioting hordes made the book a huge seller. Its publication coincided with two months of the worst weather anyone could remember. Huxley's pipes froze, and the cold, angry jobless frightened his middle-class constituency. *Darkest England*'s promise of deliverance ensured that the funds flowed in; £750,000 found their way into the General's military chest. Riots and strikes threatened the well-to-do, who turned against the means-testing miserliness of the existing Charity Organisation Society, with its targeting of the deserving poor.[7] More and more went over to the Army.

A philanthropic Mrs Crawshaw was set to buy her place in heaven by popping £1,000 into Booth's account. But she asked Huxley to vet the scheme first, and thereby triggered the chain of events. The lack of safeguards for Booth's projected Poor Man's Bank were not what really frightened Huxley when he started digging. It was the scale of its 'socialist' organization. Beneath this cymbal-bashing 'corybantic Christianity' was a regimentation of enthusiasts 'pledged to blind and unhesitating obedience'. He cynically imagined a runaway machine, powered by 'unchastened religious fanaticism', drawing on slush funds and using 'Sicilian Mafia' tactics. The nightmare scenario culminated in evangelical socialist cadres 'with barracks in every town' threatening the liberal State itself. He told Jack Collier that

> The ultimate object of their plots is the establishment of a sort of Methodist Jacobin club with vigilance committees, under the name of 'Salvation Army corps' scattered all over the country. Decent men would not be able to call their souls their own if the plot succeeded – and Stead would have his Laboratories for Experimental investigation of the possibilities of Rapes all over the country.[8]

Why this extreme reaction? Was it because the tables had been turned: the ascetic scientist had been outmanoeuvred by a worldly salvationist? Whistle-blowing pamphlets encouraged the paranoia. Even some rival missionaries denounced Booth's 'dangerous autocracy'. Army watching became a national pastime, but then the uniforms were so visible on the streets. Continual scuffles in Huxley's own seaside town of Eastbourne between Salvationists and goading youths made the daily papers and led to calls for bans on Army marches (the *Eastbourne Gazette* spotted Huxley on the edge of a crowd watching one brawl). Even the socialists eyed the Salvationists warily. Booth, rather than saving the deserving paupers in the pool, like the charities committed to the free market, or fishing out the activists, as the socialists were doing, would share his resources with the 'dregs' at the very bottom.[9] It smacked of primitive Christian communism.

Years of political bickering had affected Huxley. He had seen the newly created London County Council fall to 'Radicals and Socialists', heard the curdling yells against the 'robber knights of capital' and 'brigand aristocracy of the Stock Exchange'. Socialism was evocative, and it was moving the masses. His fears heightened with trade-unionist hopes that Booth's 'autocratic Socialism' would eventually lose its '"fantastic" religious skin' to leave a standing Red Army. Already the socialists were emulating Booth by setting up their rival 'Labour Army' and heralding a quasi-religious new dawn to rival Christianity's. But Huxley's was a bizarre nightmare: it had Booth centralizing power, controlling the press and floating his own bank to process the millions and finance his militias. Letters from disaffected Army lieutenants told of vigilantes. The highest-ranking defector, a Major, Booth's private secretary, exposed the cashiering practices of the Chiefs of Staff. But only Huxley saw the Red menace. To the end he was telling Hooker that 'the Papistical & Socialistic schemers who were rubbing their hands in the hope of profiting by his mad project & the "Army" organization, are sold'.[10]

He sent a stream of letters to the *Times* on the Army in December. It was no good telling him to 'neglect it & so give it the best chance of an earlier death', as Knowles tried. Knowles refused to dignify that 'blackguard Stead's last swindle' by printing a rebuttal. So Huxley took up the street technique; he turned the letters into a shilling pamphlet. These could be shifted in huge numbers at these evangelical moments. Macmillan had 2,000 out by January 1891, with a second edition in February. And in reply came the 'heaps of abusive letters'. 'I have not been so well abused for an age', Huxley claimed, revelling in it. 'It's quite like old times'.[11]

The Darwinian 'workhouse' solution was to help the deserving fight their own way out. Do not herd the moral sheep into Booth's 'narrow theological' pen, pleaded Huxley: 'self-respect and thrift are the rungs of the ladder by which men may most surely climb out of the slough of despond'.[12] Liberalism had been hardened on the Darwinian proving ground.

But through the crises a more sympathetic explanation of the hovel-dwellers was growing. The poor were not moral cretins, not atavists by 'nature'; in the socialists' view they were stunted by their 'nurture'. They were deprived rather than depraved. The State had to better their squalid conditions, lest the whole race 'degenerate'. Others thought that the race would degenerate if the slum-dwellers *were* cosseted in an egalitarian society. There was the apocalyptic backdrop to the *fin de siècle*. Huxley had emphasized the 'persistence' of life – how a living Mesozoic world might survive in the unchanging oceanic depths. But as the decadent art of Beardsley and Oscar Wilde shocked and Lankester saw stagnation as the fate awaiting a society that failed the industrial race, another pupil raised on Huxley's proving ground projected a different collapse. The leisured classes would degenerate into effete Eloi, taking to 'art and eroticism . . . languor and decay', to be bred in herds and devoured by the troglodyte masses.[13] H. G. Wells – having absorbed Huxley's message of a hostile universe honing mankind – had begun his book in Huxley's nemesis year, 1887. It would become *The Time Machine*. Science fiction was coloured by Huxley's pessimism.

By now Nettie was begging him 'to give up controversy'. But to no avail, and March 1891 found him settling 'accounts with that little cad of a duke & the G.O.M.' In the *Nineteenth Century* he was still running rings around Gladstone as he had once Owen, with that facetious glee in the face of grave absurdity. Policing the intellect, he called it. He was now carving ideological weapons from the esoteric work of the assyriologists. He used the Babylonian myths of a flood and half-mile-long ark to discredit the Biblical plagiarism. Gladstone 'you will find like a dead dog with a stone tied to his neck in March number of XIX', he alerted Hooker. And then he declared himself 'as sick of controversy as a confectioners boy of tarts'. Lord Armstrong did not believe it for a minute. He knew that this intellectual Gordon would '"die happy" on the field of literary battles'.[14]

The 74-year-old secularist George Holyoake watched Huxley's five-year 'duel with Gladstone, Wace and the Duke of Argyll', staggered at the impunity of it – the way Huxley made Christianity just another regional religion, with a largely borrowed mythological base. What was atheist fanaticism in the 1840s had become mainstream pulp by the 1890s. Holyoake had been jailed 50 years earlier (to deny God then was treasonous in an Anglican State). Now working-class political weaponry had become middle-class professional ideology, and he gave up editing the *Reasoner* 'because his views were abundantly advocated in the most respectable Quarterlies'. There was no incarceration for Huxley. Science, the professions and suffrage had etched away so many Anglican-State standards that pious blasphemers were now patted. Hence his gall in telling Holyoake that this fighting was 'hard upon a poor man who has retired to "make his sowl" as the Irish say, in the sea side hermitage'.[15]

His 'sowl' had all the security of home life. Nothing was allowed to disturb it. Privacy meant keeping out the searching spotlights. And with his refusal to expose himself in an autobiography or be featured in the *World*'s 'Celebrities at Home' spot, it was maintained.[16]

Large Victorian families were always edged by grief. The Huxleys were reminded of Mady every day. The fair-haired Joyce was her spitting image. The seven-year-old spent six months of each year at Eastbourne, trailing around as grandmoo's 'constant companion'. Not that a bundle of fun couldn't try the pensioners, especially given her 'rich inheritance of the family volition'.[17] Joyce had her own sage observations on being brought up by ageing grandparents. She declared her intention to remain a child, noticing 'that grown-up people have a great deal of trouble'.

Once a visitor chanced on Huxley and Joyce, lying on the floor, moving planetary pellets of paper around a large screwed-up ball of a Sun. On clear nights he would take the little girl out with a telescope to show her the other worlds.[18] The old hulk had 'come about' in an emotional calm after her mother's death. Retirement brought a certain equanimity, and with it his awe at this great universe returned.

> If there is anything I thank the Gods for (I am not sure there is, for as the old woman said when reminded of the goodness of Providence: 'Ah but he takes it out of me in the corns') it is a wide diversity of tastes [he told the 75-year-old public health campaigner Sir John Simon]. Barred from scientific work, I should be miserable, if there were not heaps of other topics that interest me, from Gadarene pigs & Gladstonian psychology, upwards. No one who has lived in the world as long as you & I have, can entertain the pious delusion that it is engineered upon principles of benevolence – and I suppose I may assume you to have reached my conviction that of all the fiends dangled before us as by hope, the 'peaceful old age' delusion is one of the most fraudulent. But for all that, the cosmos remains always beautiful and profoundly interesting in every corner – and if I had as many lives as a cat I would leave no corner unexplored.[19]

With equanimity came reflection. He was hanging photos and paintings above his chimney breast: *Rattlesnake* on top, Darwin on the bottom, von Baer (the founder of developmental biology) and Faraday (without whom Nettie would not have the 'unspeakable convenience' of electric lights) to the left, Hooker and Sir John Richardson, the 'founder of my fortunes', to the right. And in the middle? – the man who had taken Hal to Hell and back, Dante.[20]

The Huxleys visited Downe for the first time in years, but it was 'rather sad' – even if Parslow the butler, looking in on old Emma, reminded them of the glory days. 'What times those days were!' Huxley reminisced.[21] He conjured up Homeric images, as if 'warfare has been my business', something forced on him by the times. In a sense it had been: hadn't the great generals been thrown up by Dissent's industrious ranks to lead its New Model Army? He was the Puritan strategist to substitute its cause-and-effect universe for the supernaturally sanctioned Anglican status quo. He was the man who had symbolized the hopes of the Unitarian and secularist manufacturers, the man whose coming had been dreaded by the old Iron Duke of Wellington. But in the naughty nineties no one cared – except, it seems, the new cook. She walked out on learning of the godless household she was expected to cater to.

At least the life in debt ended. The two mortgages were paid off with the sale of Marlborough Place and Rich's bequest. The eccentric died in April 1891, leaving them his bachelor house along the coast, much as a devoted parishioner would leave the Church his worldly goods. Hooker ribbed Huxley about his 'estate', bemused by his evangelical power to fill the platter. 'My "estate" is somewhat of a white elephant', Huxley replied, 'unluckily, in building the house dear old Rich thought of his own convenience & not mine'. But there was an attraction, not three acres and a cow, as the Irish tenants demanded, but two acres and a coach house. Shrubberies and forest bordered beautiful lawns, which looked across to a church. 'What could pious reclusives desire more?' he asked the publisher Macmillan, who was searching for a seaside house. It fetched a handsome £2,800 and Huxley ploughed some of the money into a piece of land, 'a Naboth's vineyard' adjacent to Hodeslea, so he could 'turn horticulturist. I find nailing up creepers a delightful occupation'.[22] But he still thought of little Joyce and the stars – he drew up a new will, leaving her £500 in trust.[23]

The garden became the old man's love, and summers were for showing visitors around. Down came the men of their age. It 'would amuse you to see him going about with the hose and watering pot', Hooker told Tyndall, 'petting weak plants . . . and coaxing shrubs'. Hours were lost in the sunshine, potting the saxifrages from Kew.

The sanctuary was a far cry from the bitter streets, and the 'insane' acts of the 'new unionism', whose bus strikes for a 12-hour day could cripple a city.[24] Labour was making its own history now and passing him by. To talk of it there was John Morley, radical Liberal MP, down in the recess. And a decrepit Benjamin Jowett visited, the old *Essays* author, pleading that Huxley's last task was to locate the foundations of a humanistic morality outside of the old theological traditions. Perhaps that was what Huxley thought of as he contemplated extinction. Not that it held any terrors; humour as always deflected thoughts on that final 'small & commodious residence 7 feet by 2'.[25]

'Dad', he was signing himself now to the children, in that modern middle-class way. They were scattering. Harry the doctor got £500 for six winter weeks in Egypt with a wealthy patient, 'which is not bad for a beginner'.[26] Egypt was even more fashionable now. Young Nettie's husband Harold was out too, photographing the pharaonic frescoes for a British Museum book.

Dad was seeing too many of London's own fashionable Sphinx tombs through yellowy eyes. Hirst, his mind wandering in February 1892, had had his last smoke with the X. His life of unfulfilled promise had been 'more or less of a tragedy' after the early loss of his wife. The mathematician had typified the X as untrammelled by theology. Huxley was fittingly in a *Times* dispute on Genesis when news of Hirst's death from prostate cancer came. Tyndall was affected most. He too was ill, 'another fallen leaf'; another preparing to send his enriched atoms back to the sun: 'it will be neck and neck . . . which of us will reach the winning post . . . of the gate of Heaven', he wrote gamely to Hooker.[27] 'If I get in first . . . I shall take care to prepare comfortable berths for you and Huxley'.

But Huxley's mortal fears had moved closer to home. 'With the best will a man is but a helpless creature', he admitted as Nettie started suffering from stabbing pains (diagnosed as a 'loose kidney'). Blinding giddiness knocked her down and she had to have morphine injections. The stern patriarch was unnerved. 'I keep my head level about most things', he told Ethel, 'but I am afraid not when your mother is ill'.[28]

Spring 1992 was divided between the fruit trees in his kitchen garden and devotions in his private chapel, his stained-glass study. Here he collected his polemics against Gladstone, Wace and Argyll into what the *Times* described as a 'fugitive' volume of daring opinions, *Essays upon some Controverted Questions*. Conscious of the last grains slipping through the timer he took great pains over the

Prologue. It was eloquent on the continuing exorcism of the ghosts of medieval Christianity by a 'scientific Naturalism', and on the Victorian Reformation which illegitimated this old 'Supernature'. Ultimately it made 'intelligent work . . . the only acceptable worship'.[29] His own veneration told in the Prologue's final mythopoeic history of mankind's rise from savagery. The last revises were posted on 4 May 1892, his 67th birthday.

George Romanes was a tragic soul, terrified at his own atheism. He gazed forlornly on a godless universe which had 'lost its soul of loveliness'.[30] Yet Sunday had remained a Church day and in the decade after Darwin's death the despair had slowly subsided. His return to an appreciation of Christian moral beauty made his rehabilitation at Oxford possible. Even now he was joining Christ Church High Table and moving into Cardinal Wolsey's old oak-beamed house opposite the College.

Darwin's tortured protégé had been *plus loyal que le roi*. If Romanes had quibbled with August Weismann's theory of the continuity of germ-plasm (which denied that bodily changes during an individual's life can influence the offspring: variations result only from the 'spontaneous variation' in the chromosomes of the cell nucleus), he still saw himself holding Darwin's brief. Huxley had no truck with Lamarck's (and Darwin's) inheritance of acquired characters, unlike Spencer, who was 'bound to it *a priori* – his psychology goes to pieces without it'. Romanes sent Huxley his historical *Darwin and After Darwin* to prove 'that I have no way departed from my allegiance to Darwinism'. And he made Huxley an offer he could not refuse. Wealth had allowed Romanes to endow an Oxford lectureship, like the yearly 'Rede Lecture' at Cambridge.

> Mr. Gladstone has agreed to give the lecture for this year next term; and if you could possibly bring yourself to address once more a cultivated audience, there would not only be something appropriate in your following the champion of Adam and of swine, but you might really do much good in this seminary of ecclesiasticism. Actual theology is excluded by the Statute; but much may be consigned under 'Science' and 'Philosophy'.[31]

Dangling Gladstone hooked Huxley. He was lured out by his political contempt for the G.O.M. – despite deafness, despite a fading voice, and his blanket ban on lecturing for five years, on doctor's orders. ('Hames will countersign that statement if necessary'.) Huxley drolly told Frank Darwin that a 'Puck like spirit of mischief' forced him on, but he added seriously that 'he did want to say this thing about Ethics'.[32] And this was the other draw: he and Spencer were now 'speculatively poles asunder' and it would be a chance to voice his opposition to the 'ethical & political' nonsense stemming from Spencer's ultra-*laissez-faire* world-view.[33] So Huxley accepted his first lecture since Manchester and Mady's death.

Romanes was haunted by the moral meaning of evolution. He took a quintessential Darwinian approach, dispatching intimate questionnaires to see if there were racial differences to suffering, death and release, and immersing himself in books on the *Ethical Purport of Darwinism*. All the time he was moving from Darwin's racial cost–benefit explanation of morality to a more feeling religious understanding. So he was euphoric that Huxley's 'Romanes Lecture' would be a *fin de siècle* statement on 'Evolution and Ethics'. Given a looming election and Gladstone's age, he even begged Huxley to ready himself as the Grand Old Man's stand-in. For Huxley, doubling for Gladstone was a piquant thought. And were it to happen, Romanes 'would not be altogether sorry'.[34]

Salisbury's Tories had survived on a wafer-thin majority, helped by Parnell's divorce scandal. The Huxley–Tyndall–Hooker triumvirate gloated as 'the Gladstone-Parnell bubble burst' and the Irish alliance exploded from the 'pressure of the mephitic gases' built up by its 'internal putrefaction'.[35] Parnell had died exhausted after marrying his mistress, leaving Gladstone to fight the Tories.

Another trough in the terrible Depression brought a new extremism. In the 1892 election Gladstone was deserted by the 'Classes' and appealed to the 'Masses' – those who had told Huxley that they would soon be running the country,[36] and proved it by electing a Scottish miner, Keir Hardie, as the first Independent Labour MP. Gladstone half believed his own pandering promises of reform, disestablishment and suffrage. 'If the devil that is in him could be transferred', Huxley told Tyndall, 'there would be enough to send 2,000,000 pigs headlong, instead of a poor 2000!'[37] He hoped for a tiny Liberal majority, to keep the G.O.M.'s hands tied by the Unionists.

On 18 June 1892 Romanes thanked Huxley 'for the large and latest instalment of your wisdom'. *Controverted Questions* was out. It was a huge book, 625 pages of gilded controversy, a piece of evangelic rationalism that had one worshipper demanding a society be formed to propagate Huxley's wisdom.[38] Ironically, after a life in science, his biggest book was of Biblical criticism. But it left an overall impression of ridiculing, not clerical naivety so much as Gladstone's obscurantism.

Two days later Lord Salisbury's Tory government sounded him out about a Privy Councillorship. Donnelly had tipped Salisbury off, even telling him that he was sure Huxley would accept, 'so', he said, 'do not through any blooming *agnostic* ideas make me look a fool'.[39] Donnelly wanted 'such a note of acceptance' as he could send on. 'You have been and done me', Huxley replied, which was hardly the word to pass on, never mind his banter on this reward for the 'wicked'.

He was to be the first Crown adviser on science. Nominally, at least, this was an office, a seat in that great baronial chamber, not a title (something he had always refused); and although that might salve the conscience of a Puritan 'dead against' decorations, it was still very nominal. Knowing Huxley's predilection, the physicist William Thomson, now Lord Kelvin and 'the biggest of all the big swells', assured him that it was something he could accept. And for all the Rt Hon.'s merriment at the etiquette – searching for a 'table of precedence' to see who passed through the door first – Nettie revelled in it: sister Lizzie heard that it ranks 'above Baronetcies & titular Lordships'.[40] 'You never thought Lizzie when you threw y^{r} slipper after the boy . . .'

Parliament dissolved on 29 June amid election fever. Gladstone called again for Home Rule, and the Queen called the prospect of an 82-year-old governing 'with the miserable democrats . . . a bad joke'. The Liberals won, with more than the sliver Huxley had hoped for. Salisbury stood down on 11 August and five days later he told Huxley that his PC would be 'public evidence that the Government which is now resigning are not insensible to the great renown which you have conferred on English science, or to the services which you have rendered to your country more'.[41] Huxley had made science patriotic in the industrial 'war' with Germany, raising it with the Union Jack. So in a feverish election period, with the Grand Old Man committed to hauling down the flag, the Tories' last act was to put Huxley on the Honours List.

He and 'Mrs. Right Honourable' were away touring Wales, and 'every now and then had to laugh' at this reward for 'plain-spoken wickedness'. He declared the 'Archbishopric of Canterbury' his only ambition left, and so saying ran off into scorching parody. Of course Salisbury had no need to press for that particular spiritual peerage, knowing that

> as Evolutionism is rapidly gaining ground among the people who have votes [working classes] . . . his eminent successor [the 'demagogue' Gladstone] . . . would become a hot evolutionist . . . And when [Gladstone] goes out, my bishopric will be among the Dissolution Honours. If H.M. objects she will be threatened with the immediate abolition of the H. of Lords, and the institution of a social democratic federation of counties.[42]

A Wonderland world of Archbishop Huxley in a socialist arcadia highlighted the underlying fears as the country continued its Leftward drift.

It was an edifying spectacle on 25 August 1892: Huxley, rigged up in his Court dress 'ablaze with gold', gilt sword, the lot 'costing a sum with which I could buy, oh! so many books'. The royal train, the grand procession of officers at Osborne House (Her Majesty's Palazzo Mansion): it was so quaint. 'We knelt as if we were going to say our prayers', he recounted, as though reporting the latest dance steps; swore an oath, 'advanced to the Queen, knelt and kissed her hand, retired backwards, and got sworn over again (Lord knows what I promised and vowed this time also)'. With natural irreverence he glanced up at Queen Victoria – only, to his 'great discomforture',[43] to find her studying this interloper from another culture.

Here was final proof that he was no social pariah: science was being fêted. Not that smashing Gladstone's *Impregnable Rock* had harmed him; nor had his disbarring of socialism gone unnoticed. Of course Huxley saw nothing 'queerer' than 'that a Tory & Church Government should have delighted to honour the worst famed heretic in the three Kingdoms' – and truly it must have made some back-benchers crawl.[44] But at the end of the day, although the PC was given for Huxley's scientific status, party tensions and fear of socialism made it easier for the Conservatives. They were themselves pledged to private property and the Union.

> It is just thirty years now since I published 'Man's Place in Nature' which some of my anxious friends declared would ruin me altogether. And considering my long series of aggravated offenses since that time I should have expected the offer of a bishopric as soon as that of a Privy Councillorship.[45]

But their Lordships leaving the Dispatch Box were happy to honour the Devil, so long as he tormented 'pious William' and played havoc with the socialists. The 'anomaly' simply ignores the increasingly conservative function of Huxley's agnostic science. This particular Liberal Unionist had been making a wasteland of the Grand Old Man's scripturalism for seven years – impugning the Home Ruler's judgment in the best part of 600 reprinted pages. And who mistook Huxley's company at Court?[46] The other PCs were political functionaries, a Liberal Unionist MP and the next Tory Home Secretary. That made 'three hot Unionists' and the gift more than politically suspect. Gladstone, hearing of Salisbury's gesture, was livid.

It was The Right Honourable T. H. Huxley who attended Tennyson's funeral two months later. Tennyson had found Huxley 'chivalrous, wide, and earnest', and the Volunteer had raised his rifle in one hand and *Idylls* in the other. In June he had sent the poet his *Controverted Questions*. Now he joined the Royal Society elite over his bier. 'Tennyson had a right to that as the first poet since Lucretius who has understood the drift of science'.[47]

Huxley did not double for Gladstone at Oxford. Ten days later the Prime Minister delivered the first 'Romanes Lecture'. Under penalty to avoid religion, he dressed up his 'impassioned plea for conservative ways of thinking about Religion and Morals' as a pandering history of university education. It drew chauvinistic cheers. Lankester called it 'George's Show' for its stagey enthusiasm, and 'as a show it was well worth seeing', added Romanes. But away from the scene Huxley wondered how the great orator could say so much 'without ever rising above the level of antiquarian gossip'. The worst of it was Gladstone's leading the church parade and reading the lessons! That had Huxley pleading that 'I couldn't – really'. The horrified clergy excused him, being happily 'disposed to regard such an exhibition as the profanation of Scripture'.[48]

With the last rays of Autumn sunshine came a restless desire to re-enter the fray. He started lobbying for the reform of that colossus which bestrode the Empire, London University. He wanted a tighter co-ordination between the scattered teaching colleges and examining Senate House, to be achieved by increasing the professors' power on the executive. He busied himself so much, leading deputations and presenting evidence to the Gresham Commission on London University (indeed suggesting the Commissioners), that he seemed his old self. He told the professors 'that this old hulk is ready to be towed out into line of battle, if they think fit', which was more public-spirited than prudent. They thought him 'seaworthy enough to fly the admiral's flag' and made him President of a group intent on marshalling the 'chaotic' London colleges into a coherent whole.

From the prow the deaf Admiral led the motley flotilla towards his modern university ideal. *His* university was not to train clerics, lawyers or doctors, but 'pioneers in the exploration and settlement of new regions' of knowledge.[49]

The smart PC suit could not mask the Rt Hon.'s irreverence. 'Don't ask anybody above the younger son of a peer', he told Romanes, referring to the lecture, 'because I shall not be able to go into dinner before him'.[50]

With socialism strengthening, the first Independent Labour member in Parliament, and Kropotkin stealing the nation's heart, the great argument was the sort of ethics and evolution a democratic nation should adopt. Huxley would talk at Oxford, not on the evolution of ethics, but the ethics of evolution. He would look at whether Darwin's Nature gave any sanction to human values. It is 'very courageous of you to lecture on Morals & Evolution', said Benjamin Jowett. 'No one has yet expressed adequately the antithesis of the moral & the physical'.[51] For Jowett a weak-to-the-wall Darwinism was countered by society's wall to protect the weak.

After the blistering attacks on Gladstone's demonology Oxford was petrified at what Huxley might say. Having encouraged him, Romanes got cold feet and reminded him of the prohibition on religion and politics. If people applied what he said to religion, replied Huxley, 'that is not my affair. To be honest, however, unless I thought they would, I should never have taken all the pains'. That unleashed two more letters begging him to be circumspect. Only the arrival of Huxley's manuscript allayed the fears. It was so discursive that not even Mrs Romanes' 'fine nose for heresy' could sniff any.[52] Oxford's sensibilities were respected.

On his 68th birthday, 4 May, Nettie was in bed, the stabbing pains eased by morphine. Huxley was readying the typescript, which was to be printed and 1,000 copies put on sale prior to the lecture. Three days before the event he posted one to Tyndall. 'There are not many apples (& those mostly of the crab sort) left upon the old tree but I send you the product of the last shaking'.[53]

It was his first time on any stage for six years, and on *that* stage since 1860. The 'flu had left him a red-nosed 'disreputable Captain Costigan-looking' character, and reduced his weak voice to a whisper. Romanes had the Public Orator stand by, just in case.[54]

At 2.15 on Thursday 18 May 1893 the last students piled in to the Sheldonian Theatre. They were after 'splendid rhetoric' more than angst and insight, and more had turned out for the sacerdotal Prime

Minister than science's 'High Priest'. Huxley, silver hair flowing over his 'gorgeous D.C.L. robes', proceeded in a quiet voice. Romanes called it 'genial and "mellow"'. The students called it 'almost inaudible' and cries of 'speak up' accompanied a shuffling as they migrated forward.[55] But those in front of the stage appreciated how skilfully the injunction to avoid politics had been skirted.

The cunning disguise of 'Evolution and Ethics' was completed by its sparkling language: it was 'one of the most brilliant gems in the prose literature of the nineteenth century'. But still 'a regular egg-dance' for all that, as Huxley admitted. He was staking his Liberal political ethics midway between the Spencerian and socialist extremes without being able to mention either. The dance said less about the dons' sensibilities than Huxley's. At bottom of it he was responding to the politics of the age – to the socialism that had almost crushed him in his bus, to communist cooks who damned his uncaring Darwinism, to Labour's attacks on his Malthusian views. He was meeting the calls to pronounce on 'Socialism and Darwinism'.[56]

The theme had been set in the dark days of Mady's death. But a deeper theme was older. Fifty years on, he was still rationalizing a planet which had seen so much pleasure and pain without merit or desert. Suffering evolved with consciousness; it appeared, not because of a Fall, but with the rise of brain complexity. Sacrifice and death were the 'necessary concomitant' of evolutionary progress, part of an amoral Darwinian process. But for Huxley the price of progress had become too high.

He portrayed ethical man revolting 'against the moral indifference of nature'.[57] Care had replaced the crushing competition, altruism the competitive aggression. The flight was not to the swift, nor the battle to the strong; among humans a mitigating ethics dictated that the weak be rescued from the wall. 'Evolution and Ethics' was the missing chapter of *Man's Place in Nature*, filled in after 30 years' digestion of Darwinism.

The justice Huxley and Carlyle had seen in the soul of the universe was gone. The truth of Darwinism and fear of Socialism had forced Huxley to demur. Natural Selection, that 'calm strong angel' who had once played chess for love, had crashed in tatters, feathers scattering. And beneath them he found 'Satan, the Prince of this world'. Nature's vicious disregard in killing his daughter among the unsung myriads in the Depression was the tragedy that gave his lecture its poignancy. Still, the bitterness of 1887 was softening. That 'bloody rum world' was receding, and he was levelling out in 1893. He now bolstered a competitive Darwinism, to make it immune to mutualist attacks, while denying that it could provide any natural basis for our ethics of love. 'Evolution and Ethics' split the world; it separated a wild zoological nature from our ethical existence. 'Social progress means a checking of the cosmic process'. It selects not the 'fittest' but 'ethically the best'.[58] Man came of age when he ceased emulating Nature and started 'combating it'.

It wasn't what was being said, but *who* was saying it: the 'prophet of evolution', as *Blackwood's Magazine* called him. Spencer bristled at this further onslaught on his naturalistic ethics – his belief that the struggle for survival could be the only true foundation for ethics. He called Huxley's distinction between cosmic strife and a combating morality his own 'Pauline dogma of nature and grace'.[59]

At the end of his days Huxley could find no 'sanction for morality in the ways of the cosmos'. He had come full circle to Southwood Smith's *Divine Government*, which had taught the boy that tackling social evil was a divine responsibility. Huxley's whole life had revolved around pain and duty. He had taken the hard road back to his Unitarian and Latitudinarian allies, to Kingsley's refusal to sacrifice humanity in Nature's arena. 'Just so!' cried Mivart, with a hint of glee. Wasn't Huxley admitting an Absolute ethics outside Nature? Wasn't it *really* grace from God? Of course Huxley saw human ethics still as 'part and parcel of the general process of evolution', evolved by natural selection to defy natural selection. Man's 'nature within nature' was a strange microcosm spinning counter-clockwise. But by refusing to see human ethics as Absolute or God-given, he nonplussed many critics, who saw him plunging into paradox.[60]

Huxley the political animal was facing up to Darwin's dog-eat-dog Nature. Instinctive man was at war with ethical man in the same corporeal frame. It was no good cutting the umbilical cord to the cosmos like the Buddhists (suddenly fashionable in a humanistic age), or trying for salvation by total renunciation. Man had the mark of Cain; beneath the civil surface lay the bestiality of his savage forebears. The ferocious instincts of his 'hot youth' were struggling against his social upbringing. Huxley had internalized the 'war', satisfying his battling mentality to the end. The pugilist was leading a new fight against the savage within. Owen had once talked of original sin as the malingering ape in our constitution.[61] But the bestiality had not quite washed off with our social baptism. The old General on Oxford's stage had an air of 'militant heroism' as he faced an unequal battle against overpowering cosmic forces.

Nature's injustice 'has burned itself deeply into the writer's soul', said one critic. Some took his talk of suffering as a 'scathing attack' on 'all possible Theodices'. Others saw it as an 'indictment' of the Darwinian terrors.[62] They were too close to see him bolstering the Darwinian cosmos, whose ruthlessness could now be accepted because he had detached human ethics.

He *needed* a competitive Nature. He needed to undercut the socialist legions. 'Evolution and Ethics' was the General's final effort to save the political day. The essay was conceived in terms of competition and struggle, as were all his anti-socialist essays. He ignored 'adaptation': only in a published note did he admit that human social cohesion was of use, 'just as the gregarious habit of innumerable plants and animals . . . has been of immense advantage to them'. Ethics had evolved, Leslie Stephen said, expanding on Huxley's note, on 'purely prudential grounds', as a sort of parental altruism writ large. Our welfare, our sanitary reforms, our smallpox vaccines, all increased the health of the species. Morality benefited us. But Stephen, just as aware of the political undercurrent, was quite happy to 'stimulate "collectivism" at the expense of a crude individualism'.[63] Huxley was on harder ground. Though a little mutualism might bolster his professional State bureaucracy against Spencer, he knew from experience that too much might justify Wallace's and Kropotkin's collectivist ideals – the very targets he was trying to destroy by strengthening Darwinian nature.

He was boxed in, surrounded by invisible political walls. Praised for his stand against the 'fanaticism of individualism',[64] congratulated for his buttress against socialism in this 'muddled and aspiring epoch', he showed how difficult it was to steer a straight course. Struggling in white water, avoiding the eddies of Spencer's ultra-selfish ethics, and the whirlpool of Wallace's and Kropotkin's harmonious socialist Nature, Huxley was forcing his ethical Ark against the Darwinian current which had brought him so far.

11

Fighting unto Death

THE OLD INTELLECTUALS were in their red-brick homes. Out in the sticks, away from London. Out of time now. Doomed like Beardsley and Wilde, in a moribund decade, watching decadent London living frantically as if on borrowed time. The naughty nineties, reacting so raucously against their staid Puritanism, seemed like a distant country. Huxley escaped the shallowness in Eastbourne. Here the anatomist watched his body crumble. His yearly fights against 'flu had become a wretched struggle. The old man, huddled over the winter fire devouring Aristotle, was buying time.[1]

No manor retreats for the X-Club stragglers, no grand piles. Huxley's house on the corner of Staveley Road was overlooked on two sides. The tormented, sleepless Tyndall in the Devil's Punch Bowl of Hindhead was an equal prey to peeping fans and screened off the bottom of his garden. They seemed such ordinary men gone such ordinary ways.

And yet Huxley the ageing matinée idol still made guest appearances. At Gonville and Caius College in Cambridge he played the part and 'Loaded himself with champagne' before another Harvey dinner on 21 June 1893.[2] He looked 'tired out'. But with his tubes lubricated he could still evoke the old scientific patriotism in his homage to the discoverer of the blood's circulation.

Death's hand touched them all. Almost monthly it left friends to be mourned and memories to be enshrined. Huxley helped Lord Coleridge arrange a 'Jowett Memorial Fund'. He was astonished that his old society doctor Sir Andrew Clark, grown 'pompous' since his Haslar days, had left £250,000 from the practice among the swells. Annihilation had once filled Huxley with 'horror unspeakable': 'whether or not Nature abhors a vacuum', Romanes remembered him saying, 'I know that the soul of man does'.[3] But age had bred a certain equanimity. And anyway in 1893 it seemed to the old war-horse that 'F.M. General Death had forgotten me'.

Immortality – if Weismann was right – was a little of one's chromosomes corrupting slowly through the generations.[4] Or perhaps it was a larger uncorrupted corpus of published work. Macmillan had remained with Huxley, liberal to the century's end. Now the publisher would see a lifetime's proselytizing capped by the obligatory *Collected Essays*. Huxley joined Arnold, Kingsley and Morley, with nine volumes – a million words – the first off the press in September 1893, 40 years of bread-and-butter journalism amassed into canonical form. They ranged from Darwin's defence to the agnostic's pology, the sea of doubt to the sin of faith, from the vivid opening of the dinosaurian past to the veiling off of an immortal future. No set so amply testified to the Victorian naturalistic world and its meaning. For his prose alone he was lauded as 'perhaps the greatest virtuoso of plain English who has ever lived'.[5] The style was the man – the *bon viveur*, the twinkling, the suave hectoring, the apology that of course he was really peace-loving. Such prose only made the message more beguiling; here was the emergent scientist ratifying a new social order. Critics read the 5*s* volumes as war memoirs by a valiant 'old contemptible' (with all the propagandist connotations of that Great War image). And by the *fin de siècle* it was obvious that the moralizing Huxley had inherited the natural theologian's mantle: the publicist was appearing in new red covers to reassure another disorientated generation.

If sin did not bring its own desert, the avenging Huxley was on hand to help. It was Sir Richard Owen's misfortune to die first. They had preyed on the same fossil animals, but run with diametric packs across a changing social landscape. The sad old man was 88, demented at the end, destroyed by his only son's suicide. That was December 1892. It should have ended the hatreds. Indeed Huxley accepted an invitation to the Black Knight's funeral. But biting winds brought the reflection that Owen would end up killing him too, and so he telegraphed his apologies.[6]

Diplomacy did dictate his presence at a memorial – and a few words. But though he came to praise Owen, not to bury him, there was grim hypocrisy in his seconding the proposal for a statue in the Natural History Museum. Even his admission that the man 'did a lot of first rate work and now that he can do no more mischief he has a right to his wages',[7] made it sound like the wages of sin. The blackened bronze statue close to Darwin's shining white marble only served to rub in Owen's tarnished reputation. In truth, the great cathedral of a museum was his monument.

Owen's grandchildren buried the old man better than they knew. 'Three, or thirty, guesses & you shall not guess', Huxley wrote to Hooker. 'Rev Richard Owen has written to me to ask me to write a concluding chapter for the biography of his grand father – containing a "critical estimate" of him & his work!!!!!' There was no crueller irony. The simple curate knew little of Owen, nothing of biography, and he was 'incompetent to deal with his Grandsire's character under any aspect'. Owen's successor at the museum, Sir William Henry Flower, had refused any help. And so the Revd Richard had turned to Huxley to make the biography 'as impartial & authentic as possible'! The hapless curate should never have asked, and Huxley should never have accepted. He did turn down a personal estimate as 'I was never in your grandfather's house nor he in mine', but after twinges of doubt he agreed to assess Owen's science – and he expected 'poor old Richard's ghost' to haunt him for his pains.[8]

Luck had distributed the last spoils of victory. Huxley stopped planting his rockery to inter Owen properly. Few scientists could see past Owen's quirks to his wondrous world of dinosaurs (his word) and mammal ancestors (his work): the Grand Old Man of palaeontology had opened up the lost tropical planet during the Age of Reptiles. But Nettie revealed the home spirit. 'It is quite comic', she said of the offer: this the 'man who did his best, to prevent Hal from coming to the front, in every mean, & untruthful way'. The phobia turned on the biography itself. Flower was suspicious. Hooker had heard that it 'is likely to bubble over with unveracity – being grounded on R.O.'s estimate of his modest self & his intercourse with mankind, as contained in an autobiography which he has left'.[9] It conditioned Huxley's mood, as he imagined Owen's 'ghost in Hades' preparing a posthumous strike. In reality there was no autobiography; no stabbing from beyond the grave. The grandson simply turned the old man into a laughable 'social fop'.[10] But fear of the dead scorpion's sting affected Huxley's writing.

He wrote watching his back. In 1894 new radical evangelicals, admitting that 'Evolution is . . . a Vision – which is revolutionizing the world of Nature', were cashing in. In the age of the New Woman, the hot author Henry Drummond – Moody and Sankey's scientist – saw the *Ascent of Man* culminate in motherly love, and through the altruism of the 'Holy Family' the perfection of morality. 'Nature is the Garment of God', Drummond claimed, as Owen might have, its process His 'Eternal Will'. To naturalize the spirit – to make 'Christianity . . . as old as Nature' – was to contest secular authority once more. From another side came Benjamin Kidd's denunciation of dry agnosticism in *Social Evolution* (1894). Where the novelist Grant Allen had called religion a 'grotesque fungoid growth' disguising a primeval 'Ancestor Worship', Kidd would treat it seriously as the ethical regulator of social evolution. Such books might have been an 'anaesthetic which a clement Providence has administered to orthodoxy during the excision of its diseased organs',[11] but they were the backdrop to Owen's autopsy. The split-loyalty spiritualizers were vipers at the biologist's bosom.

Huxley finished his Darwinian business by burying Owen's Nature of Divine Archetypes. He strained to be fair and let the strain show. Even knowing that 'all the things we fought about, belong to antiquity', he continued to reslay the slain. To old hands like Flower it was the only way: 'You have been very judicious in devoting 31 out of your 57 pages to Owen's predecessors, and thus avoiding all details regarding your hero'.[12] But young adjutants who had seen victory a thousand times over wondered at the sods being thrown onto Owen's white face.

> Pp. 1–40 – very good and very interesting.
> 41–8 you praise Richard *seven pages*
> 48–66 *18 pages*(!), you damn him

Better not to 'dwell on his philosophy', thought Foster, who knew that Huxley should have concentrated on the crowning fossil edifice.[13] But 'the Apostle Paul of the new teaching' was performing the last rite of purification. The remnants of a rival Coleridgean world were destroyed – a might-have-been Nature, obeying the divine Edict, legitimating the National Church. Huxley was finishing what the industrial Unitarians had begun with their resistance 60 years earlier to a reactionary old S. T. Coleridge, who had damned the Dissenting technocracy and 'Ouran Outang theology'.[14] The 'new Nature' – that lawful, causal, agnostic bundle – had triumphed. It was called Science.

And so Huxley left the late twentieth century with the daunting task of hacking through the partisan myths to rehabilitate that giant of modern palaeontology, Richard Owen.[15]

Wednesday morning's paper, 6 December 1893, said that Tyndall had taken an overdose of drugs and there would be an inquest. 'I suppose it was Chloral at the last – & all along', Hooker sighed. It was. Louisa telegraphed the Huxleys on Thursday night and the next morning they were at Hindhead. 'Poor woman, it was a terrible meeting', said Nettie, 'She clung to us'. 'The circumstances of his death were so ghastly'.[16] Louisa had mixed up John's medicine bottles on Monday morning and given him a massive dose of the opiate sleeping draught chloral by mistake. Stomach pumps, emetics and coffee failed to keep him conscious. He had died that night.

On Saturday Huxley walked behind the hearse to Haslemere churchyard. Louisa poured out her heart about 'John's love for you & me beyond any others', Hooker told Huxley, but the tragedy left her in a 'dangerous' traumatic state. Huxley went to see a half-finished Tyndall bust for Louisa, but it only helped 'to tear her to pieces', and it was heart-rending for him. He placed a remembrance in the *Nineteenth Century* – a final board report on the 40-year-old 'firm'. Castor and Pollux had had their adventures, and come a long way since losing their Toronto chairs – through the *Reader* and X-Club to the joint LL.D.s and North Stars. One 'abusive sermon on the subject of the "late Professor Huxley"' showed that even in death they could not part. The firm had been the defining voice of the new scientific naturalism, that religion of cosmic evolution. 'People don't get their heart-strings tugged at my time of life without knowing about it',[17] Huxley said as he sipped his own tonic and spent Christmas week in bed, 'running up a little account over poor old Tyndall'.

Age brought a numbing resignation, and the Spring saw him out hoeing his sylvan patch on Staveley Road. After three years of clearing and planting, the old gardener had the rustic metaphor to introduce his 'Evolution and Ethics' in the ninth volume of essays, due out on 28 August 1894. His Kew outpost of foreign delicate shrubs was maintained against an encroaching Nature, just as care for the weak made human ethics an exotic nook in a brutal cosmos. Even this ethical corner was held like a valiant imperial conquest. Huxley's life had been a homage to heroism, and at the end he stood for man's epic fight against the universe. Nettie thought it 'a gem of [an] argument'.[18]

He was received as a hero himself now. A cameo appearance was called for at the BAAS in August 1894, which after 34 years was returning to Oxford. The students were steeped in the mythology of 1860. Revd George Brodrick, the Warden of Merton, had the Huxleys' room ready and headed a new phalanx of liberal dons ready to be 'signally honoured' by a visit. Even if Brodrick was no more 'sound on the doctrine of Evolution' than his liberal predecessors in 1860, he appreciated 'how many doors it has appeared to unlock'.[19] Hesitancy had been Oxford's lot. It still was.

Huxley should have been the silent star bathing in the adulation. But the gods had a way of intervening, and at the last moment he was asked to second the vote of thanks for Lord Salisbury's Presidential speech. 'Hal's wrath was great', said Nettie, as he read the draft with its backhanded compliment to evolution and slight on natural selection. On the platform, Salisbury talked of that 'comforting word, evolution', although he took more comfort from the latest disputes over heredity which made the thing look tottery. Huxley sank into his chair. At the end the ovation for him began. He stood, 'looking kinglike in his red gown', said a proud Nettie: 'the applause was deafening – again & again it rose & fell'. He was on the stump again, managing the crowd. And on this occasion the *Times* reported every word of clever repartee in the face of aristocratic ignorance. He spoke amid laughter as one who 'had made a pretty free use of the comfortable word "evolution"'. Then he politely rapped Salisbury's knuckles for confusing Darwin's and Weismann's theories with the historical fact of evolution, and went on to welcome 'so distinguished a convert' to his comfortable world. He sat down drowned by cheers. For a last time he was the 'hero of the day in the Sheldonian Theatre'.[20]

The 'old Adam' reconstructed himself in these mythic moments. He retailed the day's events to Louisa Tyndall (and Hooker, and Lockyer, and Lewis Campbell), overplaying them awfully:

> Lord Salisbury was clever as usual; but knowing nothing about the topic, in reality, he makes an awful hash of this attempt to deal with Darwins views. If the address had only been a paper in section D [the working Zoology Section], I think the massacre would have been worse than that of 'Sammy' 34 years ago – always excepting that Ld Salisbury was courteous & indeed generous to Darwin personally.

But for all of Salisbury's caveats Huxley took satisfaction in His Lordship's acceptance of evolution, telling Hooker, 'It was very queer to sit there and hear the doctrines you & I were damned for advocating 34 years ago at Oxford, enunciated as matters of course – disputed by no reasonable man! – in the Sheldonian theatre by the Chancellor'.[21]

It was clearly 'rather a risky thing to entrust the Presidentship to a layman'.[22] *Lay* said it all: after 34 years the professionals no longer needed these stately sanctions.

The next afternoon at Christ's garden party – as if to remind them of the passing time – they were handed tea by the son of Hal's *Rattlesnake* superior, John Thomson. A baby then, he was in his 50s now and had Nettie reminiscing about all the shore leave his father had given Hal to 'come & see me'.[23] Those courting days seemed far off to the bundled old lady, now with 14 grandchildren (Aldous had been born to Len and Julia two weeks earlier).

Every event was to be Huxley's last, but the indomitable old chap had become a stately institution. Up to town he would trot, there to be cared for by the Donnellys 'as if I were a piece of old china'. His 'swellness' would don his gilt sword to dine with the Prime Minister, Lord Rosebery. The puffing reached gigantic proportions after the Liberal PM begged 'the smallest of your works with my name written in it', to be 'cherished by your . . . lifelong admirer'.[24] (After 30 years Huxley thought an original *Man's Place in Nature* suitable for the Head of State.) He made an appearance at the Savoy to mark the 25th anniversary of *Nature*. In a quarter of a century he had seen his broad-forum weekly become the organ of the specialist. But no more romantic aphorisms of Goethe's and accusations of madness; he marked the completion of 50 volumes with a rallying retrospective of evolution. It was his 'anti Salisbury manifesto', to counter Oxford's faint praise – a rummage through his old scientific drawers to peruse the fossil title deeds once more.[25]

Up he went again to collect his long-service award. He had hoped that the Royal Society's new Darwin Medal would be used to fire the young bloods, not bedeck the 'useless old extinct volcanoes'. But the prize went to him anyway for his comparative anatomy and 'intimate association with Mr Darwin' – 'it was inevitable', said Foster by way of comprehensive explanation.[26] It showed that he was not quite shelved. 'Old age brings mere calm isolation to us all', he mused in the New Year 1895. 'When I am well, I am capable of forgetting my antiquity and then the many reminders that I am regarded by my younger contemporaries as a relic of the past (more or less venerable) have a very droll effect'.[27] And in that vein he gamely led a London University deputation to Lord Rosebery at No 10 through the January snow, which of course gave him a chill and put him in bed. It was the chance to plan a tenth volume of essays.

Meanwhile students at the College of Surgeons were arguing over an extraordinary monograph just received from Java. A short, bow-legged, heavy-browed ape-human had been announced by Eugène Dubois. Haeckel had guessed that a hypothetical '*Pithecanthropus*' would be found in the East, and Dubois, inspired to search, accordingly named his find *Pithecanthropus erectus*. He placed it close to the ape-human fork. But the skullcap, said Arthur Keith – a latter-day impecunious Huxley hoping to make a penny popularizing this 'real "missing link"' – showed it to be a true early human, with a 900cc brain, midway between a chimpanzee's and a modern human's. On 13 February young Keith read a paper at Bart's on it. The next day Huxley wrote to Hooker that 'The Dutchman seems to have turned up something like the "missing link" in Java . . . I expect he was a Socratic party with his hair rather low down on his forehead'.[28] By 1895 it was so matter-of-fact. Huxley had lived long enough to see the first ape-man – indeed hear about a Far Eastern cradle for humankind, where these bent, small-brained ape-people had retreated in the face of the northern ice sheets. Suddenly the Owen fracas seemed positively prehistoric.

Oscar Wilde's decadence was a release from two decades of Puritanism. But there was a final and more pointed challenge to Huxley's moral agnosticism. In February 1895, as the students contemplated Java Man's villainous low brow, the high-brow Arthur Balfour on the Tory Front Bench delivered the strongest rebuttal yet. An aristocrat, 'bolder but less brilliant' than his uncle Lord Salisbury (or so said Gladstone), Balfour was destined to succeed him as Tory Prime Minister. The agnostics related his metaphysical *excursus* to the milk-and-water Oxford praise. 'He & Salisbury run on the same lines'. 'Is this the basis of Conservative statesmanship?' asked Foster. 'Thank Ether I am a radical'.[29]

In ten years the Tories, unsettled by Fenian terrorism, socialism, secularism and other manifestations of the 'class war' (Salisbury's term), had become the Law and Order party of the Union. 'Bloody Balfour's' bolstering of United Kingdom should have endeared him to the X-Club. They shared interests – indeed as extreme Unionists the Xs even deplored his sop to the Nationalists in the shape of a proposed Irish Catholic University. And the collectivist threat to property struck Tory Anglicans and Liberal Scientists alike. But Huxley's men were themselves targeted by Balfour's Conservatives. Scientific 'Naturalism' was thought to feed Socialism. It reduced morale and an effective theological policing, destroying the safeguards of the established order. Balfour had already dubbed it a 'contemptible fetish' at that famous 1888 Church Congress.[30] By removing God's Personal sanction and the threat of His punishment, Naturalism opened the gates to the gothic hordes.

Balfour's *Foundations of Belief* was a Shadow Cabinet censure motion on all the secular '-isms'. The book berated Huxley's regrounding of morality and association of agnosticism with 'real' science. An election was looming; *Foundations* spoke for moral fibre, Anglican authority and a higher sphere of class union. It attempted to unstitch the scientific warp from the naturalistic weave (by questioning Huxley's own faith in an undeviating causality and uniform nature), and then reweave science into a supernatural pattern.

Politicians held sway with the 'wandering British public', said Knowles. 'Since you have forsaken the Constable's Beat the loose characters of thought have plucked up too much courage'. Gagged at Oxford before Balfour's uncle, Huxley did not need luring. Feeling chipper, already thinking about a summer holiday in Wiesbaden, he was eager to respond to the *Foundations*. The *Times* on 8 February had incensed him with its talk of the 'little Bethels of . . . Agnosticism' quaking in Balfour's wake.[31] Balfour liked his rapier with its button off; for all his breeding, he held Dr Johnson's belief that to respect an enemy is to give him the edge. He deplored the agnostics' 'parasitic' moral life on the Christian rump; and like all Tories he thought that without Christian blood the parasite would perish.[32] *Christ* was Morality. Huxley took his own button off. The professional 'Constable' was not prepared to see Tory recidivists go about questioning the new State of science.

Fashionably elegant, one of the wealthiest men in England (he had inherited £4 million on coming of age), Balfour had patronized Drummond's evangelical lectures. He had been active in cultivated Cambridge, itself resisting the vulgar professionals. The counter-'Revolution of the Dons' saw them infiltrating the Cavendish Laboratory and endorsing a Physics based on that universal supramundane stuff, the 'ether' (which could knit the seen and unseen kingdoms into the 'living garment of God'). The physicists in the Society for Psychical Research used Cambridge's scientific apparatus to probe the unseen, invoking a sort of 'transcendent naturalism' to trump the Londoners' materialism. By 1895 Balfour was 'President of the Spook Society' and Knowles expected Huxley's blow against 'Spook-speculation, in all its forms'.[33] He would not be disappointed.

With Naturalism hurting Tory Anglican interests, Balfour gave it a tinny materialistic ring. Old Huxley put on his spectacles and repolished his trumpet. Agnosticism had been his strength in an alien world – his moral shield against the medieval powers – and it had inspired his Cossacks. This time 'Mr. Balfour has acted like the French in 1870', he observed, and 'gone to war without any ordinance maps'. Clamping his teeth on, Huxley found 'the cleverest exhibition of philosophical ineptitude'. But his teeth were false now, the book was gristly, and chewing would be a long process. So he split his review into two. He posted the first part on 18 February. 'I think the cavalry charge in this months XIX will amuse you', he told Ethel in March.[34]

The indignant General laid about the *fin de siècle* with a vengeance. In the 1890s everything seemed up for grabs. A restlessness gripped the nation. Hedonism and theosophy railed against the Puritan years. Socialism had weakened the political structures as well as science's voice. Nietzsche was making 'truth' another moral prejudice, and Ibsen saw the need for 'vital lies' to enrich life. Everywhere was change and disillusionment, while the people looked 'in vain to science and authority for any hint as to duty'. Victorian Science and Victorian Statesmen, Huxley and Balfour, were like dinosaurs, struggling in their dying world. Huxley was 'fighting for his life'.[35] As evening crowns the day so 'Mr. Balfour's Attack on Agnosticism' would be his last testament.

Foster wanted 'a parody on B's book bolstering up some d—d idiocy'. Huxley gave him a Swiftian satire on the whole d—d society. He made profligate Imperial Rome stand for Balfour's Britain, in which the 'refined depravity among the upper classes' was matched by the hypocritical priests' winking as they performed sacred rites, no longer believing their own fables. With the moral rot had come the barbarian superstitions, Oriental religions and 'criminal impostures, analogous to so much of modern spirit-rapping' (the 'Spooks'). In his bankrupt Rome, the 'half-cretinised products of over-civilisation' had become sensually indulgent, 'flabby' and 'weak minded', led by clever *littérateurs* who substituted smart prose for substance (Wilde was about to be sentenced to hard labour in Pentonville for homosexuality).[36] Never had he crafted such blistering Swiftian prose. The tables were turned on an effete Establishment (Balfour himself had been accused of effeminacy). It dwarfed the critique of the Eloi's decadent eroticism in *The Time Machine*, which his old boy H. G. Wells would post him in three months.[37]

Balfour's society smelt of decay. By substituting illicit faith for pious ignorance it had kicked away its foundations in 'solid and stern' reality and abdicated its moral responsibility. Even now the 'shepherds of the people' would jeopardize the 'future of our civilisation' by reinstating the old pagan gods.[38]

'Delightful', said Donnelly of the therapeutic rant. But even if Hooker assured Huxley that 'You have probed his weak places with effect', it was a wonderfully quixotic tilt. Not that this was true disembowelling, he told Ethel: the proper 'bayonets will be brought into play next month'.[39] Then he would slice through Balfour's misreading of 'Agnosticism' line by line.

But the Winter 'flu swept through Eastbourne. Nettie caught it in late February and took to her bed. Hal struggled on, 'so anxious to finish the 2nd part of his article on Balfours book, that he fought against the pains in his limbs'.[40] He posted off Part II early in March only to collapse into bed. There he stayed, with no heart for the proofs.

The weathercocks pointed due east. The 'flu turned into bronchitis and 14-hour bouts of coughing damaged his weak heart. Night and day the nurses tended him. Always there was Brace, the sweet maid, smiling through her hospital chores. The 'anxiety & misery' reached a peak for Nettie as Hal's lungs became infected. It left him sitting up all night, deranged by fevers and head pains. Harry's wife Sophie – a former nurse – came to help. Three times – 'three terrible scares' – he seemed on a knife's edge and the girls telegraphed Harry.[41]

All the while Sophie and Ethel intercepted the mail, only to discover how much of it was malignant. The fanatics had heard that Huxley was dying and on his way to Hell.

The shock of white hair tossed and turned on the pillow. For 29 days in bed, hallucinating, sweating, the back of his head pounding, he fought the lung infection. Wasted and weak, he nevertheless survived, a 'mere carcass, which has to be tended by other people'. The children had taken shifts, with Harry and Ethel coming down as Sophie and Rachel left. By his 70th birthday on 4 May 1895 he could just about walk from the terrace to the lawn in the sunshine to see his saxifrages. Foster and the faithful had watched 'from afar all these dreadful weeks'.[42] They feared the General had reached his Khartoum.

Half a century earlier, Huxley used to wake in his *Rattlesnake* alcove on stormy nights and, hearing the duty officers coping, fall asleep again. In the same way he trusted the doctors. But he watched his decline and wondered why the kidney complications had not put him in a coma. The country watched too. After an alarming report in the *Times* he wrote to Hooker on 26 June that he didn't 'feel at all like "sending in my checks"'.[43]

The two old salts were the last of the '"thick and thin" companions'. The surgeon's mates would reminisce about wooden ships and weevily biscuits, and Huxley's terrace at Hodeslea became his 'Quarterdeck', where he paced in the sea breeze. There was no pacing now. Each day in June he had been borne down to a garden tent, where he basked in the sun. It had been a lovely hot Summer and he thought he was mending, despite the 'beastly nausea' on any exertion. The nurses knew he was dying. Hooker guessed it too from Nettie's scribbled words on his 26 June envelope.

Huxley was 'still clinging to hope', but his was a 'sad hand'. The last news was of Rachel's husband dying of yellow fever in San Salvador, like so many sons of the Empire – leaving her and the three children with little provision. Grief would be Hal's to the end. For two days the agnostic 'stood alone with his dead before the abyss of the Eternal'.[44]

For those 48 hours nausea would strike him for long periods. In between he was indomitable. He read, seemingly equanimical about stepping into Nature's vacuum. Nettie fussed about him; she had waited almost as long as Rachel to marry her Jacob and the tenderness showed them as 'lovers to the end'. On the summery Saturday morning, 29 June 1895, he had a heart attack. Painkillers eased his last seven hours.[45] The doctors declared him dead at 3.30 in the afternoon.

Rachel had lost her Jacob. 'May we love to grow old together and dying may we meet again in Heaven', the star-crossed lover had written almost 50 years earlier. 'I am alone!' the old lady scribbled against these words. She was lost in his love letters, as if Sydney was more tangible than Heaven. Then in Hal's secret belongings she came across a 48-year-old bloom.[46] It was the red camellia that the black-eyed surgeon had begged after their parsonage dance.

How to honour 'the Apostle Paul of the new teaching'? Some proposed a State funeral in Westminster Abbey, where he might join Darwin. But Huxley had anticipated and scotched that idea. It might have been fitting for the Pope of Science, but it was absurd in its way. Wilder calls were heard for a Pantheon for these new men,[47] but that was very unBritish, and there was a stubborn Britishness to Huxley.

Nor would Highgate's infidel plot do. Clifford, George Eliot and G. H. Lewes had already colonized the north-east corner, ultimately to be joined by Spencer, Holyoake and Watt's agnostics. But Huxley had been the intelligentsia's 'finest free lance',[48] and a lifetime's lonely furrow in gentlemanly engagement would have made him uncomfortable there too.

His own 35-year wish would be respected – to lie alongside his little son Noel. And so on Thursday morning, 4 July, the wreath-covered oak coffin travelled by train to London Bridge, thence by hearse past quiet fields to Finchley.

There was 'no pageantry', no eulogy, the *Times* noted, and 'little that was even official'.[49] A simple blessing was given by that stalwart friend Revd Llewelyn Davies, who had come down from his parish in Westmorland. Heterodox himself, Davies was that last remnant of Christian Socialist stock with no scruples about evolution or emancipation, and no notion that his prayers could alter the physical universe.[50]

The *Telegraph* noted that the grave had been 'deeply excavated'.[51] Of course, the golden-haired three-year-old had been interred 12 feet down that his father and mother might rest just above him. It had always been intended as a family plot. At 3 o'clock Huxley was laid close by his brother George, next to his son Noel.

No invitations had been sent out. It was to have been a quiet funeral for the family. But the veiled Nettie, standing beneath the oak that had been a sapling at Noel's death, turned round to see the last and greatest constellation of Victorian scientists ever to gather on one spot. Two hundred had made their individual ways there. In front stood Sir Joseph Hooker, Lord Kelvin, Sir Joseph Lister, Michael Foster and Ray Lankester. With them were sombre heads of untold Physics, Chemistry and Biology Labs, the 'Professors', the South Kensington militia led by Major-General Sir John Donnelly, Sir William Henry Flower and the museum directors, Presidents and Councils of every learned society, the great hospital surgeons: all friends who were positively embarrassed by their admiration. Then the faceless men from the institutes, trainloads from the Midlands and North. It became a 'military' burial in Science, missing only a fusillade from the Royal Engineers. There was no government or Church presence, and none was wanted, the obituarists agreed. During an election, mud-slinging politicians would have sullied the agnostic shroud. Instead artists mixed with writers, Alma-Tadema with Henry James; 'the commanding figure of Lecky' was spotted,[52] sad-faced at the Christian recital, the fine-browed Leslie Stephen, and Darwin's sons. And, to comfort Nettie, Lucy Clifford and Louisa Tyndall.

Unknown mourners mingled, covens from the *Agnostic Journal* and *Liberty Review* and Rationalist Press, there to record events in reverent detail. For them it was 'painful' to hear the '*sure and certain*' when Huxley was so unsure and so uncertain – a 'cruel mockery' one called it. With fine-honed sarcasm Moncure Conway, reading the lesson from Huxley's works at his South Place Chapel, found that the doctrine '"he that believeth not shall be damned" – is reserved for common people; it does not apply to Fellows of the Royal Society'.[53]

Had they returned a few days later, they would have found the wreaths removed to Huxley's old hospital, Charing Cross.[54] And carved on the tombstone were lines from Nettie's poem on 'Browning's Funeral'. The original had begun appropriately

And if there be no meeting past the grave,
If all is darkness, silence, yet 'tis rest.

But there followed the three lines on the headstone:

Be not afraid, ye waiting hearts that weep;
For still He giveth His beloved sleep,
And if an endless sleep He wills, so best.

Nettie, still with that 'sneaking love for the old story', had covered her options.[55]

The sects were already tugging at Huxley's corpse, with the *Freethinker* laughing at the *Catholic Review*'s comment, 'He is no longer an Agnostic; he knows now that the Christian revelation is true'. But a grief-stricken Nettie jealously guarded Hal's intellectual remains. Through his Eastbourne retirement she had begged him to give up controversy.[56] Now she would see it stopped at the grave. That Swiftian satire would have no conclusion.

The old story jostled uncomfortably with the new in her mind. No cajoling could persuade her to release the unrevised Balfour finale. There would be no last charge, no bayoneting from beyond the grave. Knowles' plea that Hal had been 'fighting even *with* Death to accomplish it' had no effect.[57] Huxley had gone down like his hero Gordon, sword in hand, and death brought all controversies to rest.

Afterword

Huxley in Perspective

'READ NO HISTORY', advised Disraeli, only 'biography, for that is life without theory'. Good enough, perhaps, for the posing *littérateur*; but it would be a rash biographer today who ignored the new contextual and sociological approaches to science in 'Darwin's Century'. Isn't the modern function of biography to carve a path through brambly contexts? To become a part of history? Without comprehending Huxley, the *Times* said, no one could estimate the century's intellectual and social transformation. And isn't that our ultimate aim, to understand the making of our world?

Not only did the cultural landscape transform between 1840 and 1890, along with the city skyline – indeed the emergence of South Kensington testified to the rise of the professional and decline of the gentleman – but 'the very foundations of human thought' were 'rebuilt'. One Victorian concept above all would shake the complacency of ages. Evolution, Benjamin Kidd said, 'has affected the entire intellectual life of our Western civilization'.[1] At its visceral edge was T. H. Huxley – evolutionary propagandist and proselytizer of a new scientific authority – and it is impossible to separate his story from that of the 'Wonderful Century'.

Huxley is part of the new contextual history of science. This itself is a reaction to the old history of ideas, which *dis*placed the person, made him or her a disembodied ghost, a flash of transcendent genius. Only by embedding Huxley can we appreciate his role in the vast transformation that staggered our great-grandfathers. It is an irony that many historians who gravitated to the sociology of knowledge in the 1980s, trying to understand why different sorts of knowledge were produced by different social groups, have come out seeing their subjects as individuals. For me this is particularly true. Perhaps it is because, as a beleaguered minority, we have been forced to follow our subjects so closely – the onus lay on us to prove that science really was socially contingent.[2] It meant ever more microscopic examination of unique contexts, leading 'to the point at which each individual has "his" science – almost a pulverizing pluralization of the concept'.[3] This put the burden back on biography to explain scientific originality in terms of individual social trajectories. The upshot is a revitalized interest in scientific biography in the 1990s.[4]

At the same time a recognition that there is no such thing as value-free history has made biographies more personal. Given my apprenticeship – charting the radicals' fight against Anglican monopoly in *Politics of Evolution*, the street use of science in 'Artisan Resistance and Evolution', and the way Victorians reconstructed their dinosaurs using social cement in *Archetypes and Ancestors* – *Huxley* had to be an ideological portrait. While 'confrontationist' histories ('Science vs. Religion') are deeply unfashionable, it unashamedly digs into the roots of Huxley's gladiatorial antagonism. It is a book about Class and Power.

Frank Turner rightly berates an older genre, based on the Victorian *Lives and Letters*, which themselves assumed an ahistorical and hagiographical air.[5] Today's goal is to relate Huxley to the alienated Dissenters, to the rising industrialists and to the retrenching gentry who sought safety in Church. We have to understand his origins and audience. We must travel incognito on mud-spattered streets, pick up our *National Reformer* and don our wideawake hats to appreciate his workers' lectures, or buy a *Macmillan's Magazine* and mingle with the feather and sable fashionables at the Royal Institution. More than anything we have to understand how the man of science rode the political and religious crest to power.

'Servants talk about People: Gentlefolk discuss Things' ran the Victorian proverb. And since my grandparents and their parents were cooks and grooms in the great manors, my history is a maelstrom of motivated people and social action.

HUXLEY'S SOCIAL HISTORY

[The *Origin of Species* and *Man's Place in Nature*], which were anathema to the generation passing away, have become the standards of scientific thought to-day, blessed by bishops and quoted by rural deans. The times are changed more than we can appreciate.

Pall Mall Gazette, 1 July 1895

The 1850s were the time to be young, wrote G. M. Young in *Portrait of an Age* – to be one of Thackeray's flashing blades. Tom Huxley had the keenest edge of them all, honed to a glint in the hungry forties. The 1860s and 1870s were the 'glorious hour of crowded life' – the years of the liberal intelligentsia, the *Origin of Species* and *Essays and Reviews* and the fall of Anglican monopoly. Then came the storm clouds of the recessionary 1880s with their socialist riots. This is our time – a huge span. Just as the Chartists of the forties seemed remote from the equipoised Darwinians of the sixties, so Britain in the 1890s with its secularism, socialism and rediscovery of sexuality seemed another world again. Each age shocked, and was shocked in turn. 'To dip into the current literature of the "sixties"', said the *Pall Mall Gazette* on Huxley's death, 'is like plugging into a burning fiery furnace'.[6] I have tried to show the famous rapier being tempered in this oven: to grasp T. H. Huxley's role in half a century which saw the emancipation of Dissent and rise of the professions.

He lived long enough to see the scandalous sexual experimentation. The naughty nineties arrived after decades of belief that morality was fixed. Women in knickerbockers on bikes, women climbing the winding stairs of open-top buses, men complaining that 'their privileges are going'. The hedonism of Wilde's London was a furious reaction to the old guard's Puritanism. The long years of salvation by reason had led the unsatisfied spirit to try salvation by sin. Or salvation by social action, or spiritualism – Huxley bowed out amid the decadence, the new mystifications, Annie Besant's final migration to theosophy, and science going private as political activism assumed its public function. He left amid the *fin de siècle* restlessness, 'pregnant of great changes'.[7]

There was a flawed perfection to his messy life: the conquering heights, the prehistoric visions, the quixotic tilts and medieval excursions, the visionary who 'dreams strange things', the inward collapses and outward bravura. His life was lived like a hurtling express, and it periodically careened off the tracks. The speed and sublimation, Beatrice Webb thought, were something to do with 'his early life' being 'supremely sad'. Speed from a full head of steam was his diversion. But the energy he expended on School Boards, Commissions and intellectual theatricality left everyone excusing the defects; anyway, said Moncure Conway echoing Shakespeare, 'Best men are moulded of their faults'. For Webb they were what made Huxley fascinating. Even Catholic contessas were drawn to this religious smiter of Papal perversions, to this Reformer from the North with no god and no heaven; and still there was 'something so attractive in Prof Huxley'.[8]

To many the assertive 'masculine' prose suggested that there were no hidden depths. Steely imagery for the Victorians meant intellectual power and virility (an equation itself that was no longer adding up by the 1890s).[9] 'Pope Huxley' exuded certainty and reassurance. He provided the totemic strength to face up to our animal past and face down an Immortal future. It was a magnificently efficient façade, put up to comply with Victorian codes of behaviour. Men did not gush out their feelings in public; and when one did, like Froude, Carlyle cursed him for 'vomiting up his interior crudities'. But an acute Beatrice Webb saw the frail veneer over the seething depths, while Len's sister-in-law Mrs Humphry Ward extracted Huxley's revealing self-perception:

> Beneath the cooled logical upper strata of my microcosm, there is a fused mass of prophetism and mysticism, and Lord knows what might happen to me, in case a moral earthquake cracked the superincumbent deposits, and permitted an eruption of the demonic element below.[10]

The currents visible in the 1850s were still swirling after a generation.

Always the self-perceived 'plebeian',[11] Huxley was a prey to the pressures of Victorian uprightness. Using Darwinism to claw more power only exacerbated his predicament. With evolutionists widely held to be wicked, his life had to be an exemplary open book. Hence the appearance of a model family, above reproach. Indeed it was a stable, close-knit, free household glossed by Pater's 'warm, indulgent, loving nature',[12] even if, as Webb said, none of the children understood his intellectual struggle.

It explains why the sober Huxley, keeper of the agnostic moral flame, was wary of the family skeletons rattling in the closet. The poor boy was conscious of his origins. George's banking scandal and Ellen's drunken debauchery threatened him like a dropped accent. Ellen's and Polly's deaths removed the peril of exposure, but only their gin-sodden corpses explained his accepting an Honorary Membership of the suitably distant 'American Society for the Study and Cure of Inebriety' in 1893, with a coy admission that he knew something 'of its very worst consequences'. Still, 'No scandal ever had the name' of Huxley 'for its butt', concluded one admirer.[13] And from our century there never did appear 'such worthy representatives of frock-coated respectability as those terrible scientists'. But the struggle for respectability had taken its toll.

He had to erect formidable defences. A lacerating tongue was for conquering and repelling; a scalpelled pen saw him cutting up men more than monkeys. Many approached but few touched him. There was a frightening presence. Young Oliver Lodge felt it. He once plucked up courage at a soirée to ask Mrs Huxley about the dying Clifford. Through the noise she thought he was asking about the children, and the 'General' 'stiffened in a manner appropriate'. Poor Lodge, 'too shy to explain, slunk away' and it took him 20 years to overcome the 'twinge' and write to explain.[14]

Only to strong women did Huxley open up – the dark priestesses like gutsy Ellen Busk, to be adored and feared. George Eliot in the 1850s saw him blindly driven, aloof, while Beatrice Webb in the 1880s penetrated the smouldering vulnerability. She saw the insecurities beneath the life of conquest. His were philosophic dashes between disabling fits. Just as he had no time to earn money, he had no money to buy him time: he could never luxuriate like Darwin in sustained research. It was all *ad hoc*, squeezed in. His science suffered. 'He is greater as a man than as a scientific thinker', Webb said, and more interesting. He had 'None of the enthusiasm for "what is", or the silent persistency in grasping truth'. His was 'the eager rush of the conquering mind, loving the fact of conquest more than the land conquered'. And behind him was a trail littered with half-finished work which generations would try to mop up.[15] Publishers understood and cajoled him: Macmillan once sent him a bound, embossed *Lessons in Elementary Physiology* – completely blank-leaved, with a reminder to write the book. But the dashes enabled Huxley to scout beyond society into strange regions, back to ape-men, forward to the ice death of planet, out to the lonely cosmos, inward to the 'abyss of the Eternal'.[16]

The voyager acquired a cynicism as he was blown about 'among the grains of human dust on our speck of a planet'. The anguished soul had discovered the gloomy wastes of an uncaring cosmos and was venting his evangelical anger. This was Victorian man on the edge, lashing out, as George Eliot noted. Such 'melancholy has haunted his whole life', Webb added. Hence the paradox: he was 'never at peace unless he was fighting', never alive unless he was slaying. The poor boy broke lances in religious aggression. And the alienated outsiders who had risen with him indulged his mock modesty. 'What an unfortunate man you are!' said Lecky as Huxley stood before the Salvation Army. And 'With your deep "sense of the blessedness of peace"'. Ultimately his 'controversial manner' became as 'polished as his literary style',[17] but that does not disguise his religious need to engage.

Science did bring the 'solace of fame', but it barely satisfied. Huxley, the most ascetic of sceptics, the most relativistic of agnostics, laughing at materialism, knowing nothing of necessity, the man who stood alone with no Humanist Church or Agnostic Temple, found less and less to cling to. He had left the 'Unknowable' a desert, the Laws of Nature merely the relations of events passing our vision. Yet through all, the 'Cynic and sceptic' clung to love as the one 'mysterious reality'.[18] It was this that pulled him back from the brink. And it was this that saved mankind in 'Evolution and Ethics'.

But personality is not the most interesting level of explanation. 'Men of genius', said the *Times*, contemplating Huxley's shooting star, 'come no one knows whence or when'.[19] But we can appreciate the social forces they ride to power. To start, we might ask why the *enfant terrible* felt himself part of excluded England, alienated and angry. And why he felt the need to forge *Science* as his rapier.

THE ROUNDHEAD WHO LOST HIS FAITH

> The question . . . is how British intellectual life marked by a predominance of Anglican institutions, ideas, and ideology in 1830 moved by 1870 to a culture in which Nonconformity . . . played an important part and one in which scientific naturalism had replaced natural theology.
>
> Frank Turner[20]

Twenty years ago Arnold Thackray brilliantly analysed Manchester's Unitarians. He made their Dissenting drive the motor force of the 'transformation of natural knowledge'.[21] In the industrial heartland, the Chapel elite had developed a wheeze-and-snort Nature wilfully at odds with the supernatural props of Anglican power. The Black Country democrats legally bound Nature, made it subject to law and order. The most radical of them denied that it was subject to Divine aristocratic whim. Thus they refused any miraculous support for the bishops' status quo. With the institutions of power – the universities, the bench and the hospitals – in Anglican hands, these *arriviste* industrialists forged a rival outsider-knowledge. To these excluded, marginal men the democratic republic of science was appealing.

Now consider Huxley. True, his father – that shadowy presence – taught in an Anglican public school (taught the future Cardinal Newman no less). But if Ealing School had been part of the nation's evangelical backbone, it was in decline in Tom's day and 'as bad as any of them'.[22] Nor should this blind us to the teenager's sensitivity to religious injustice. It was shown in the ease with which he learnt the morality of resistance from the handicapped Dissenters. Those are the unexplored years of Huxley biographies: the lost background, the missing key, the trajectory away from Anglicanism. The years in cotton-spinning Coventry reading Southwood Smith's fatalistic, reforming Unitarian bible, *The Divine Government*, and in Marshall Hall's cut-price medical school, cast a new light on the development of Huxley's science and agnosticism. No one had even correctly identified Huxley's first anatomy school before, the short-lived 'Sydenham College' in London. And yet it was the institution that pioneered the study of reflex arcs and automaton biology and led the dirty war against Anglican privilege.

Huxley's radical teachers were waging a campaign of disobedience against the Anglican-run, power-grabbing College of Physicians. Huxley in the forties was among radical Methodists and rational Dissenters – activists whose culture of resistance and scientific Calvinism had matured around the Lord's table. Houston Peterson once said that Huxley's mind was fixed about 1840. Peterson knew nothing of Huxley's radical schooling, but I think he was right.[23] Young Huxley became heir to the Dissenting resistance of cotton kings and medical activists. Without this insight his lifelong struggle simply makes no sense.

The ultra-radicals accepted a sovereign, self-regulating Nature. Not for them a supernatural command structure descending from the Godhead through the State priesthood (as L. S. Jacyna has shown in a series of stunning papers). The radical Dissenters were disabling this divine sanction of Anglican repression. They were taking their orders direct from God's Works, His natural order. The new causal, natural science became the 'social legitimation of marginal men', their 'mode of cultural self-expression', the means to paint Tory Anglicans themselves as idolatrous '*pagani*'.[24] Huxley and Spencer would make it the cosmic norm; and with Darwin's competitive *Origin of Species* sanctioning the Nonconformist meritocratic ideal, a new intellectual aristocracy would be born around Science.

In the 1840s evolution had been a nail-studded club hidden in the street atheist's coal-hole; by 1870 it was being polished as a Whitworth gun in the imperial armoury. By any account this was a telling crossover. Thirty years of Dissenting liberation and professional changes had eased the way for Darwin's *Origin of Species*. Jim Secord calls Darwin's the 'palace coup'.[25] It took the winter palace after the battle had been won by the urban Dissenters and professionals.

Twentieth-century scientists have taken Huxley's non-partisan self-image on trust. He became iconic as *the* ideologically untainted Scientist. But historians have become cautious. Bernie Lightman has pointed out the theological structures behind Huxley's thought. Lightman's *Origins of Agnosticism* makes Huxley a transitional figure whose agnosticism had *religious* qualities. And this was how Huxley was seen in his own day – as 'a lineal descendant of the Protestant Reformation', steeped in Biblical lore. 'He may have inverted orthodox theology, he may have blessed what it bans', said the *Times*, but he shared its 'temper'.[26] He commanded 'the sect of the Darwinian evolutionists', whose converts would revere evolution's 'grandeur and power'. In short, he made an undercast feel first class through his holier-than-thou attitude. Scientists, he said, had a higher 'standard of veracity'. That in itself, critics argued, bred a 'spirit of latent intolerance':

> his nature is essentially Puritanic, if not Calvinistic. He has the moral earnestness, the volitional energy, the absolute confidence in his own convictions, the desire and determination to impress them upon all mankind, which are the essential marks of Puritan character. His whole temper and spirit is essentially dogmatic of the Presbyterian or Independent type, and he might fairly be described as a Roundhead who had lost his faith.[27]

So we have Huxley decrying the 'sin of faith', descending on the apostate Mivart. We have the righteousness, the prophetic 'tide of matter' drowning unregenerate 'souls'. He was a good hater, with a 'scientific hell, to which the finally impenitent, those who persist in rejecting the new physical gospel, might be condemned'.[28] We have to beware of this Dissenting imagery becoming one-sided. What he actually retained was the 'temper' and the deconsecrated theological shell, a sort of evacuated Calvinistic antigen in the shape of a deterministic Nature.[29] But mate this Dissenting husk to Turner's Carlylean living host, fire it with the residual romanticism described by James Paradis in his superb *T. H. Huxley: Man's Place in Nature*, and you have the roots of young Huxley's scientific secularism.

It went to cement his Cromwellian image – and Chamberlain's Unitarian Birmingham loved him for it. But it was a religious reputation he had to shake if Science was to seem untarnished. Not that that was hard. Ultimately, with the success of Dissent, his Nonconformist virtues – earnestness, duty, moralism – became the middle-class norm in the Victorian Noon. They no longer stood out.

PROFESSOR HUXLEY, LL.D., F.R.S., L.S.D.,

13. The Scientist as Public Servant. With a radical Home Secretary discriminating to get scientists jobs, Huxley added the Inspectorship of Fisheries in 1881 to his teaching load and Royal Commissions. *Punch* cynically appended '£.s.d' to his name, but the extra work drained his energy and drove him towards another breakdown.

14. The reclusive Darwin became a commanding public figure in Boehm's statue. Placing it in Owen's Cathedral of Science – the Natural History Museum – was a political sign that London's last bastion had fallen.

15. Huxley's true heir was his talented, unstable daughter Marian ('Mady'). She was an inspired artist – a girl, admitted her paternalist father, with a 'career' before her. She married the artist John Collier, shown here painting her – but the painting itself is by Mady. She would die mad in 1887.

16. (*Above*) Huxley's daughters were all artists and favourites at the Slade. Here the burnt-out old man is caught snoozing by young Nettie.

17. (*Opposite*) H.G. Wells was among Huxley's last students. He is apeing Huxley, who mesmerized his class by lecturing with his arms around the gorilla.

18. (*Above*) The Huxleys' drawing room. The portraits are all by Collier: left, Huxley's daughter Nettie, painted in 1885; centre, Ethel Huxley, painted in 1887 (three years later she would become Collier's second wife after Mady died); and right, Huxley the patriarch, painted in 1883.

19. (*Opposite*) The Right Honourable T. H. Huxley, spokesman for Science at the Councils of the State. Having ridiculed Gladstone's Scripturalism and impugned the Home Ruler's judgment, Huxley was made a Privy Councillor by Lord Salisbury's Tories in 1893.

20. Behind the stern portraits of the savage controversialist lay the droll, good-natured chap of this rare photograph.

In some ways Agnosticism *was* the apotheosis of Dissent. It was the last act of the Protestant Reformation. To that other Ealing graduate John Henry Newman it was as '*clear as day*' in 1840 'that Protestantism leads to infidelity'. By then Huxley – that most 'radical among Protestant Whigs', as Chalmers Mitchell called him – was treading the path.[30] He was cutting and trimming to the knowable border. He carried freedom of conscience to the limit. This was his 'New Reformation' – the freeing of Nonconformity from its final idolatrous anchor.

From dog-collar to white-collar: subtly his 'sect' absorbed the old priesthood's functions. Morality became acquiescence to scientific evidence. The social order was sustained by the Laws of Biology. The unemancipated women and workers were held to their stations. Order remained as the classes toppled one another (or ultimately merged into a higher hegemony). Industrial-age Science, hitching itself to the State, was called upon to curb insurrection and maintain national security. It explains why the pious old 'Pope' – who castigated the clergy for climbing over their side of the fence – felt free to roam into politics, theology, morality and education himself. And why it was impossible to open a journal 'without feeling his hand in all the moving subjects of the day'.[31]

The Nonconformist motor had carried Huxley to power. And Nonconformist money kept him there – bequests from Quaker manufacturers, Cobden's free-traders and Congregationalist steel barons, all of whom understood his *Lay Sermons*. The seditious Unitarian science of 1800 had become the deconsecrated universal by 1900. Southwood Smith's deterministic *Divine Government* became Huxley's *Natural Government*. (Not for nothing was Huxley's Jubilee address on the 'Progress of Science in the last Half Century' cemented into the foundation of the All Souls Universalist Church in Grand Rapids, Michigan, by a 'thorough evolutionist' pastor who preached humanitarian sermons.[32]) By 1887 the Nonconformists had their open society, their access to power. Indeed, they had their new universities in the industrial towns, Birmingham, Liverpool, Manchester, Leeds, Nottingham, Sheffield, all giving science prominence and Huxley his due.[33]

So Huxley's 'New Reformation' was synonymous with the liberation of the industrial and professional classes. It made evolutionary naturalism the serviceable way of thought in a free-trading nation. As he modernized history – making ape ancestors for mankind as unproblematic as dinosaur ancestors for birds – he camouflaged the tainting metaphysics while putting the 'new Nature' into the professionals' hands. He left an image of neutral science soaring like Pegasus to unknown regions.

All of this suggests that Evolution had an overriding social importance. While he had difficulty reconciling himself to Darwin's bloody Natural Selection in biology, the competitive struggle could legitimate a meritocratic order or combat socialism. To this extent 'Darwin's Bulldog' was a misnomer (as Michael Bartholomew said long ago). In the final analysis Huxley comes across as a complex figure coping with the shift from a Romantic 1840s to a Socialist 1880s. He repackaged Darwinism for his dissolvent armoury. Both to fire off its shells at a rival Anglican edifice, and to sustain a form of Calvinist fatalism: justifying resignation on earth rather than redemption in heaven. His prose was called 'masculine English' because it squared up to the 'abysmal griefs hidden under the current of daily life'.[34] His 'masculine vigour' was a hard-edged uncompromising style, a clenched-jaw attitude to the horror of pain and death in nature and the sentimental supernatural fictions which surround it. His evolutionary Nature was harsher than Calvin's, and his hard-nosed science hinted at a similar religious forbearance.

A SALVATION ARMY OF HUXLEYS

We begin to sense how science in Huxley's hands had a religious potency. The fact that it acquired a non-aligned image made it even better to ratify the new social order and sanction the seizing of Church assets. The State Church, portrayed as a rival 'branch of the Civil Service',[35] lost its monopoly on Oxbridge, the bench and the hospitals.

Huxley's men were being puffed as a 'priesthood of science' as early as 1868 by the secularist George Holyoake. Not only were they usurping Dissent's dispute with the Anglicans, they were turning it into a territorial claim over health, education and morality (making the common culture of scientific, social and sectarian thought at once larger than R. M. Young envisaged in *Darwin's Metaphor*). This explains why Huxley so easily turned theological questions into scientific ones, why he plumbed 'the whence and whither of mankind, the limitations of knowledge, the sanctions of conduct', while challenging the Church's 'monopoly of serious and constant reflection upon the terrible problems of existence'.[36] Even the title of his book *Lay Sermons* said so much: a century later it sounds plummy, strange, even dusty for a *scientist's* work, but its double meaning was provocative in 1870: suggesting secular sermons to rival those from the pulpit, or professional addresses to the laity adoring at the scientific altar. Like the old Paleyites who had made known God's way through Nature, Huxley was making Nature's known through Science. The 'garment of God' had become the scientific priest's robe. And like the old priesthood he saw nothing insignificant in nature. Every coral polyp in a reef or *Globigerina* in the Chalk was pregnant with moral meaning.

The outsiders hitched their demands for State employment to an image of science as a national asset.[37] The result was a swelling 'Salvation Army of Huxleys': a middle-class profession. It was self-sustaining through its teacher-training programme, and self-validating through its university restructuring. It left a growing corps of biology professors who swore (as an eavesdropping Chalmers Mitchell heard at a Royal Society soirée) that 'it was Huxley who made all of us possible'.[38]

Scientific research became free-ranging, open-ended, itself a novel concept. Huxley's professionals in their 'knowledge factories' would become 'pioneers in the exploration and settlement of new regions'. It was exciting, modern. H. G. Wells tingled at the thought that he might 'do Research. Research!' A buzz surrounded the word. Wells was in awe of Huxley, and the frisson shows at his prospect of voyaging into the unknown, at 'any moment' to 'make a Discovery!!!' Such open-ended research broke the seminary tradition of incestuously-recycled Classicism. Vulgar nature had been by-passed by the Classics-dominated Anglican Universities, with their dedication to rank and wealth. But Huxley exploited this shunned and sordid Nature to legitimate his scientific 'priesthood', using it to build a rival base in secular London and the industrial Midlands. From here he turned the instruments of government against the Anglican universities. The Classics *had* been the mark of a Gentleman, but the 'Gentleman' as an occupational category was dead. And as Ruth Barton says, Huxley portrayed Science as more rigorous, more critical, and equally character-forming.[39]

This was already evident when 'Theology' was 'massacred', as the legend had it, at the 1860 Oxford British Association meeting. In fact, Archdeacon Farrar remembered it as a question of manners. Wilberforce's 'flippant' question on grandma Huxley's descent from apes showed that the 'the Bp. had forgotten to behave like a gentleman'. Huxley for once refused to cap the tackiness, leaving a question hanging about the bishop's taste. An Oxford audience of 'gentlefolk, not prepared to endorse anything vulgar', contrasted the worldly bishop, his 'splendid nature debauched by society', with this plain-dressed Puritanical unknown. The manners themselves reflected a wide sectarian divide. The jest was innocuous to Wilberforce because his distinguished grandmother was related to bankers and archbishops. The venerable old lady being akin to apes was ludicrous. But Huxley knew nothing of his grandmother, and it stung to be the brunt of High Church hauteur. Puritans made virtue the true nobility; and Huxley's gravity showed the man of science, Cockshut said in *The Unbelievers*, to be 'the more faithful heir of the heroes of the Reformation and Civil War'.[40]

The Puritans slid their men into the Oxbridge seminaries. Here the professionals created a unique space for themselves. Laboratories were built to enclose Nature. The 'field' reappeared under the lens, as Graeme Gooday puts it. Here the 'new Nature' could be jealously guarded. But the laboratory's deadroom air gave it a very different feel from Paley's happy parsonage. That is because Huxley's 'Biology' – that unique South Kensington development – was carved out of medical comparative anatomy.[41] It remained a dead, dissected nature, relocated from the anatomy schools, and simplified by means of 'type' specimens so that it could be transmitted to the schoolmasters. The geography of science had changed dramatically by the mid-1870s. The industrial fringes had coalesced into centres of laboratory excellence within the old universities.

Huxley called the 'Victorian epoch' the 'age of science'. It was only a beginning, he argued. Since 'Nature is limitless', the free-roaming enquirer would never come up against a boundary.[42] Securely institutionalized in the universities, funded by the State, the emergent scientific enterprise had become a self-sustaining exploration.

Inside its great institutions, the 'scientific priesthood', quasi-autonomous like so much of the civil service, would continue the old patrician ethos. There was a grand imperial, paternal arrogance in Victorian Britain. It was not only the age of science, but the Age of the Father.[43] The *men* of science were chary of letting even their talented daughters near the altar or workers do more than swing thuribles. Against this backdrop one has to judge Huxley's attitude to women.

Evelleen Richards talks of the 'scientific onslaught' on women's emancipation. The onslaught was sanctioned by a nascent, worried profession backed by Darwin's *Descent of Man*, and it was the Darwinians who 'articulated the dominant constructions of feminimity . . . and naturalized the barriers against feminine intellectual and social equality'. Women bought the Darwinian commodity, figuratively and literally. Despite the stereotype of stay-at-home, religiously demure wives, many paid for the *The Descent of Man*, even if they had 'to order it on the sly!' And amid the 'pretty hubbub' at Huxley's Royal Institution talks Tyndall was 'torn to pieces by women in search of tickets. Anything that touches progenitorship interests them'. But for all that was religiously liberating or titillating (it is difficult to capture the frisson about 'evolution' except by this word), would-be emancipists were being bound by its prejudicial laws. They had a doubly hard time of it. Darwin had branded them as biologically inferior because of their exclusion from the competitive arena, yet in medicine they were seen as undesirable economic competitors, rivalling men for the few paying jobs. The men simply did not want them as contenders.

But women were prising open the doors – Huxley even thought his talented Mady had a brilliant 'career' in prospect. In the 1860s he had put biological limitations on women's capacity; but as a liberal paternalist he was willing to grant them the privilege of sitting in class.[44] And *yet*, allowed to compete, the women came off well, confounding his stereotype: the sole woman in his first practical class at South Kensington took the prize. And Huxley soon had Miss McConnish demonstrating. By H. G. Wells' day Huxley's audience was a normal cross-section, including women, vegetarians and socialists. Interestingly, when Huxley died the papers juxtaposed the successive Darwinian and suffragettist revolutions: 'we have now got over' the shock of the *Origin of Species* and *Man's Place*, said a syndicated obituary, 'just as we . . . may, perchance, get used to the "new woman"'.[45] It was as if Huxley was responsible for the first and consumed by the second.

The Nemesis of growing knowledge was its fractionalization. Huxley's age had created the specialists. In the 1860s came a few Generals. By the 1890s whole squads of sappers were spending their lives watching amoebas or weighing gases, their research papers being valued 'in proportion as the corner of the world with which they deal is dark and minute'. Knowledge, said the *Times*, had 'already become too vast to be manageable'. Huxley had been the last to manage it, indeed the last to view Art, Literature and Science as a whole. In Royal Academy talks he visualized each of them stopping the flux of life to fix its order and beauty momentarily. David Roos has him keeping faith with the broad-based monthly magazines and demanding a larger purview for culture. Out there, in public, as Edward Clodd observed, Huxley was 'free from that curse of specialism which kills all sense of proportion'.[46] But that was ironic, because it was Huxley's training that created the boffins.

Of course he outlived his time, and it showed in his superannuated Church-bashing in these monthlies. He 'continued his method of controversy after its justification had ceased', unable to shake off his old political mentality. Even as the Right Honourable T. H. Huxley grew staid he clung to an old radical sectarianism. A second generation never followed him. His students were the specialists now: winning their own Royal Medals or studying heredity in Weismann's Germany. They kept their religious sense of belonging to him. As was true 'of Pius IX when he wrote to the Emperor of Germany, saying "everyone who was baptised belonged to the Pope"', wrote one admirer, 'so every student of science belongs to you'. But few became miracle-denouncing publicists, and he lamented the fact. They were professionally secure, with his scientific naturalism written into their accredition procedures.

The years of science's heady excitement were over. After he died, there was only the 'deadly dulness of the mere workshop'.[47] On the eve of the twentieth century science was specialized and esoteric; it shut itself away in the laboratory and lost its public appeal. Its radicalism passed to politics, its moral drive to humanism; and the poison bombs raining death in the Great War finally killed its nineteenth-century promise.

AGNOSTICISM

. . . the word had to him a deep and solemn meaning.

Michael Foster[48]

Something more surrounded the man of science's credentials – an agnostic moral aura. 'Pope Huxley' had fused the little sciences into a universal corpus – the One Catholic Apostolic Church of True Knowledge. Science, with a capital 'S' now, a monolithic entity matched by a name for its acolyte, the 'Scientist'. Its method of enquiry set limits to the knowable, and acquiescence to those limits earned initiates moral dispensation. Indeed the acceptance of physical evidence became a religious imperative itself. It was what gave Huxley, in Bishop Magee's words, his 'bumptious air of omniscience'. Huxley had at last found his 'saving belief'.[49]

Agnosticism was a product of circumstance. It was already evident in the young surgeon's letters of 1847. Here it appears as much a response to the seditious street atheists, bent on destroying the social fabric, as to Carlyle's ideal of a theology-less religion. Frank Turner sees the 'cultural apostasy' of the Arnolds and Stephens as 'different from the direct social and political protests' of the 1840s. So it was for them, but Huxley's outsider education put him closer to the protesters. If Matthew Arnold's 'cultural apostates' were fifth columnists destroying the Church from within, Huxley was digging up the foundations from without. He *would* later seek a gentlemanly engagement, but the boy among cotton spinners and medical destructives was steeped in the dissident sub-culture. It had turned him into an 'agnostic' in all but name before he set foot on the *Rattlesnake*. From the chaos of the 1840s came a Calvinistic upstart quoting Luther, a sceptic who sought the burden of evidence, a nonconformist who refused to equate the 'Truth' with Anglican authority.[50] Agnosticism was fashioned from a Dissenting lawful secularism to give the State Church its moral come-uppance.

Twenty years later, in 1869, the word was added to the deed. 'Agnosticism' became his 'apologetic tool', Lightman says. He consecrated doubt and wielded it with political bravado. In those 20 years the tainting sectarian connotations had started to wear off. The word would appear *de novo*, signifying the scientist with clean hands. It would make the agnostic a moral cut above all the sectarian 'ists' – Atheist or Anglican, Positivist or Spiritualist. 'What does nature want with me?' the young romantic had asked in 1851.[51] By 1869 he knew; he had become Nature's prophet, Her voice in the wilderness of men.

Agnosticism became a secure port, Tennyson's 'golden harbour'. Scientific method defined the limits to the sensory orb, beyond which it was immoral to stray. Acquiescence to the unpalatable sublunary truths about apes or ancestors became a baptism by fire for tyros, and for them 'veracity [lay at] the heart of morality' and at the centre of a new religion. While Mallock and Hutton slashed at secularism for making life meaningless,[52] Huxley put the meaning back with his essays, equating worth and purpose with duty and honesty.

Science's *method*, not its glitzy applications. offered redemption. It became a harder and harder line to hold. Faced with the technological marvels of the 1880s and 1890s – motorbikes, the first petrol-driven cars, moving pictures and electric underground trains – he had to ensure the purity of Science. Where once he had attacked 'aristocratic flunkeyism' in the Royal Society, now he lashed the techno-flunkeys from the temple – the 'Engineers, Chemical traders

& "Experts" (who have sold their souls for a good price) and who find it helps them to appear to the public as if they were men of science'. He feared the veneration switching to Science's products – 'its froth and scum', its engines and telegraphs, as he angrily put it answering Disraeli. Science's ascetic method was the real 'foundation of its human worth'. Science had been sanctified for its agnostic moral purity. It had acquired something of the holy. 'Science takes the place of dogmatic religion', noted the *Tablet* in 1871, 'Mr. Huxley is the favourite and popular apostle of this new creed'.[53] And the 'holy' had to be preserved to bind the profession in an age of religious revivals.

Method and agnostic moralism were his professionals' *raison d'être*. Science was no longer a revelation of God's handiwork, but a search for the Eternal in a fact. It was an image powerful enough to make agnosticism the intellectual's credentials by the 1880s. Huxley took it 'out of the wilderness of Sinai', said a follower.[54] He made a Promised Land of Science.

KENSINGTON BARRACKS: THE SOCIAL ROOTS OF THE MILITARY METAPHOR

> The ascendancy of an unambiguously militaristic ethos [in the Department of Science and Art] . . . raises a number of troubling questions . . .
>
> Rafael Cardoso Denis on the role of the Royal Engineers at South Kensington[55]

There is no doubt that Frank Turner is right: the 'war' between science and religion was a professional territorial dispute. By the 1870s this 'military' image was being hyped by Huxley's group and universalized by Draper's blockbuster *History of the Conflict Between Religion and Science* into the battle of all time. Jim Moore decisively deconstructed the 'war' scenario in his 'non-violent' *Post-Darwinian Controversies* (1979). It was a book born of the anti-Vietnam War years, as he says himself. And he has gone on to give a more gutsy political *re*construction. Through the 1980s, while I was looking at the medical radicals for *Politics of Evolution* – the antagonistic under-class – Moore was re-evaluating the intellectuals' crisis of faith. He saw it as a result of the elite's attempt to rationalize the industrial dislocations while retaining their grip on power. The Victorians created and resolved their crisis by naturalizing religious beliefs, putting God's power into Nature and making Scientists the new priests. Moore too saw it as a case of new physical gospels for a new social order.[56] We arrived at the same spot, which is why we could sit down to collaborate on *Darwin*.

But what stimulated this 'War' propaganda? Why did students dub Huxley the 'General'? Why did he see himself as a shilling sergeant, enlisting men 'into the army of science'? We need to get back beyond the 1870s. Too much talk of the 'military metaphor' has been about a bloodless paper war. Not only must we penetrate the radical Dissenting campaign headquarters, but we need to look at real warfare. For the slippage between a metaphoric and literal militarism was surprising; indeed there was a common basis. While Huxley called evolution his Whitworth gun, he aligned himself with the gunsmiths. South Kensington had its military underbelly.

We must go back further still, to Huxley the young war reporter on the *Westminster Review*. Already we see the metaphor acquiring its military edge as he identified with Sultan Schamyl's guerrilla resistance to the Cossacks. This was more than reportage in 1854, in the patriotic prelude to the Crimean War. Huxley *lived* the Islamic *jihad*, contrasting Islam's 'youthful vigour' with the 'degraded idolatry' of the Russian Orthodox Church. He sided with the ascetic Sufi, who damned Orthodoxy's 'besotted priests' with their 'gew-gaw saints'. His report was a displaced attack on a corrupt theology at home. He had Schamyl standing 'beside our own Cromwell' as a liberator. Huxley was already deep in his own holy war. The 'prophet-warrior' taught that to resist oppression was a religious duty, and Huxley sought to bind his 'scientific Young England' as the Sultan was uniting his Muslim nation, by meeting an orthodox 'threat'.[57]

Huxley the teacher was surrounded by Crimea veterans. Troops fresh from the front were seconded as free labour to the Kensington site. The Royal Engineers turned the 'sword into the reap-hook' and gave the Department of Science and Art its military mind. The DSA had Major-General Donnelly as chief of staff, and six similar ranking officers among its inspectors by the 1880s. With War Office personnel, and soldiers patrolling the exam halls, the regimental colours waved over South Kensington. Huxley was a War Department examiner himself. He lectured at the Royal Engineer Institute in Chatham (making the Forces the naturalist's eyes abroad) and was 'all for an R.E.' to drill the students.[58] The uniform suited his purpose. In an age when the Salvation Army cadres were setting up their own recruiting tents, Science acquired real military authority and an air of national purpose.

The Whitworth gun was a product of Dissenting industry, and its designer backed the Kensington corps. Sir Joseph Whitworth put £100,000 into the DSA's science scholarships and joined the steel magnate Sir William Armstrong to fill Huxley's purse. This was armaments money. While the gun-toting Volunteer put Darwin's Whitworth into the liberal armoury, his sponsors were producing weapons to police an empire. Whitworth and Armstrong supported Huxley's technical education, and in return got science teachers for their factory towns. The Huxleys would enjoy a wing in Whitworth's Matlock mansion. Working trips to Newcastle, to pore over Permian reptiles, gave way to annual holidays at Armstrong's Gothic manor. The *paterfamilias* toured the plants, looking at the experimental breech-loaders and iron-clad cruisers. The families became close – Lady Armstrong was Ethel's godmother – while the misses donned mob caps to go dancing with Captain Noble's daughter.

The metaphor of the *Origin* as a 'Whitworth gun in the armoury of liberalism' – the Darwinian muzzle-loader to keep Britain Great – had complex social roots in an age of gun-toting Volunteers. Huxley was updating Dissent's intellectual weaponry. He was allying the *Origin* to patriotism and secular competitive progress – shouldering his .45 to shoot over the ranks of obstructive Anglicans. Society's 'crisis of faith' was a collision of creeds accompanying the professionalizing of society. Huxley's evolutionary oiling of the industrial rents both speeded the cultural transition and made the crisis so much worse for many. It goes to reinforce the image of Science's 'war' with the Church as an extension of industrial Dissent's struggle, born of an era, in Gilley and Loades' words, when the Churches themselves 'were at war'. It was 'part of a wider battle'.[59]

Dissent's demand for fair competition – meritocracy rather than Anglican monopoly – was fulfilled by the *Origin of Species* (1859). But then that too was a belated piece of Reform Age business, crafted in 1837–9 when the Dissenting struggle was at its height (and supported by Darwin's Whigs). Darwin's book was itself built on 'death, famine, rapine, and the concealed war of nature' (as he said in that turbulent year 1842). It gave a scientific sanction to competition; the best survived to carry the species forward, both among animals and humans. Darwin had been bathed in economic individualism; the *Origin* recast Nature in its light, and in 1872 he was expressing dismay that the unions opposed piece-work and competition, and that so many saw the 'Cooperative Societies . . . as the main hope for the future'. Given all this it was easy for Huxley to re-politicize the *Origin*'s competitive aspect a decade later to use against the socialists who had attacked his bus. New contexts required new conceptualizations of Darwin's opus, and the 'new debates', as Asa Briggs has called them, were 'about the nature not of the Universe but of society'. Huxley turned full circle and used Darwin's 'neutral' science to justify a property-owning capitalist economy. It was at this point, around 1890, as the Malthusian aspects of the *Origin of Species* were being used to quell the socialist masses, that the term 'Social Darwinism' was first coined.[60] The very words had anti-socialist connotations.

The international situation was by then becoming tense. The 'war' – initially between a competitive, evolutionary Science and a monopolistic Anglicanism – was extended yet again. Huxley now *nationalized* the Darwinian struggle. There were dangerous currents beneath the gay nineties. Paul Crook has dipped his toes into these darker waters in *Darwinism, War and History*: the arms race was on, military budgets were staggering and peace seemed increasingly dependent on 'sheer force'. This was the age of Krupp's Ruhr works; Germany had the best-equipped army in the world, and its militarists would come to see war as a civilized nation's 'highest expression of strength'. Europe's industrial growth supported the scramble for Africa (in the last 15 years of the century Germany and France added 4.5 million square miles of colonial territory). The flood of imports marked 'Made in Germany' left Britons with a foreboding. In 1887 Huxley called this competition among the great powers industrial 'warfare'. A 'war' footing demanded better technical education and the stabilizing of class relations within a capitalist economy. British universities would have to become 'the drill-grounds of the army of industry'.[61] A former Minister of War echoed Huxley's warning that 'famine, indigence, and starvation' would accompany economic defeat.

Crook's analysis of the 'peace' books of the period – which declared war to be economically unviable and genocidal – showed the fears as Anglo-German relations deteriorated after 1893. This was the backdrop to the final act in Huxley's 'war' drama. Or rather the final proof that there were practical ramifications of his Darwinian 'war' metaphor. For in 1894 he refused to sign a moratorium on the European arms race. Though an 'International Arbitration' agreement had the backing of trade unions and Churches, he declined to sign because industrial competition was natural and Darwinian – 'merely the superficial expression of social forces the operation of which can not be sensibly affected by agreements between governments'.[62]

His belief that governments could not moderate these large-scale Darwinian struggles forces us to re-evaluate his ethical position at the end. Clearly the post-Mady Huxley was restricting mankind's anti-Darwinian ethics (care rather than competition) to a very tight *personal* sphere. Not even governments could take a moral stand (that smacked of socialism). Michael Helfand called 'Evolution and Ethics' an essay on the 'limits of political activism', and he is right.[63] And there was a sad irony to it all. The romantic who was originally so suspicious of Darwin's bloody Malthusianism was trapped by it at the end. Hatred of socialism had him bowing to an inevitable Darwinian arms race 20 years before the Great War.

Huxley slid easily from one 'war' footing to another. Perhaps it is too glib to make the 'war' between Science and Theology a transformed case of the radical Dissenting campaign of the hungry thirties, with its demand for fair competition to free up a static Anglican society. Perhaps it is too ambitious to see the same political Dissent create the structure for Huxley's Darwinian and International 'war' images, to make them all of a piece. Yet surely some such larger picture will ultimately prove more satisfying than simply accepting Science's 'War' with Theology as an inevitable development of the rational mind.

SCIENCE ON THE STUMP

> In England when people say 'science' they commonly mean an article by Professor Huxley in the *Nineteenth Century*.[64]

Canvassing votes for the profession – by selling the *Origin of Species* or condemning a benighted theology – meant reaching out. Almost all of Huxley's famous articles were campaign speeches, positively plebeian and crafted for accessibility. They were beguiling, having that 'telepathic effect which enables you at once to perceive his meaning'[65] – an apparent opaqueness suggesting that he was a neutral conduit for the social precepts of the 'new Nature'.

Historians have long accepted Huxley's claim that the 'work of the popular expositor' was simply the conversion 'of the hieratic language of the experts into the demotic vulgar tongue'.[66] Nothing more. It was to retail the latest discoveries, package them in paper of 'colourless brilliancy' which declared a transparent intent. Such diffusion required a sponge-like absorption by the audience. That is what he meant by oiling the bolus of evolution to stuff into the 'ecclesiastical swallow'.

But surely there was much more than a simple *diffusion*.[67] Neither

Huxley nor his audience was disinterested. He was refracting the light of science through an ideological lens. The Huxleys and Tyndalls were reaching out with evangelical fervour, outdoing the pamphleteering Methodist fanatics. This is how people knew them, on the stump: 'Science' was the latest harangue in the *Nineteenth Century*. Ray Lankester went so far as to call his hero only 'accidentally a zoologist'. Huxley's real work was as a publicist – a one-man lobbying machine.[68]

It helped that Huxley and Tyndall were among the few scientists who could actually turn a phrase. In an age when the ubiquitous W. T. Stead, editor of *Cassell's Magazine*, *Pall Mall Gazette* and *Review of Reviews*, refused to commission scientists because they talked gobbledegook, Huxley's scintillating prose was converting mundane matters into thrilling parable. He did not need an interpreter. A *Daily News* wag said that Huxley 'would have known how to make Herbert Spencer readable'.[69] It reinforced the belief that Science was coming undiluted from the fountainhead. The message was made more pleasurable by Huxley's Ciceronian irony and cautious claims dressed in outrageous garb. Not to mention his wit, the distanced intellectual word-play that punctuated his essays. Even ticklish events, like Hooker's son Brian falling into a salt vat, would have Huxley waxing:

> Abram, Abraham became
>   By will divine:
> Let pickled Brian's name
>   Be changed to Brine![70]

This fast wit weaving around Old Testament allusions greased a social edge; it made the prose frictionless. 'I always admire & envy you', Leslie Stephen wrote; 'no English writer, alive or dead, could ever put his points better'. His seemingly see-through style was designed to keep the spotlight on the dramatization of Nature in his 'proletarian theatre', where, as Paradis says, it was reworked in the way of an old morality play. He saw himself merely encapsulating 'great emotions & great thoughts in such form that they touch the heart'.[71]

For him popular lectures were never hors-d'œuvres but meals in their own right. Even the act of reaching out was seen to be virtuous: the *Illustrated London News* praised him for not joining those who 'keep their name as scientific hierophants unsullied'. The fine-honed prose made his worldwide reputation. But if he was the man 'who brought down science from the skies',[72] he distributed his manna in revealing ways. From the young Volunteer's patriotic panegyric on Science as his profession formed,

> Cherish her, venerate her, [or] . . . the day will come when our children will see the glory of England vanishing like Arthur in the mist[73]

to the pensioner's use of Social Darwinism to debunk

> that Liberty Equality & Fraternity to which many look as to a new Heaven & new Earth[74]

the last thing he was selling was disinterested science. His science was instrumental, it had a political payoff that changed with the context. He was cajoling, social grooming, promising greatness, pacifying or damning. The world's greatest scientific synthesizer was easing the social dislocations of industrial society. His common-sense cleverness was committed to the creation of a new moral society, a New Reformation.

HUXLEY AND HIS WORKERS

> 'Did they get "the message"?'
>
> Roger Cooter and Stephen Pumfrey challenging the traditional 'diffusionist' model of popular science.[75] How did Huxley's workers take his parables?

If one element missing from studies of science and religion is radical Dissent, another is the political atheism of the workers. The factory hands are still ignored by historians of science. The absence is more glaring for the fact that they were Huxley's sounding board.

The curiosity is not that Victorians lectured the workers, but that the bearded men turned up in droves. It suggests that they weren't passive recipients, but that they *wanted* something. And their penny prints showed what it was. In a growing democracy they saw themselves preparing for power. The labour elite knew that 'political freedom and general ignorance are incompatible' and that to redirect industrial society they needed to be masters of politics and science.[76] Flaming democrats growled that science was 'a matter of traffic and trade among the *savants* . . . who are interested in keeping up the usual common-place *go* in society'.[77] So the workers appropriated it, turning it into the scientific patois of the street prints. Early socialists harnessed social Lamarckism to justify co-operation and female emancipation. They made it an anti-Creationist force to overthrow 'Priestcraft' and 'Old Corruption'. Into the 1860s they exploited any materialistic science with socially-regenerative properties. Huxley's talk of the rising underworld of life suited perfectly.

Even in the 1840s the convicted agitator Richard Carlile was looking to 'bring the Spiritual World and all Religion within the boundaries of science'.[78] No wonder that his heirs saw Huxley 'confirming our own view of the universe'.[79] Both Huxley, gaining a constituency, and his workers, gaining a serviceable science, benefited by the transaction.[80]

Because (as Cooter and Pumfrey say) so little is known of what *audiences* got out of science lectures, I have broached Huxley's workers and their indigenous literature throughout. We can triangulate to determine their beliefs, knowing that Huxley's tickets were touted at secular societies, his books were shifted in the Socialist Halls of Science, his 'brigandlike' auditors were largely freethinkers, and his lectures were reported in the *Reasoner* and *National Reformer*.[81] In the 1860s he made evolution appeal to this radical interest. He enlisted its support in his territorial dispute with the clergy and put its strength behind his nascent profession. Opposed by the powerful Church and Anglican universities, he had to be able to speak in the name of the nation and its people. He talked the radicals' language, duplicated their cynicism (to the extent that he was accused of nihilism) and depicted a history of revolutionary scientific bursts. In turn they reshaped his progressive evolution on their co-operative march to the Millennium. It dignified humble origins and allowed them to project 'forward, with inexorable confidence to the achievements of the future'.[82] 'Darwinism' was continually reconfigured as it passed across these political boundaries. A self-propelling evolution was stirred into the old seditious literature of innately-powered atoms. The result was a science to liberate the sovereign 'social atoms' from spiritual tyranny and sanctify democratic equality.

It gave Huxley a ready-made street audience, unlike, say, Matthew Arnold or Leslie Stephen. His Darwinians captured this constituency so successfully through the 1870s that the workers' old pirated literature was pushed to the back shelves. Mechanics' Institutes traded up to Darwin's *Descent of Man*, Huxley's *Man's Place in Nature* and *Lay Sermons*, as well as Wallace, Haeckel and the International Scientific Series. John Laurent shows that Huxley's *Physiography* was possibly the most borrowed book in the northern institutes. Later Huxley even projected workers' lectures on the New Testament, portraying the Bible as the Magna Carta 'of the poor and the oppressed', to stir them to insurrection 'against the worst forms of clerical and political despotism'.[83]

One understands how he became a working-class hero, why cabbies refused his fare and delegations petitioned him as they once would have nobility – supplication that showed the tremendous power acquired by the scientist. In Manchester the old Chartist George Howell, soon to be a Trade Union MP, would be stopped by cheers mid-lecture when he mentioned Huxley's name. (More touching still, Howell's son died tragically asking his father to thank Huxley for the pleasure his talks had given him.) In the 1860s an uplifting evolution filled an almost religious need among the oppressed. Science became a devotion, and one chemist's dispenser, in awe of Huxley's books, willed his body to Huxley for dissection.[84]

There was no doubting Huxley's sincerity. His belief that Science would uplift the masses was genuine. He put it with his usual apocalyptic flair: if the conquest of Nature could not better mankind's condition, he intended to hail 'some kindly comet which would sweep the whole affair away as a desirable consummation'. 'When the poor have cried, Caesar hath wept', said an admirer.[85] The legend grew with his largesse. Like his kindness in 1894 to the pound-a-week coffee unloader in Southampton docks, George Sparks. The casual docker had sent him such promising observations of the fission of pond organisms (made with a sixpenny 'toy-glass') that Huxley pulled strings to locate the man (who had given no address). The two regional networks – Donnelly's School Inspectors and the Solent clergy – were co-opted, and the local St Luke's vicar reported back on finding Sparks, clearly captivated himself. Here was a self-educated haulier, with a knowledge of advanced biology that was 'something astounding'. He was, 'as one might expect, a socialist in politics', the vicar said, 'and in religion as one would also expect, a free-thinker . . . But what does that matter! He is a truly sincere seeker after demonstrable Truth'. Having tracked down his docker, Huxley sent books and an achromatic compound microscope through the priest, marking them 'from a friend'. 'Ah', said the docker, 'I know who that must be; it can be no other than the greatest of living scientists'. Then came Huxley's own telescope to enable him to see the sun spots – and 'I', said Sparks, moved by it all, 'who carries nothing but negative recommendations, such as poverty and obscurity'.[86] The rapport was unfeigned, whatever the ideological cross-currents.

And yet those cross-currents were already evident during the dock strikes, as Huxley's *ad hoc* coalition with the workers peeled apart.

From the late 1880s he met the reinvigorated socialism by emphasizing the Malthusian competitive aspects of Darwinism. The old man was seeming to harden – but in truth it was working-class society changing, drifting to the Left and forcing a reaction. Letters began to complain that he was looking, not from 'the point of view of the "masses" [but] rather of the "classes"'.[87] He ended the scientific *alter ego* of Joseph Chamberlain, a 'benevolent Conservative', said the *Spectator*'s R. H. Hutton with satisfaction. But it was with a very small 'c', and of the most idiosyncratic sort. Like Chamberlain Huxley had been pushed into conservative Unionism by Home Rule, and to a defence of property by socialism. The old bull elephants of the X-Club found themselves in unfamiliar terrain, surrounded by Hooker's 'dirty Radicals'. The lab doors shut and the profession became unresponsive to the needs of women and workers. New flanking dissidents accused his Royal Society of elitism, of becoming a professors' forum. Huxley's response made him sound like his old Hero-worshipping self: he defended the high institutions inside science; while outside he wanted the municipal 'laboratories' of politics (as he called the town halls) to breed decisive leaders for the Commons, men 'who have clear heads, a strong sense of right, and the courage to stand alone with their backs to the wall'.[88] By the new democratic standards, his out-of-step Puritans had become old reactionary patriarchs. Science had lost its street credibility.

Huxley made 'Social Darwinism' the stern taskmaster to reconcile the workbench to capitalism. He still promised melioration through technical education, but even that was challenged. Can 'pauperism . . . be cured by technical education'? the socialist Walter Crane asked him. By 1890 the intellectual and political freedoms had eroded faith in a Divinely or even Darwinianly-instituted social order. Kropotkin, Henry George and the Fabians jostled on the institutes' shelves with tracts on 'Evolution and Socialism'.[89] The masses were on the move, pointing the way to a Labour twentieth century.

The class divide was glaringly obvious even in 1883, when the crude G. W. Foote was jailed for blasphemy while Lord Justice Coleridge declared Huxley's reverent agnosticism no offence. The cultured and now powerful professionals had switched their coalition partners, and high society threw its protective cloak around them. Science no longer needed its old bedraggled backers. The red line was redrawn as the aristocrats of intellect were permitted to question Christianity, while street scurrility commanded a year in prison.

The agnostics had became part of the new class hegemony. The second-generation Dissenters were entrenched at Oxbridge; the industrialists were living a baronial life on big profits (which, as Martin Wiener says in *English Culture and the Decline of the Industrial Spirit*, was the start of the rot – that developing 'culture of containment' which saw the bourgeoisie absorbed and gentrified and industrialism arrested by the patrician order).[90] The politicized workers had become a liability to Science. As natural history overtly resumed its old policing function, Darwin's influence declined on the street. There was even a residual bitterness at the greats around Huxley's grave. One radical stated starkly that, had Huxley

> put forward his Agnosticism . . . in some mere penny journal, had he, instead of occupying a Government Professorship, and writing in the leading (*i.e.* high-priced) reviews, addressed the democracy, not only would there have been no such funeral demonstration, but, on the contrary, he would have stood a remarkably good chance of interviewing some Justice North or other at the Old Bailey, and of enjoying subsequently a twelvemonth's hospitality at the expense of his country at Holloway or Pentonville.[91]

Huxley died in honour, not in Holloway jail, because he had so successfully consolidated science as a civil service profession. He had made it part of the State apparatus, and Roy MacLeod has shown the extent of its tentacles in Whitehall. In 1890 Huxley's 'Normal School' (the French name never took) had become the impressively titled Royal College of Science, its walls adorned with portraits of Huxley and Tyndall and the old professorate. Rising status was revealed in the Honours Lists. The men heading up the big institutions were dubbed, from that 'over-rated old Saint Flower', through Sr'enery at Manchester, and Sir Archibald Geikie at the Geological Survey, to Sir John Donnelly at South Ken.[92] Their prestige showed at that other social node of Victorian Science, the Athenaeum Club. By the nineties his scientists were no longer an indistinguishable part of the general culture, as they had been 60 years earlier. Now they acted as a bloc to elect representatives on the Club's committees.

As the specialists looked inwards, Huxley's romantic mantle was assumed by the novelists. It became the new science fiction. H. G. Wells' *Time Machine* explored the theme of human degeneration in a society stripped of competition. The dark side of the deranged automaton was exploited in Stevenson's *Dr Jekyll and Mr Hyde*. While the lost worlds motif was plumbed by Conan Doyle, whose

Sherlock Holmes became the apotheosis of Zadig's clinical detective, the scientist-sleuth as a 'fictional superman'.[93]

As the superman in Huxley becomes fictional, we begin to see the flawed greatness of this Schamyl binding his nation through science. He was an intellectual bruiser who 'warmed both hands at the fire of life'. That, ultimately, is what makes Thomas Henry Huxley so interesting. He was in the thick of the nineteenth century. He was crucial to that social transformation towards the modern world. Without comprehending his Darwinian campaigns or agnostic polemics, the *Times* wrote, it would be impossible 'to estimate the forces which have been at work to mould the intellectual, moral, and social life of the century'. He shaped our vision, closing one window onto future immortality as he opened another on our prehistoric past. There was no looking beyond for him. And yet, *Punch* said in the best epitaph, when he magically carried readers to exotic dinosaurian worlds, or conjured up pithecoid people,

> The great Agnostic, clear, brave, true,
> Taught more things may be, than he deemed he knew.[94]

Abbreviations

CORRESPONDENTS

AD	Anton Dohrn
BJ	Benjamin Jowett
CD	Charles Darwin
CK	Charles Kingsley
CL	Charles Lyell
CWT	Charles Wyville Thomson
ERL	Edwin Ray Lankester
ES	Eliza Salt, later Scott (sister)
FD	Frederick Dyster
GJR	George James Romanes
GR	George Rolleston
HAH	Henrietta Anne Huxley (née Heathorn)
HS	Herbert Spencer
JD	John Donnelly
JH	Joseph Dalton Hooker
JK	James Knowles
JM	John Morley
JT	John Tyndall
MF	Michael Foster
NL	Norman Lockyer
RIM	Roderick Impey Murchison
WBC	William Benjamin Carpenter
WHF	William Henry Flower

Abbreviations

MANUSCRIPT SOURCES

AD	Huxley family letters being transcribed by Angela Darwin
APS	American Philosophical Society
BL	British Library
BM(NH)	British Museum (Natural History)
CUL	Cambridge University Library
HH	T. H. Huxley–Henrietta Heathorn Correspondence, Imperial College, Huxley Archives (catalogued in Pingree, *T. H. Huxley: Correspondence with Henrietta Heathorn*)
HM	T. H. Huxley Manuscripts, Imperial College, Huxley Archives (catalogued in Pingree, *T. H. Huxley: List of his Scientific Notebooks*) HM series:volume:folio
HP	T. H. Huxley Papers, Imperial College, Huxley Archives (catalogued in Dawson, *Huxley Papers*)
OUM	Oxford University Museum
ZSL	Zoological Society of London

PRINTED SOURCES

CCD	F. Burkhardt and S. Smith, eds, *The Correspondence of Charles Darwin* 9 vols (Cambridge, Cambridge University Press, 1985–1994).
CE	T. H. Huxley, *Collected Essays* 9 vols (Macmillan, 1893).
LCK	F. Kingsley, ed., *Charles Kingsley: His Letters and Memories of his Life* 2 vols (Kegan Paul, 1881).
LGR	E. Romanes, ed., *The Life and Letters of George John Romanes* (Longmans, Green, 1896).
LHS	D. Duncan, ed., *The Life and Letters of Herbert Spencer* (Methuen, 1908).
LJH	L. Huxley, ed., *Life and Letters of Joseph Dalton Hooker* 2 vols (Murray, 1918).
LJT	A. S. Eve and C. H. Creasey, eds, *Life and Work of John Tyndall* (Macmillan, 1945).
LLD	F. Darwin, ed., *Life and Letters of Charles Darwin* 3 vols (Murray, 1887).
LLL	K. Lyell, ed., *Life, Letters and Journals of Sir Charles Lyell* 2 vols (Murray, 1881).
LRO	R. S. Owen, ed., *The Life of Richard Owen* 2 vols (Murray, 1894).
LTH	L. Huxley, ed., *Life and Letters of Thomas Henry Huxley* 2 vols (Macmillan, 1900).
MLD	F. Darwin and A. C. Seward, eds, *More Letters of Charles Darwin* 2 vols (Murray, 1903).
SM	M. Foster and E. R. Lankester, eds, *The Scientific Memoirs of Thomas Henry Huxley* 5 vols (Macmillan, 1898–1902).

Notes

THE APOSTLE PAUL OF THE NEW TEACHING

1. As David Knight spotted: 'Huxley', 34.
2. Or so Bourdieu, *Outline*, 177ff puts it in his study of archaic economies.
3. Van Riper, *Men among the Mammoths*, on the inception of this long pre-history.
4. Harris, *Private Lives*, 19.
5. *Pall Mall Gazette*, 1 July 1895; *Times*, 1 July 1895.
6. Turner, *Contesting*, 39–40; Wilde: Young, *Portrait*, 143. MacLeod, *Public Science*, on science becoming an arm of the State. E. Richards, 'Huxley', on the anti-feminist ethos among the Darwinians. Lightman, *Origins*, 117–21, 146 on deflecting the spotlight from evolutionary naturalism.
7. J. R. Moore, 'Metabiographical Reflections'; Desmond, 'Author's Response'.
8. Setting scientific ideas back in their original production sites in order to understand them is now a prime concern of historians: Ophir and Shapin, 'Place of Knowledge', for an overview.
9. Roderick and Stephens, *Scientific*, 29–31; 'Apostle': Clodd, 'Huxley'.
10. Pedersen, 'Rathbone'. Angela Darwin's transcriptions of the Huxley women's letters is beginning to shine a light on the family relations.
11. Webb, *Diary*, 202.

1 THE GUN IN THE LIBERAL ARMOURY

1. 'Men of the Day, No. 19', *Vanity Fair*, 28 Jan. 1871; *Illustrated London News*, 17 Sept. 1870; 'noble': TH to MF, 2 Oct. 1875, HP 4.109; 'great': HAH to ES, 8 Feb. 1871, AD.
2. Dennis and Skilton, *Reform*, 104.
3. TH to unknown corres., 8 Jan. 1871, APS; G. M. Young, *Portrait*, 83.
4. HAH to ES, 8 Feb. 1871, AD.
5. HAH to ES, 8 Feb. 1871, AD; T. A. Hirst, Journal 15, 13 Mar., 14 June 1884: Royal Institution; *LJT*, 200; wing: J. Whitworth to TH, 3 May 1873, HP 29.20.
6. HAH to ES, 8 Feb. 1871, 22 Sept. 1872, AD; Rolt, *Victorian Engineering*,

216; Underground: TH to JK, 9 Jan. 1871, APS; 'Modern': Huxley, 'Professor Huxley at Manchester'.

7. *CE*, 3:104; Brock, 'Patronage', 174; Cardwell, *Organisation*, 111–26; Dennis and Skilton, *Reform*, 188; Turner, 'Public Science', 592; Alter, *Reluctant Patron*, chap. 2.
8. Bibby, 'South London', 213; F. Palgrave to TH, 6 Jan. 1867 [1868], HP 24.16; on Palgrave: TH to JH, 15 July 1865, HP 2.134; 'queer': TH to G. J. Holyoake, 2 Aug. 1873, Holyoake Collection 2178, Co-Operative Union, Manchester.
9. MacLeod, 'Support', 202–7; MacLeod, 'Ayrton', 46–7; Cardwell, *Organisation* 125; 'you', 'most': E. Lankester, 'Representation', 509.
10. Fiske, 'Reminiscences'; HAH's Godparents Notebook, AD; Bibby, *Huxley*, 151.
11. HAH to ES, 8 Feb. 1871, 22 Sept. 1872, 16 Apr. 1874, AD; 'ought': 20 Sept. 1869, HP 31.40; A. Huxley, 'Grandfather', 147; Fiske, 'Reminiscences'. Huxley's solicitor E. F. Burton (17 Aug. 1870, HP 11.199) made it plain that Duffy's 'Cash and Catholicism' were the jarring points. McClatchie is presumably the 'shipmate' whose wife was 'a very old & dear friend of my wifes', referred to in TH to WHF, 17 Oct. 1871, APS.
12. Osborn, 'Enduring Recollections' 727; HAH's Reminiscences, HP 62.1.
13. Brown, *Metaphysical*, 10, 23, 29, 32, 41, 111–12; *LTH*, 1:313–21.
14. Brown, *Metaphysical*, 50–56, 65, 94, 103, 139–40, 318–20; *CE* 6:201; 'Oecumenical': TH to JK, 27 Apr. 1870, APS; J. R. Moore, 'Deconstructing Darwinism', 365. Tener and Woodfield, *Victorian Spectator*, 180 reprint Hutton's 'Pope Huxley' article. Lightman, *Origins*, on Huxley's resistance to analysing his own axioms.
15. A. Clark to TH, [pre-1874], HP 12.198. Gladstone was present at Huxley's 17 Nov. 1869 talk: Brown, *Metaphysical*, 146, 319; 'A': TH to JK, 15 Nov. 1869, APS.
16. M. Arnold to TH, [1870], HP 10.151. *Lay Sermons* was published in July 1870; by 15 November there were 'not more than 150 copies left'. In 1871 came the abridged *Essays Selected from Lay Sermons, Addresses and Reviews*: HP 52.1–4; 'will': JT to TH, 16 June 1870, HP 1.67.
17. ES to HAH, 4 Mar. 1869, AD; *LTH*, 1:323.
18. Youmans' prospectus, HP 21.262; E. L. Youmans to TH, [Aug. 1871], HP 29.261–2. Henry S. King was to publish the books in England first, then send the plates to Appleton, see HP 19.145ff; TH to JT, 31 Oct. 1874, HP 8.167; 'has': HAH to ES, 8 Feb. 1871, AD; TH to E. Delafield, 24 Aug. 1870, APS.
19. Circular 'To British Scientific Authors', 28 Dec. 1871, HP 30.92; MacLeod, 'Evolutionism', 65, 67–72; Youmans: Fiske, *Century*, 71; TH to NL, 21 Nov. 1868. HP 21.248.
20. HAH to ES, 8 Feb. 1871, AD; 'ignorant': JT to TH, 24 Sept. 1873, HP 1.113; encl. 1870 letter 1.115; 'rapidly': F. V. Hayden to TH, 20 Dec. 1869, HP 18.89: Goetzmann, *Exploration*, 406–7, 490–502; Appleton: E. L. Youmans to TH, 7 Apr. 1868, 28 Apr. 1871, HP 29.259, 10.105–7.
21. J. R. Moore, 'Deconstructing', 365.
22. J. R. Moore, 'Wallace's Malthusian Moment' on the original Darwin–Wallace common culture; Wallace, 'Principles', 392; R. Smith, 'Wallace'; and Kottler, 'Wallace' on its break-up.
23. Bartholomew, 'Huxley's Defence'; Desmond, *Archetypes*, chap. 3; di

Gregorio, *Huxley*, 60–8; Lyons, 'Origins', on Huxley's saltationism as an attempt to square evolution with an older morphology based on discrete types.

24. TH to JH, 10 Aug. 1870, HP 2.163. The institutional aspects are nicely brought out in James Strick's Princeton Ph.D. thesis on the spontaneous generation debates in 1860–80. *CE*, 8:136; *LTH*, 1:333; 'going': TH to NL, 8 Oct. 1870, HP 21.252; 'not': TH's annotation on H. C. Bastian to TH, 2, 12 May 1870, HP 10.238–40; Bastian, 'Reply'.

25. TH to MF, 2 Jan. 1871, HP 22.27; HM 2:3; *CE*, 8:110; bacteria as mould: TH to JH, 20 July 1870, HP 2.157; *SM*, 3:606; HM 1:1:1–66, 2:1:1ff.

26. R. E. Grant to H. Bastian, 26 June 1872, Wellcome Institute Library, London. Grant, *Tabular View*, 3, 5–6, 9, had a continually originating microbial life giving rise to independent 'trees of life', a strikingly pre-Darwinian concept, as explained in Hodge, 'Universal'. Farley, *Spontaneous*, 124, on Bastian's Lamarckism. Bastian won Grant's gold medal in 1859; Grant's previous winner, the revolutionary's son Alexander Herzen, offered to translate Bastian into French: A. Herzen to H. Bastian, 15 Dec. 1877, Wellcome Institute. *LTH*, 1:168.

27. E. R. Lankester, 'Instruction', 362; Gooday, 'Nature'; Barton, 'Scientific Opposition'; Chadarevian, 'Laboratory'; Meadows, *Science*, 84–5.

28. Forgan and Gooday, 'Constructing South Kensington'.

29. Forgan and Gooday, 'Constructing South Kensington'; Girouard, *Waterhouse*, 26–33; *Survey of London*, 74; Rupke, *Owen*, 36ff. Huxley's Devonshire Commission examined the plans for the Natural History Museum, which led to a scrap when Owen the 'old fool' appeared: TH to JH, 18 Mar. 1871, HP 2.172.

30. On the cognitive and architectural changes accompanying the switch from museum to lab, which was not so much a replacement as an expansion: Pickstone, 'Ways of Knowing', 442–52; Forgan and Gooday, 'Fungoid Assemblage', 158–60; Nyhart, 'Natural History'. In some senses Huxley's lab for beginners was a simplified museum laid open, with the corpses made accessible to trainees. It was not designed for control over, or alteration of, Nature (as in the later, research-driven, vivisection programmes), even if it did foster new manipulative skills. This blurs the socio-cognitive categories in 1870: Pickstone, 'Museological Science', 113, 131–2.

31. The voice was that of the Middlesbrough ironmaster, and shortly Huxley's fellow Devonshire Commissioner, Bernhard Samuelson MP: *Hansard*, 198 (19 July 1869), 160; L. Goschen to HAH, 1 Aug. [1871], 24 June [1871–4], HP 17.94–7; G. Goschen to TH, n.d. [*c*.1870?], HP 17.89; *Survey of London*, 234.

32. TH to JH, 7 Jan. 1872, HP 2.189; Forgan and Gooday, 'Constructing South Kensington'; Meadows, *Science*, 85–7; TH to NL, 20 Apr. 1871, HP 21.270; Bibby, *Huxley*, 116.

33. Huxley, 'Royal School of Mines', *Times*, 11 Apr. 1871; TH to NL, 20 Apr. 1871, HP 21.270; Gooday, 'Nature', 334; Bibby, *Huxley*, 113.

34. Forgan, 'Architecture', 154.

35. *Survey of London*, 234–7; 'The Creation of Albertopolis', *Jarvis Journal*, 54 (1978), 4–6; 'New Science Schools for the Department of Science and Art, South Kensington', *Builder*, (2 Sept. 1871), 687; Forgan and Gooday, 'Fungoid Assemblage', 162–4. Huxley's friend, the chemist A. W. von Hofmann, had visited the German laboratories and reported back to Cole.

36. TH to AD, 7 July 1871, HP 13.202; *LTH*, 1:361.

37. TH to MF, 5 Jan. 1871, HP 4.29; 'The Creation of Albertopolis', *Jarvis Journal*, 54 (1978), 4–6; Gooday, 'Nature', 334–5; *CE*, 3:45.
38. TH to MF, 5 Jan. 1871, HP 4.29, initially projected 15 microscopes; Gooday, 'Nature', 336; E. R. Lankester, 'Instruction', 362; Geison, *Foster*, 132; *LTH*, 1:378. These were possibly Hartnack microscopes (mentioned in JD to TH, 27 Jan. 1894, HP 14.171) – cheap students' models of typical Continental design, made by Edmund Hartnack in Paris until 1870 and then in Potsdam (Eric Hollowday, pers. comm.).
39. Haters of Oxbridge-exclusivity such as the radical Methodist Marshall Hall and Unitarian W. B. Carpenter also saw their sons at Cambridge (Philip Carpenter won a scholarship to Trinity College in 1871). Lankester studied zoology under Huxley's plummy protégé George Rolleston in the new University Museum, but why he chose Oxford rather than University College or Jermyn Street is puzzling. Wiener, *English Culture*, 13–14 on this dilution of Nonconformity. Howarth, 'Science Education', 334–5.
40. Lester and Bowler, *Lankester*, 19.
41. E. R. Lankester, 'Use', 34–5; Desmond, *Archetypes*, 138. He purged the idealist word 'homology', which took its meaning from Owen's Platonic archetype, replacing it with 'homogeny', meaning structural affinity through descent.
42. ERL to TH, 18 Dec. [1872], HP 21.39; Lester and Bowler, *Lankester*, 23, 27, 39.
43. E. R. Lankester, 'Instruction', 362–4; Gooday, 'Nature', 336.
44. Denis, 'Brompton Barracks'; Cardwell, *Organisation*, 116.
45. Huxley, 'President's Address', *Journal of the Quekett Microscopical Club*, 6 (1879), 251; Denis, 'Brompton Barracks', 11–12. J. R. Moore, *Post-Darwinian Controversies* on the 'military metaphor'.
46. JD to TH, 22 Sept. 1871, HP 14.4; *Survey of London*, 86ff; Denis, 'Brompton Barracks', 11–14. *LTH*, 1:415; T. J. Parker, *Parker*, 31–2; Desmond, *Archetypes*, 51, 216–17.
47. Huxley, 'Contemporary Literature', *West. Rev.*, 65 (1856), 269. Huxley had the UCL physiology professor Burdon Sanderson and hygiene professor at the Army Medical School Edmund Parkes appointed to Liverpool's health authority: E. A. Parkes to TH, 3 Dec. 1870, HP 24.62. MacLeod, 'Support', 212, 224.
48. Fuegians, Maltese and British Columbian 'Indians' refused to be photographed nude: HM 1:15:158–9; HM 1:16:1, 180. The Central Board for Aborigines in Melbourne would only photograph willing subjects naked: HM 1:15:117. Chains: HM 1:15:2–8, 155. See HM 1:15:4, 113–52; also HM 1:16:23, 60, 85–6, 118, 186, 196; photographs in HM Boxes G and H. Di Gregorio, *Huxley*, 175.
49. HM 1:16:172. Ethnological Society talk, 7 June 1870, HM 2:103:170; *SM*, 3:564; Huxley's race typology: Lorimer, 'Theoretical Racism', 408–13; di Gregorio, *Huxley*, 162ff; his sexism: E. Richards, 'Huxley'; paternalism: Lorimer, *Colour*, 148–9. On the geopolitical aspects of ethnography and biogeography: Browne, 'Biogeography', 314; Desmond, *Archetypes*, 102–3; and the origin of questionnaire-type collations in government surveying voyages: Beer, 'Travelling', 327; Bravo, 'Ethnological', 344.
50. BJ to TH, 14 Jan. 1870, HP 7.3; Howarth, 'Science Education', 335; *LTH*, 1:330.
51. M. Foster Sr to TH, 3 May 1870, HP 4.176; 'two': MF to HAH, 10 Feb.

1870, HP 16.205; Huxley's influence: W. G. Clark to TH, 2 Apr. [1870], HP 4.172; Geison, *Foster*, 76–7, 100.

52. G. Young to TH, 17 Jan. 1879, HP 29.266; T. J. P. Jodrell to TH, [1872?], HP 19.70–2; Huxley's 1872 Diary, HP 70.12 (26 Nov. 1872). On Jodrell's chairs: Bibby, *Huxley*, 216–17; Harte, *World*, 86.
53. A. W. Williamson to TH, 8 July [1870], HP 29.58; *CE*, 3:308ff; Bibby, 'Huxley and Medical Education', 193.
54. HAH to AD, 20 May 1872, postscript to HP 13.214; HAH to ES, 8 Feb. 1871, 22 Sept. 1872, AD.
55. Godlee, 'Jones', 102.
56. M. Fox to TH, 16 Mar. 1871, HP 16.245. Morley, *Recollections*, 1:88–90; Jacyna, 'Science'. Huxley's radical social and scientific blend was reflected in his alignments. When a new club, designed 'to bring into contact the Radical members of the House of Commons, the representatives of the Liberal press, and the leaders of liberal thought in the universities & elsewhere' (circular HP 16.52) was mooted, with Mill, Cairnes, Morley, Stephen and Dilke signed up, Huxley was invited to join: H. Fawcett to TH, 14 Jan. 1870, HP 16.51.
57. *LJH*, 2:125; Burkhardt and Smith, *Calendar*, 7323; Darwin, *Descent*, 62, 95–6; Desmond and Moore, *Darwin*, chap. 38.
58. Greene, 'Darwin', 7–16; Gruber and Barrett, *Darwin*, 24; Durant, 'Ascent', 285; G. Jones, 'Social Darwinism Revisited', 771.
59. This was W. B. Dawkins ('Darwin', 195–6), the Huxley-nominated geology curator at Owen's College, Manchester. E. Richards, 'Darwin' and 'Redrawing the Boundaries'; Erskine, '*Origin*'; and Jann, 'Darwin', for the most recent feminist studies on Darwin's selection scenario which upheld the Victorian commonplace of female inferiority.
60. TH to AD, 18 July, 17 Nov. 1870, 7 Jan. 1871, HP 13.177, 183, 189; *LTH*, 1:334, 336–7, 361; 'bloody': TH to JH, 20 July 1870, HP 2.157 – and on 10 Aug. 1870, HP 2.163, he was wishing 'they would hang the Emperor at the nearest Camp'; JD to TH, 19 July 1870, HP 14.1. Kovalevskii: CD to TH, 1 Oct. [1869], HP 5.275.
61. Bibby, *Huxley*, 144; Owen, 'Fate'.
62. Todes, 'Kovalevskii', 119; Horne, *Fall*, 45–6, 229–31, 246ff, 341.
63. St G. Mivart to CD, 24 Jan. 1871, DAR 171, CUL; Horne, *Fall*, 520, 556; *Times*, 8 Apr. 1871, 5; *LTH*, 1:359.
64. 'The Pedigree of the Horse', (Royal Institution Lecture, 8 Apr. 1870), HP 44.7–42, ff.14 ('one'), 18, 30; *CE*, 8:358–61. Huxley was following the French – Albert Gaudry, Paul Gervais and Edouard Lartet – and Richard Owen (*Anatomy*, 3:825): on which see Ospovat, *Development*, 137–40, and Desmond, *Archetypes*, 165–9. HM 2:100 notebook; 'torn': JT to TH, 6 Apr. 1870, HP 1.65; *LTH*, 1:329; Ritvo, *Animal Estate*, 18–20; Read, *England*, 61–3.
65. Kovalevskii, 'Osteology', 21; Todes , 'Kovalevskii', 130–3.
66. Bibby, *Huxley*, 146–7. Committee and speeches: 'Election of London School Board. Addresses to the Ratepayers of the Marylebone Division from T. H. Huxley and W. R. Cremer', HM 3:122:11.
67. MF to HAH, 28 Nov. [1870], HP 16.211; curriculum: 'Election of London School Board . . .', HM 3:122:11, also *CE*, 3:389ff; *LTH*, 1:338; 'with': HAH to ES, 8 Feb. 1871, AD.
68. HAH to ES, 8 Feb. 1871, AD; Bibby, 'Huxley and Medical Education', 194; Blake, *Charge*, 62.

69. J. A. Picton to TH, 24 Mar. 1873, HP 24.126; Davies, *Heterodox London*, 1:351–5.
70. TH to G. Dixon, 20 Feb. 1871, APS; referring to Genesis 19:32, 37:12; 'without': Huxley, 'Election of London School Board . . .', HM 3:122.11. The Bible-reading compromise that won was brought in by W. H. Smith, son of the newsagent, which allowed for principles of religion and morality suitable to the children to be drawn from the readings: Coleman and Mansell, 'Science'; Bibby, *Huxley*, 150, 153; *LTH*, 1:346; *CE*, 3:396ff.
71. MF to HAH, 26 Feb. 1871, HP 16.213; *CE*, 3:395; 'should': Mivart, 'Reminiscences', 993; Tom: TH to ES, 26 Nov. 1854, AD.
72. TH to AD, 7 Jan. 1871, HP 13.189; *LTH*, 1:361; 'to': TH to G. Dixon, 20 Feb. 1871, APS; 'really': Conway, 'Huxley', 73–4.
73. TH to G. J. Holyoake, 21 Apr. 1871, Holyoake Collection 2001, Co-Operative Union, Manchester; 2 Aug. 1873, Holyoake Collection 2178, on protecting freethinkers, funding; 'your': G. J. Holyoake to TH, 21 June 1871, HP 18.211. The divide between the scientific agnostics and Holyoake's secularists was shown in Holyoake's ill-treatment by the BAAS in 1870, even though Holyoake was there to report Huxley's Presidential Address.
74. TH to F. Sandford, 5 Dec. 1870, HP 26.21; T. Carlyle to TH, 5 Jan. 1871, HP 12.33. George Eliot recommended John Nassau Senior (whose wife was a close friend) for Chief Secretary of the School Board: G. E. Lewes to TH, 2 Jan. 1871, HP 21.221; Haight, *Eliot Letters*, 9:5–6.
75. JD to MF, 20 Feb. 1872, HP 14.8; HP 70.14 ff.1–28; HM 2:65; *LTH*, 1:309–10; Huxley, *Physiography*, vii; *CE* 6:282, 8:137; HP 39.58; A. Buckley to TH, 22 May 1871, HP 11.182; HP 52.4–5; J. C. Brough to TH, 10 Aug. 1870, HP 11.97.
76. TH to JK, 9 Jan. 1871, APS; I. Turguenieff to TH, 10 Jan. 1871, HP 28.43; HAH to ES, 8 Feb. 1871, AD.
77. *LTH*, 1:360–1; Slade: HAH to ES, 22 Sept. 1872, AD; HAH to AD, 19 Jan. 1872, HP 13.205. Huxley was introducing Riviere with his sketch pad at the Zoo: B. Riviere to TH, 9 May 1871, 30 Apr. 1873, HP 25.92–3; RA: HP 49.36; HM 3:122:13; Roos, 'Arnold', 316.
78. TH to E. F. Burton, 20 Mar. 1871, HP 11.198; TH to JK, 8 July 1871, APS; *LTH*, 1:383; HAH to ES, 22 Sept. 1872, AD.
79. H. A. Bruce/TH, 14 Nov. 1870, HP 11.132.
80. Huxley *et al.*, *School Board*, 2–6; Bibby, *Huxley*, 155–60; Coleman and Mansell, 'Science', 150.
81. TH to AD, 7 July 1871, HP 13.202, *LTH*, 1:362; *LJH*, 2:125; Burkhardt and Smith, *Calendar*, 7627; *CE*, 3:424.
82. H. E. Roscoe to TH, 10 Aug., 19 Oct. 1871, HP 25.267, 273; *LTH*, 1:360; 'interpreter': undated fragment, HP 49.55. Children's popularizations: Lightman, 'Voices'; Tener and Woodfield, *Victorian Spectator*, 169.
83. MF to HAH, 10 Feb. 1870, HP 16.205.
84. W. Thomson to TH, 9 Apr. 1871, HP 27.265. They also dined 'without ceremony' at the Taits, and Nettie too liked 'Mrs Tait very much for so short an acquaintance': HAH to AD, 6, 8 Sept. 1871, HP 13.209.
85. Smith and Wise, *Energy*, 633–45; *CE*, 8:256–7; *SM*, 3:607.
86. TH to JH, 11, 28 Aug. 1871, HP 2.177–9; *LJH*, 2:126–7, 165–6; Burkhardt and Smith, *Calendar*, 7905; Ellegard, *Darwin*, 89.

87. HAH to AD, 6, 8 Sept. 1871, HP 13.209; 'tons': TH to JH, 11 Sept. 1871, HP 2.181; *LTH*, 1:363; Collie, *Huxley*, 135–6.
88. Baynes, 'Darwin', 502–6.
89. TH to JH, 11 Sept. 1871, HP 2.181; *LTH*, 1:364; *LLD*, 3:147; Mivart, *Genesis*, 19, 67–73, 239, 302; Gruber, *Conscience*, 52ff; Vorzimmer, *Darwin*, 230ff; Hull, *Darwin*, 351; J. R. Moore, *Post-Darwinian Controversies*, 62–4; *CE*, 2:125ff; Huxley, *Critiques*, ix–xi.
90. CD to TH, 21, 30 Sept. 1871, HP 5:279, 283; *LLD*, 3:148–9; *LTH*, 1:365; 'clever': TH to JH, 11 Sept. 1871, HP 2.181.
91. E. R. Lankester, 'Use of the Term', 342; Flower, 'Introductory', 199; Desmond, *Archetypes*, 138–9; *LJH*, 2:128–30; 'limbo': *Times*, 1 July 1895; 'sect': Baynes, 'Darwin', 506; 'sin': CD to TH, 5 Oct. [1871], HP 5.287; JK to TH, 22 Sept. 1871, HP 20.1.
92. This was 'Administrative Nihilism', delivered in Chamberlain's Birmingham on 9 Oct. 1871, to be discussed below. Manchester: Huxley's Diary, HP 70.11 (6 Oct. 1871); H. E. Roscoe to TH, 15 Oct. 1871, HP 25.269; governor, chloral: HAH to ES, 8 Feb. 1871, AD; 'as': TH to JH, 11 Aug. 1871, HP 2.177.
93. M. Foster Sr to TH, 30 Oct. 1871, HP 4.180; *LTH*, 1:349–55; Bibby, *Huxley*, 153–5; C. J. Herries to TH, 28 Oct. 1871, HP 18.137.
94. TH to J. Carr, 18 Nov. 1871, HP 9.249; published in the *Daily News* and reproduced in the *Reasoner*, (Dec. 1871), 183, which identifies the recipient.
95. TH to JH, 7 Jan. 1872, HP 2.189; A. Hobhouse to TH, 25, 29 July, 15, 24 Nov. 1871, HP 18.188–92, 196; bones: TH to J. Phillips, 10 Nov. 1871, OUM 1871/66.
96. JH to TH, 25 Oct. 1871, HP 3.153; Brown, *Metaphysical*, 118, 139, 323; JK to TH, [Nov. 1871], HP 20.2.
97. TH to MF, 27 Oct. 1871, HP 4.31; Bibby, *Huxley*, 54.
98. Knowles had him write up 'Yeast' for the next *Contemporary* number: JK to TH, [Nov. 1871], HP 20.2; *CE*, 8:110.
99. MF to HAH, 28 Jan. 1870, HP 16.202; 'Don't': TH to JH, 31 Dec. 1871, HP 2.187; Huxley's 1871 Diary, HP 70.11; 'seedy': TH to MF, 18 Dec. 1871, HP 4.34. Mind: *CE* 1:240; London Institution lectures on 'Bodily Motion and Consciousness', 30 Oct.–4 Dec. 1871: HM 2:67; HP 70.14, ff.1–23.
100. JT to TH, 24 Dec. [1871], HP 1.79; TH to JH, 22 Dec. 1871, HP 2.185; TH to JT, 22 Dec. 1871, HP 9.48.
101. TH to AD, 3 Jan 1872, HP 13.213; *LTH*, 1:367–8; Burkhardt and Smith, *Calendar*, 8136, 8139; F. Brady to TH, 23 Nov. 1871, HP 11.65; H. T. Stainton to TH, 3, 22 Dec. 1871, HP 26.211–12; Huxley's notes HP 26.214–16; '&': HAH to AD, 19 Jan. 1872, HP 13.205.
102. HAH to ES, 22 Sept. 1872, 16 Apr. 1874, AD.
103. *LTH*, 1:351; J. H. Lawrence to TH, 9 Jan. 1871, HP 21.178; replying to 6 Jan. 1872, HP 21.176; HAH to AD, 19 Jan. 1872, HP 13.205.
104. TH to JH, 7 Jan. 1872, HP 2.189.
105. TH to MF, 8 Jan. 1872, HP 4.35; MF to HAH, 12 Jan. 1872, HP 16.219.

2 *FROM THE CITY OF THE DEAD TO THE CITY OF SCIENCE*

1. Notes on Egypt, 11 Jan.–16 Mar. 1872, HP 70.13, ff.1–6; HAH to AD, 19, 24 Jan. 1872, HP 13.205; *LTH*, 1:367.
2. Notes on Egypt, HP 70.13, ff.6–8. JH to HAH, 3 Feb. 1872, HP 3.154; TH to JH, 9 Apr. 1872, HP 2.192; *LTH*, 1:368; 'springs': TH to FD, 9 June 1875, HP 1.135. Sir John would dine with the Huxleys in London: TH to JT, 28 May 1872, HP 9.54; J. D. Hay to HAH, [May 1872], HP 18.87.
3. Notes on Egypt, HP 70.13, ff.9–11; 'disagreeable', 'muddy': HAH to AD, 13 Feb. 1872, HP 13.207.
4. Pang, 'Social Event', 264; Blake, *Disraeli*, 581–7; Morris, *Heaven's Command*, 290–5, 417–19.
5. Notes on Egypt, HP 70.13, ff.12–22; Drower, *Petrie*, 35–6. Sir William Gregory would later ask Huxley's advice on a Director for his proposed natural history museum in Colombo: TH to AD, 20 May, 5 June 1872, HP 13.214–18; *LTH*, 1:374.
6. JT to [HAH], endorsed 23 Feb. 1872, HP 1.82; JK to HAH, 26 Jan., 16, 20 Feb. 1872, HP 20.6–10; JK to TH, 23 Feb. 1872, HP 20.12; 'Cairo': HAH to AD, 13 Feb., 20 May 1872, HP 13.207, 214; JT to TH, 14 Feb. 1872, HP 1.80; HAH to ES, 22 Sept. 1872, AD; 'Friend', 'Huxley's Homes'.
7. TH to JT, 31 Mar. 1872, HP 9.50; *LTH*, 1:371; TH to HAH, 11 Feb. 1872, AD; Notes on Egypt, HP 70.13, ff.30–42; C. Ellis to TH, n.d., HP 18.180.
8. Notes on Egypt, HP 70.13, ff.44–56; *LTH*, 1:370; Drower, *Petrie*, 36, 56, 112–14, 221; Kamil, *Luxor*, 112; 'always': TH to JT, 31 Mar. 1872, HP 9.50; TH to MF, 5 Apr. 1872, HP 4.36.
9. Notes on Egypt, HP 70.13, ff.56–9, 63–4; TH to JT, 31 Mar. 1872, HP 9.50; *LTH*, 1:371.
10. TH to JT, 31 Mar. 1872, HP 9.50; *LTH*, 1:371–3; Huxley's Diary, HP 70.12; TH to AD, 20 May 1872, HP 13.214; AD to HAH, 7 Mar. 1872, HP 13.210; Lester and Bowler, *Lankester*, 42–7.
11. HAH to ES, 22 Sept. 1872, AD; Huxley's Diary, HP 70.12; TH to MF, 5 Apr. 1872, HP 4.36.
12. TH to JT, 31 Mar. 1872, HP 9.50; *LTH*, 1:371; 'like': TH/HAH to MF, 21 Apr. 1872, HP 4.39; 'took': HAH to AD, 20 May 1872, HP 13.214; 'I am': TH to JH, 9 Apr. 1872, HP 2.192.

    Delegating proved a disaster. His *Introductory Science Primer* for children was not finished. Roscoe's chemistry volume and Stewart's physics were ready, and Geikie was writing on geology. They needed Huxley's to launch the series. He tried farming it out to James Ward, but Ward's work was useless, so Huxley had to take it up again later: H. E. Roscoe to HAH, 20 Feb. 1872, HP 25.275; J. C. Ward to TH, 1 Apr. 1873–14 Mar. 1874, HP 28.157–65; A. Macmillan to TH, 31 May, 3 June 1872, HP 22.144–6; *LTH*, 1:381.
13. Denis, 'Brompton Barracks', 12–15, 19, 22; Stoddart, 'That Victorian Science', 23. *Physiography*'s popularity in the Mechanics' Institutes also testified to Huxley's pedagogical success: Laurent, 'Science', 592; Becker, *Scientific London*, 156; Meadows, *Science*, 84.
14. MF to HAH, [Jan. 1872], HP 16.217; HAH to MF, 21 Apr. 1872, HP 4.39;

'missile': TH to MF, 15, 21 Apr. 1872, HP 4.38–9; 'young': TH to D. C. Gilman, 20 Feb. 1876, Milton S. Eisenhower Library, Johns Hopkins University.

15. TH to JT, 4 June 1872, HP 9.56; *LTH*, 1:379; JT to TH, 3 June [1872], HP 1.105.

16. ERL to TH, 18 Dec. [1872], HP 21.39. Lankester was cranky, but others too told of how alien the science Fellow felt at Exeter College, which belied the talk of Oxford's scientific promise: Howarth, 'Science Education', 334–5, 348, 353. 'I should': TH to AD, 5, 22 June 1872, HP 13.218, 222.

17. Lester and Bowler, *Lankester*, 47–57; Gooday, 'Nature', 334.

18. TH to MF, 5 Apr. 1872, HP 4.36; skeleton: G. H. Richards to TH, 22, 24 June 1872, HP 25.66–7; also HP 19.3–5, 25.5, 33.70–2.

19. TH to ES, 22 Sept. 1872, AD; Bibby, *Huxley*, 117; Gooday, 'Nature', 334; Forgan and Gooday, 'Constructing South Kensington'.

20. Caron, 'Biology', 240–53, relates the emergence of 'biology' to Huxley's 'vocal and aggressive group' at South Kensington. But he fails to note that it was forged as part of Huxley's strategy for the remoulding of State education. Huxley was designing a transmittable basic biology for the new school curriculum. That explains Caron's otherwise anomalous observation that this 'biology' was 'introductive and elementary' and spawned no research tradition. It *had* to be simple, synthetic and assimilable. It was to train teachers and had no other heuristic function. (In the same way, Gooday, 'Precision', 48–50, shows how the new school physics teachers were part of the driving force for the creation of the physics labs.)

    Huxley's comprehensive 'biology' united a study of plants and animals on the basis of their common protoplasmic structure and function. It was formed not from natural history but from physiology, structural botany, and pre-eminently comparative anatomy, which gave the new 'biology' its distinctive morphological aspect. 'Biology' retained medical comparative anatomy's lineaments as analytic and descriptive (Desmond, *Politics*), even as it moved sites from the anatomy theatre and Professor-only museum to trainee-accessible laboratory. Indeed this comparative-analytic approach dominated medicine itself until the mid nineteenth century: Pickstone, 'Ways of Knowing', 437, 442–9.

    But then the 'lab' culture itself developed largely from medicine. The General Medical Council had first recommended compulsory physiology practicals for student MDs in 1869. (Butler, 'Centers', 475; Geison, *Foster*, 148–56) The College of Surgeons followed suit in 1870 and UCL in 1871 (after receiving Huxley's report: 'Human Physiology', [1870] HP 42.34).

21. Gooday, 'Nature', 313. Of course there was a long haul between 'real' nature and the enclosure of the 'field' under the microscope. In between lay the more visible enclosures in zoos and museum gardens and galleries (Outram, 'New Spaces', 251–3) as well in as the medical theatres noted above.

22. Thiselton-Dyer, 'Plant', 711; Bower, 'Teaching', 712; 'not': Huxley, 'Distribution of Awards'; Forgan and Gooday, 'Constructing South Kensington'; Gooday, 'Nature', 327, 332; *CE*, 3:284–5. The come-apart papier-mâché models were from L. Auzoux's workshop in Paris. Later glass animals were added as teaching aids, supplied by Leopold Blaschka's Dresden works (pers. comm. Anne Barrett). The British and Continental dealers who supplied specimens are listed in HM 2:71:2.

23. Fiske, 'Reminiscences'; Mairet, *Pioneer*, 1, 15; Geddes, 'Huxley', 742; 'glad': Osborn, 'Memorial Tribute', 46; Gooday, 'Nature', 330–40; Howarth, 'Science Education' 349.
24. Forgan, 'Architecture', 149, 153.
25. Grant, 'Lectures'.
26. E. R. Lankester, 'Instruction', 362–3; Huxley and Martin, *Course*, v–vi; *LTH*, 1:378; Lester and Bowler, *Lankester*, 41. That Huxley had access to quantities of seaside and field animals is obvious from his 1873 Diary (HP 70.15A): 'Ask Lloyd about getting Hydra/ Hydratula/ Actinia/ Ascidian/ Green Lizards / . . . / Whelks /Cephalopods /Echinoderms /Dogfish'.

    Physiological experiments followed the anatomical dissections: the masters experimented on the frogs' heartbeats and so forth.
27. Huxley, *Manual of the Anatomy of Invertebrated Animals*, 4; Lyons, 'Origins', 466–7. Ironically, it was the young T. J. Parker ('Huxley', 163) who 'saw' these evolutionary connections and Parker who insisted on reversing the order: *LTH*, 2:405, 411.
28. *Survey of London*, 234–5; Whitrow, *Centenary*, 14; cod: HM 2:31.
29. TH to JH, 11, 28 Aug. 1871, HP 2.177–9; JH to TH, 2, 19, 31 Aug. 1871, HP 3.142–6; *LJH*, 2:59, 161, 165; MacLeod, 'Ayrton Incident', 51–7; 'live': TH to MF, 5 Apr. 1872, HP 4.36.
30. TH to R. Lowe, 4 May 1872, HP 22.22. He had dined with Lowe in Nelson's Bay, Sydney, along with Nicholson (the future Speaker), Donaldson (the future Premier of New South Wales) and W. S. Macleay (or perhaps his brother George Macleay, the then Speaker). 'I have met with many of the best men of my time since – but I have never listened to better talk than at that table': TH to A. P. Martin, 14 Nov. 1893, HP 22.176. A. P. Martin to TH, 13 Nov. 1893, HP 22.174 on Lowe's visit to Darwin, whom he came to 'hero-worship'. MacLeod, 'Ayrton', 59–69; MacLeod, 'Science and the Treasury', 138; Wiener, *English Culture*, 15; TH to AD, 5 Aug. 1872, HP 13.226.
31. TH to AD, 23 Aug. 1872, HP 13.232; 'Like': TH to JH, 31 Dec. 1871, HP 2.187; *LTH*, 1:376.
32. He targeted the *Telegraph*, *Daily News* and *Spectator*, and Hutton 'had very great pleasure in firing off a double shot at that wretch Ayrton, one in this paper & one in the Economist': TH to R. H. Hutton, 9 July 1872, APS; reply 12 July 1872, HP 18.364. JT to TH, 19, 20 June [1872], HP 9.56, 1.109–11; TH to JT, 20 June 1872, APS; JH to JT, 9 May 1872, HP 1.246; MacLeod, 'Ayrton', 58, 61; *LTH*, 2:112.
33. TH to JH, 11 Sept. 1871, HP 2.181; MacLeod, 'Ayrton', 70, 72 n9; 'craven': JH to HAH, 19 Apr. 1872, HP 3.156. On Lubbock's role: HP 22.72–9; 1.110, 248; *LJH*, 2:171.
34. MacLeod, 'Ayrton', 61–5; *LJH*, 2:176; Huxley, 'Kew', which shows how much Owen's intervention polarized the community. Owen's act finally appalled Tyndall. He had remained friendly with Owen through the ape-brain fiasco, and had even urged him to heal the breach with Huxley (R. Owen to JT, 14 June 1871, BM(NH) Owen Corres., vol. 21, f.28; Desmond, *Archetypes*, 143; Rupke, *Owen*, 295). 'I never broke with that man, as you know', he told Huxley. 'But this last trick makes me feel that those who broke with him knew him better than I did. It will greatly augment his isolation': JT to TH, 5 Sept. 1872, HP 1.87; reply HP 9.58.

35. G. J. Goschen to TH, 19 June [1872], HP 17.85; TH to G. J. Goschen, 30 Nov. 1872, HP 17.87; Huxley's Diary, HP 70.12 (28 Nov. 1872); TH to JT, 1 Jan. 1872 [1873], HP 9.63; *LTH*, 1:389; T. A. Hirst to TH, 9 Dec. 1872, HP 18.174; 'Oh': TH to JH, [June 1873], HP 2.208; Burkhardt and Smith, *Calendar*, 8761; 'dreads': Barton, 'Influential', 66–9, 73–5; *LJH*, 2:135. Barton sees Hooker's Presidency as the reforming high spot of the Xs' term of office.

    Ironically, the Naval College had originally been destined for the 'Science Schools' building that Huxley was now in. On Huxley as RS Secretary: T. A. Hirst to TH, 20 June 1872, HP 18.173; *LTH*, 2:451; Hall, 'Royal Society', 157. He succeeded William Sharpey.

36. TH to AD, 24 Feb. 1873, HP 13.236; 'no': 15 Nov. 1873, HP 13.249; 'each': 24 June 1874, HP 13.268; *LTH*, 1:400, 417; Desmond and Moore, *Darwin*, 601.

37. Burkhardt, 'England', 33–8.

38. Turner, 'Victorian Conflict', 367; MacLeod, 'Royal Society', 341.

39. G. G. Stokes to TH, 16 Jan. 1873, HP 27.87. Huxley read the paper on 6 February 1873. The referees, W. H. Flower and W. B. Dawkins, were both comfortable with evolution (RR 7.250–1, RS). Kovalevskii, 'Osteology', 20; Todes, 'Kovalevskii', 128.

40. JT to TH, 3, 19, 20 June [1872], HP 1.105, 110–11; TH to JT, 20 June 1872, APS. The £1,000 was repaid on 11 Jan. 1875, HP 9.90. £4,000: Huxley's 1872 Diary, HP 70.12; JK to TH, 23 Feb. 1872, HP 20.12; wine cellar: Angela Darwin, pers. comm.

41. TH to MF, [Sept. 1872], HP 4.57; 'head': TH to AD, 5 Aug. 1872, HP 13.226; *LTH*, 1:375; 'damnable': TH to JT, 9 Sept. 1872, HP 9.58.

42. TH to JT, 1 Jan. 1872 [1873], HP 9.63; 'meat': TH to MF, [Sept. 1872], HP 4.57; TH to JK, 18 Sept. 1872, APS; 'recover': TH to JT, 9 Sept. 1872, HP 9.58; *LTH*, 1:382, 388. The beneficial effect of Huxley's 'cocoa and Revalenta' diet could support Fabienne Smith's belief ('Darwin's Ill Health') that Huxley, like so many Victorians, suffered from an allergenic disorder, which was aggravated by stress.

43. Friend, 'Huxley's Homes'; CD to HAH, 16 Oct. [1872], HP 5.291; 'stupid': TH to JT, 1 Jan. 1872 [1873], HP 9.63; 'joy': TH to JK, 18 Sept., 2 Nov. 1872, 25 Apr. 1873, APS; TH to AD, 24 Feb. 1873, HP 13.236; TH to MF, 28 Apr. 1873, HP 4.53; *LTH*, 1:383, 388, 399, 403. R. Browning to HAH, 1875–8, HP 11.118–21; H. F. Martin to HAH, 17 Feb. [1875], HP 22.181.

44. TH to JK, 2 Nov. 1872, APS; 'such': 18 Sept. 1872, APS; TH to AD, 24 Feb. 1873, HP 13.236; 'Fancy': TH to JT, 1 Jan. 1872 [1873], HP 9.63; *LTH*, 1:384, 388, 399; HAH to ES, 29 Mar. 1873, AD for the details of the case.

45. TH to JH, n.d., HP 2.208; TH to AD, 24 Feb. 1873, HP 13.236; E. F. Burton (Huxley's Solicitor) to TH, 19 Feb. 1873, HP 12.318; M. H. Cookson (Counsel) to E. F. Burton, 19 Feb. 1873, HP 12.318; E. F. Burton to HAH, 'Monday night', HP 11.201; *LTH*, 1:384, 399.

46. *CE*, 8:37–8, 41, 48, 52–60; 'best': Huxley, 'First Volume'; Deacon, *Scientists*, chap. 15; Linklater, *Voyage*, 15–16; 'Rice, 'Oceanographic', 213; Rehbock, *At Sea*; MacLeod, 'Ayrton', 46–7; Morrell, 'Patronage', 356–7, 383–4. Poems: M. Arnold to TH, 22 Nov. [1873], HP 10.157.

47. C. G. Ehrenberg to TH, 13 Jan. 1873, HP 15.172; TH to MF, 2 Mar. 1873, HP 4.44, 47; Rehbock, 'Huxley', 519–29. Others who had Huxley's Atlantic

mud samples were not too sure of *Bathybius* either: Huxley, 'Deep-Sea Soundings'.

48. TH to JH, 25 July 1871, HP 2.174; C. W. Thomson to TH, 23 Sept. n.y., n.d., 13 Oct. 1871, 10 Oct. 1872, HP 27.283–7, 291; Morrell, 'Patronage', 383. Huxley's word had put Thomson in the chair: H. A. Bruce to TH, 26 Oct. 1870, HP 11.131.
49. C. W. Thomson to TH, 19 May [1873], HP 27.303; see 13 Feb. [1873] on, HP 27.293ff; 'literary': JK to TH, 28 Apr. 1873, HP 20.23; R. von Willemoes-Suhm to TH, 11 Feb. 1873, 5 June 1874, 2 Sept. 1874, HP 29.31–7; Huxley, 'Dinner'; Huxley, 'First Volume'; Deacon, *Scientists*, 338; Linklater, *Voyage*, 35. On the *Challenger*'s results, particularly as they affected Huxley (proving, for example, that *Globigerina* was planktonic and not benthic), see *CE*, 8:89–109.
50. HAH to ES, 29 Mar. 1873, AD; 'take': TH to MF, 2 Mar. 1873, HP 4.44; *LJH*, 2:184; Davidoff and Hall, *Family Fortunes*, 279–81, 313; bills: JK to TH, 2, 23, 28 Apr., 19 June 1873, HP 20.20–6.
51. CD to JT, 8, 11 Apr. 1873, Down House MS 8:13–14; G. H. Darwin to JT, [7 Apr. 1873], Down House MS 8:12; *LLL*, 2:451; *LJH*, 2:184; Litchfield, *Emma Darwin*, 2:212; Burkhardt and Smith, *Calendar*, 8843.
52. CD to JT, 11 Apr. 1873, Down House MS 8:14; Burkhardt and Smith, *Calendar*, 8852, 8855, 8860, 8870.
53. CD to JT, 18 Apr. [1873], Down House MS 8:15; 'be': CD to TH, 23 Apr. [1873], HP 5.295; *LTH*, 1:367; Litchfield, *Emma Darwin*, 2:212.
54. TH to CD, copy dated 'April 25th. 1873', HP 9.198.
55. TH to CD, copy dated 'April 25th. 1873', HP 9.198; 'so': CD to TH, 25 Apr. [1873], 5.297; T. Ashton to TH, 30 Apr. 1873, HP 10.171.
56. TH to MF, 25, 28 Apr. 1873, HP 4.51–3; CD to TH, 28 Apr. 1873, HP 5:299; 'old': TH to JT, 1 Apr. 1873, HP 8.138; *LHS*, 167.
57. TH to A. Clark, 8 May 1873, APS (also 'world'); 'doctor': TH to JT, 2 July 1873, HP 8.150. A. Clark to TH, 25 Sept. 1873, HP 12.199; plants: Huxley and Martin, *Course*; Desmond and Moore, *Darwin*, 601, 608; Colp, *To Be an Invalid*, 88–9; *LTH*, 1:384.
58. TH to JH, 24 Aug. 1873, HP 2.202; 'beauty', 'ashamed': TH to JT, 30 July 1873, HP 9.72; *LTH*, 1:390–5; 'wifes': TH to MF, 27 June 1873, HP 4.60.
59. TH to JT, 30 July 1873, HP 9.72; Blinderman, 'Oxford Debate', 127.
60. Hooker was for sending the ribbon back, even if it meant being in 'the black-books of all the crowned Heads': JH to TH/HAH, 4, 6, 8 Aug. 1873, HP 3.194–202; *LJH*, 2:186–7; 'good': TH to JH, 8 Aug. 1873, HP 2.200.
61. TH to JK, 18 Oct. 1873, APS; TH to JH, 25 Sept. 1873, HP 2.206; TH to Count Steenbock, [Sept. 1873], HP 30.141; 32.13–14; 'wretched': HAH to ES, 16 Apr. 1874, AD.

3 *AUTOMATONS*

1. Becker, *Scientific London*, 48–9; 'fiend': CD to TH, 5 Dec. [1873], 20 Mar. [1874], HP 5.293, 305; *LTH*, 1:418–19. Cosans, 'Anatomy', for a recent highly-charged defence of Owen's neuroanatomy and 'holistic biology'.
2. Barton, 'Tyndall'; Turner, *Contesting*, 21; Turner, 'Victorian Scientific Naturalism', 349; Lightman, *Origins*, chap. 6; Holyoake, 'Priesthood'.

   Design: *CE*, 2:86, 109; Paradis, *Huxley*, 99. Huxley talked on evolution and design in Glasgow on 15 Feb. 1876 (Diary 70.18; *LTH*, 1:456–7; J. S. Blackie to TH, 22 Feb. [1876], HM 3:121:11) and in his Working Men's College (Bibby, 'South London', 216); 'we': Thiselton-Dyer, 'Plant Biology', 711.

3. A. Thorold to TH, 27 Dec. 1871, HP 27.342; 'I have': W. H. Dalton to TH, 19 Nov. [1874], HP 13.3, endorsed 'An[d]. Dec 9th 1874'.
4. MacLeod, 'Science and the Treasury', 135; Turner, 'Public Science', 592; Turner, 'Victorian Conflict', 375.
5. Huxley, 'Science and "Church Policy"'; Barton, 'Evolution', 263–4; Jacyna, 'Immanence'; Turner, 'Victorian Scientific Naturalism', 334–42; Turner, 'Victorian Conflict', 371; Turner, *Contesting*, 157–8.
6. TH to JT, 2 July 1873, HP 8.150; Galton, 'Statistical Inquiries', 134; Turner, *Contesting*, 153–4, 162–70 for a full analysis.
7. Fiske, *Personal Letters*, 121–2, 146–8; Fiske, 'Reminiscences'; J. Fiske to TH, 22 Dec. 1873, 9 Feb. 1874, HP 16.80–3; 'condemned': Clodd, 'Huxley'; 'fresh': TH to JK, 5 Dec. 1873, APS. Tyndall wanted Huxley to write on Spinoza's 'notorious' contemporary influence: JT to TH, 29 Aug. [1875], HP 1.139, also HP 9.91; *LTH*, 1:447, 458. Jacyna, 'Physiology', 119, on the Victorian monists' love of Spinoza.
8. HAH to ES 22 Sept. 1872, AD; 7 Mar. 1875, AD. The publisher Alexander Macmillan met Sam through Nettie and used his book illustrations: A. Macmillan to HAH, 25 July, 26 Sept. 1873, HP 22.147–9. J. Fiske to TH, 31 Jan. 1875, HP 16.86; TH to AD, 24 Feb. 1873, HP 13.236; *LTH*, 1:399; JH to TH, 4 Aug. 1873, HP 3.195; *LTH*, 1:396; Len: TH to JK, 16 Mar. 1874, APS; Fiske, 'Reminiscences'.
9. There is a growing literature on the ideologies of spiritualism: Barrow, in *Independent Spirits*, investigates this plebeian and socialist road to power, and A. Owen, in *A Darkened Room*, explains the sexual politics of female mediumship.
10. A. Owen, *Darkened Room*, chap. 1; Slade: Milner, 'Darwin for the Prosecution'; sneaking admiration: Huxley, 'Spiritualism Unmasked'.
11. Tennyson, *The Princess*, quoted in Erskine, '*Origin*', 102.
12. G. Darwin to TH, [22, 28, 30 Jan. 1874], HP 13.87–91; Huxley, 'Report on Séance Jany. 27 1874', HP 49.121; CD to TH, 29 Jan. [1874], HP 5.377. Huxley's rapping: Conway, 'Huxley', 74. 'Better': *LTH*, 1:419–20; *LLD*, 3:187. W. Crookes to W. Huggins, 9 Feb. 1874, HP 12.352; W. Huggins to TH, 11 Feb. 1874, HP 18.318; H. Wedgwood to TH, [Mar. 1874], HP 28.209, 215; TH to H. Wedgwood, 14 Mar. 1874, HP 28.213; spirit photographs: HP 28.221.

    Another worry was Carpenter, who seemed 'on the brink of spiritualism or something equally absurd': JT to TH, 27 Oct. 1876, HP 1.148; reply HP 9.101.
13. Denis, 'Brompton Barracks', 14, 17–18. Sir James Kay-Shuttleworth, founder of Battersea teacher-training college, was overjoyed at the prospect of Huxley at the Department: JH to TH, [5, 14 Oct. 1873], HP 3.212–16.
14. Huxley's Aberdeen predecessor, the Under-Secretary of State for India, Grant Duff, was making his first visit to the subcontinent and Liverpool's MP offered to pay Huxley's expenses if he went along: M. Grant Duff to L. Huxley, 4 Nov. 1898, HP 30.178; other requests: HP 19.132–4, 23.17, 28.56, 187; JT to HAH, 25 Apr. 1874, HP 1.118; TH to JT, 22 July 1874, HP 9.84; *LTH*, 1:355, 410.

15. TH to AD, 5 March 1874, HP 13.260; JM to TH, 23 Dec. 1874, HP 23.21; Burkhardt and Smith, *Calendar*, 9469.
16. TH to MF, 22 Apr. 1873, HP 4.50; TH to JK, 25 Apr. 1873, APS; 'deeper': Bibby, *Huxley*, 201–11; 'stinketh': TH to JT, 1 Jan. 1872 [1873], HP 9.63; *LTH*, 1:389; 'shall': *CE*, 3:191. A. Harvey to TH, 25 Apr. 1873, HP 18.68. Huxley wanted botany and zoology removed from Aberdeen's medical examinations and put in a new Faculty of Science, to free up time for 'finger-end' clinical studies (*CE*, 3:217, 222–3; 'On the Medical Curriculum', *Nature*, 9 [1873], 21–2), and he suggested that German or French be substituted for ancient Greek.
17. TH to MF, 23 Feb. 1874, HP 4.73; Bibby, *Huxley*, 205; *CE*, 3:191, 202.
18. Becker, *Scientific London*, 185–7. Frederick Harrison, Lyell, John Chapman and Spencer had at times sat in on the workers' lectures (Peterson, *Huxley*, 139), and the student Thiselton-Dyer ('Plant Biology', 709); curate: R. England to TH, 7 Mar. 1874, HP 15.194; 'telepathic': HAH to ES, 31 Dec. 1865, AD.
19. Knight, 'Getting Science', 136. We have to recognize the needs of Huxley's workers in order to understand his gentle hegemonic hijacking. True, many *Reasoner* readers relished Darwinism's dissident image, seeing the *Origin* bypass the Creative props of a static Anglican society. But others saw lecturer and lectured as a sort of coalition and continued on their co-operative evolutionary track. While Huxley was trying to mobilize this constituency, radicals were incorporating the congenial parts of his science, sustaining them within socialist programmes in the Halls of Science. It was a case of working-class 'appropriation, and transformation', rather than passive diffusion: Cooter and Pumfrey, 'Separate Spheres', 242–9.
20. L. L. D., 'Huxley', cf. *CE*, 6:279, 1:241.
21. Carpenter, 'Doctrine', 400–2, reminded Huxley of his debt to Hall; *CE*, 1:191, 199ff, esp. 244; Jacyna, 'Physiology', 111–16; R. Smith, 'Human Significance'; Tyndall, *Fragments*, 92–3, 441.
22. By 1874 he had become more deterministic, making the feeling of free will an emotional warmth which accompanies some compunction (*CE*, 1:241). In 1871, his more cautious admission that the mentally-constructed world of a conscious mind was as likely as the material world of our subjective being brought jeers from the militant materialists. By making it impossible to disprove free will, he was casting 'Idealistic dust in our eyes; seemingly to prevent the bigots calling him Materialist': L. L. D., 'Huxley', cf. *CE*, 6:279.
23. TH to JT, 25 Sept. 1873, HP 9.77; *LTH*, 1:401, 418; Sopka, 'Tyndall'; Harvard: TH to C. E. Appleton, 8 July 1874, APS; *LJT*, 167–73; party: TH to MacGregor, 14 Mar. 1873, APS; £150: JK to TH, 5, 8 June 1874, HP 20.38–9. HAH to ES, 16 Apr. 1874, AD.
24. TH to JH, 4 Dec. 1874, HP 2.216; 'Sir': 31 Mar. 1874, HP 2.210; *LJH*, 2:148–9; Becker, *Scientific London*, 23–5.
25. Over 70 masters had applied for the June 1874 course; 40 were accepted, double the usual number: TH to MF, 18 May 1874, HP 4.84.
26. T. J. Parker to TH, 7 May 1875, HP 24.23; 'Elementary', 'Best': TH to MF, 5 May, 4 July 1874, HP 4.81, 86; T. J. Parker, 'Huxley', 165; O'Connor, *Founders*, 188–202.
27. W. G. Armstrong to TH, 3 July 1874, HP 10.116. Huxley tapped both Armstrong and Whitworth for the Dohrn appeal: TH to MF, 26 Apr. 1874,

HP 4.180. Heath: HAH to ES, 16 Apr. 1874, 7 Mar. 1875, AD. Huxley, 'Professor Huxley at Manchester'.

28. TH to unknown corres., 30 June 1894, APS; Briggs, *Victorian Cities*, chap. 5; G. M. Young, *Portrait*, 109.

29. *CE*, 1:256–9, 282. While there has been considerable exegesis of this essay, e.g. Helfand, 'Huxley's "Evolution"', Paradis, *Huxley*, 173–7, no one to my knowledge has emphasized its telling Birmingham location.

    For a subtle analysis of Spencer's Lamarckism and Huxley's non-Lamarckian naturalism, and the way this led to human nature being fixed for Huxley, with social progress being brought about by the 'transformation of the environment', i.e. a Chamberlainite technocracy, see Paradis, '*Evolution*', 31–5.

30. H. Cole to TH, 3 Nov. 1871, HM 3:121:43; A. R. Wallace to TH, 27 Sept. 1873, HP 28.96; 'John Bull' to TH, 16 Oct. 1871, HP 9.278; TH to AD, 3 Jan. 1872, HP 13.213; Huxley, *Critiques*, vi–ix; *LTH*, 1:368; *LHS*, 150; Spencer, *Autobiography*, 2:232.

31. K. M. Lyell to HAH, 5 Aug. 1874, HP 22.111; 'Satan': TH to JT, 22 July 1874, HP 9.84; *LTH*, 1:410; *CE*, 3:2, 30; 'hung': HAH to ES, 7 Mar. 1875, AD.

32. TH to JT, 25 Sept. 1873, HP 9.77; *LTH*, 1:401; replying to HP 1.113; JH to JT, 16 Oct. [1873], HP 8:356; *Belfast News-Letter*, 21 Aug. 1874, 5; Burkhardt and Smith, *Calendar*, 9063.

33. JT to TH, 14 May 1874, HP 1.119; 'lunatic': TH to JT, 13 Nov. 1873, HP 9.79; 'slanderous': JT to JH, 25 Oct. 1873, HP 8.357; Burkhardt and Smith, *Calendar*, 12220, 12230; M. Arnold to TH, 13 Oct. 1873, HP 10.155; Brown, *Metaphysical Society*, 65–6. Alexander Agassiz told Tyndall (10 June 1874, HP 6.143) to 'Cowhide Ruskin' the 'scientific Charlatan'.

34. *Belfast News-Letter*, 21 Aug. 1874, 5; *LTH*, 1:414.

35. *LJH*, 2:158; *LTH*, 1:413; *CE*, 1:241; 'dance': TH to MF, 12 Aug. 1874, HP 4.90; Barton, 'Tyndall', 115–16; 'those': TH to W. H. Williamson, 24 Aug. 1873, APS.

36. Barton, 'Tyndall', 113; Tyndall, *Fragments II*, 199; *LTH*, 1:413. Calderwood, 'Present Relations', 225, had long seen such imperial pretensions and the 'strong hand of conquest' in Huxley's work.

37. Livingstone, 'Darwinism', 411–12, 418; *LJT*, 187; Barton, 'Tyndall', 116; Gillespie, 'Duke', on disputes about mankind's rise from savagery; HAH to ES, 7 Mar. 1875, AD; 'as Luther', quoted by Lightman, 'Pope', 156; 'its': TH to MF, 12 Aug. 1874, HP 4.90; drafts: JT to TH, 1, 15 July 1874, HP 1.128–9.

38. Livingstone, 'Darwinism', 419; *LLL*, 2:455; Barton, 'Tyndall', 121. Tyndall's cosmos had its teleological aspect, as Huxley ('Natural History of Creation', 40–3) knew.

39. Tyndall, *Fragments*, 163–4; Barton, 'Tyndall', 117; *LJT*, 183. With Tyndall bathing Lucretius' atheistic *De rerum natura* in the new atomic light, Classicists made the Roman poet denounce a stale modern naturalism. One anonymous potboiler (written by Balfour Stewart and P. G. Tait), *The Unseen Universe*, expanded Tyndall's cosmos into a greater Whole. Here energy flowed back and forth between Providential and natural realms to square conservation principles with immortal promises: Turner, 'Lucretius', 330–8; Heimann, '*Unseen Universe*'.

40. *LTH*, 1:424; JM to TH, 12 Nov. 1874, HP 23.20; 'going': TH to P. L. Sclater, 24 Apr. 1875, APS; Brown, *Metaphysical Society*, 224–30; Morley, *Recollections*, 1:88–90.
41. Carpenter, 'Human Automatism', 397, 413–15, and esp. 943; Desmond, *Politics*, 214–15; V. M. D. Hall, 'Contribution'; Wace, 'Scientific Lectures', 42. Jacyna, 'Physiology', 111–12, 124–6, for a superb study on the new 'physiological psychology' of Spencer, Huxley, Bain, Ferrier, Clifford *et al.*, with its epiphenomenal mind and anti-Church political connections.
42. Perkins, *Origins*, 158–9; 'doll': TH to CL, 17 Mar. 1860, HP 30.34, *LTH*, 1:212; McConnish: Becker, *Scientific London*, 182. Huxley would be a Trustee for the George Henry Lewes Studentship for physiology at Cambridge in 1879, which was open to women and men: Haight, *Eliot Letters*, 7:117, 177.
43. E. Richards, 'Huxley', 276; E. Richards, 'Darwin', 60ff for a convincing study of the 'congruence of *The Descent* with dominant Victorian social and political assumptions' (79); Erskine, '*Origin*', 97–103; Jann, 'Darwin'; Darwin, *Descent*, 563–6.
44. Huxley, 'Miss Jex-Blake'; *LTH*, 1:417; Bibby, *Huxley*, 35–6.
45. HAH to ES, 10 Feb. 1883, AD; Erskine, '*Origin*', 105.
46. Dennis and Skilton, *Reform*, 148.
47. E. A. J. Wallop to HAH, 21 Oct. 1874, HP 28.107; Stevenson: HAH to ES, 16 Apr. 1874, AD. For the Huxleys at the Earl of Portsmouth's mansion: *Brighton Herald* press cutting, July 1895, HP 81.94.
48. Blake, *Charge*, 90–2, 96, 104, 114, 123.
49. One was Mary Whitfield: M. Whitfield to TH, 9 Aug. 1894, HP 29.14; *LTH*, 1:386–7; E. Richards, 'Huxley', 278; Blake, *Charge*, 117–18.
50. 'X.Y.Z.' to *Times*, 2 June 1874.
51. JH to TH, 25 Nov. 1874, HP 3.222; 'University': TH to MF, 1 Dec. 1874, HP 4.100; L. Playfair to HAH, 30 Nov. 1874, HP 24.140.
52. Harte, *University*, 126–8; Blake, *Charge*, 135, 167; *LTH*, 1:417.
53. HAH to ES, 7 Mar. 1875, AD; 'not': TH to AD, 24 Feb. 1873, HP 13.236; *LTH*, 1:400. Nettie's submergence matched Emma's in Charles Darwin (E. Richards, 'Darwin', 80), even though she too disagreed with her husband on religious matters. Despite writing to Lizzie, 'You touched me deeply when you said that you believed dear Hal's "principles aims & hopes and mine were the same" – I can truly say that indeed they are' (HAH to ES, 8 Feb. 1871, AD), there was never quite the congruence that she implied on the deepest issue, agnosticism.
54. HAH to ES, 13 Sept. 1879, AD. Rachel failed. The Cambridge local exams admitted women from 1865: Brock, 'School Science Examinations', 171–2. Martin Cooke is currently looking at Henrietta's Moravian education. 'Regina': TH to MF, 5 May 1874, HP 4.81; 'Few': TH to MF, 5 Apr. 1872, HP 4.36.
55. M. G. Grey to HAH/TH, 12 June, 13 July 1871, HP 17.144–8; Bibby, *Huxley*, 36.
56. HAH to TH, 7–8 July 1873, AD.
57. In HAH to TH, 7 July 1873, AD, Nettie saw Hal founding 'a new school of thought where the materialists & spiritualists shall be united in brotherhood – or if not this, your creed shall give peace to those whose souls are unsatisfied with the doctrines alike of materialist or spiritualist', which missed his

point entirely. Indeed his reply (TH to HAH, 8 Aug. 1873, AD; *LTH*, 1:397) made plain that he was not reconciling 'the antagonisms of the old schools', 'nor is any reconcilement possible between free thought and traditional authority. One or other will have to succumb', and he had no more doubt that 'freethought will win in the long run than I have that I sit here writing to you'. She evidently preferred not to see his work this way.

58. Haight, *Eliot Letters*, 5:365. But then there was the odd echo of his own reverie in 'Physical Basis of Life' in *Middlemarch*: Adam, 'Huxley'.
59. I have only been able to trace one undated HAH reminiscence on the point, written late in life (HP 62.21):

> Geo. H Lewes. Pater w[d] tease me by repeating his compliments which I loathed. – Pater goes thrice to the Lewes but not allowing me to call.

The first statement suggests Nettie's dislike of the coarse G. H. Lewes, the second that Huxley would not allow her to visit George Eliot.

60. Lightman, 'Voices'; Gates, 'Revisioning', 762ff; Cooter and Pumfrey, 'Separate Spheres'. Buckley's visits: HAH to TH, 7 July 1873, AD.
61. A. Secord, 'Science in the Pub', for a sophisticated look at the manual workers' co-operative botany in Victorian Lancashire, with its Sunday pub meetings, Methodist organization and craft pride, and the way this had once allowed the weavers to share the cultural property of the educated classes.
62. *CE*, 2:236; Weindling, *Darwinism*, 47–8; cf. Dohrn's rival work on an annelid ancestry for vertebrates: Groeben, *Darwin*, 34–5; TH to AD, 30 Apr. 1870, HP 13.174; *LTH*, 1:332; Maienschein, 'It's a Long Way'.
63. Abstract of Huxley's Lectures on Biology, South Kensington, Oct. 1874, by W. W. Cobb, HP 68.41–2; *SM*, 4:51, 128; ERL to TH, 11 June [1875], HP 21.45; 'shut', 'take': *LTH*, 1:398, 416–17, 425; HM 1:5:83, 2:16.

    Huxley was also attempting to homologize the lamprey's and tadpole's skulls, to show that the jawless fish shared the normal vertebrate plan (contra Gegenbaur and Haeckel): *SM*, 4:128–44; HM 2:17–18.
64. E. R. Lankester, 'On the Primitive', 'Notes on the Embryology'; Lester and Bowler, *Lankester*, 82–3. Haeckel, 'Scientific Worthies', was quick to point out that Huxley's suggestion that the two layers of the coelenterates were analogous to the germinal layers of the vertebrate embryo was at the root of his 'Gastraea' theory in 1874, which hypothesized a two-layered remote ancestor for all metazoa (Gould, *Ontogeny*, 170).
65. *SM*, 4:66ff, esp. 82–3, 175, 227–32. For a study of the meaning of Huxley's crocodile work and its contrast to Owen's, see Desmond, *Archetypes*, 170–4; also Collie, *Huxley*, 60ff; and di Gregorio, *Huxley*, 95–7.
66. Ruse, 'Booknotes', 250.
67. HM 2:69:24ff.
68. *CE*, 8:176. Huxley's was also partly influenced by Haeckel's monographs on the 'monera'; hence his own work on the ciliates in late 1874. He was cadging *Paramecium* from Foster (who had a Muscovy duck pond), and devising new techniques to preserve the related unicellular *Nyctotherus* and *Balantidium*: TH to MF, 20 Oct. 1874, HP 4.94; HM 2:6:2, 5, 7ff.
69. Cobb's notes, HP 69.8. By 1879 – after America and Marsh's horses – he was prepared to use the 'good servants and bad masters' metaphor in a way more positive to evolution: Huxley, 'Prefatory Note', xi.

70. Mivart, 'Reminiscences', 996; St G. Mivart to TH, 6 Oct. 1874, HP 22.261; Gruber, *Conscience*, 237 n32.
71. *LTH*, 1:425; 'Papist': TH to JH, 27 Dec. 1874, HP 2.220; Gruber, *Conscience*, 99–101; G. Darwin to TH, 28 Dec. 1874, HP 13.94.
72. TH to C. E. Appleton, 28 Jan. 1875, APS; 'leave': TH to JH, 27 Dec. 1874, HP 2.220; Gruber, *Conscience*, 102–4; *LTH*, 1:425; also HP 2.218, 3.225. Huxley only caught up with the offending review on 17 December 1874: TH to JH, 19 Dec. 1874, HP 2.214.
73. J. Fiske to TH, 31 Jan. 1875, HP 16.86; CD to TH, 24 Dec. [1874], HP 5.311; G. Darwin to TH, 28 Dec. 1874, HP 13.94; Huxley, 'Anthropogenie', 16–17; Gruber, *Conscience*, 102, 109.
74. Mivart, 'Reminiscences', 994, 997; St G. Mivart to TH, 20, 24 Dec. 1874, HP 22.263, 267; reply HP 22.265; Burkhardt and Smith, *Calendar*, 9768, 9770, 9777, 9780, 9800; CD to TH, 6 Jan. 1875, HP 5.313; TH to JH, 27 Dec. 1874, HP 2.220; JH to TH, 28 Dec. 1874, HP 3.229; Gruber, *Conscience*, 102–10.
75. MF to TH, 19, 27, 31 Jan. [1875], HP 4.192–4, 200; TH to MF, 1 Feb. 1875, HP 4.102; Geison, *Foster*, 142–3. Foster thought Martin's name on the cover would increase his job prospects; that it did was evident from Huxley's sending Johns Hopkins a copy in 1876, as a reference for Martin. He became the biology professor there: Benson, 'American', 166–7.

    'Lord how I wish that I had gone through such a course', said Darwin as he read it (CD to TH, 12 Nov. [1875], HP 5.324). In fact Darwin was being polite – his morphologically-undisciplined mind would have hated it, and his stomach would have reacted to the gore, as it did during his student days in Edinburgh.
76. Poore, 'Grant'; Schafer, 'Sharpey'.
77. ERL to TH, 11 June [1875], HP 21.45; Lankester was appointed on 20 Feb. 1875; 'life': ERL to TH, [*c.* 1873], HP 21.48; 'like': Lester and Bowler, *Lankester*, 61–7.
78. *LLL*, 2:452, 460; bedside: Judd, *Coming*, 80; *LTH*, 1:361, 448; *LJH*, 2:199; *LCK*, 2:343; 'You': F. Kingsley to TH, 16 Nov. 1876, HP 19.261; 'pain': HAH to ES, 7 Mar. 1875, AD.
79. Tener and Woodfield, *Victorian Spectator*, 28; desert: *CE*, 6:319.
80. H. E. Roscoe to TH, 24 Jan. 1875, HP 25.277; E. Becker to TH, Feb. 1875, HP 10.261–2 on the *Primers*' German translation; MacLeod, 'Evolutionism', 74. Book list: HP 52.9, cf. 30.92.
81. Meadows, *Science*, 88–92; TH to NL, 31 Jan., 3 Feb. 1875, HP 21.266–7.
82. 'Thank': TH to P. L. Sclater, 22 Jan., 14 Aug. 1875, ZSL; 29 Apr., 11 May 1875, APS; TH to JH, 3 Nov. 1875, APS; *LTH*, 1:447, 450; Burkhardt and Smith, *Calendar*, 9827, 9831, 9843. The Polar Committee also fought for Treasury funding to make Carpenter's son Philip the naturalist on the 1875 *Valorous* expedition to the Arctic: WBC to TH, 20 Jan. 1876, HP 12.105; A. Gunther to TH, 1 Dec. 1875, BM(NH) L MSS Gunther Coll. 27, box 1, folder 9. Huxley had already backed a private attempt to get a screw steamer through the Spitzbergen ice to the unconquered Pole: *Proposed Arctic Expedition, via Spitzbergen* (Jan. 1873): flyer in BM(NH), Z. Keeper's Archives 1.1.

    And he encouraged military efforts to record information. At the Royal Engineer Institute, Chatham, he talked on 'The geographical distribution of animals; and on collecting and observing . . . ', 3 Apr 1878, HM 1:4:131.

83. TH to FD, 9 June 1875, HP 1.135; antivivisection flyers: HP 49.143; 'or else': MF to TH, 27 Jan. [1875], HP 4.194; Ritvo, *Animal Estate*, 160–4; 'alleviating': TH to JD, 12 Feb. 1874, HP 30.85; *LTH*, 1:431; Harrison, 'Animals', 791; O'Connor, *Founders*, 132; French, *Antivivisection*, 100.

84. TH to MF, 16 Apr. 1875, HP 4.106. The Council on Education minute on vivisection was recorded on 10 Feb. 1874 and evidently changed to cover only conscious animals after Huxley protested: TH to Lord Aberdare (H. A. Bruce), 14 Feb. 1874, HP 30.87; TH to JD, 12 Feb. 1874, HP 30.85; *LTH*, 1:430–3; French, *Antivivisection*, 95; '*parvenu*': Ritvo, *Animal Estate*, 157–65; E. Richards, 'Redrawing the Boundary' on the class edge to Cobbe's feminist attack.

Ironically, having clawed State funding, the Xs were soon to start worrying that it might bring with it State interference: Barton, 'Influential', 76–7.

85. To explain the sympathy of women with the antivivisectionist movement one must look to Evelleen Richards' work on the Victorian categorizing of women, as a lower form, like 'dogs' possessing 'dangerous sexualities that necessitated control'. Women accepted that inferior position, while sharing a sympathy with other denigrated races brutalized by men: E. Richards, 'Redrawing the Boundary'. Coral Lansbury, 'Gynaecology', goes further to suggest slippage between the anti-pornography and antivivisectionist protest, in both cases the victims being tied down and violated.

86. Burkhardt and Smith, *Calendar*, 9849, 9916, 9923, 9933–5, 9938, 9948; *LLD*, 3:204; French, *Antivivisection*, 62–79; *LGR*, 7–8, 15–22; R. Richards, *Darwin*, 334ff; sermon: Countess Camperdown to TH, 7 July [1875], HP 15.23–5. Playfair's reworded Bill in the Commons proved unsatisfactory: a clause allowing vivisection only for the purpose of scientific discovery would have outlawed Huxley's schoolmasters' demonstrations: *LTH*, 1:436–9; CD to TH, 21 May 1875, HP 5.316.

87. R. A. Cross to TH, June 1875, HP 12.353–6; *LTH*, 1:438–9; HP 10.204–6; E. Cardwell to TH, 1, 6 July 1875, HP 12.29–32; French, *Antivivisection*, 91ff, and 93 on the fox-hunting MPs on the Commission.

88. Huxley, Edinburgh lectures, 3 May–23 July 1875, HM 2:70:4; 'University of Edinburgh – Opening of the Natural History Class by Professor Huxley', newspaper cutting, HM 2:70:4a. Cf. his letter to Spencer, in which he jokingly claimed that he had warned the students 'to keep free of the infidel speculations which are current under the name of evolution': Caron, 'Biology', 250. TH to FD, 9 June 1875, HP 1.135; 'still': TH to JH, 10 Oct. 1875, HP 2.222. Rice, 'Oceanographic', 216. Morrell, 'Patronage' 360–78; autograph hunters: J. E. Millais, HP 22.232–3; also HP 15.224, 22.12.

89. TH to JT, 13 Aug. 1875, HP 9.91; *LTH*, 1:443–6.

90. CWT to TH, 9 June 1875, HP 27.312; 'horrid': 5 Sept. 1874, HP 27.310; Rehbock, 'Huxley', 527–9; Linklater, *Voyage*, 121ff.

91. Rehbock, 'Huxley', 528–9; Rupke, '*Bathybius*', 60; Rice, 'Huxley', 173; Huxley, 'Notes from the "Challenger"'; *LTH*, 1:480; 'My': TH to NL, 13 Aug. 1875, HP 21.268; Meadows, *Science*, 31–6.

92. TH to MF, 29 Nov., 1 Dec. 1874, HP 4.96, 100; ERL to TH, 11 June [1875], HP 21.45; HAH to ES, 3 Apr. 1876, AD.

93. TH to JK, 14 June 1875, APS; 'white': JK to TH, 9 June 1875, HP 20.42; 'refreshing': TH to JK, 5 June 1875, APS; Catlett, 'Huxley', 184–6; 'gentle': Tener and Woodfield, *Victorian Spectator*, 9.

94. CD to TH, 1 Nov. [1875], HP 5.322; *LTH*, 1:440; sheep-pox: TH to JT, 9 Nov. [1874], HP 9.88; O'Connor, *Founders*, 133, 137, 155–7, 254; Harte, *University*, 125–6; Litchfield, *Emma Darwin*, 2:221; French, *Antivivisection*, 103–6. Klein, Burdon-Sanderson, Brunton and Foster, *Handbook for the Physiological Laboratory* (1873) was the standard text on the experimental method.

4 THE AMERICAN DREAM

1. F. Harrison to TH, 30 Aug. 1876, HP 18.48 (also 'whole'); Martin, 'flying': TH to D. C. Gilman, 20 Feb., 23 Apr. 1876, Milton S. Eisenhower Library, Johns Hopkins University; D. C. Gilman to TH, 14 Mar. 1876, HP 17.51; 'heart', 'glorious': J. Fiske to TH, 1 Mar. 1876, HP 16.89; 'thirty': TH to ES, 8 June 1876, HP 31.44; Jensen, 'Huxley's Address', 259; *LTH*, 1:446, 459–60.
2. TH to JK, 4 Dec. 1875, APS, reply, 7 Dec., HP 20.44; M. Arnold to TH, 8 Dec. 1875, HP 10.159; *LTH*, 1:319, 448, 457; 'up': TH to MF, 4 Dec. 1875, HP 4.111.
3. HAH to ES, 3 Apr. 1876, 2 Sept. 1878, AD; creditors: J. W. Johnson to TH, 15 Nov. 1875, HP 19.79; W. C. Norton to TH, 16 Nov. 1875, HP 23.230.
4. TH to JK, 4, 31 Dec. 1875, APS.
5. *SM*, 4:36, 84–124, esp. 101, 121; Woodward, 'Contributions', 729; di Gregorio, *Huxley*, 72–4. Yet he suggests elsewhere that, despite the remarkable similarity to the Devonian fringe-finned fish *Dipterus* (now known to be a lungfish), *Ceratodus* was possibly not related to it 'in the way of ancestry': *SM*, 4:166.

   Nyhart, *Biology*, 251–62 on Gegenbaur's 'archipterygium' theory: his attempt to show how *Ceratodus*' 'archetypal fin' had developed; Huxley was not too happy about Gegenbaur's conclusion: *SM*, 4:118. Di Gregorio, 'Wolf', on Gegenbaur as a go-between bridging the archetypal idealists such as Owen and the Darwinians with their evolutionary theory.
6. TH to P. L. Sclater, 21, 31 Dec. 1875, APS; Len: TH to A. Gunther, 3 Jan. 1876, Z Keeper's Archives 1.9, Letters 1876 no 279; *LTH*, 1:398; Drawings of *Polypterus*, 1 Jan. 1875, HM Box D:54; Notes on *Ceratodus Forsteri*, HM 2:22:1.
7. Brown, *Metaphysical*, 31, 89, 140, 329; *LTH*, 1:319, 457; JK to L. Huxley, 23 Feb. 1899 HP 20.200; Conway, 'Huxley', 74; Peterson, *Huxley*, 170.
8. Anne Evans' Diary, HP 31.105; Magnus, *Gladstone*, 229, 233–7; W. E. Gladstone to TH, 24 Feb. 1876, HP 17.67; Huxley's Diary, 2 March 1876, HP 70.18.
9. JM to TH, 9 Jan. 1876, HP 23.24; *LTH*, 1:458. Huxley (Diary, HP 70.18) met Morley on 18 January 1876 and presumably discussed the paper. W. K. Clifford to HAH, 7, 19 Apr. 1876, HP 12.240–2; J. L. Richards, 'Reception', 152–6.
10. HAH to ES, 3 Apr. 1876, 14 Nov. 1877, AD; 'face': TH to AD, 13 Jan. 1877, HP 13.272; JH to HAH, 1 July 1876, HP 3.245; Countess of Portsmouth to HAH, 2 Aug. 1876, HP 28.109; TH to JT, 13 Aug. 1875, HP 9.91; *LTH*, 1:447. Huxley was soon introducing Waller to the people of note: TH to H. Cole, 6 July 1877, APS.
11. JT to TH, 15 Oct. [1875], HP 1.92, also 1.91–7; 9.38, 94–6; *LTH*, 1:449;

Friday, 'Microscopic Incident', 65–9; TH's notes, HM 1:1:67, 2:2; *CE*, 3:280.

12. *LJT*, xxi, 202–6; *LHS*, 182; 'After': JT to TH, 4 Feb. 1876, HP 1.141–3, also 1.145, 151; JH to JT, 10 Mar. 1876, HP 8.368; 'considering', 'D[r]': HAH to ES, 3 Apr. 1876, AD.
13. HAH to ES, 3 Apr. 1876, AD; J. P. Thomasson to TH, 20 Mar. 1876, HP 27.243, see also 244–7; W. Brimelow to TH, 30 Mar. 1876, HP 11.76; Morley, *Cobden*, 687.
14. Huxley was awarded the Geological Society's Wollaston Medal in 1876: H. Woodward to TH, 2 Feb. 1876, HP 29.92.
15. TH to MF, 25 May 1876, HP 4.120 (also 'pietistic'); *Times*, 23 May 1876; Huxley's letter, *Times*, 26 May; Shaftesbury's reply, *Times*, 27 May, in HP 49.140–2; TH to Shaftesbury, 29 May 1876, HP 12.320; *LTH*, 1:427–30; *CE*, 3:310. Sir William Smith urged Huxley (21 Feb.–19 Mar. 1876, HP 26.131–49) to write on vivisection in the *Quarterly* to sway Parliament.
16. HAH to ES, 3 Apr., 9 Aug. 1876, AD; Huxley's Diary HP 70.18; *LTH*, 1:460. Hooker: *LJH*, 2:202; JH to JT, 26 June 1876, HP 8.369; JH to HAH, 1, 4 July 1876, HP 3.245–6.
17. HAH to ES, 9 Aug. 1876, AD; cartoon of ship, 2 Aug. 1876, Huxley's Diary HP 70.19; 'must': ES to TH, 26 June 1876, AD. They sailed with friends, George Smalley of the *New York Tribune* and Newell Martin, on his way to Johns Hopkins: Maienschein, *Transforming*, 25; *LTH*, 1:461.
18. King, 'Catastrophism', 469–70; Pfeifer, 'United States', 199–200; Irvine, *Apes*, 289; MacLeod, 'Evolutionism', 66; Hofstadter, *Social Darwinism*, 6–10, 41; F. Harrison to TH, 30 Aug. 1876, HP 18.48; *LTH*, 1:460.
19. Randel, 'Huxley', 75–81; *LTH*, 1:461, 463; 'beautiful': HAH to ES, 9 Aug. 1876, AD; Hofstadter, *Social Darwinism*, 24.
20. W. H. Appleton to HAH, 22 Aug. 1876, HP. 10.108; 'to': TH to ES, 8 June 1876, HP 31.44.
21. Marsh, *Introduction*; Marsh, *Odontornithes*; and Marsh, 'Discovery', 56–7 – a paper earmarked in Huxley's Diary HP 70.15A: 'Marsh – Bird from Upper Cretaceous shale of Kansas . . . Annals Jny 1873'. *LTH*, 1:462–3; Randel, 'Huxley', 78–80. Background: Schuchert and LeVene, *Marsh*; Ostrom and McIntosh, *Marsh's Dinosaurs*; Goetzmann, *Exploration*, 421–9.

    After Huxley left America Marsh continued to work on the toothed, flightless *Hesperornis* and to reaffirm that its primitive characters were those of ratites, in effect confirming Huxley's dinosaur–*Hesperornis*–ostrich link: O. C. Marsh to TH, 12 Jan. 1877, Yale University Library.
22. Dinosaurs alone were responsible for the prints, Marsh now believed: *Introduction*, 11; Dean, 'Hitchcock's Tracks'; Desmond, *Archetypes*, 129; Randel, 'Huxley', 80; *LTH*, 1:462.
23. Schuchert and LeVene, *Marsh*, 236–7; 'more': TH to O. C. Marsh, 17 Aug. 1876, Yale University Library; *LTH*, 1:463; 'red-faced': HP 89.39.
24. Marsh, *Introduction*, 27; Marsh, 'Huxley'; Marsh, 'Notice', 255; *LTH*, 1:463; Rainger, 'Paleontology', 282–4.
25. J. Fiske to TH, 1 Mar. 1876, HP 16.89; Fiske, *Darwinism*, 54. Fiske named his own son Herbert Huxley: Randel, 'Huxley', 75, 82; 'driven': A. Agassiz to TH, 14 July 1874, HP 6.144; Winsor, *Reading*, chaps 5–6; Desmond and Moore, *Darwin*, 562–3; Dupree, *Gray*, 337–41.
26. HAH to ES, 2 Sept. 1876, AD; 'thin': ES to TH, 26 June 1876, AD; Randel,

'Huxley', 82–4. Winsor, *Reading*, 42. The Director of Buffalo Museum wrote of how the 'pulpiteers' struck up after Huxley left. Their arguments 'smell badly' and it takes 'all Moody & Sankey and Mrs. Van Cott can do to make them neutral in their odor'. A. R. Grote to TH, 13 Mar. 1878, HP 17.149. On Moody and evolution: J. R. Moore, *Post-Darwinian Controversies*, 55; J. R. Moore, *Darwin Legend*, 83ff.

27. Summerville, 'Roberts', 18–22, 30–6, 180–2; J. M. Smith, 'Huxley', 191–8; 'most': ES to HAH, 30 Oct. 1876, AD. The 'buckle on the Bible belt' is Jim Moore's expression.
28. ES to TH, 6 July 1874, 26 June 1876, AD; 'George': TH to ES, 8 June 1876, HP 31.44; 'drink': HAH to ES, 3 Apr. 1876, AD; J. M. Smith, 'Huxley', 193.
29. Randel, 'Huxley', 85–6; J. M. Smith, 'Huxley', 200–1, 322–7, 330–40; 'pugilistic': ES to HAH, 30 Oct. 1876, AD. Fisk: Lorimer, *Colour*, 63.
30. HAH to ES, 17 Sept. 1876, AD; 'page': ES to HAH, 30 Oct. 1876, AD; J. M. Smith, 'Huxley', 334, 336; Flexner, *Gilman*, 35.
31. Randel, 'Huxley', 88–9; Jensen, 'Huxley's Address', 257–64; Flexner, *Gilman*, 23–5, 35, 48, 50, 55–9, 63–4; White, *History*, 22ff; and see J. R. Moore, *Post-Darwinian Controversies* on White's military metaphor.
32. *CE*, 3:236, 256, 260–1; 'vigorous': HAH to ES, 17 Sept. 1876, AD; Jensen, *Huxley*, 98; Jensen, 'Huxley's Address', 265; Huxley, 'How to Become', 2.
33. TH to H. N. Martin, 2 Apr. [1879], Milton S. Eisenhower Library, Johns Hopkins University; Jensen, 'Huxley's Address', 258–60; Randel, 'Huxley', 90; Caron, 'Biology', 243–5. On Martin at Hopkins, and his lab-based physiological approach: Pauly, 'Appearance', 378–9; Benson, 'American', 166–7; Benson, 'Museum Research', 66ff. As in London, so Martin here too started practical lab classes for teachers with a microscope as the exam prize: Maienschein, *Transforming*, 27–8.
34. HAH to ES, 17 Sept. 1876, AD. The Smithsonian zoologist Spencer Fullerton Baird (the man who commissioned the Centennial *Hadrosaurus*) escorted Hal and Nettie around the exhibits. Rainger, 'Rise', 9–12. Huxley presumably never met the Philadelphian E. D. Cope. Even Agassiz had warned him off the erratic Cope, who had gained 'the contempt of all the scientific men of the country': A. Agassiz to TH, 14 July 1874, HP 6.144.
35. HAH to ES, 17 Sept. 1876, AD. Requests: HP 11.106, 13.135, 15.7, 15.36, 15.223, 21.173, 23.207, 24.108, 24.192, 25.1, 26.159, 27.121, 29.100.
36. Randel, 'Huxley', 91–3. Greeley himself had been ever ready to 'lend an attentive and unprejudiced ear to the bold speculations of our Darwins and Huxleys, wherein they almost seem to lay a confident finger on the very heart of the great mysteries of life', quoted in *New-York Daily Tribune*, 18 Sept. 1876.
37. Randel, 'Huxley', 92–4; *New-York Daily Tribune*, 19 Sept. 1876; *Daily Graphic*, 27 Sept. 1876, HP 79.16.
38. Huxley, 'Evidences'. This press transcript differs from Huxley's MS (HM 2:82:38ff), showing that he extemporized on the night. He modified the text further for *American Addresses*. He changed the expression to 'extranatural', and strengthened it by talking of supposed events 'many thousand years ago . . . utterly foreign to and inconsistent with the existing laws of Nature': *CE*, 4:48–9. This pointed reference to the miraculous base of Christianity was not made on the night.
39. Jensen, *Huxley*, 101–4; Randel, 'Huxley', 93–5; *New York Daily Tribune*, 19 Sept. 1876; Huxley, 'Evidences'; *CE*, 4:53–4.

40. Desmond, *Archetypes*, 128–30. The suggestion that *Archaeopteryx* was an 'intercalary' (not a 'linear') type was not made on the night but appeared in print in *American Addresses*. Cf. *CE*, 4:102ff with Huxley, 'Evidences'. *Compsognathus* diagram: TH to O. C. Marsh, 17 Aug. 1876, Yale University Library.
41. Marsh, *Introduction*; *CE*, 4:132; *New-York Daily Tribune*, 23 Sept. 1876; Randel, 'Huxley', 96; Pfeifer, 'United States', 197. Desmond, *Archetypes*, 167, and Bowler, *Fossils*, 132, for the scientific context of Huxley's discourse.
42. Huxley, 'Evidences'; *CE*, 4:137. The *Times* (23 Aug. 1878, p.10) called the word 'scientist' 'a horrible, but handy Americanism'. In fact the word had been coined by William Whewell in Britain in 1834, but it only caught on in the US in the 1870s.
43. HAH to ES, 23 Sept. 1876, 4 Jan. 1877, AD; E. L. Youmans to TH, 17 Nov. 1876, HM 3:121:122; 'profound': P. Jackson to TH, 22 Sept. 1876, HP 19.11.
44. HAH to ES, 8 Oct. 1876, AD; 'dear': Clark, *Huxleys*, 93; 'Wife': TH to MF, 12 Oct. 1876, HP 4.133; '£600': Huxley's Diary, 70.19; Randel, 'Huxley', 96; Jensen, *Huxley*, 109.

5 *A TOUCH OF THE WHIP*

1. HAH to ES, 4 Jan. 1877, AD; Burkhardt and Smith, *Calendar*, 10873.
2. *LTH*, 1:477–8; Bibby, *Huxley*, 211–14; expenses: HP 30.105–12; 'Government': HAH to ES, 3 Apr. 1876, AD; 'that': Huxley, [Speech], *Journal of the Quekett Microscopical Club*, 5 (1878), 48; Deanery: A. Stanley to TH, 18 Oct. 1876, HP 26.237; HAH to ES, 4 Jan. 1877, AD.
3. TH to MF, 29 June 1876, HP 4.129; 'rushing': HAH to ES, 4 Jan. 1877, AD; A. Russell to HAH, 4 Jan. 1877, HP 25.309.
4. Plates of *Spirula*: CWT to TH, 1877/8, HP 9.314–18, 27.322, 326; Huxley, 'Dinner'; drawings, HP 78; MS: HP 40.1–53; J. P. Hennessy to TH, 30 Jan. 1877, HP 18.112; 6257: Huxley, 'First Volume'; 'debt': Anne Evans' Diary, HP 31.105; Manual: HAH to ES, 4 Jan. 1877, AD; *LTH*, 1:399, 491. Seventeen years later (by which time the old Huxley seems to have forgotten that he had written this much manuscript) the plates were turned over to P. Pelseneer, who started afresh: J. Murray/TH, 29, 30 Sept. 1894, HP 23.190; *LTH*, 2:361–2.
5. TH to JT, 7 Dec. 1877, HP 8.203; JM to TH, 14 Dec. 1877, HP 23.36; *LTH*, 1:476–7; HAH to ES, 14 Nov. 1877, AD; ES to HAH, 11 Feb. 1879, AD; J. A. Froude to TH, 3 June 1877, HP 16.284; Stoddart, 'That Victorian Science', 18–22; Jensen, *Huxley*, 108. Marsh completed the horse teeth-and-toes diagram in *American Addresses* by putting the pattern on the grinders: TH to O. C. Marsh, 27 Dec. 1876, Yale University Library.
6. HAH to ES, 13 Sept. 1879, AD; walk: 7 Mar. 1875; godfather: HAH's Godparent's Notebook, AD. The switch occurred late in 1876: Duckworth christened Alice Heath's baby (with Nettie godmother) on 26 December 1876: HAH to ES, 4 Jan. 1877, AD; 'self', 'Their': Anne Evans' Diary, HP 31.105. Pevsner, *Buildings*, 330.
7. O. C. Marsh to TH, 12 Jan. 1877, Yale University Library; E. L. Youmans to TH, 17 Nov. 1876, HM 3:121:122. Marsh had also worked out ancestries for tapirs and rhinoceroses, and Huxley incorporated them into his lectures: 'The Succession in Time of the Form of Ungulata' (HM 1:10:37–45).

8. Huxley, 'Prefatory Note', xiv. (In 1892 he was still assuming that our primate ancestors would be found in the strata that yielded the horses: *Controverted Questions* 45.) Cartoon, HP 79.18; Marsh, *Introduction*; 'inexhaustibility': TH to O. C. Marsh, 27 Dec. 1876, Yale University Library; *LTH*, 1:469.
9. TH to A. W. Williamson, 27 June 1877, APS.
10. *CE*, 2:187; *LTH*, 449–54; HM 2:32; CD to TH, 11 June [1878], HP 5.331; Hooker's address: TH to JH, 8 Dec. 1877, HP 2.227; Star: *LJH*, 2:147, 150. The way evolution triumphed without natural selection is chronicled in Bowler, *Non-Darwinian Revolution*.
11. TH to CD, 28 Dec. 1878, CUL DAR 210.12:8 (my thanks to Perry O'Donovan for sending me a transcription). Darwin's maintenance of respectability is at the crux of Desmond and Moore, *Darwin*.
12. TH to CD, 6 Mar. 1881, HP 9.209; gave: CD to TH, 29 Dec. 1878, HP 5.329.
13. Burkhardt and Smith, *Calendar*, 10933; TH to H. Milne Edwards, 1 June 1877, HP 30.102, 22.248–52; F. Lacaze-Duthiers to TH, 21 June 1877, HP 22.250.
14. Colp, 'Notes on Gladstone', 181–2; Irvine, *Apes*, 211; Huxley's Diary, 10 Mar. 1877, HP 70.20.
15. Tennyson, 'Prefatory Poem'; Brown, *Metaphysical*, 180ff; JK to TH, 26 Apr. 1876, HP 20.46.
16. Huxley, 'Modern "Symposium"'; HAH to ES, 15 July 1877, AD. Huxley also became a fixture on the 'Recent Science' column: TH to JT, 2 Dec. 1880, HP 9.130, also 1.173.
17. JM to TH, 16 Jan. 1878, HP 23.39; 'ravening': 27 Nov. 1877, HP 23.33; Bibby, *Huxley*, 104; *LTH*, 1:483; 'occupy': TH to AD, 12 June 1880, HP 13.289.
18. *LTH*, 1:485–8; *SM*, 4:319–44; Huxley, 'Scientific Worthies'. Darwin had been hurt by the slurs about his 'anti-Baconian' method. J. S. Mill had early defended him (*CCD*, 9:204) and now Huxley used 'Harvey' to show that '*the worm has turned*', implying that Darwin's was *the* scientific method. J. Spedding to TH, 28 Jan. 1878, HP 26.179, 181.
19. *CE*, 3:407–8; HAH to ES, 14–27 Dec. 1877, AD; *LTH*, 1:488.
20. Barton, 'Scientific Opposition', 16; W. G. Armstrong to TH, 26 Nov. 1877, HP 10.118; *CE*, 3:425; *LTH*, 1:474, 484; Grocers: TH to JT, 19 May 1883, 22 May 1884, HP 9.136, 146; Cardwell, *Organisation*, 139.
21. HAH to ES, 3 Apr. 1876, 4 Jan., 15 July 1877, 2 July 1878, 13 Sept. 1879, AD; *LTH*, 2:35; Clark, *Huxleys*, 99.
22. Anne Evans' Diary, HP 31.105; HAH to ES, 3 Apr. 1876, 14 Nov. 1877, AD; also 15 July 1877, 2 July, 2 Sept. 1878, AD.
23. HAH to ES, 4 Jan., 15 July 1877, AD. AnneMarie Robinson, University of London Archives, provided confirmation of Leonard Huxley's matriculation. On the practice of using the university's 'highly valued' matriculation exam to gain a proficiency certificate, see Brock, 'School Science Examinations', 173.
24. HAH to ES, 26 Nov. 1878, AD; Jowett's role: HAH to ES, 15 July, 14 Nov. 1877, AD; 'on': BJ to TH/HAH, 23 Apr., 6 May 1877, HP 7.9–11; 'so': 19 July 1877, HP 7.13; tutors: 7, 23 May [1878], HP 7.15–17; Howarth, 'Science Education', 364–5.
25. Howarth, 'Science Education', 335, 347, 353; *CE*, 3:214.

26. Mairet, *Pioneer*, 19ff; 'sharp': TH to MF, 12 Oct. 1876, HP 4.133; H. N. Martin, Sydney Vines, Emily Munn came down from Cambridge.
27. O'Connor, *Founders*, 162–3; exams: Ruse, *Darwinian Revolution*, 262.
28. TH to AD, 5–6 Mar. 1874, HP 13.260–2; 'dash': *LTH*, 2:37; HAH to ES, 3 Sept. 1882, AD; *viva*: MF to TH, 1 Oct. [1874], HP 4.188; Bowler, 'Development', 290.
29. TH to AD, 21 Nov. 1877, HP 13.280; Desmond and Moore, *Darwin*, 629–30; 'University': HP 41.151; *LTH*, 1:479–81; *CCD*, 7:396.
30. CD to TH, 19 Nov. [1877], HP 5.328; 'Mr': HP 41.151; *LTH*, 1:479–80, 483.
31. 'The Extinct Animals termed Belemnites and their Ancient & Modern Allies', London Institution, 17 Dec. 1877, HM 2:82:16–37, ff.20–8. See also HM 1:3:179, 189; *CE*, 4:14–16; HP 40.64–9; Naples: HP 13.272, 280; 'growing': Huxley, *Anatomy of Invertebrated Animals*, 4 (only days after the publication of this book he delivered his 'Extinct Animals' talk). Huxley, 'New Arrangement of Lenses'; *SM*, 4:316–18; G. B. Howes to L. Huxley, 9 Jan. 1900, HP 18.264; Hollowday, 'Huxley', 451–2.
32. Interestingly Robert Louis Stevenson's *Strange Case of Dr Jekyll and Mr Hyde* (1886) could have been based on the case studies popularized by Huxley in his famous 1874 essay on 'Automatism' (*CE*, 1:235). Stevenson was an Edinburgh University engineer by training and a close friend of Huxley's 'Tall Teas' regular Henry James.
33. Marsh, 'Huxley', HP 82; *LTH*, 1:494; W. T. Roden to TH, 16 Jan. 1879, HP 25.129, also 131–3; S. Evans to TH, 31 Dec. 1881–4 Jan. 1882, HP 15.220–2; Anne Evans' Diary, HP 31.105; T. Woolner to HAH, 5 Dec. 1877, HP 29.95, also 96; 'large': HAH to ES, 14 Nov. 1877, AD. An analogy of phylogenetic trees with the ephemeral 'fabled "bean-stalk"' was drawn by Mivart, '*Lepilemur*', 506.
34. L. Stephen to HAH, 28 Nov., 18 Dec. 1877, HP 27.44–6; correspondents, HAH to ES, 4 Jan. 1877, AD; Stanley: Anne Evans' Diary, HP 31.105.
35. Anne Evans' Diary, HP 31.105; *LTH*, 1:488–9; HAH to ES, 4 Jan. 1880, AD.
36. Marian Huxley to ES, 26 Nov. 1878, AD; A. Forbes to TH, n.d. [1878], HP 16.143; *LTH*, 1:489; Frere: JM to TH, 16 Mar. 1879, HP 23.57. Morris, *Heaven's Command*, 384; Magnus, *Gladstone*, 261–4.

    Huxley met war veterans at Forbes' house and had explorers to his own, including the small, taciturn Henry Morton Stanley – who left with egg on his face, having brought two chimpanzee skulls in bandboxes, only to have them pronounced human, 'with some amusement': Anne Evans' Diary, HP 31.105; H. M. Stanley to TH, [Mar. 1878], HP 26.270. The Queen asked Huxley about Stanley's skulls: F. I. Edwards to TH, 18 Feb. 1880, HP 15.162.
37. H. W. Smith/TH, 27, 28 Jan. 1881, HP 26.123; maths at Eton: Revd R. Okes to TH, 18 June 1881, HP 23.232; 'I': E. Clayton, 29 Sept. 1890, HP 12.220; Bibby, *Huxley*, 172–5.
38. TH to JH, 9 Nov. 1878, HP 2.229; 'Victor, Comte de Veysey' to TH, 19 Sept., 26 Oct. 1878, HP 28.69–70; also HP 2.236, 11.111, 24.278. The *Globe*, 14 Mar. 1879, reported Veysey in a Rome jail. Crown Prince: Viscountess Goschen to HAH, 28 May 1878, HP 17.99. *LTH*, 1:445, 458.

6 A PERSON OF RESPECTABILITY

1. HS to HAH, n.d., HP 7.143; 'grey': HAH to ES, 2 July 1878, 8 July 1879, AD; *LTH*, 1:492; 'as': JT to TH, 3 May 1878, HP 1.152.
2. Parker, 'Huxley', 166; *LTH*, 1:492–4; 'worn': TH to AD, 16 Feb. 1879, HP 13.284; TH to JT, TH to JT, 16–20 May 1878, HP 9.112–16; 'Married', 'lost', 'for': Marian Huxley/HAH to ES, 2 July, 2 Sept. 1878, AD. Parker was about to go out to New Zealand as the first Professor of Zoology at Otago University: CWT to TH, 14 Jan. 1880, 27.324; HM 3:121:99
3. TH to JT, 20 May 1878, HP 9.114–16; CD to TH, 11 Aug. [1878], HP 5.326; Huxley, Davis Lectures, ZSL, 17 May–21 June 1878, HM 1:4:2–13; 'speak': 'FZS' to Council, 23 May 1878, ZSL; farm: HAH to ES, 2 July 1878, AD; *LTH*, 1:492–4.
4. He did pick up *Spirula* in Summer 1880, but the momentum was lost (HM 2:15). *LTH*, 1:399–401.
5. Huxley, 'President's Address' (1879), 255; 'Morphological': Huxley, Davis Lectures, ZSL, HM 1:4:5, 'Phylogeny', f.8: this genealogy is reproduced in di Gregorio, *Huxley*, 110, who gives a detailed discussion; cf. *SM*, 4:300–14.
6. Plan for an educational series, 9 Oct. 1878, HP 52.11; Huxley's 1878 Diary, HP 70.21; 'mightier': MacLeod, 'Evolutionism', 72; Hofstadter, *Social Darwinism*, 33ff; Draper, *History*, iv, viii. For contextual studies of Draper's 'conflict' thesis, see Brooke, *Science*, 34ff; Barton, 'Creation'; and esp. J. R. Moore, *Post-Darwinian Controversies*, 20ff.

   In Huxley's popular ISS book, *The Crayfish*, 320–46, the evolution of the crays takes on a diffusionist, geographical orientation, in line with his growing 'physiographic' approach. The increasing biogeographic interest also reveals Wallace's influence. Indeed, Jane Camerini ('Evolution', 700 n1) suggests that it was Huxley who coined the term 'Wallace's Line' (dividing the Australian and Asian faunal zones), in his work on the classification of gallinaceous birds in 1868. And significantly, shortly after this, Huxley began to use global maps of human stocks to accompany his Ethnological Society lectures.
7. He did start a sort of Darwinian programme in late 1879 as a prelude to writing this book. He collated information on domestic breeds from Hungary to India, and had expats searching for Bengal foxes, Burmese jackals and African foxes for his ultimate canine pedigree (HM 1:12:105–216; 1:13:1–14; *SM*, 4:404). He talked on 'Dogs and their History' at the London and Royal Institutions (HP 39.198; HM 1:12:216ff, 2:56), or 'Dogs and their Forefathers', as he called it in his more homely 'anthropological' style in his working-class lectures in February 1880. But the book itself remained unwritten.
8. JM to TH, 28 Mar., 29 Sept. 1878, HP 23.41, 47; *LTH*, 1:424–5, 495–7.
9. Huxley, 'Prefatory Note', xvi–ix; 'fleck': McCabe's introduction to Haeckel, *Evolution*, ix; *LTH*, 1:492; Tyndall, *Fragments II*, 397; Wace, 'Scientific Lectures', 52–61. Haeckel was to complain of Virchow's blocking his access to funds: TH to CD, 28 June 1881, HP 9.211, 5.364. Huxley, *Physiography*, v; this book was reprinted yearly until 1885. By 30 July 1878 (HP 12.326) his Macmillan statement was looking eminently 'respectable'.
10. *CE*, 6:51, 61–3, 69–70, chaps 5, 7–8, esp. 152, 166.

11. HAH to ES, 2 Sept. 1878, AD (also 'See', on which cf. HP 62.1); 2 July, 26 Nov. 1878, AD; *SM*, 4:265; 'and': Osborn, 'Enduring Recollections', 728; Webb, *Diary*, 203.
12. Yet *Hume* never quite made contact with Darwin. At one of Huxley's 'Tall Teas' Romanes questioned 'the omission of the inheritance-theory of innate ideas [from *Hume*]', having heard Huxley criticize 'the lack of that idea in J. S. Mill's "Utilitarianism"': Anne Evans' Diary, HP 31.105. 'Pudding': *CE*, 3:272, 280; Paradis, '*Evolution*', 22–34 on Huxley's later revolt against utilitarianism in the moral realm.
13. JM to TH, 26 Oct., 6 Nov. 1878, HP 23.49–50; *CE*, 6:211, 226.
14. JM to TH, 26 Jan. 1879, HP 23.54; 'I'm': 26 Oct. 1878, HP 23.49; 10,000: 25 Sept. 1880, HP 23.64; 'measure': Anne Evans' Diary, HP 31.105; *LTH*, 1:496–7; *CE*, 6:43.
15. H. F. Peck to TH, n.d., HP 24.93; JM to TH, 14, 26 Jan. 1879, HP 23.53–4; CD to TH, 18 Jan. 1879, HP 5.333; *MLD*, 1:381; *LTH*, 1:501; dogmatism: Veitch, 'Huxley's Hume'; 'Twenty': TH to H. N. Martin, 2 Apr. [1879], Milton S. Eisenhower Library, Johns Hopkins University. List of recipients: HP 31.109. M. Arnold to TH, 17 Oct. 1880, HP 10.163. G. G. Stokes to TH, 10, 13 Jan. 1882, HP 30.190–1. Revd Henry Wace even quoted *Hume* in his Bampton lectures: Wace to TH, 23 June 1881, HP 28.84.
16. TH/JT, HP 9.118–26; 1.160–3; *LTH*, 1:498–500; projected series: HP 52.12. Huxley himself was set to turn in a volume on William Harvey: HP 39.154ff. H. E. Roscoe to TH, 24 Dec. 1878, HP 25.281. Collini, *Public Moralists*, 316.
17. TH to J. S. Stone, 31 Jan. 1875, HP 27.103, replying to HP 27.102; 'with': TH to G. J. Holyoake, 2 Nov. 1875, Holyoake Collection 2338, Co-Operative Union, Manchester, replying to HP 18.213.
18. Haeckel, *Freedom*, xxvii; Huxley, 'Prefatory Note', xviii–xx; R. Richards, *Darwin*, 526–8; Kelly, *Descent*, 123–41; 'Socialism': Wace, 'Scientific Lectures', 59.
19. TH to HAH, 8 Aug. 1873, AD; *LTH*, 1:397; 'sowing': HAH to TH, 7 July 1873, AD; 'No': HAH to ES, 26 Nov. 1878, AD.
20. M. Conway to TH, 13 Nov 1878, HP 12.298, also 12.300–12; Conway, 'Huxley', 73; broadsheet HP 30.10. The Old Testament scholar Marcus Kalisch (to TH, 17 Jan. 1879, HP 19.124) wanted 'the principles of the "Lay Sermons" . . . acted upon', but Huxley had his own agenda for that. Doubts: L. Stephen to TH, 19 Nov.–17 Jan. 1878, HP 27.50–3; JM to TH, 26 Jan. 1878, HP 23.54: JT/Louisa Tyndall to TH, 25 Jan., 7 Feb. 1879, HP 1.167, 179; TH to M. Conway, 24 Feb. 1879, HP 12.311; *LTH*, 2:3–4.
21. *LTH*, 2:4; J. Power to TH, 12 May 1879, 24.193–4, also 30.113; Bibby, *Huxley*, 187.
22. BJ to HAH, 21 Dec. 1879, HP 7.26; tutor A. M. Bell: 22 Apr., 5 Aug. 1879, HP 7.22–4; BJ to A. M. Bell, 13 Aug. [1879], HP 7.21. At St Andrews Leonard gained the Guthrie Scholarship: L. Campbell to TH, 5, 11 Apr. 1879, HP 12.12; *LTH*, 2:8; F. Pollock to TH, 22 Apr. [1879], HP 24.158. Exhibition: GR to TH, 27 Nov. 1879, HP 25.195; HAH to ES, 4 Jan. 1880, AD; 'monks': *CE*, 3:214. Hooker's son Reggie would also go to Cambridge: JH to TH, 19 June 1889, HP 3.344.
23. J. Hardcastle to E. Hardcastle, 12 Sept. 1874; bishops: R. Collier to J. Collier, 1 May 1836, both in the possession of William Collier; Collier, *Religion*, 56; 'friend': HAH to ES, 8 July, 1879, AD; *LTH*, 1:454.

24. *LTH*, 1:495–6, 501–2; 'moo': W. K. Clifford to HAH, 25 June 1878, HP 12.244; 'you', 7 Apr. 1876, HP 12.240; JM to TH, 3 Apr. 1878, HP 23.44; TH to JT, 2 Apr., 6 May 1878, HP 9.108, 110.
25. HAH to ES, 8 July, 28 Sept. 1879, 4 Jan. 1880, AD.
26. HAH to ES, 13 Sept. 1879, AD; *SM*, 4:380; HM 2:106.
27. H. E. Roscoe to TH, 24 Jan. 1875, HP 25.277; JD to TH, 16 Sept. 1879, HP 14.18; *LTH*, 2:2; Lightman, 'Voices'; Cooter and Pumfrey, 'Separate Spheres', for an exceptional study of science popularization.
28. Wace, 'Scientific Lectures', 36, 45–6; tram: WBC to TH, 29 Nov. 1883, HP 12.113; HAH to ES, 2, 13, 28 Sept., 26 Nov. 1879, AD.
29. Tyndall quoted in Wace, 'Scientific Lectures', 51.
30. Marsh, 'Notice of a New and Gigantic Dinosaur'; Marsh, 'A New Order'; Schuchert and LeVene, *Marsh*, 189ff; Ostrom and McIntosh, *Marsh's Dinosaurs*, 2–47; Colbert, *Men*, 82ff; King, 'Catastrophism', 469.
31. Marsh, 'Fossil Mammal' 459. In England in 1879 the Platonist and Archetypalist Harry Seeley ('Note on a Femur'), happy with a 'grade' concept of organization, (Desmond, *Archetypes*, chap. 6; Padian, 'Pterosaurs') relocated these early mammals into a low, sub-marsupial, 'generalized order'. Marsh ('Notice of Jurassic Mammals') followed suit, calling them 'Pantotheria'.
32. Forking phylogenetic tree, 29 Jan. 1879: HM 1:10:5. It shows the 'Monocondylia' passing from the Amphibia to the Sauropsida (reptiles and birds), and the 'Dicondylia' leading via 'Promammalia unknown' to the monotremes. (The monotremes, incidentally, give rise independently to the edentates and marsupials – and, through the latter, the rest of the mammals.) He read a paper at the Royal Society on 3 February giving this conclusion: Huxley, 'Characters of the Pelvis', 404. Haeckel, *History*, 2:233 on 'Promammalia'.

    Winsor, 'Impact', 78–82 has looked at Huxley's attempt at an evolutionary classification of the mammals (Huxley, 'Application', 658–9). Her analysis suggests that he was addressing the issues of species' multiple origins and convergence (then being discussed by P. M. Duncan, St G. Mivart, H. Seeley and E. D. Cope: Duncan, 'Anniversary Address', 85–7; Mivart, '*Lepilemur*', 506–10; Desmond, *Archetypes*, 183–4; Bowler, 'Cope'). But Huxley's notes with their branching trees show, I think, that he was engaged in a 'conventional' Haeckelian phylogenetic programme. He simply allowed that each group, like his paradigm, the horse, had a long 'peculiar line of ancestry', and that the common ancestors lay deep in the past – and that classification must reflect this.
33. T. Bain to R. Owen, 15 Dec. 1878, BM(NH), Owen Corres. vol. 2, f.61; Owen, *Descriptive*, iii–iv, 76; Owen, 'Evidence of a Carnivorous Reptile'; Desmond, *Archetypes*, 197–9. John Evans, the President, was praising Owen's work at the Geological Society (*Quart. J. Geol. Soc.*, 32 [1876], 112) the day Huxley was awarded its Wollaston Medal.
34. Hooker's election: JT to JH, 17 Feb. 1879, HP 8.388; Huxley's: JH to TH, 26 Feb. 1884, HP 3.279; reply, 27 Feb. 1884, HP 2.446 on potential blackballing; P. G. Hewett to TH, 2 Apr. 1884, HP 18.166. Rupke, *Owen*, 56–8 for interesting insights on Owen's four decades in The Club.
35. Even if Huxley noted some 'Simosaurian and Nothosaurian analogies' (*SM* 3:117) of Owen's paradigm specimen, the weasel-reptile *Galesaurus*, presumably in an attempt to undermine their mammal-likeness.

36. Seeley, 'Ornithosaurian', 238; Cope, 'Descriptions', 529; Cope, 'Second Contribution', 38–40. Desmond, *Archetypes*, chap. 6; and Padian, 'Pterosaurs', for the way social and biological philosophy prestructures perceptions of fossils.
37. Cope, 'Relations', 480. Although in Huxley's lectures on 'Sauropsida', Feb. 1882 (HM 2:75:10) he includes

    Theriodontia?? Copes Pelycosauria [*Dimetrodon*] comp[are]
    Protorosauria
    Anomodontia [i.e. Rhynchosaurus]?

    with the dinosaurs (his old view, lumping *all* reptiles as Sauropsida), his '??' show his growing uncertainty, and indeed in pencil next to them is written 'doubtful'. He was moving to a recognition that some reptiles might not be sauropsids, but be on a line to mammals.

    Later in the 1880s teeth were detected beneath the bony plate of the duck-billed platypus and its egg-laying was confirmed. This evidence for its reptilian ancestry swayed Mivart ('Possibly Dual Origin') among Huxley's disciples.
38. *LTH*, 1:476; G. G. Stokes to TH, 14 Jan. 1878, HP 30.180; 'to': Wace, 'Scientific Lectures', 35; University College: W. D. Halliburton to TH, 8 May 1878, HP 17.236.
39. A. Macmillan to TH, 23 Apr. 1880, HP 22.154.
40. Forgan and Gooday, 'Constructing South Kensington', 'Fungoid Assemblage', 166–9; Barton, 'Scientific Opposition'; *Survey of London*, 237–42; 'pet': JD to TH, 13 Feb. 1885, HP 14.48; on trade schools next to factories: HP 42.52–7; 'Art': Denis, 'Brompton Barracks', 17; 'if': *LTH*, 1:476, reply from the labour leader George Howell, 26 Jan. 1880, HP 18.241.
41. *LTH*, 1:398, 455, 2:62

7 *THE SCIENTIFIC WOOLSACK*

1. TH to FD, 30 Dec. 1881, HP 15.138.
2. Desmond, *Archetypes*, 58–9; *CE*, 2:230–1; '&': CD to TH, 11 [Apr.] 1880, HP 5.340; *LLD*, 3:240; *LTH*, 2:416; 'very': HAH to ES, 4 Apr. 1880, AD. Murchison was the elite geologist who came closest to retaining a catastrophic impression of the past.
3. E. g. Grant Allen cited in MacLeod, 'Evolutionism', 76.
4. Anne Evans' Diary, HP 31.105; 'Professor Huxley on the Origin of Species', *Standard*, 10 Apr. 1880; HM 1:12:198; *CE*, 2:227.
5. J. A. Froude to TH, 3 June 1877, HP 16.284; *CE*, 2:229; CD to TH, 11 May [1880], HP 5.342; *LTH*, 2:12–13.
6. Brown, *Metaphysical*, 34, 104.
7. TH to CD, 8 Jan. 1881, HP 9:203; *LTH*, 2:14; Burkhardt and Smith, *Calendar*, 12815; Darwin, *Autobiography*, 211; Butler, *Evolution*, 346; H. F. Jones, *Butler*, 1:272, 277, 291, 299ff, 318–28, 340–4, 349, 372, 385.
8. *CE*, 2:241, 4:6, 18, 44; HP 44.118, 59.40; Paradis, *Huxley*, 34. T. Chenery to TH, 28 Apr.–31 Aug. 1880, HP 12.179–82; A. Macmillan to TH, 23 Apr. 1880, HP 22.154; Escott, *Masters*, 183; CD to TH, [24 Dec. 1880], HP 5.363; Becker, *Scientific London*, 48–9.
9. Osborn, 'Memorial Tribute', 47; Marsh, 'Huxley'.

10. J. R. Lowell to TH, 27 Aug. 1880, HP 22.29, reply 22.30; H. James to TH, 17, 28 Nov. [1880], HP 19.23; Huxley, 'Olive Branch', 620–4; *LTH*, 2:15.
11. Osborn, 'Enduring Recollections', 728; Rainger, 'Vertebrate Paleontology' on the American institutional infrastructure created by Osborn and his 'Huxley method', which made palaeontology more zoology than geology. Munn: TH to AD, 18 Jan. 1882, HP 13.291; 'clever', 'pleasant': HAH to ES, 4 Jan. 1880, 8 Feb. 1882, AD.
12. Chlorodyne – containing morphia, chloroform and hemp – was in vogue among women, who became habituated and constantly increased their dosage. Addicts 'behave like morphinists', and in extreme cases 'women sell . . . property and steal in order to obtain the drug': Lewin, *Phantastica*, 75; White, *Materia Medica*, 618–19; sources provided by Ralph Colp.
13. Ellen begged money to bury her grandson: HAH to ES, 15 Jan., 3 Sept. 1882, 6 Dec. 1885, 1 July 1887, AD.
14. Friend, 'Huxley's Homes'; 'easy': HAH to ES, 4 Jan., 4 Apr. 1880, AD. William Collier kindly identified the subject of 'The Sins' for me.
15. T. A. Hirst, Journal XV (1884), 2151, Royal Institution.
16. And also of the peculiar *Peripatus* sent by Lloyd Morgan, who had worked in Huxley's lab: L. Morgan to TH, 2 Aug. 1880, HP 23.5; R. Trimen to TH, 19 Aug.–30 Dec. 1880, HP 28.39–42, 6 Jan. 1881, HM:4:59ff: 'workaday': HAH to ES, 13 Aug. 1880, AD; Home Office: R. Strachey, 14, 19 Aug. 1880, HP 27.106–9.
17. HAH to ES, 13 Aug. 1880, AD; J. R. Moore, 'Theodicy', 160.
18. W. Spottiswoode to HAH, 13 Aug. 1881, HP 26.203; Hall, 'Royal Society', 137; Jones, *Butler*, 294; Barton, 'Scientific Opposition'.
19. Morley, *Recollections*, 1:150–3; Spencer, *Autobiography*, 2:206; tea: J. Chamberlain to HAH, 23 Feb. 1881, HP 12.159; 'parked': Briggs, *Victorian Cities*, 231.
20. *CE*, 3:135–7, 140–50, 153, 158, 290; Paradis, *Huxley*, 166–8, 177, 188; Roos, 'Arnold', 317; Sanderson, 'English Civic Universities', 92–5.
21. JH to TH, 26 Nov. 1880, HP 3.259; JH to CD/CD to TH, 26 Nov. 1880, HP 5.349; *LTH*, 2:14–15. Huxley was still exposing Carpenter's demonstrations by card-sharps of the supposed transference of thought, never mind Wallace's full-blown spiritualism: WBC to TH, 16 June 1881, HP 12.108.
22. Wallace, *My Life*, 2: chap. 34; Durant, 'Scientific Naturalism'.
23. A. F. Walter to TH, 6 Jan. 1881, HP 28.155; HAH to ES, 18 Jan. 1881, AD; HM 2:46–52.
24. TH to CD, 24 Jan. 1881, HP 9.205; W. Harcourt/TH, 23 Dec. 1880 on, HP 18.5–18; 'carping': ERL to TH, 23 Jan. [1881], HP 21.77; warrant, 29 Jan. 1881: HP 32.(27). MacLeod, 'Government', on the State's use of expertise to investigate pollution and fish stocks.
25. *LTH*, 2:21–2; S. Walpole to TH, 17 Feb 1881, HP 28.122 (Spencer Walpole was his fellow Inspector); 'to make': HAH to ES, 18 Jan. 1881, AD; 'So': TH to CD, 24 Jan. 1881, HP 9.205.
26. Clipping from *Pall Mall Gazette* [1880], quoting Huxley in regard to the Evicted Tenants Bill, HP 49.62; Magnus, *Gladstone*, 295–8. The day after Gladstone introduced his new Land Bill, Disraeli (Lord Beaconsfield as he had become) was in communication with the Huxleys and discussing the question: J. Hawthorne to HAH, 8 Apr. 1881, HP 18.84.

27. TH to CD, 6 Mar. 1881, HP 9.209; CD to TH, 5 Mar. 1881, HP 5.359; Burkhardt and Smith, *Calendar*, 13046, 13071–2, 13080.
28. *LTH*, 2:27–9; *SM*, 4:473–92; HM 2:27–9; TH to H. G. Hensmen, 5 July 1881, APS; MacLeod, 'Government', 140.
29. HAH to ES, 14 Aug. 1881, AD. Trips: Burkhardt and Smith, *Calendar*, 13202; CD to TH, 9 Sept. 1881, HP 5.368; HS to HAH, 6 July 1881, HP 7.149. R. Browning to TH, 8, 10 Feb. 1880, HP 11.122–4. Bust: L. Russell to TH, 20 May 1881, HP 25.321 (it was Lady Laura Russell who also had Huxley ask Darwin to sit); TH to J. E. Boehm, 31 May 1881, HP 11.23; J. E. Boehm to HAH, 12 May 1882, HP 11.25; G. Howell to TH, 3 May 1882, HP 18.247.
30. HAH to ES, 14 Aug. 1881, AD; *LTH*, 2:36, 40–1; J. P. Spencer to TH, 30 Mar. 1881, HP 26.190. While not exactly endorsing a free-market approach to medicine, Huxley thought that attaching Medical Council examiners to each licensing board would be a less disruptive way to obtain the minimum qualifications than to start afresh with State 'Divisional Boards': *CE*, 3:323; cf. Cowen, 'Liberty', 34–5.
31. BJ to L. Huxley, n.d., HP 7.47; BJ to HAH, 8 May 1881, HP 7.29; HAH to ES, 14 Aug. 1881, AD. Congress: *SM*, 4:493–507; HP 59.41; *LTH*, 2:33–4.
32. HAH to ES, 14 Aug. 1881, AD; G. G. Bradley to TH, 24 Mar. 1881, HM 3:121:19; J. R. Moore, 'Darwin Lies', 99; 'that': TH to J. H. Thompson, 19 Dec. 1880, HP 30.119.
33. G. C. Broderick to TH, 21 June 1881, HP 11.85; 'spirit', 'very': BJ to HAH, 17 June, 4 July 1881, HP 7.35–7; H. J. S. Smith to TH, 10 June, 12 July 1881, HP 26.118–19; *LTH*, 2:30; 'We': HAH to ES, 14 Aug. 1881, AD.
34. HAH to ES, 14 Aug. 1881, AD.
35. *Prospectus of the Normal School*, 5; E. Frankland to TH, 11 Oct. 1882, HP 16.252. Dean: J. P. Spencer to TH, 18 Aug. 1881, HP 26.192; *LTH*, 2:36; salaries: TH to C. J. Faulkner, 9 Oct. 1881, HP 16.34 (£1,500 a year: £800 at the Normal School and £700 as Inspector: *LTH*, 2:20); 'after': HAH to ES, 14 Aug. 1881, AD.
36. A. Agassiz to TH, 8 Nov. 1882, HP 6.146, reply in Clark, *Huxleys*, 93; Winsor, *Reading*, 133; Oxford: C. J. Faulkner/TH, 9–18 Oct. 1881, HP 16.34–50; Howarth, 'Science Education', 351; *LTH*, 2:32.
37. MF to TH, 3 Jan. 1881, HP 4.216; TH to W. Spottiswoode, 15 Feb., 7 Oct. 1881, HP 26.203–6; TH to J. Paget, 27 Apr. 1881, Sir James Paget Papers, APS; 'I find': TH to FD, 30 Dec. 1881, HP 15.138; Bibby, 'South London', 216.
38. *LTH*, 2:24; 'ten': TH to FD, 30 Dec. 1881, HP 15.138. Disease: HP 15.3–5, 23.188; HM 1:1:88, 1:7:230, 2:57; *SM*, 4:520–8, 540–62; Huxley, *Twenty First Annual Report*, 11.
39. Lester and Bowler, *Lankester*, 98–101; 'far': GJR to TH, 25 Dec. 1881, HP 25.210; ERL to TH, 17 Apr. [1882], HP 30.122; W. Thiselton-Dyer to TH, 18 Apr. 1882, HP 27.193. TH to *Scotsman*, 22 Apr. 1882, HP 21.81; in the *Scotsman* he praised Rosebery, who remained cordial (Lord Rosebery to TH, 26 Apr. 1882, HP 24.209).
40. HM 1:9:99; HM 2:36:14; HM 2:37; HM 2:39:12, 16, 22–45; *SM*, 4:529; HM 2:75.
41. TH to FD, 30 Dec. 1881, HP 15.138; 'peculiar': G. H. Inskip to TH, 13 June 1881, HP 19.9; 'I': HAH to ES, 8 Feb., 3 Sept. 1882, AD.

42. CD to TH, 12 Jan. 1882, HP 5.370; *LLD*, 3:251; *LTH*, 2:38; Desmond and Moore, *Darwin*, 652; HAH to ES, 8 Feb. 1882, AD.
43. CD to TH, 27 Mar. 1882, HP 5.371; *LLD*, 3:358; Desmond and Moore, *Darwin*, 659.
44. F. Darwin to TH, [20 Apr. 1882], HP 13.10.
45. TH to JH, 21 Apr. 1882, HP 2.240; JH to TH, 21 Apr. 1882, HP 3.261, also 263; *LJH*, 2:259; '50': JD to J. P. Spencer, 26 Aug. 1882, HP 30.131; J. R. Moore, 'Darwin Lies', 98ff.
46. G. Darwin to TH, [22 Apr. 1882], HP 13.96; TH to JH, 23 Apr. 1882, HP 2.238; *CE*, 2:244–7; GJR to TH, 25 Apr. 1882, HP 25.216–18; J. R. Moore, 'Darwin Lies', 102.
47. J. R. Moore, 'Darwin Lies', 98–110; Desmond and Moore, *Darwin*, 677; F. W. Farrar to TH, [Apr. 1882], HP 16.26; Chartist: G. Howell to TH, 28 Apr. 1882, HP 18.246.
48. TH to NL, 11, 16 July 1883, HP 21.283–5; J. Evans to TH, 12 July 1883, HP 15.208; Stearn, *Museum*, 73; J. R. Moore, 'Darwin Lies', 107; Moore, pers. comm.; W. E. Darwin to TH, 28 Apr., 6 July 1882, 2 May [1883], HP 13.106–9; *CE*, 2:247.

    Closer to home, son-in-law Jack Collier was ploughing £500 into having his 1881 portrait of Darwin etched, and Huxley used Marsh to open up the American market for these prints of the fallen hero: TH to O. C. Marsh, 17 June 1882, Yale University Library.
49. GJR to TH, 25 Apr. 1882, 10 Nov., 6 Dec. 1883, HP 25.218–22 (also 'sorrow'); *LTH*, 2:39; *CE*, 2:245–7; R. Richards, *Darwin*, 339–52; *LGR*, 71–88, 135–6; Schwartz, 'Romanes's Defense', 307; Teas: Anne Evans' Diary, HP 31.105; 'man': *Times*, 22 Aug. 1878, 8.
50. HAH to ES, 3 Sept. 1882, 29 Jan. 1883, 21 June 1885; and Mady's psychology: 27 June 1865, AD. Ralph Colp (pers. comm.) suggests that this violent attack of 'hysteria' in a young and peculiarly sensitive girl, stressed perhaps by leaving home and her new marriage, reflected the onset of acute schizophrenia, which would become chronic with her approaching insanity and death.
51. Address, 13 May 1882, HP 49.31; J. E. Millais to TH, 20 Jan., 14 May 1882, HP 22.233–6.
52. He told Edward Aveling, then writing on Darwin in the *Reformer* and soon to be Besant's lover: Tribe, *Bradlaugh*, 220, 227; Desmond and Moore, *Darwin*, 643–5; TH, Physiology course, 28 June–18 [20th practicals] July 1882, HM 2:76–7; *LTH*, 2:56.
53. HAH to ES, 3 Sept. 1882, AD; TH to AD, 24 Sept. [1882], HP 13.293; *LTH*, 2:37–8; TH to JH, 28 July 1882, HP 2.246.
54. TH to HAH, 12 Jan. 1883, AD; *LTH*, 2:48; HM 1:7:26–7; HM 2:21, 23–4, 26; *SM*, 4:563–609; E. Johnson to TH, 28 Oct. 1882, HM 1:3:161–3.
55. HAH to ES, 18 July 1883, 21 June 1885, AD.
56. *LTH*, 2:63; HAH to ES, 10 Feb. 1883, AD; group: W. P. Frith to TH, Feb. 1882, HP 16.282–3.
57. BJ to L. Huxley, [21 Nov. 1881], HP 7.40; BJ to HAH, n.d., HP 7.49; Clark, *Huxleys*, 99; Webb, *Diary*, 203; HAH to ES, 3 Sept., 8 Feb. 1882, 7 Feb. 1884, AD. Matthew Arnold was a regular diner at the Huxleys': e.g. 4 July 1884, with Hirst, Noble and Alma-Tadema: T. A. Hirst, Journal XV (1884), 2150, Royal Institution.

58. Huxley, 'English Literature'; Huxley, 'Prize Distribution'; *CE*, 3:163; Roos, 'Arnold', 319–22; Bibby, 'Huxley and University', 102. This was a response to Oxford's manoeuvre of putting a *philologist* into the new Chair of English Language and Literature (which had been endowed in response to Royal Commission suggestions).
59. Howarth, 'Science Education', 351.
60. JT to TH, 24 Mar. 1884, HP 1.171; JH to JT, 20 May 1882, HP 8.401; *LJH*, 2:246; HAH to ES, 10 Feb. 1883, AD; 'rogue': TH to JH, 30 June 1883, HP 2.250; also HP 11.70, 21.282, 26.209, 27.95; 'poor: JH to TH, 29 June 1883, HP 3.268; *LJH*, 2:256.
61. M. Holzmann to TH, 9 Mar 1882, HP 18.223; Court: F. Lowell to HAH, 25 Feb. [1883], HP 22.27; Lord Kenmore to J. R. Lowell, 5 May 1883, HP 11.117; J. R. Lowell to HAH, 7 May 1883, HP 22.34; HAH to ES, 25 Jan. 1885, AD; screen: W. Spottiswoode to TH, 6 July 1882, HP 26.207.
62. G. G. Bradley to TH, 9 July 1883, HP 11.59, also 61.
63. C. J. Steinberg to TH, 8 Feb. 1883, HP 27.38; reply, 12 Mar. 1883, HP 27.40; *LTH*, 2:406; J. Sully to L. Huxley, [1900], HP 27.131; H. T. Mosley to TH, 4 Apr. 1884, HP 23.100; reply, 8 Apr. 1884, HP 23.101; Lightman, 'Ideology', 301.
64. J. R. Moore, *Religion*, 339–40, 353–60, esp. 357; 'ghoul-like': J. R. Moore, 'Freethought', 313; Tribe, *Bradlaugh*, 224–6; Foote, *Defence*, 9, 25: I should like to thank Jim Moore for showing me a copy of this book.
65. J. D. Coleridge to TH, 19 Dec. 1869, HP 12.276; Lord Coleridge had been sponsored for the FRS in 1877 by Huxley, Hooker, Galton and Spottiswoode among others: Certificate at Election, X.292, Royal Society Archives. Foote, *Defence*, 9. Jowett would invite the Huxleys to Oxford to dine with Coleridge and his daughter: BJ to HAH, 16 Apr. [1880], HP 7.28.
66. E. Scammell to TH, 25 Nov., 31 Dec. 1881, HP 26.39–41; 'The': TH to JH, 10 Nov. 1887, HP 2.295.
67. TH to HS, 27 Dec. 1880, HP 7.247; *LTH*, 2:18, 31, replying to HS to TH, 24 Dec. 1880, HP 7.246; Haight, *Eliot*, 548–50.
68. TH to C. A. Watts, 10 Sept. 1883, HP 28.196 (draft, the final version was longer and printed in *Agnostic Annual*, 1 (1884), 5–6); 'paraded', TH to JT, 25 Nov. 1883, HP 9.144; 'that': TH to G. J. Holyoake, 9 May 1884, Holyoake Collection 2935, Co-Operative Union, Manchester. Lightman, 'Ideology', 286; J. R. Moore, 'Freethought', 308. Huxley's protest about the use of his letter gave Annie Besant on the *National Reformer* an excuse to return Watts' advert for the new edition of the *Agnostic Annual*, marking it 'declined on account of the fraud on Prof. Huxley': A. Besant to TH, 22 Dec. 1883, HP 10.307; reply, 24 Dec., HP 10.308. As Bernie Lightman points out to me, ten years later Watts was still using Huxley's name as bait to catch writers of Karl Pearson's calibre: K. Pearson to TH, 15, 20 July 1894, HP 24.89–90.
69. TH to C. A. Watts, 10 Sept. 1883, HP 28.196; '*must*': TH to JT, 25 Nov. 1883, HP 9.144. Temple: *Agnostic Annual*, (1885), 54, back cover – Bernie Lightman kindly provided this reference, and his 'Ideology', 288–301 and *Origins*, 116ff are my main sources. On the need for agnostic 'books of reference': R. T. Wright to TH, 22 July 1882, HP 29.240. So little faith did Huxley have in Watts that he later refused to back him as Finsbury's Secular Education Candidate to the School Board: R. Bithell to TH, 30 Sept. 1894, HP 11.5; reply, 22 Sept., HP 11.6.

70. Bonner, *Bradlaugh*, 1:26, 41, 75, 98, 192; Tribe, *Bradlaugh*, 210–11.
71. Besant, *Law*, 6, 10, 14, 17; *CE*, 9:210; *LGR*, 145; Jones, *Outcast London*, chap. 11; Desmond, 'Artisan Resistance', 79; 'Bradlaugh': TH to G. J. Holyoake, 2 Aug. 1873, Holyoake Collection 2178, Co-Operative Union, Manchester; 'not only': TH to C. A. Watts, 10 Sept. 1883, HP 28.196; *LTH*, 1:56. E. Richards, 'Gendering', is a rich study of Besant, Aveling, birth control and the socialists' use of Darwin.
72. A. Besant to JH, 23 Oct. [1882], Director's Corres., 79 (386), Archives of the Royal Botanic Gardens, Kew; Tribe, *Bradlaugh*, 178–83; Royle, *Radicals*, 12–19; J. R. Moore, 'Freethought', 305–7; Desmond and Moore, *Darwin*, 627–8.
73. Tribe, *Bradlaugh*, 220, 226–7; *LTH*, 2:56; 'without': memorial signed by Huxley (a UCL Councillor) and other members of University College: College Correspondence AM/C/125, 160, UCL: E. W. Aveling to the Council, 23 June 1883, University College London. There was a plethora of complaints about the exclusion, and Huxley had to keep on the right side of the Council, and at the same time try to elicit acceptable reasons for the banning order.
74. *LTH*, 2:56–7.
75. Huxley, 'Unwritten History'; cf. Besant, 'Egypt', in *Selection*; Tribe, *Bradlaugh*, 221; 'every': Huxley, 'Prize Distribution'. Huxley ('President's Address' (1883), 66), also took advantage of the Egyptian occupation by having the War Office begin a series of geological borings in the Delta.

    Huxley's clever rhetorical stance and changing alliances help to explain why he was invited to deliver the annual Rede Lecture at Cambridge in 1883. It was 'the cordial manner' in which he spoke of the university during a talk at the Cambridge Philosophical Society in 1881 (where he had been invited by Frank Balfour [F. M. Balfour to TH, 4 Nov. 1881, HM 3:121:6]) that had the Vice-Chancellor issuing the invitation (Revd J. Porter to TH, 7 Dec. 1881, HP 24.171).
76. H. J. S. Smith to TH, 5 May 1878, HP 26.112. Huxley was eased into the Presidency by Hooker, Foster and John Evans: JH to TH, 1, 6 July 1883, HP 3.270, 274; Becker, *Scientific London*, 22–5.
77. HAH to ES, 19 Apr. 1884, AD; 'that', 'keep', 'dead': TH to JH, 30 June, 6 July 1883, HP 2.250, 256; 'cold': TH to WHF, 8 July 1883, APS; *LTH*, 2:52–3; 'like': TH to FD, 10 July 1883, HP 15.141; 'certain': FD to TH, 6 July 1883, HP 15.140; 'Lord': H. E. Roscoe to TH, 13 Nov. 1887, 25.287. Barton, 'Influential', 70.
78. TH to JH, 23 Oct. 1883, HP 2.262, also 3.277; 'all': MF to TH, 22 Sept. 1883, HP 4.218, also 220–5; 'family': J. E. Huxley to TH, 7 July 1883, HP 31.59. Barton, 'Influential', 71.
79. TH to A. J. Mundella, [1884], HP 23.130; TH to Marquis of Salisbury, 29 Nov. 1885, HP 12.146; WHF to TH, 28 Nov. 1883, 16.125, and TH to WHF, 3 Dec. 1883, APS (marked 'Privatissime') for the manoeuvring to get Flower into Owen's old job; *LTH*, 2:66; J. R. Moore, 'Darwin Lies', 107; Stearn, *Natural History Museum*, chap. 7.
80. *LTH*, 2:69; TH to JH, 6 Dec. 1883, HP 2.266.
81. MF to TH, 7 Feb., 8, 20 Mar. 1885, HP 4.246, 250–2. W. G. Armstrong to TH, 25 Oct., 9 Nov., 1 Dec. 1885, HP 10.128–32, HM 3:121:1; Huxley, 'President's Address' (1885), 283. TH to 'Her Royal Highness', 6 Feb. 1884,

HP 9.259. Becker, *Scientific London*, 22. As Barton, 'Influential', 79, says, Huxley's absence made his term an anticlimax, and it was Foster who took the smoking-room and library initiative.

82. *LTH*, 2:60–1; *LJT*, 232; 'vies': E. Hamilton to HAH, 5 Feb. 1881, HP 17.246; TH to JT, 9 Nov. 1883, HP 9.138; 8.234–7. Morley, *Recollections*, 1:184–5, 201; Magnus, *Gladstone*, 277, 339. The changes were reflected in the birth of the Liberal Club in 1883, whose building, thanks to Nettie's whispers in influential ears, and Huxley's and Hooker's testimonials, was designed by son-in-law Fred Waller: HAH to ES, 10 Feb. 1883, AD.
83. TH to JH, 22 Aug. 1883, HP 2.260; JH to TH, 23 Aug. 1883, HP 3.276; *LJH*, 2:264; 'content': R. Strachey to TH, 23 Aug. [1883], HP 27.109; Magnus, *Gladstone*, 207.
84. J. Fiske to TH, 17 Sept. 1883, HP 16.101; *LTH*, 2:50; *LJH*, 2:265; sanitation: A. Wills to TH, 4, 6, 10 Mar. 1881, 26 Mar. 1882, HP 29.66–72; pests: H. M. Jenkins, 28 Apr. 1883, HP 19.50–2.
85. G. G. Leveson-Gower, Earl Granville, to TH, [25–8], 28 July 1883, HP 21.212–13; *LTH*, 2:59; Harte, *University*, 127–37.
86. MF to TH, 18 Sept. 1884, HP 4.227; *LTH*, 2:49; TH to F. Knollys, 7 May 1883, HP 19.268, also 270–2, 30.134.
87. ERL to TH, 12 Oct. [1883], 19 June 1884, HP 21.83–7; TH to President of the Zoological Society, 30 July 1884, ZSL; Lester and Bowler, *Lankester*, chap. 9.
88. HAH to ES, 9 Apr., 19 Aug. 1883, 19 Apr., 24 May, 9, 14 Sept. 1884, 3, 25 Jan. 1885, AD; *LTH*, 2:20, 42, 71–6. 'Huxley': T. A. Hirst Journal, XV (1884), 2145, 2147, Royal Institution; lab: Osborn, 'Enduring Recollections', 726. Buying a farm: Angela Darwin, pers. comm. Home Office letters continued to report the squabblings while he was away: HP 16.293–303, 22.106.

8 POLISHING OFF THE G.O.M.

1. A. J. Mundella to JD, 10 Oct. 1884, HP 23.132. The radical Mundella, who had pushed through the 1881 Compulsory Education Act, 'could not more *earnestly* express my wishes for Huxleys health . . . if I filled a sheet of foolscap'. *LTH*, 2:81; 'great': HAH to ES, 3 Jan. 1885, AD; Arnold: Peterson, *Huxley*, 219; Notebook of journey: HM 3:128.
2. J. W. Ramsay to TH, 16 Oct. 1884, HP 25.25; S. Walpole to HAH, 15, 20 Oct. 1884, HP 28.125–8; *LTH*, 2:81–2; 'Between': HAH to ES, 11 Sept. 1885, AD; wedding: 25 Jan. 1885, AD; Ralph Colp, pers. comm.
3. MF to TH/HAH, Nov. 1884–Jan. 1885, HP 16.228, 4.238–43; JD to TH, 27 Dec. 1884, 13 Jan. 1885, HP 14.42,46; *LTH*, 2:82, 110. Clark's word in official ears helped, and the doctor cannily applied for a Fellowship of the Royal Society at the same moment, which put the returning President in a quandary: TH to JH, 25 Apr. 1885, HP 2.274.
4. TH to Ethel Huxley, 18 Nov. 1884, APS; *LTH*, 2:83–5; HAH to ES, 3 Jan. 1884, AD.
5. J. Evans to TH, 30 Oct. 1884, HP 15.210; 'seemed': MF to HAH, 21 Nov. [1884], HP 16.228; 'what': JD to TH, 18 Sept. 1884, HP 14.34, 'I won't have Lankester', Donnelly continued.
6. HAH to ES, 25 Jan. 1885, AD; TH to Ethel Huxley, 22 Dec. 1884, APS;

LTH, 2:85–90. A tonic, quinine was also used for bad digestion ('dyspepsia'), coughs and debilitation: Estes, *Dictionary*, 48; Ralph Colp, personal communication.

7. *LTH*, 2:86–92, 113; HAH to ES, 25 Jan. 1885, AD. Galileo: TH to St G. Mivart, [12 Nov. 1885], HP 22.272; reply 13 Nov. 1885, HP 22.274.
8. *LTH*, 1:94–5, 139; 'great': JD to TH, 13 Feb. 1885, HP 14.48; C. Gordon to TH, 17 Jan. 1882, HP 17.81; 'mourning': MF to TH/HAH, 7 Feb. 1885, HP 4.246. The relief expenses: J. W. Ramsay to TH, 27 Dec. 1884, HP 25.27. Morris, *Heaven's Command*, 496–7.
9. He sensed how cocaine worked: he talked in the wake of Mady's death of the 'moral coca' which sanitary reformers needed to stomach the stinking ghettoes: *CE*, 9:217; 'plant': HAH to ES, 21 June 1885, AD; 'fully': TH to Ethel Huxley, 30 Mar. 1885, APS; *LTH*, 2:100–1; HM 2:101; HP 31.113.
10. HAH to ES, 8 Feb. 1882, 28 Mar. 1886, AD; BJ to L. Huxley, 17 Mar. 1885, HP 7.56; Webb, *Diary*, 203.
11. HM 2:79:51, 2:80. This was the course H. G. Wells sat.
12. Wells, *Experiment*, 1:201, 207; 'yellow', 'excessively', research: Wells, 'Huxley', 210. Wells studied Biology Part 1 at the Normal School in December 1884 (while Huxley was away) and Part 2 beginning February 1885; and Advanced Zoology in June 1885. So he was describing Huxley during his last term of teaching (pers. comm. Anne Barrett).
13. Clark, *Huxleys*, 111; Jackson, *Eighteen Nineties*, 62, 69–72, 106–7; 'mad': Webb, *Diary*, 203. Sketching: TH to P. L. Sclater, 28 Mar. 1884, ZSL; Nettie's sketches of Huxley are in the possession of Hilary Buzzard.
14. *LTH*, 2:106, 109; TH to C. S. Parkinson-Fortescue, 11 May 1885, HP 30.137; TH to W. Harcourt, 11 May 1885, HP 30.136; 'So': MF to TH, 4 May 1885, HP 4.254; 'enduring': Huxley, 'Contemporary Literature', *Westminster Review*, 64 (1855), 241.
15. S. H. Northcote/TH, 20, 24 Nov. 1885, 23.227–8; HAH to ES, 6 Dec. 1885, AD; A. J. Mundella/TH, 19, 20 June 1885, HP 23.134–5; JD to C. S. Parkinson-Fortescue, 18 May 1885, HP 24.64; HP 30.138–40; 'sort': TH to B. Price, 20 May 1885, HP 24.206; *LTH*, 2:107–10; MacLeod, 'Science and the Civil List', 51.
16. F. Harris to TH, 7 Dec. 1886, HP 18.38; *CE*, 9:117. As Darwin in the *Origin* had traded off familiarity (e.g. pigeon selection) rather than novelty to get his message across (Ritvo, 'Classification', 60), so Huxley hoodwinked conservatives that there was nothing new, philosophically, under the Empire's never-setting Sun.
17. JD to J. P. Spencer, [sent 15 May 1885], HP 30.131. Hooker had always wanted Huxley 'made a P. C., on public grounds': JH to TH, 27 Dec. 1883, HP 3.278. Soon the Prime Minister would be sounding Huxley out on instituting a new honour as a 'formal recognition of distinguished service in Science Letters & Art': Lord Salisbury to TH, May–June 1887, HP 12.148–53; *LTH*, 2:164.
18. Huxley's assistant T. G. B. Howes became his successor, amid opposition, and the botanist D. H. Scott, who was promoted by Thiselton-Dyer, became one of the two assistant professors: W. Thiselton-Dyer/TH, 15 Aug., 4 Sept. 1885, HP 27.201–5; D. H. Scott to TH, 8 Aug 1885, HP 26.49.
19. HAH to ES, 11 Sept. 1885, AD; budget: JD to TH, 13 Feb. 1885, HP 14.48; 'Providence': 16 Feb. 1888, HP 14.91.

20. *CE*, 2:248–52; J. R. Moore, 'Darwin Lies', 107; Minutes of 'Special General Meeting, 9th June, 1885', BM(NH).
21. TH to St G. Mivart, [12 Nov. 1885], HP 22.272, also 22.271, 274–8; *LTH*, 2:113, 123; Notes on Dentalium, 31 Aug. 1885, HM 1:3:171; 'away': HAH to ES, 21 June 1885, AD.
22. *Times*, 1 Dec. 1885; Huxley, 'President's Address (1885), 294; L. Playfair to TH, 7 Dec. 1885, HP 24.142; 'Since': ERL to TH, 8 Nov. 1885, HP 21.88; Royal Society: W. G. Armstrong to TH, 28 May, 9 Nov. 1885, HP 10.126, HM 3:121:1; MF to HAH, 21 Sept. [1885], HP 4.263.
23. E. R. Lankester, *Advancement*, 89; *LTH*, 2:309–10; Desmond, *Politics*, 254–75.
24. *LTH*, 2:106; HAH to ES, 11–16 Sept., 6 Dec. 1885, AD.
25. HAH to ES, 6 Dec. 1885, AD; J. E. Carpenter to TH, 15 Nov. 1885, HP 12.35; JT to TH, 24 Mar. 1884, 5 May, 22 Aug. [1886], HP 1.180–2; 8:241; TH to JH, 24 Oct. 1885, HP 2.276; *LJT*, 253. Kew: JH to TH, 9 May 1884, HP 8.405; 'thraldom': JH to JT, 26 Mar. 1887, HP 8.408.
26. TH to F. Max Müller, 1 Nov. 1885, HP 23.118; *LTH*, 2:115; 'Even': HAH to ES, 6 Dec. 1885, AD; *CE*, 4:141; J. R. Moore, *Post-Darwinian Controversies*, 65; Magnus, *Gladstone*, 333–40. Gladstone was taking Sir William Dawson's line.
27. *CE*, 4:145–7, 151, 156–7, 171; 'brain': F. Max Müller to TH, 6 Nov. 1885, HP 23.120; HAH to ES, 6 Dec. 1885, AD; *LTH*, 2:115, 122.
28. JK to TH, 12 Nov. 1885, HP 20.50; HP 44.162; *CE*, 4:148–9; *LTH*, 2:114.
29. St G. Mivart to TH, 31 Mar. 1886, HP 22.280; Revd C. F. Gunton, 5 May 1886, HP 17.162; Revd R. M. Spence to TH, 9 Jan. 1886, HP 26.185; HS to TH, 19 Jan. 1881, 7 Dec. 1885, HP 7.146, 168; *LTH*, 2:115; JK to TH, 16 Dec. 1885, HP 20.51.
30. R. Owen to W. E. Gladstone, 5 Jan. 1884, 7, 14 Dec. 1885, BL Add. MS 44,485, f.32, 44,493, ff.188, 223; Foot and Matthew, *Gladstone*, 11:445; Desmond, *Archetypes*, 196–203, 218; Rupke, *Owen*, 340–1; Gruber, 'Owen and his Correspondents', 45–6; Owen, 'Description of . . . an Anomodont', 423; Owen, 'Order Theriodontia'; Association: R. Owen to J. K. Langdon Edis, 1882–5, BM(NH) Owen Corres.; 'Alas': W. Armstrong to TH, 3 Dec. 1885, HP 10.132.
31. *CE*, 4:180; *LTH*, 2:116, 122; 'pulverizing', 'be': JK to TH, 31 Dec. 1885, 6, 14 Jan. 1886, HP 50.52, 55, 58; Magnus, *Gladstone*, 340; Peterson, *Huxley*, 229 on Gladstone's additional paragraph after hearing from Owen.
32. Which reflected as much in global human architecture. Huxley, back from Italy, explained to children how today's Papuan pile-dwellers were at the same 'grade' as the hut-builders of Stone Age Italy who would one day build the Parthenon: Huxley, 'From the Hut', 282. *CE*, 4:290, 301, 308, 350–2; '40': JK to TH, 1, 6 Jan., 10 Feb. 1886, HP 20.53–5, 61; Magnus, *Gladstone*, 341–3.

    Churchill: TH to A. Grey; Huxley, 'Home-Rule Bill'; *LTH*, 2:125; 'Lord Randolph Churchill on Science and Art Instruction', *Times*, 27 Oct. 1887.
33. ['The Natural History of Christianity'], HP 48, f.5, 30. This was intended to be bound as a book with the 'Evolution of Theology' (f.15). The evidence suggests that he may only have started, or continued, this book after 1889 (e.g. *LTH*, 2:229). *CE*, 4:349, 354, 358, 361–2.

    A. Edwards to TH, 28 July, 11 Sept. 1886, HP 15.154–6. In 1887 Huxley was drafting Royal Society reports on future borings in the Delta to date the Nile deposits, and suggesting that its Delta Committee work with the Egypt Exploration Fund (HM 2:85:2–6).

34. JK to TH, 10 Feb. 1886, HP 20.61. Foot and Matthew, *Gladstone*, 11:505.
35. L. Carpenter to HAH, [Feb.1886], HP 12.48; 8 Mar. [1886], HP 12.50 on Leeds; G. S. Jones, *Outcast London*, 227, 291, 344–5; Wallace, *My Life*, 2:104, 240; 'earth': TH, 'Olive Branch', 620–1.
36. *CE*, 1:43, 51, 108; commissioned: J. Caird to TH, 12 Dec. 1885, HP 12.2; *LTH*, 2:146–7; Besant, 'Why I am a Socialist', 2–3, in *Selection*; Tribe, *Bradlaugh*, 229–52.
37. Tyndall, 'Political Situation'.
38. A. Grey to TH, 19, 23 Mar. 1886, HP 17.128, 123; 'cowardly', 'government': TH to A. Grey, 21 Mar. 1886, HP 17.132; Huxley, 'Home-Rule Bill'; *LTH*, 2:124; 'profligate': TH to JT, 7 May 1886, HP 9.150; 'Professor Huxley on Government', *Monthly Record of the Protestant Evangelical Mission*, Aug. 1887, p.122, HP 49.65; Escott, *Masters*, 193, 202–3.
39. Magnus, *Gladstone*, 345–9; 'unimpassioned': A. Grey to TH, [1886], HP 17.142. The Liberal Unionists begged him to join their committee: A. Grey to TH, 24 Apr. 1886, HP 17.140; 'quintessence': G. Smith to TH, 12 Apr. 1886, HP 26.109; 'outrage': E. A. J. Wallop to TH, 16 Apr. 1886, HP 28.113; *LTH*, 2:168.
40. Huxley, 'British Race-Types'; Rich, 'Social Darwinism', for the wider basis of the shifting attitudes towards the Celtic and Saxon 'races'. Huxley had long dismissed the idea of pure 'Celtic blood' or distinct Celt and Saxon 'races' (breaking Europeans down instead into broader morphological groups – the northern fair Xanthochroi and southern darker Melanochroi). But he had always done this against the explicit backdrop of the Irish question: e.g. in 1870 when he transferred his 'Sunday Evenings for the People' to Moncure Conway's South Place Chapel and talked on 'The Forefathers . . . of the English People' (9 Jan. 1870: HM 2:61:16; *CE*, 7:260; Huxley, 'Forefathers'; Keith, 'Huxley', 722). And by 1886 Huxley was arguing that something other than 'race' explained the negative Irish traits.

    By removing 'race', he undercut Nationalist demands for a homeland while leaving English prejudices intact. That spare-time anthropologist John Lubbock knew that, as a Liberal Unionist MP, his science would be discredited if he talked in the House on race, so he asked Huxley to point out the 'large admixture of Celtic, Scandinavian & Germanic' blood throughout England and Ireland, which he (Lubbock) could then quote in Parliament in order to assert one 'nationality': J. Lubbock to TH, 24 Jan. 1887, HP 22.96. Darwin, *Descent*, 138; Desmond and Moore, *Darwin*, 557; di Gregorio, *Huxley*, 178.
41. TH to A. Grey, 21 Mar. 1886, HP 17.132; Huxley, 'Home-Rule Bill'; *LTH*, 2:45, 124; 'ingrained': TH to JH, 2 Dec. 1890, 2.373.
42. JT/TH, 27 Dec. 1887, 1, 4, 8 Jan. 1888, HP 1.199, 102, 9.166–8; E. Frankland to TH, 5 Nov. 1887, HP 16.272.

    Contrast the support for this political 'scientific declaration' with the furore when Stokes, Huxley's Presidential successor at the Royal Society, ran for Parliament. Up went cries that science was 'above' politics and that Stokes was compromising his office. Huxley's Liberal academics advised the President to resign, rather than have 'all the dirt of politics imported into

Science'. (TH to NL, 6, 10 Nov. 1887, HP 21.291; TH to JH, 6 Nov. 1887, HP 2.293, reply 3.305, also 9.224–6, 25.287, 1.198.) Although Huxley's group was opposed by Evans' businessmen, Lubbock's MPs and Conservative FRSs: HP 3.316, 4.294–307, 21.297, 22.98–100, 27.209. The problem was partly Stokes' *Tory* candidature. After reading Stokes' election address, Huxley deemed that the President – who had already 'abused us' by accepting the Chair of the Victoria Institute, founded in defence of Revealed Truth – was pulling the Society behind 'everything Churchy & reactionary', and he even vented his feelings in an anonymous leader in *Nature*, 'drawn mild but with a head to it!' (TH to NL, 10, 13 Nov. 1887, HP 21.293–5; reply 21.296; Huxley, 'M. P.'; TH to JH, 6, 14 Nov. 1889, HP 2.293, 297, reply 3.308; TH to G. G. Stokes, 1 Dec. 1887, HP 30.192; *LTH*, 2:173–5; Meadows, *Science*, 226).

43. TH to JH, 11 Sept. 1886, HP 2.280, reply 3.288; T. A. Hirst to TH, 9 May 1886, HP 18.177; yacht: JH to TH, 27 Mar., 6, 7 July 1886, HP 3.281, 284–7; TH to JH, 26 Mar. 1886, HP 2.272; HS to TH, 19, 23, 24 Mar., 19 May, 11 Oct. 1886, HP 7.172–83; *LTH*, 2:119, 127; 'bear': JH to TH, 30 Apr. 1886, HP 3.283; 'doleful': TH to JH, 3 May 1886, HP 2.278; *LJH*, 2:1–7

44. G. B. Howes on Huxley's unconventionality, HP 40.282; *SM*, 4:612; 'amazed': JH to TH, 12 Sept. 1886, HP 3.288; 'catch': MF to TH, [12 Sept. 1886], HP 4.275; 'madly': HAH to ES, 8 Oct. 1886, AD; HM 2:107–11; *LJT*, 391; *LTH*, 2:137–8; 'suits', 'I have': TH to JT, 19 Aug. 1886, HP 9.152; Cook: JT to TH, 22 Aug. [1886], HP 1.182. Huxley's Diary, 1887, HP 70.30 – this also contains a heart-rending account of the English climber whose life Huxley tried to save. On the agnostics and the Alps: Lightman, *Origins*, 150.

45. TH to JH, 20 Oct. 1886, HP 2.287; *LTH*, 2:144; Browne, 'Charles Darwin', 361–2 on the making of the Oxford legend. Hooker concurred with Huxley: 'The Quarterly does not get one iota more than it deserves, or than the public should see it gets': JH to TH, 21 Oct. 1886, HP 3.292; *LJH*, 2:301. Wilberforce's 1860 query – 'How would the Professor like to reckon apes among the progenitors of his father or mother?' – was routinely recounted during the Huxleys' 'Tall Teas': Anne Evans' Diary, HP 31.105. Huxley's 1887 'Reception' caused a sharp exchange in the *Times* with Wilberforce's son: R. G. Wilberforce, 'Professor Huxley'; Huxley, 'Bishop Wilberforce'.

46. *CE*, 9:146; Lilly, 'Materialism', 576, 586; Paradis, *Huxley*, 43–5; 'of': HS to TH, 11 Dec. 1886, HP 7.189.

47. Gruber, *Conscience*, 153–70; St G. Mivart to TH, 31 Dec. 1886, HP 22.284; 'I': TH to JT, 24 Nov. 1886, HP 9.154. Mivart was *still* being blackballed at the Athenaeum for his sins: JH to TH, 28 Nov. 1888, HP 3.335. Mivart's undoing in the eyes of the Church came with his 'Happiness in Hell' in 1892. No sooner was it out in the *Nineteenth Century* than Knowles was trying to goad Huxley into responding to it: JK to TH, 6 Dec 1892, HP 20.166.

48. W. Huxley to TH, 24 Nov. 1886, HP 31.64, reply 65.

49. Huxley, 'Queen's Jubilee'; L. Playfair to TH, 1 Jan. 1886 [1887], HP 24.144, also 146. The notion of institutional struggle was taken up by another moderate State interventionist, D. G. Ritchie, in *Darwinism and Politics* (1891): Paradis, '*Evolution*', 40; G. Jones, *Social Darwinism*, 57–62.

50. E. L. Scott to TH, 15 July 1887, HP 26.51.

51. Huxley, 'Organization'; editorial, *Times*, 18 Mar. 1887; 'Lord Hartington on our Industrial Position', *Times*, 18 Mar. 1887; 'Messrs. Goschen and Huxley on English Culture', *Nature*, 37 (1888), 337–8.

52. J. R. Moore, *Post-Darwinian Controversies*, 51–3ff, is still brilliant on this imagery; Denis, 'Brompton Barracks'; Crook, *Darwinism*, 12ff for a counterbalance to the 'war' image; Beer, *Darwin's Plots*, 9; Stauffer, *Natural Selection*, 92–4, 134–8, 214, 223–4, 380.
53. Huxley, 'Imperial Institute', *Times*, 20 Jan., 19 Feb. 1887; *LTH*, 2:151; *Times*, 17 Feb. 1887, HP 42.159; also HP 14.76, 12.189, 23.191, 18.139; Huxley, 'Queen's Jubilee'; 'odour': HAH to ES, 1 July 1887, AD; Harris, *Private Lives*, 19.
54. Webb, *Diary*, 202–3; Nettie: HAH to ES, 6, 28 Apr. 1887, AD; A. Agassiz to TH, 31 Jan., 8 Mar. 1887, HP 6.159, 163; J. R. Lowell to HAH, 23 May 1887, HP 22.45; E. C. C. Agassiz to HAH, 19 Apr. [1887], HP 10.25.
55. Or rather belligerently reattribute a skull – which 83-year-old Owen had just diagnosed as the remains of an extinct Australian monitor lizard – as a turtle's skull. Owen responded, showing that rivalries still existed: HM 2:99 notebook on *Ceratochelys*; *SM*, 4:232.
56. TH to G. J. Holyoake, 24 Apr. 1887, Holyoake Collection 3080, Co-Operative Union, Manchester; *CE*, 5:122, 4:284; 'guess': G. J. D. Campbell (Argyll) to R. Owen, 27 Feb. 1863, BM(NH) Owen Corres. vol. 1, f.230; 'got': JK to TH, 18 Mar. 1887, HP 20.70; G. J. D. Campbell to TH, 4 Mar., 3 Apr. 1886, HM 3:121:32, HP 12.4, for their disagreement on Argyll's 'Predestined Potentiality' of evolving life – whatever its potentiality, Huxley did not think it was 'predestined'.
57. J. Skelton to TH, 7 Mar. 1887, HP 26.93; *CE*, 5:69–75; Jacyna, 'Immanence'; Desmond, *Politics*, 114–16, 216, 257, 263.
58. *CE*, 5:75–80, 104–16; Argyll, *Reign*, 294. Owen praised the *Reign* as a 'wholesome antidote': R. Owen, 'The Reign of Law' (1867), 'Autograph Manuscripts of Sir R. Owen', BM(NH) OC 59. R. Smith, 'Background', 97–105, on the distinction between Huxley's use of Hume's 'constant conjunction' theory of causation, and the Romantic belief in law as an efficient cause equivalent to a Divine force.
59. Huxley, 'Free Libraries'; HP 42.168–75. Huxley's Working Men's College had amalgamated with the South London Free Library on his retirement in 1880: W. Rossiter to TH, 7 Dec. 1880, HP 25.300; Bibby, 'South London', 216–17. 'I may': TH to G. J. Holyoake, 24 Apr. 1887, Holyoake Collection 3080, Co-Operative Union, Manchester, reply to HP 18.216; 'abused': J. Skelton to TH, 7 Mar. 1887, HP 26.93.
60. Clark, *Huxleys*, 109; 'smiled', 'worst': TH to FD, 25 Nov. 1887, 15.143; 'She', 'down': TH to JH, 21 Nov. 1887, HP 2.299; HAH to ES, 11 May 1886, AD.
61. HAH to ES, 11 May 1886, 6 Apr., 1, 24 July 1887, 4 Mar. 1888, AD; E. A. J. Wallop to HAH, 29 Oct. 1887, HP 28.118; JD to TH, 22 June 1887, HP 14.79. Charcot: TH to JT, 26 Nov. 1887, HP 9.164; Sulloway, *Freud*, 15–35.
62. HAH to ES. 15 Dec. 1887, AD (also 'Oh'); TH to JH, 21 Nov. 1887, HP 2.299; 'beyond': JK to TH, 23 Nov. 1887, HP 20.77; TH to JT, 26 Nov. 1887, HP 9.164. Manchester: A. H. D. Ackland to TH, 24 Oct. 1887, HP 10.6; H. E. Roscoe to TH, 13 Nov. 1887, HP 25.287.
63. JT to TH, 23 Nov. 1887, HP 1.196; picture: 'Friend', 'Huxley's Homes'.
64. Huxley, draft of Manchester Address 1887, HP 42.58–67, f.61; 'envy': HAH to ES, 15 Dec. 1887, AD; TH to NL, 27 Nov. 1887, HP 21.297, reply 299; JD to TH, 21, 23 Nov. 1887, HP 14.83–5; TH to JH, 21 Nov. 1887, HP 2.299;

LTH, 2:180. Paradis, *Huxley*, 142–8 considers Huxley's 'Evolution and Ethics' the culmination of alienation, but surely it lies here, in 1887, rather than in a mellower 1893.

65. Huxley, 'Apologetic', 569.
66. Huxley, early draft of Manchester Address 1887, HP 42.58–67, f.67. Helfand, 'Huxley's "Evolution"', 167–8; R. Richards, *Darwin*, 331–2.
67. TH to JH, 4 Dec. 1887, HP 2.301; *LTH*, 2:181; *Manchester Guardian*, 30 Nov. 1887; 'later': TH to FD, 25 Nov. 1887, 15.143.
68. Huxley's working title had been 'Programme of Industrial Development'. It pushed February's *Nineteenth Century* into an immediate second edition and was 'greatly talked about': JK to TH, 12 Dec. 1887, 4 Feb. 1888, HP 20.83, 90.
69. McCready, 'Worship'; *CE*, 9:196, 199–200, 210–11, 229, 232; 'Huxley': Gilley and Loades, 'Huxley', 303, 307.
70. HAH to ES, 15 Dec. 1887, AD; *CE*, 9:202–5; Helfand, 'Huxley's "Evolution"', 169–70.

9 CHRIST WAS NO CHRISTIAN

1. *LTH*, 2:186, 198–9; TH to JH, 29 Jan., 12 Apr. 1888, HP 2.309, 318.
2. HAH to ES, 4 Mar., 29 July 1888, 2 Jan. 1889, AD; J. Paget to TH, 28 Apr. 1888, HP 24.12; TH to J. J. Horny, 5 Nov. 1888, HP 18.226. In an age of civic pride and acquisition, 'The Death of Cleopatra' was bought by the Municipal Art Gallery in Oldham: William Collier, pers. comm.
3. ERL to TH, 1885–8, HP 21.90–121, 30.146, Lester and Bowler, *Lankester*, 110–13. But he was still dogged by controversy in the MBA. With the government mooting a Fisheries Department, Lankester – more a corporatist than Huxley – canvassed so raucously for a staff of scientists that Huxley had to slap him down in the *Times* (Huxley, 'Proposed Fishery Board'; *LTH*, 2:128). Huxley's 'Don't Meddle' policy was due in part to his *laissez-faire* heritage; but it was also the pragmatic response of an inspector who knew that trawlermen paid no heed to scientists. He thought that biologists should be sought for advice, not to run the Fisheries Department. See TH/A. J. Mundella, 15, 16, 18 Mar. 1886, HP 30.142, 23.137–9; H. T. Wood to TH, 23 Mar. 1886, HP 29.87; MF to TH, 3 Apr. [1886], HP 4.271.

   The President permanently teetered in his inclination to resign over Lankester's bull-headedness. But he was convinced to stay on to keep Lankester in check until the Plymouth lab was functioning. (J. Evans to TH, 19 June 1887, HP 15.218; TH to H. N. Moseley, 20 June 1887, HP 23.98–9; MF to TH, 9 Apr. [1888], HP 4.325.)
4. MF to TH, 14 Apr. 1888, HP 4.328; 'hermit': HAH to ES, 4 Mar. 1888, AD; 'Origin': TH to JH, 23 Mar. 1888, HP 2.316; *LTH*, 2:190–3.
5. TH to JH, 4 May 1888, HP 2.322; *CE*, 2:258–61, 270; F. Darwin to TH, 10 Apr. 1888, HP 13.72 supplied the details; '4': P. G. King to TH, 8 Feb. 1888, HP 19.152; *LTH*, 2:183. Leslie Stephen shortly asked Huxley to write Darwin's entry in the *Dictionary of National Biography*, but Huxley had clearly had enough: L. Stephen to TH, [1889], HP 27.61.
6. *LTH*, 2:184–8; HS/TH, 6, 9, 10 Feb. 1888, HP 7.209–12; 'hammock': HS to TH, 16 Nov. 1887, HP 7.204.
7. L. Boguslavsky to TH, 12 Sept. 1888, HP 11.27. Woodcock, *Anarchism*, 172–6, 190–5, 206; Todes, 'Darwin's Malthusian Metaphor', 545–8 on

mutualist biology as both the Russian socialist 'national style' and a response to life on the tundra wastes.

8. *CE*, 9:200, 204; 'one': JK to TH, 27 Oct. 1890, HP 20.139.
9. Paradis, *Huxley*, 149–50; Kropotkin, 'Mutual Aid'.
10. *LTH*, 2:199; JK to TH, 2 June 1888, HP 20.93. Crook, *Darwinism*, 106–9 discusses 'peace' biology's debt to Kropotkin in his opposition to Huxley's industrial 'war'.
11. HAH to ES, 29 July 1888, 2 Jan. 1889, AD; TH to JH, 23 Oct. 1888, HP 2.326; *LTH*, 2:206–7, 210. Huxley was using Oertel's graduated exercise technique to strengthen his heart: *British Medical J.*, 6 July 1895.
12. TH to JH, 15 Nov. 1888, 6, 9 May, 19 June 1889, HP 2.332, 342–4; *LTH*, 2:211; MacLeod, 'Of Medals', 83–99; HM 3:121:92.
13. L. Playfair to TH, 3 Jan. 1889, HP 24.147; J. R. Moore, *Darwin Legend*, 82–3, 143; Huxley, 'Sea Fisheries'; H. Ffennell to TH, 9 Jan. 1889, HP 16.68; Huxley, 'Spiritualism Unmasked'; HP 49.128–33; 'age': TH to AD, 1 Dec. 1886, HP 13.299; 'It': TH to JH, 28 Oct. 1888, HP 2.328; *LTH*, 2:148, 208.
14. [Ross], 'Huxley', HP 47.62–3; W. S. Ross to TH, 25 Apr. 1889, HP 25.297; Lightman, 'Ideology', 291, 296, 301; Lightman, *Origins*, 143–4; *CE*, 1:421, 5:245–6. Only when Huxley published 'Agnosticism' in 1889 did Watts' group really begin to appreciate his distance from Spencer and his 'Unknowable Noumenon': F. J. Gould/TH, 23 Dec. 1889, 2 Jan. 1890, HP 17.106–8.
15. Eisen, 'Huxley', 352; Ashforth, *Huxley*, 117–22; *CE*, 5:239, 245; *LTH*, 2:221. Dockrill, 'Huxley', 461, is right: this was only a different emphasis from his 1869 understanding, when his focus was on the outer veil this method revealed. He had not switched definitions. Indeed, the letters show Huxley still defining 'agnostic' as a 'confession of ignorance': TH to J. A. Skilton, 10 Dec. 1889, HP 30.152.
16. JK to TH, 14 Jan. 1889, HP 20.99; Lightman, *Origins*, 141; *CE*, 5:255; Eisen, 'Huxley', 351. Sir Spencer Walpole wondered why Achilles was bothering with the 'small fry of the Trojan Army' (Positivism) when he should be sticking to his battle with Hector (Christianity): S. Walpole to HAH, 10 Feb. 1889, HP 28.143. But Huxley was in continual engagement with the Positivist Frederic Harrison, who defined agnosticism as a 'paralysis of religious faith' (Harrison, 'Future', 144). Huxley was showing by contrast that it was an active, elevating moral position.
17. *CE*, 5:218, 230–1; *LTH*, 2:70–1; TH to MF, 9 Aug. 1884; Barton, 'Evolution'.
18. One second-eleven exception was Huxley's Methodist friend William Kitchen Parker, a rustic pietist and anatomical pedant whose every second was coloured by an 'abiding sense of the Divine Presence'. He alone could believe that Elisha's axe-head swam and that no law of hydrostatics could explain it. There being no rationale, he compartmentalized his beliefs and accepted Huxley's positivist biology. More, he idolized Huxley, naming one son after him, and putting another, Jeffrey, under him. And all along the 'cunningly contrived deceptions of the four gospels', which according to Huxley 'it is immoral to believe . . . have been the strength of my life': T. J. Parker, *Parker*, 125; T. J. Parker, 'Huxley', 125; Desmond, *Archetypes*, 51–2.
19. G. A. Kendall to TH, 6 Apr. 1889, HP 19.127; Gladstone's enquiry after Dawson: E. W. Hamilton/TH, 15 July 1884, HP 17.248–9; Livingstone, *Darwin's Forgotten Defenders*, 80–5.

20. Jacyna, 'Science', 13, 21; Jacyna, 'Immanence'; Peterson, *Huxley*, 236, 251. Turner, *Contesting*, and MacLeod, *Public Science*, are collected essays exploring these larger themes.
21. Huxley's 'private conscience' Protestantism never went so far as to support anarchism or ultra-democracy. He was scathing on 'the coach-dog theory of premiership', where the Prime Minister seems 'to look sharp for the way the social coach is driving, and then run in front and bark loud' (*CE*, 5:252).
22. BJ to HAH, 26 Feb. 1889, HP 7.66; *CE*, 5:242; *LTH*, 2:289.
23. HAH to ES, 22 Jan. 1889, AD; JK to TH, 13 Feb. 1889, HP 20.102; *CE*, 5:160.
24. JH to TH, 25 Jan. 1889, HP 3.339; M. Armstrong to HAH, 15 Jan. 1889, HP 10.114; W. G. Armstrong, 23 June 1887, HP 10.133.
25. TH to JH, 14 Jan. 1889, HP 2.336; JH to TH, 25 Jan. 1889, HP 3.339; *LTH*, 2:217; 'Bishops': TH to P. Allen, 28 Mar. 1889, HP 30.163; HAH to ES, 25 Jan. 1885, 22 Jan., 19 Mar. 1889, AD.
26. HAH to ES, 21 June 1885, 2, 22 Jan., 3 Nov. 1889, AD; TH to G. H. Hames, 20 Aug. 1889, HP 17.242; Huxley's 1889 Diary, HP 70.33; *LTH*, 2:221, 229.
27. *LTH*, 2:216–17; Lightman, *Origins*, 149–52; 'waking': Huxley, 'Prize Distribution'; HP 42.153; *CE*, 3:164–5.
28. HAH to ES, 15 Feb. 1883, 22 Jan., 19 Mar., 3 Nov. 1889, 10 Nov. 1890, 15 Jan. 1891, AD; TH to JH, 25 June 1889, HP 2.346; HP 62.6 Eastbourne house advert; *LTH*, 2:277.
29. *LTH*, 2:230, 265; TH to HAH, 2 Mar. 1889, AD; H. von Herkomer to TH, 23 May 1890, HP 18.135; *CE*, 1:1–17; Roos, 'Neglected', 405–6. The autobiography was 'rather too short', said Hooker in a masterly understatement (JH to TH, 28 Sept. 1893, HP 3.328). It was read aloud in one biology society, like some venerable text, to cries of 'Huxley has not done himself justice' (S. F. Clarke to TH, 17 Sept. 1894, HP 12.214).

    Another autobiography was commissioned by the 'British Biographical Company': E. W. Scott Martin to TH, 1 Aug. 1894, HP 22.179; reply 11 Nov. 1894, APS.
30. *LTH*, 2:221–4; 'witness-box', Christie's: JK to TH, 1, 9, 17 Mar., 18 Nov. 1889, HP 20.103–6, 114; *CE*, 5:262; 'Editors': JH to JT, 11 Dec. 1889, HP 8.421. *Robert Elsmere*'s hero was like one of Huxley's apostate Anglican vicars imploring his help (in the novel he ended up a Unitarian doing social work). The novel explored the value of testimony to the miraculous, Huxley's monthly theme in the *Nineteenth Century*: Peterson, *Huxley*, 243–4.
31. HAH to ES, 19 Mar. 1889, AD; M. Armstrong to HAH, 15 Jan. 1889, HP 10.114; *LTH*, 2:224; Huxley's 1889 Diary, HP 70.33.
32. *CE*, 5:270, 285, 289–97; *LTH*, 2:223, 228–30; JK to TH, 9 Mar., 11, 22 Apr. 1889, HP 20.104, 108, 110.
33. *CE*, 1:176, 5:73, 6:153, 9:121; Lightman, *Origins*, chap. 6; Gospel: JK to TH, 17 Mar. 1889, HP 20.106.
34. J. Chamberlain to TH, 14 Apr. 1889, HP 12.162; JD to TH, 21 Apr. 1889, HP 14.101, also 103; *LTH*, 2:219; R. A. T. G. Cavendish (Hartington) to TH, 7 May 1889, HP 12.145; *LTH*, 2:219; 'fanatics': HAH to ES, 19 Mar. 1889, AD; 'unfitting': TH to JH, 22 Mar. 1889, HP 2.338; Huxley's 1889 Diary, HP 70.33. William Collier, pers. comm., assumes that it was a civil ceremony.

35. *LTH*, 2:223–7, 234; Eisen, 'Huxley', 351; 'hacking': Lightman, *Origins*, 141; 'you': JH to TH, 19 June 1889, HP 3.344; L. Stephen to TH, 8 Apr., 5 May 1889, HP 27.57–9; TH to JH, 30 May 1889, HP 2.344; *CE*, 5:334.
36. TH to W. T. Stead, 8 July 1890, HP 27.5–9. Tunnel: Bradlaugh, *Channel*; JK to TH, 6 June 1890, HP 20.134; 'dirty': JH to JT, 14 Nov. 1891, HP 8.429.
37. *Hansard*, 335 (13 April 1889), 459; *LTH*, 2:225. By contrast, the socialist atheists wanted all blasphemy laws swept away: Royle, *Radicals*, 274. Huxley tried to indict Gladstone for justifying the loss of a pig herd (a violation of property) to score a point: it was Gladstone the Home Ruler who would dispossess the great estate owners in Ireland (*CE*, 5:369).
38. JH to TH, 4, 25 Mar., 11 Apr. 1888, HP 3.320–1, 260; *LJH*, 2:304–5.
39. HS to JH, 5 Dec. 1889, HP 7.243. Huxley, 'Mr. Spencer', 'Political Ethics', 'Ownership'; TH to HS, 19 Oct. 1889, HP 7.230 (not sent); *LTH*, 2:242–3. On Spencer's early belief in land socialism, which came back to haunt him: *CE*, 1:297.
40. JH to TH, 6 Dec. 1889, HP 3.352; JH to JT, 6, 11 Dec. 1889, 1 Jan. 1890, HP 8.420–2; HS to JH, 5 Dec. 1889, HP 7.243; TH to HS, 9 Dec. 1889, HP 7.244; 'abruptly': TH to F. H. Collins, 3 Dec. 1889, HP 12.286.
41. TH to JH, 1 June, 26, 29 Sept. 1890, HP 2.361, 365–7.
42. Huxley too had planned to republish his political essays as *Letters to Working Men*. It was Nettie's idea again: a socially-quieting 'Primer of Politics' for the masses. (And the come-hither '*Letters*', said Knowles, was 'a bit of inspiration in itself'.) JK to TH, 18 Nov., 13, 16 Dec. 1889, HP 20.114–19; *LTH*, 2:223–5, 245; TH to JH, 17 Jan. 1890, HP 2.346.

    A. R. Wallace to TH, 22 Nov. 1891, HP 28.100; Wallace, *My Life*, 2:14, 38–9; Wallace, 'Human', 336–7; Helfand, 'Huxley's "Evolution"', 163–6; E. Richards, 'Gendering', on Wallace the feminist.
43. Flürscheim, 'Huxley's Attacks'; *CE*, 291–3, 308–9, 313; *LTH*, 2:245.
44. M. Halboister to TH, 18 Feb. 1894, HP 17.229–231; also A. Tille to TH, 20 Jan.–14 Dec. 1894, HP 28.6–9. J. R. Moore, 'Socializing Darwinism', 61–6.
45. Huxley was not to know that middle-class family sizes would decrease continually from that time on: Ashworth, *Economic History*, 41; *CE*, 9:20–2.
46. *CE*, 9:39 is a very subtle piece of autobiography.
47. Helfand, 'Huxley's "Evolution"', 170. Geddes' book, co-authored with his pupil J. Arthur Thomson – himself critical of the Romanes lecture (J. A. Thomson, 'Huxley') – is all but ignored in Mairet, *Pioneer*, 45–50, 61–9, 100. E. Richards, 'Gendering'.
48. TH to JH, 13 Jan. 1890, HP 2.354; Spencer, 'Absolute Political Ethics'; JK to TH, 27 Oct. 1890, HP 20.139.
49. Buchanan, 'Are Men Born Free'; E. Jeffrey to TH, 29 Sept. 1890, HP 19.42; 'seems': A. Herbert to TH, 17 Feb. 1890, HP 18.126; *CE*, 9:216.
50. Christie, 'Working Man's Reply'; 'passionate': JK to TH, 20 Mar. 1890, HP 20.129; 'poor': 20 Jan. 1890, HP 20.123; *LTH*, 2:219; G. A. Gaskell to TH, 23 Jan. 1891, HP 17.20.
51. Buchanan, 'Are Men Born Free'; 'servant': JK to TH, 3 Feb. 1890, HP 20.125; Huxley, 'Are Men Born Free'. Lafargue, 'Primitive Communism'; the SDF *Commonweal* was captured by the anarchists in 1889: Cole and Postgate, *Common People*, 422.
52. *CE*, 1:336–58, 428, 9:154: 'men's': JK to TH, 20 Jan. 1890, HP 20.123.

53. On his resignation, HP 21.135–50; 10.265–6; HM 3:121:16; Lester and Bowler, *Lankester*, 110–12. HAH to ES, 19 Mar. 1890, AD; *LTH*, 2:251–7; JK to TH, 26 Mar., 3 Apr. 1890, HP 20.131–2.
54. *CE*, 1:393–5, 402, 424–5; Paradis, *Huxley*, 182; botany reading: W. T. Thiselton-Dyer to TH, 12 Jan. 1890, HP 27.222; 'head': TH to HAH, 3 May 1890, AD.
55. TH to HAH, 3 May 1890, AD; TH to Ethel Collier, 6 May 1890, APS; TH to JH, 18 May 1890, HP 2.359; HAH to ES, 19 Mar. 1890, AD; *LTH*, 2:252, 255–7; 'worthy': Webb, *Diary*, 203.
56. TH to A. L. Moore, 15 Mar. 1888, APS on Moore's *Guardian* review of Darwin's *Life and Letters*; A. L. Moore, 'Evolution', 154; A. L. Moore, *Science*, 184ff; J. R. Moore, *Post-Darwinian*, 259–69; 'itch': JK to TH, 19 May 1890, HP 20.133.
57. *CE*, 1:210, 232–3, 237. He had set out to write exclusively on *Lux Mundi* (his MS, 'Educated Circles; and their Modes of Reasoning', is in HP 46.125) but presumably reset his sights after reading Liddon's sermon in 1890.
58. As he told Carpenter's son Estlin (*LTH*, 2:266), a Unitarian minister whose *First Three Gospels* he rated 'the best popular statement I know of the result of criticism': TH to JH, 29 Nov. 1890, HP 2.371. Romanes too saw Christ's personality securing the acceptance of his ethical teachings (*LGR*, 227).
59. *LTH*, 1:321–2, 343; P. Bayne to TH, 1892–4, HP 10.248–55; C. A. Watts to TH, 23 May 1892, HP 28.199. Funding: Agnosco, 'Huxley'; TH to Leicester Secular Society, 12, 17 Feb. 1891, Holyoake Collection 3307, Co-Operative Union, Manchester, also HP 9.262–3; G. J. Holyoake to TH, 26 Mar. 1891, HP 18.218. William Collier, pers. comm., on Jack Collier's paintings.
60. E. Clayton interview, 29 Sept. 1890, HP 12.220 (also 'military', '30'); *CE*, 1:207–29; *LGR*, 160; JK to TH, 8 July 1890, HP 20.135. 'The Lights of the Church' probably caused more stir in the Hispanic American magazine *El Pensamiento Contemporánea*: A. Llano to TH, 10 Dec. 1891, HP 21.229.
61. Jackson, *Eighteen Nineties*, 17–26.
62. Reviving Latham's 'Sarmation hypothesis', which he had first met as a young *Westminster* reviewer: this disputed a dispersal point in the 'Hindoo-Koosh'; *CE*, 7:305–6; HP 33.156ff; *LTH*, 2:259–60; di Gregorio, *Huxley*, 181. Classics: Burrow, *Evolution*, 238.
63. TH to JH, 29 Sept. 1890, HP 2.367; *LTH*, 2:269; *CE*, 7:321–2; Bowler, *Theories*, 34, 81; Burrow, *Evolution*, 263.
64. TH to JH, 26 Sept. 1890, HP 2.365; *LTH*, 2:221, 263, 267, 274, 277; HAH to ES, 19 Mar., 10 Nov. 1890, AD; garden: HP 31.123; 'one': JK to TH, 8 July 1890, HP 20.135.
65. HAH to ES, 22 Jan. 1889, 20 July 1890, 15 Nov. 1891, AD; Jackson, *Eighteen Nineties*, 106–10.
66. TH to JH, 2 Nov. 1890, HP 2.369; reply 3 Nov. 1890, HP 3.365; *LJH*, 2:346.
67. JT to TH, 20 Dec. 1890, HP 1.205; *CE*, 5:374, 393, 415; ''ome': TH to JH, 29 Sept. 1890, HP 2.367; *LTH*, 2:269; 'spread eagling': TH to J. Collier, 16 Dec. 1890, in the possession of Hilary Buzzard.
68. TH to JH, 29 Sept. 1890, HP 2.367; *LTH*, 2:269. Church: *Sussex Daily News*, 15 Oct. 1890: cutting courtesy of Angela Darwin. The Wallers, Jess and Fred, were Christians, and Fred was finishing the house.

10 COMBATING THE COSMOS

1. H. G. Sharp to TH, 23 Jan. 1891, HP 26.61.
2. JK to TH, 9 Dec. 1890, HP 20.144; Huxley, *Social Diseases*, 54–5, 63, 73.
3. Hodges, *Booth*, 12–13, 27; Huxley, *Social Diseases*, 44. On Hall and the New Connexion: C. Hall, *Hall*, 1–4; Hepton, *Methodism*, 67–9, 104; Desmond, *Politics*, 156, 184.
4. Greenwood, *Booth*, 44–5; Huxley, *Social Diseases*, 66; J. R. Moore, *Religion*, 305; Briggs, *Victorian Cities*, 314.
5. W. T. Stead to TH, 22 Oct. 1890, HP 27.11; evidently Booth 'drafted' the book and Stead 'settled' it: Greenwood, *Booth*, 98; 'gulf': 29 Oct. 1890, HP 27.12; 'filthy': JK to TH, 8 Jan., 9, 12 Dec. 1890, HP 20.121, 144–6.
6. The Colonial Office was shortly to tax Huxley on this part of Booth's scheme: C. E. H. Hobhouse/TH, 28, 30 Oct. 1892, HP 18.198–200.
7. Huxley was familiar with the work of C. S. Loch and the Charity Organisation Society: *Social Diseases*, 55, 61, 106; TH to J. Collier, 16 Dec. 1890, in the possession of Hilary Buzzard; 'sensational': 'Watchman', *Darkest England*, 5; worst weather: TH to JH, 2 Dec. 1890, HP 2.373; T. A. Hirst to TH, 20 Jan. 1891, HP 18.183.
8. TH to J. Collier, 16 Dec. 1890, in the possession of Hilary Buzzard; Huxley, *Social Diseases*, 10–11, 53–8. Mrs Crawshaw was possibly Catherine Crawshaw, wife of the Liberal Unionist Thomas Crawshaw: TH to JH, 2 Dec. 1890, HP 2.373; *LTH*, 2:271–3; JK to TH, 12 Dec. 1890, HP 20.146.
9. Greenwood, *Booth*, 29, 82; Hodges, *Booth*, 38ff; Eastbourne: R. P. Martin to TH, 12 Mar. 1892, HP 22.183; *Eastbourne Gazette*, 3 July 1895. Tyndall's alignment: TH to JT, 18 Dec. 1890, HP 9.176; 'dangerous': 'Watchman', *Darkest England*, 14.
10. TH to JH, 4 Jan. 1891, HP 2.375; Huxley, *Social Diseases*, 7, 72–9; Hodges, *Booth*, 52; Kidd, *Social Evolution*, 9; 'Labour Army': Yeo, 'New Life', 27. Talk by the dock-strike leader John Burns, on the London County Council's far Left, of 'corybantic' conservatives hampering the LCC (Briggs, *Victorian Cities*, 334–9), suggests that the socialists were still reading Huxley.
11. TH to JH, 30 Jan., 17 Feb. 1891, HP 2.377–9; *LTH*, 2:274; T. A. Hirst to TH, 20 Jan. 1891, HP 18.183; 'heaps': HAH to ES, 15 Jan. 1891, AD; 'neglect': JK to TH, 9 Dec. 1890, HP 20.144. Greenwood's pamphlet on *General Booth and . . . the Criticisms of Professor Huxley* had advance orders for 10,000.
12. Huxley, *Social Diseases*, 65.
13. Bowler, 'Holding', 332, 336–8; E. R. Lankester, *Degeneration*; E. R. Lankester, *Advancement*, 349–50; Desmond, *Archetypes*, 108; Jones, *Outcast London*, 313.
14. W. G. Armstrong to TH, 8 Jan. 1891, HP 10.138; 'accounts', 'you': TH to JH, 30 Jan., 17 Feb. 1891, HP 2.377–9; *LTH*, 2:274–6; *CE*, 5:414; 'to give': HAH to ES, 5 Apr. 1891, AD.
15. TH to G. J. Holyoake, 1 Apr. 1891, Holyoake Collection 3293, Co-Operative Union, Manchester; 'because': TH to H. Thompson, 27 Aug. 1892, APS. Huxley was discussing Holyoake and the rationalism of the times with the surgeon Henry Thompson, who had started the infamous 'Prayer Gauge Debate' in 1872: Turner, *Contesting*, 151.

16. J. F. Boyes/TH, 12, 13 Nov. 1892, HP 11.57–8.
17. TH to J. Collier, 16 Dec. 1890, in the possession of Hilary Buzzard; 'constant': TH to E. Collier, 4 May 1891, APS; 'that': TH to JH, 27 Mar 1892, HP 2.411; *LTH*, 2:333; TH to JT, 14 Feb 1892, HP 8.275.
18. TH to E. Collier, 14 Aug. 1891, APS; *LTH*, 2:435; Joyce Kilburn, letter in *Sunday Times*, 19 Apr. 1870; *LTH*, 2:293.
19. TH to J. Simon, 11 Mar. 1891, HP 26.82.
20. TH to JH, 17 May 1891, HP 2.383; HAH to ES, 10 Nov. 1890, AD.
21. TH to JH, 3 July 1891, 11 Jan. 1892, HP 2.385, 395; *LTH*, 2:213, 232, 287, 291.
22. TH to JH, 17 May, 3 July 1891, HP 2.383–5; 'What': TH to [F. or G. A.] Macmillan, 26 Apr. 1891, APS; *LTH*, 2:286–7; mortgages: HAH to ES, 12 July 1891, AD.
23. 'Professor Huxley's Will', *Globe*, 5 Aug. 1895. Will dated 29 Oct. 1891. He died leaving £8,907, wealth by his standards.
24. Huxley, [Bus Strike], *Trade Unionist*, 20 June 1891; 'Professor Huxley on the Bus Strike', *Pall Mall Gazette*, 27 June 1891; HP 49.117; Pelling, *History*, 97–102; 'would': JH to JT, 20 June 1892, HP 8.439; JH to TH, 27 June, 15 Aug. 1892, HP 3.392–4; JH to TH, 29 June 1892, HP 2.417.
25. TH to JH, 10 July 1891, HP 2.389; BJ to HAH/TH, 4 Aug. 1891, 3, 9 Feb., 8 July 1892, HP 7.77, 81–3, 88; JM to TH, 13, 15 June 1891, 5 Mar. 1892, HP 23.83–5.
26. TH to JH, 27 Nov. 1891, HP 2.391; HAH to ES, 5 Jan. 1892, AD; TH to E. Collier, 17 May 1892, APS.
27. JT to JH, 21 June 1892, HP 8.440; 'more': JT to TH, 18, 19 Feb. 1892, HP 1.211; reply, HP 9.182; also HP 8.434–6, 3.381–4. Genesis: *LTH*, 2:296–7; HM 3:121:72, 88–90, 97–8.
28. TH to E. Collier, 28 May 1892, APS; 'With': 18 Mar. 1892, APS; HAH to ES, 24 Apr., 22 Aug. 1892; TH to JH, 26 May 1892, HP 2.415.
29. Huxley, *Controverted*, 7, 35; TH to E. Collier, 5 May 1892, APS; Prologue: TH to N. P. Clayton, 4 Jan. 1893, HP 12.231; *LTH*, 2:298; *Times*, 1 July 1895. Lightman, 'Fighting', Paradis, *Huxley*, 178, and Turner, *Between*, 11, on the introduction of the word 'Naturalism'. While many intellectuals saw *Controverted Questions* as a superannuated book by an old general wallowing in past campaigns, it did have influence in unsuspected areas. It taught the new men like Ben Tillett, the 1889 dock-strike leader, 'to puzzle my ill-trained brain': Laurent, 'Science', 607.
30. *LGR*, 87–8, 153–6, 256–7; Desmond and Moore, *Darwin*, 632–4.
31. GJR to TH, 31 May 1892, HP 25.232; *LGR*, 240, 274–6; *LTH*, 2:267; Spencer's Lamarckism: Freeman, 'Evolutionary Theories', 216–17; TH to JH, 30 Dec. 1893, HP 2.440, where Huxley calls Spencer (who was disagreeing with Weismann) a 'poor fool of [a] man . . . He does not know what he is talking about'. Schwartz, 'Romanes's Defense', 314–15, on Romanes' denial, too, that non-adaptive traits were a refutation of natural selection.

   The freethought journalist W. Platt Ball wrote what Huxley considered an excellent book against the inheritance of acquired characteristics (*Are the Effects of Use and Disuse Inherited*), while defending Huxley in the *National Reformer*: Ball, 'Hebrew Prophecy'; W. P. Ball to TH, 24 Oct. 1890, HP 10.217; F. Darwin to TH, 15 Nov. 1890, HP 13.76. On Romanes and acquired characteristics: Ridley, 'Coadaptation', 59–63; R. Richards, *Darwin*, 350–2.

32. Marginalia in F. Darwin's copy of *The Romanes Lecture*, DAR pamphlet G2136, CUL (Perry O'Donovan's transcription). Mario di Gregorio kindly alerted me to this note. Hames: TH to J. Collier, 16 Dec. 1890, in the possession of Hilary Buzzard; *LTH*, 2:350.
33. Huxley, 'Mr. Balfour's Attack on Agnosticism II', MS HP 47.73–4; Peterson, *Huxley*, 315–16; Huxley, 'Apologetic', 568; Gilbert, 'Altruism'; Paradis, '*Evolution*', 31–4. Three weeks after accepting Romanes' offer, Huxley received Spencer's *Principles of Ethics* and a note from Spencer trying to heal the breach. But it was too late 'for I really do not care one straw about his friendship or his enmity now': TH to JH, 29 June 1892, HP 2.417; HS to TH, 2 July 1892, HP 7.231. The rupture became final as Huxley composed 'Evolution and Ethics': TH to HS, 20 Oct. 1893, HP 7.242; TH/JH, 20, 25, 27, 29 Oct. 1893, HP 2.433, 3.410, 2.435, 3.412.
34. GJR to TH, 5, 10 June 1892, HP 25.234–6; Schurmann's *Ethical Purport*: 4 Jan. 1888, HP 25.224; *LGR*, 144, 188; *LTH*, 2:350; R. Richards, *Darwin*, 332.
35. TH to JT, 18 Dec. 1890, HP 9.176.
36. Christie, 'Working Man's Reply'; G. A. Gaskell to TH, 23 Jan. 1891, HP 17.20.
37. TH to JT, 10 July 1892, HP 9.186. On the rise of Keir Hardie: S. Walpole to TH, 23 Aug. 1892, HP 28.146.
38. F. C. Holland to TH, 27 Sept. 1892, HP 18.210; 'for': GJR to TH, 18 June 1892, HP 25.238.
39. JD to TH, 20 June 1892, HP 14.136–8; *LTH*, 2:323–4.
40. HAH to ES, 22 Aug. 1892, AD; *LTH*, 2:322–3; W. Thomson to TH, 21 Aug. 1892, HP 27.275; 'biggest': *LGR*, 91; H. Roscoe to TH, 25 Aug. 1892, HP 25.294; 'table': TH to E. Collier, 22 Aug. 1892, APS.
41. Lord Salisbury to TH, 16 Aug. 1892, HP 12.153–5; 'with': Magnus, *Gladstone*, 397.
42. *LTH*, 2:323–5; TH to JH, 20 Aug. 1892, HP 2.419.
43. *Westminster Budget*, 8 August 1895: *LTH*, 2:324–8; *LGR*, 287; HP 32.95–6.
44. TH to E. Collier, 22 Aug. 1892, APS; *LTH*, 2:345; Jacyna, 'Science', 20ff. The science should not be underplayed; Salisbury, on Huxley's long-standing recommendation, now gave Flower, up to this point a CB, his KCB – although even this was for heading the Natural History Museum, rather than for actual scientific work.
45. TH to H. Thompson, 27 Aug. 1892, APS.
46. Donnelly did not: 'I wish you were not mixed up with a lot of *your* politicians', he said after seeing the Honours List in the *Times*: JD to TH, 19 Aug. 1892, HP 14.140; *LTH*, 2:329; Magnus, *Gladstone*, 407; 'pious': TH to JT, 7 May 1886, HP 9.150. There were five PCs, and the *Times* (19 August 1892) allowed that 'The Privy Councillors are interesting, if only because they include the name of Professor Huxley. We are far from the Platonic ideal State in which philosophers shall be Kings; but it is something to find the foremost man of science . . . becoming a Councillor of the Queen'.
47. TH to JT, 15 Oct. 1892, HP 9.188; *LTH*, 2:337–8; A. Tennyson to TH, 21 June 1892, HP 27.166.
48. GJR to TH, 25, 31 Oct. 1892, HP 25.242–4; *LTH*, 2:350; *LGR*, 286; Magnus, *Gladstone*, 404; 'impassioned': *Oxford Magazine*, 11 (24 May 1893), 380.
49. On this Association for Promoting a Teaching University in London,

Huxley, 'Professorial University'; HP 42.93–144. Commissioners: JD to TH, 29 Mar. 1892, HP 14.118, reply *LTH*, 2:311, 333; Harte, *University*, 150–6; Bibby, *Huxley*, 221–30 ('seaworthy', 225) for a full discussion.

50. *LGR*, 287; *LTH*, 2:352.

51. BJ to TH, 18 Apr. 1893, HP 7.91.

52. GJR to TH, 21, 25, 27 Apr. 1893, HP 25.250–4; *LTH*, 2:353–4.

53. TH to JT, 15 May 1893, HP 9.190; *LTH*, 2:356; GJR to TH, 19 Apr. 1893, HP 25.248; TH to E. Collier, 4 May 1893, APS; 2,673 copies of the 'Evolution and Ethics' pamphlet sold in a month: F. Macmillan to TH, 16 June 1893, HP 22.156.

54. GJR to TH, 27 Apr. 1893, HP 25.254. TH to J. Collier, 9 May 1893, APS; TH to JT, 15 May 1893, HP 9.190; *LTH*, 2:355–6.

55. 'The Romanes Lecture', *Oxford Magazine*, 11 (24 May 1893), 376, 380–1; *LGR*, 303; 'voice was weak from Influenza – couldn't be heard', was Frank Darwin's comment: marginalia in Darwin's copy of 'Evolution and Ethics', DAR pamphlet G2136, CUL (Perry O'Donovan's transcription).

56. H. de Varigny to TH, 8 Nov. 1892, HP 28.67; 'one': 'The Romanes Lecture', *Oxford Magazine*, 11 (24 May 1893), 376, 380–1; HP 45.28; 'regular': TH to J. Collier, 9 May 1893, APS; *LTH*, 2:355; Helfand, 'Huxley's "Evolution"', 159–60. Paradis, '*Evolution*', 6–7, 33, dissents from much of Helfand's thesis. For him the thrust of 'Evolution and Ethics' is against 'the romantic a priori arguments of the social idealists', whether of Right or Left (in line with his political writings of the 1880s). In the end Paradis (p.55) sees (as I do) Huxley fighting for the political 'middle ground'. He was neutralizing nature's restraints to allow the technocratic transformation of society.

57. *CE*, 9:58–9; Huxley, *Controverted Questions*, 44.

58. *CE*, 9:81–3; Paradis, *Huxley*, 148; Gilley and Loades, 'Huxley', 305; Turner, 'Victorian Scientific Naturalism', 342; 'bloody': TH to JH, 6 Nov. 1887, HP 2:293. Evelleen Richards sees a methodological similarity between Huxley's ability to *allow* a benign human ethics, despite the lack of any Darwinian sanction, and his liberal paternalist tactic in the 1860s of *granting* the emancipation of women and workers, even though 'biology' vouched for male supremacy in a competitive Darwinian universe (E. Richards, 'Gendering'). For 30 years he had stood apart from the socialists on this score. *He* was granting a favour, against his better Darwinian Nature; *they* were demanding a right sanctioned by a different egalitarian science.

59. Seth, 'Man's Place', 823–5.

60. He was a believer in 'an *a priori* Moral law discerned by Reason', said the *Oxford Magazine*, rather than in the sensationalism of his *Hume* period (*Oxford Magazine*, 11 (24 May 1893), 381). Seth, 'Man's Place', 825; *CE*, 9:53, 114, 205; Mivart, 'Evolution', 203–6.

61. R. Owen to G. Rorison, [April 1860], BM(NH) Owen Corres., vol. 22, f.379; *CE*, 9:52; his peer-group fascination for Buddhism: JH to TH, 18 May 1893, HP 3.404; 'militant': Seth, 'Man's Place', 825. Huxley's approach to 'instinct' had changed dramatically since writing *Hume*.

62. Seth, 'Man's Place', 823; 'The Romanes Lecture', *Oxford Magazine*, 11 (24 May 1893), 380–1.

63. Stephen, 'Ethics', 163–7, 170; *CE*, 9:114–15.

64. W. P. Ward to TH, 19 May 1893, HP 28.173; *CE*, 9:82; A. M. Curtis to TH, 19 Aug. 1893, HP 12.371.

11 *FIGHTING UNTO DEATH*

1. HP 45.42–231, and HP 53–55 for his 'physiographical' or spatial, map-based, approach to the ancient philosophies.
2. Marginalia in F. Darwin's *Evolution and Ethics*, pamphlet 2136, Darwin Coll. CUL. Huxley's speech at Gonville and Caius College, 21 June 1893, HP 39.183; MF to HAH, [22 June 1893], HP 16.235. Screened: Press cutting, HP 82.32.
3. GJR to TH, 9 Oct. 1893, HP 25.265; 'pompous': JK to TH, 14 Nov. 1893, HP 20.169; *LTH*, 2:367–8; Fund: C. S. C. Bowen to TH, [Nov. 1893], HP 11.45–7.
4. Huxley had intended 'gathering up the threads of the Weismann question' and tying them together in an essay (GJR to TH, 26 Sept. 1893, HP 25.263; *LTH*, 2:368). His notes on Weismann's 'Continuity of Germ plasm' show that he was contrasting it with Owen's *Parthenogenesis*: HP 41.118.
5. H. L. Mencken, quoted in Fawcett, 'Huxley', 208; *LTH*, 2:371; Roos, 'Aims', on Huxley's steadfast public platform; R. M. Young, *Darwin's Metaphor*, 126 on the common context of early Victorian natural theology and late Victorian naturalism.
6. TH to E. Collier, 25 Dec. 1892, APS; *LTH*, 2:340.
7. TH to JH, 22 Jan. 1893, HP 2.421; MF to TH, 15 Jan. [1893], HP 4.367; J. Paget to TH, 19 Jan. 1893, HP 24.14; *LTH*, 2:340–1; Rupke, *Owen*, 3.
8. TH to JH, 1 Oct. 1893, HP 2.429; 'as': R. S. Owen to TH, 25 Sept. 1893, HP 23.251; 'I': TH to R. S. Owen to TH, 26 Sept. 1893, HP 23.253; WHF to TH, 9 Feb. 1895, HP 16.136; *LTH*, 2:364; 'incompetent': JH to TH, 8 Oct. 1893, HP 3.408.
9. JH to TH, 8 Oct. 1893, 4 Feb. 1894, HP 3.408, 444; WHF to TH, 1 May 1894, HP 16.134; 'man': HAH to ES, 29 Dec. 1893, AD; *LTH*, 2:373
10. Gruber, 'Owen Correspondence', 3–7: the *Life* was 'an unconscious parody' of filially-devoted biographies. Its bowdlerized letters were used to curry science's good favour while grandfather was jockeyed into the highest echelons – 'a successful imposture, quite worthy of the subject', said Flower: WHF to TH, 7 Feb. 1895, HP 16.135.
11. J. R. Moore, 'Evangelicals', 390, 393, 408, 412; Kidd, *Social Evolution*, 17, 21, 23, chap. 5; Drummond, *Lowell*, 9, 34, 73, 342ff, 406, 414, 426, 441.
12. WHF to TH, 1 May 1894, HP 16.134; 'all': TH to JH, 4 Feb. 1894, HP 2.444; *LTH*, 2:373.
13. MF to TH, 30 June 1894, HP 4.379; Huxley's notes on Owen's work, HP 39.186.
14. Coleridge, *Constitution*, 1972, 51–2; Desmond, *Politics*, 237; 'Apostle': Clodd, 'Huxley'.
15. The more sympathetic re-evaluation was begun in the 1970s by Dov Ospovat, 'Influence', Ospovat, *Development*. It is now a rolling movement: Desmond, *Archetypes*; Rehbock, *Philosophical*; Sloan, 'Darwin'; E. Richards, 'Question'; Desmond, *Politics*; Sloan, *Owen*; Gruber and Thackray, *Commemoration*; Rupke, *Owen*; Padian, 'Hunterian Lecture'; Desmond, 'Foreword'.
16. HAH to ES, 29 Dec. 1893, AD; TH to JH, 8 Dec. 1893, HP 2.437; 'I': JH to TH, 5 Dec. 1893, HP 3.413; JD to TH, 6 Dec. 1893, HP 14.159.

17. TH to [L. Tyndall], 9 Jan. 1894, HP 9.184; 'tear', 'abusive': TH to E. Collier, 24 Dec. 1893, APS; 'dangerous': TH to JH, 8, 15 Dec. 1893, HP 2.437–8; 'John's': JH to TH, 10 Dec. 1893, HP 3.414; *LTH*, 2:369; Huxley, 'Tyndall'; JK to TH, 15, 19, 21 Dec. 1893, HP 20.171–4; bed: HAH to ES, 29 Dec. 1893, AD.
18. HAH to ES, 6 Feb. 1895, ES; *CE*, 9:17; G. A. Macmillan to TH, 16 Aug. 1894, HP 22.156.
19. G. C. Brodrick to TH, 5 Dec. 1893, 3 Sept. 1894 HP 11.88–91.
20. G. C. Brodrick to TH, 3 Sept. 1894, HP 11.91; 'wrath', 'looking': HAH to ES, 18 Aug. 1894, AD; Osborn, 'Memorial Tribute'; J. R. Moore, 'Deconstructing', 354.
21. TH to JH, 12 Aug. 1894, HP 2.452; *LTH*, 2:378–9; Lord: TH to [L. Tyndall?], 20 Aug. 1894, HP 9.269.
22. E. Frankland to TH, 2 Sept 1894, HP 16.276.
23. HAH to ES, 18 Aug. 1894, AD.
24. A. P. Primrose/TH, 1, 2, 9 June 1894, HP 24.212–14; *LTH*, 2:362, 373.
25. Historians have disagreed about Huxley's 'Past and Present' retrospective. The letters show that he was limiting the damage done by Salisbury: 'Oh that my hands had not been tied & I could have shown up the rottenness of the thing': TH to MF, 28 Oct. 1894, HP 4.144 (also 'anti'); TH to NL, 28 Oct. 1894, HP 21.318; Turner, 'Conflict', 369, cf. Roos, 'Aims', 176, n48; Meadows, *Science*, 217.
26. MF to TH, 2 Nov. 1894, HP 4.384, also 383; Lord Rayleigh to TH, 1 Nov. 1894, HP 27.122; *LTH*, 2:386–7.
27. TH to N. P. Clayton, 2 Jan. 1895, HP 12.234; deputation: A. P. Primrose to TH, 6 Dec. 1894, HP 25.215; A. W. Rucker to TH, 10 Jan. 1895, HP 25.307; HAH to ES, 17 Dec. 1894, 6 Feb. 1895, AD.
28. TH to JH, 14 Feb. 1895, HP 2.460; *LTH*, 2:394; Keith, *Autobiography*, 172–4; Dubois, 'Place'; Bowler, *Theories*, 34–5; McCabe, *Prehistoric Man*, 17–20.
29. MF to TH, 7 Mar. 1895, HP 4.248; Magnus, *Gladstone*, 402.
30. R. F. Carpenter to TH, 10 Feb. 1889, HP 12.55; Catholic University: JH to TH, 26 Sept. 1889, HP 3.346, reply 29 Sept. 1889, HP 2.350; *LTH*, 2:241–2; Magnus, *Gladstone*, 368; Jacyna, 'Science', 20–3, 27.
31. Lightman, 'Fighting'; 'wandering': JK to TH, 13 Feb. 1895, HP 20.177. Donnelly said the reviews made *Foundations* sound like one 'long wail as to how dreadful the truth about things was and therefore it could not be true': JD to TH, 5 Mar. 1895, HP 14.188. Holiday: TH to E. Collier, 5 Feb. 1895, APS.
32. Peterson, *Huxley*, 302; Morley, *Recollections*, 1:226–7.
33. JK to TH, 9 Feb. 1895, HP 20.176; 'living': Wynne, 'Physics', 179–80; Drummond: J. R. Moore, 'Evangelicals', 389.
34. TH to E. Collier, 6 Mar 1895, APS (also 'cleverest'); JK to TH, 22, 24 Feb. 1895, HP 20.178–9; *LTH*, 2:396–8.
35. Lightman, 'Fighting'; 'look': Kidd, *Social Evolution*, 5; Turner, *Between*, 228; Jackson, *Eighteen Nineties*, 126; Peterson, *Huxley*, 195.
36. Huxley, 'Mr. Balfour's Attack', 527–9 – the 'Second Revise' is in HP 47.65; 'parody': MF to TH, 7 Mar. 1895, HP 4.248.
37. H. G. Wells to TH, May 1895, HP 28.233; effeminate: Magnus, *Gladstone*, 368.

38. Huxley, 'Mr. Balfour's Attack', 530–2.
39. TH to E. Collier, 6 Mar. 1895, APS; 'You': JH to TH, 27 Mar. 1895, HP 3.425; 'delightful': JD to TH, 28 May 1895, HP 14.194. Lightman, 'Fighting', by contrast suggests that Balfour had probed the weak spots of Naturalism – its unquestioned axioms. Peterson, *Huxley*, 315–27 finally published the galley proofs of part II; the original MS is Huxley, 'Mr. Balfour's Attack on Agnosticism II', HP 47.72.
40. HAH to ES, 30 Mar. 1895, AD; TH to E. Collier, 6 Mar. 1895, APS; cf. *LTH*, 2:400; JK to TH, 9 Mar. 1895, HP 20.182.
41. HAH to ES, 30 Mar. 1895, AD; poison pen letters (thought to have been from the Salvationists), Martin Cooke, pers. comm., and Clark, *Huxleys*, 119; Brace: TH to E. Collier, 5 Feb. 1895; E. M. Thompson to TH, 12 Mar. 1895, HP 27.248; *LTH*, 2:400.
42. MF to HAH, 26 May 1895, HP 4.390; *LTH*, 2:401–2; HAH to ES, 30 Mar. 1895, AD.
43. *LTH*, 2:402; *British Medical Journal*, 6 July 1895.
44. Clodd, 'Huxley' (the expression comes from Huxley, 'Apologetic'); *LTH*, 2:402, 442; *LJH*, 2:328, 357–9; 'beastly': TH to JH, 10 June 1895, HP 2.462. Ships: JH to TH, 7 June 1895, HP 3.427.
45. 'Death of Professor Huxley', *Observer*, 30 June 1895; 'lovers': *Daily Chronicle*, 1 July 1895. The immediate cause of death was a pulmonary embolism – a blood clot in the pulmonary artery causing a heart attack: *British Medical Journal*, 6 July 1895.
46. HAH reminiscences, HP. 62.1; HAH to TH, 23 Dec. 1847, HH 6.
47. *Folkstone Express*, 6 July 1895; Abbey: Marsh, 'Huxley'; *Daily Telegraph*, 5 July 1895; 'Apostle': Clodd, 'Huxley'.
48. Conway, 'Huxley', 75.
49. *Times*, 5 July 1895; *Eastbourne Chronicle*, 6 July 1895.
50. Revd L. Davies to TH, 2 June [1889], HP 13.123.
51. *Daily Telegraph*, 5 July 1895.
52. *Agnostic J.*, 1 Aug 1895; e.g. on politicians *Eastbourne Guardian*, 10 July 1895; list of mourners: *Times*, 5 July 1895; *Nature*, 11 July 1895.
53. Conway, 'Huxley', 73; *Agnostic J.*, 13 July, 20 July, 1 Aug. 1895; *Literary Guide*, 1 Aug. 1895.
54. *Daily Telegraph*, 5 July 1895.
55. That Nettie was still a church-goer and Hal observed the 'Christian' pieties helped to explain why their Eastbourne vicar Revd Bickersteth Ottley gave Huxley a fine memorial sermon at St Mary's Church, an 'unholy panegyric' according to one horrified member of the congregation: 'The Vicar of the Late Professor Huxley', *Eastbourne Guardian*, 10 July 1895; 'A Protest by Mr. G. F. Chambers', *Eastbourne Gazette*, 9 July 1895.
56. HAH to ES, 5 Apr. 1891, AD; 'He': HP 81.26.
57. JK to HAH, 16, 20 Aug., 11 Oct. 1895, HP 20.184 Ostensibly Nettie objected that the proof was unrevised. But I think it cut deeper. Len and Fred Pollock were certainly for publication: F. Pollock to HAH, 30 Sept. 1895, HP 24.160; Lightman, 'Fighting'.

AFTERWORD: HUXLEY IN PERSPECTIVE

1. Kidd, *Social Evolution*, v, vi.
2. Shapin, 'History'.
3. This was Grene's ('Recent Biographies', 664) comment on *Politics of Evolution*. Like other historians, I have come to see that the actors we once lumped together – the 'Darwinians' of the 1860s or the morphologists of the 1830s – consisted of heterogeneous, politically-allied individuals whose constructions of Nature were as unique as their embedding contexts.
4. It is shown in the current symposia, e.g. Shortland and Yeo, *Telling Lives in Science* (1996) and La Vergata, *Le Biografie Scientifiche* (1995).
5. Turner, *Contesting*, 40.
6. *Pall Mall Gazette*, 1 July 1895; G. M. Young, *Portrait*, 67, 145.
7. Kidd, *Social Evolution*, 3; Jackson, *Eighteen Nineties*, 30, 126; 'their': HAH to ES, 1 July 1887, AD. The old Puritans, disliking the nineties, looked back to a time of higher morality. 'I remember one exhibition in which there were portraits of FD Maurice, Carlyle, JH Newman & of J. S. Mill & each one was sadder than [the] other', said T. H. Farrer (to TH, 6 Jan. 1894, HP 16.33), '& yet' those were the men who had moved 'mankind towards better things'.
8. E. R. Pisani to HAH, 9 Mar. 1894, HP 24.129; Conway, 'Huxley', 75; Webb, *Diary*, 202.
9. Green, 'Strange [In]difference', 531.
10. Ward, *A Writer's Recollections*, quoted in Peterson, *Prophet*, 13, 268.
11. *CE*, 3:189.
12. Webb, *Diary*, 203.
13. Agnosco, 'Huxley'; Peterson, *Huxley*, 83; 'American': G. F. Ormsby/TH, [Dec. 1893], 3 Jan. 1894, HP 23.238–9.
14. O. Lodge to TH, 17 July 1893, HP 22.1.
15. Webb, *Diary*, 202; Jensen, *Huxley*, chap. 1. As late as 1899 Sclater at the Zoological Society gave young Arthur Keith (*Autobiography*, 193) four large lithograph plates of ape anatomy which Huxley had prepared in 1864 for an unwritten paper, asking him to supply the 'missing text'. It took Keith 50 years.
16. Clodd, 'Huxley'. The blank *Lessons* is now owned by Sir Andrew Huxley.
17. *Pall Mall Gazette*, 1 July 1895; 'What': W. Lecky to TH, 20 Jan. 1891, HP 21.191; 'never': Clodd, 'Huxley'; Webb, *Diary*, 202; 'among': Huxley, 'Mr. Balfour's Attack on Agnosticism II', HP 47.83.
18. TH to HAH, 28 June 1851, HH 155; desert: *CE*, 6:319; 'solace': *CE*, 5:60.
19. *Times*, 5 July 1895.
20. Turner, *Contesting*, 44.
21. A. Thackray, 'Natural Knowledge', 764.
22. TH to E. W. S. Martin, 11 Nov. 1894, APS. Huxley's mother too was High Anglican. Despite the sinking fortunes of the family, it evidently had once had gentlemanly origins, judging by the fact that Huxley's brother George was using the family crest of the Cheshire Huxleys in the 1840s: information from Angela Darwin.
23. Peterson, *Huxley*, 20; Desmond, *Politics*, chaps 3–4, on the radical medical milieu.
24. *CE*, 5:143; 'social': A. Thackray, 'Natural Knowledge', 678; Jacyna, 'Immanence', 321–8.

25. Secord, 'Behind', 166.
26. *Times*, 1 July 1895; Jensen, *Huxley*, calls Huxley a 'secular theologian', and, although one understands what he means, the term strikes me as wrong; 'lineal': Mitchell, 'Huxley', 148–9. Lightman, *Origins*, 3–5, 6–9, 30, made Huxley a transitional figure in religion as my *Archetypes and Ancestors* made him a transitional figure in palaeontology. But where Lightman emphasizes Huxley's use in 1859 of Mansel's 'orthodox' logic to chop away at Anglicanism, I see this as a late *ad hoc* sarcastic rationalization, with the real origins of his agnosticism back in the Dissenting 1840s.
27. Baynes, 'Darwin', 502–6; 'standard': *CE*, 5:140–1.
28. Baynes, 'Darwin', 506; *Times*, 1 July 1895.
29. Ruth Barton, 'Evolution', calls Huxley's a 'sterilized' Calvinism, with 'little to commend it to Calvinist theologians'; di Gregorio, *Huxley*, 192–3 for a good discussion.
30. Mitchell, 'Huxley', 148–9; '*clear*': Briggs, *Age*, 484.
31. *Pall Mall Gazette*, 1 July 1895.
32. C. Fluhrer to TH, 2 June 1892, HP 16.140.
33. Sanderson, 'English Civic Universities', 91.
34. *LTH*, 2:392; 'English': Tener and Woodfield, *Victorian Spectator*, 141; 'vigour': *Oxford Magazine*, 11 (24 May 1893), 381. Bartholomew, 'Huxley's Defence'; Barton, 'Evolution'.
35. *CE*, 5:92.
36. *CE*, 5:140; 'whence': E. R. Lankester, 'Huxley'; R. M. Young, *Darwin's Metaphor*, 23; Heyck, *Transformation*, 102. Turner talks of Huxley's men removing theology's 'social vision from the cocoon of eternity' and dragging it 'into the saeculum of history': *Contesting*, 118.
37. MacLeod, *Public Science*; Turner, *Contesting*.
38. Mitchell, 'Huxley', 147.
39. Barton, 'Scientific Opposition', 16; Wells, 'Huxley', 209; 'pioneers': Huxley, 'Professorial University'.
40. 'The worldly, flippant Anglican is being rebuked by one of the ranting Colonels of Cromwell's army': Cockshut, *Unbelievers*, 91, 93. Wilberforce's grandmother: J. Stephen, 'Wilberforce', 469–70; 'splendid': Gardiner, *Harcourt*, 1:247; 'the Bp.': A. S. Farrar to L. Huxley, 12 July 1899, HP 16.13.
41. *Standard*, 1 July 1895; Caron, 'Biology'; Gooday, 'Nature'; Forgan and Gooday, 'Constructing South Kensington'.

    While some of the best literature contrasts the science in the gentry's country house with that in the academic's laboratory (Chadarevian, 'Laboratory Science'; Secord, 'Extraordinary Experiment'), the more representative path for the social transference of science occurred lower down the social scale, between London's medical schools with their radical comparative anatomy courses (Desmond, *Politics*; Pickstone, 'Museological Science') and the laboratories of Huxley's South Kensington, Rolleston's Oxford and Foster's Cambridge.
42. Huxley, undated fragment, HP 49.55; 'age': Huxley, 'Royal Academy'.
43. Pedersen, 'Rathbone', 98–9.
44. E. Richards, 'Gendering', E. Richards, 'Huxley'; E. Richards, 'Redrawing'; E. Richards, 'Darwin'; Erskine, '*Origin*'; Blake, *Charge*; *LJH*, 2:125; 'torn': JT to TH, 6 Apr. 1870, HP 1.65; *LTH*, 1:329.
45. E. g. *Cambridge Express*, 6 July 1895; Wells, 'Huxley', 209.

46. Clodd, 'Huxley'; Roos, 'Aims', 176; 'corner': *Times*, 5 July 1895.
47. *Hospital*, 13 July 1895; 'Pius': R. T. Wright to TH, 22 July 1882, HP 29.240. News from his last group of students: H. M. Ward to TH, 20 Nov. 1893, HP 28.157; C. H. Hurst to TH, 7 Sept. 1894, HP 30.201; W. J. Sollas to TH, 14 July 1894, HP 26.167; 'continued': Mitchell, 'Huxley', 149.
48. Foster, 'Few More Words', 320.
49. Dale, *Pursuit*, 5; Peterson, *Huxley*, 253.
50. TH to HAH. 16–17 Oct. 1847, HH 2–3; Turner, *Contesting*, 44–5.
51. TH to HAH, 16 Oct. 1851, HH 169; Lightman, *Origins*, 28–9; Dockrill, 'Huxley', 470; J. R. Moore, 'Deconstructing'.
52. Tener and Woodfield, *Victorian Spectator*, 28; 'veracity': *CE*, 3:205.
53. Ellegard, *Darwin*, 61; 'froth': Huxley, 'Science and "Church Policy"'; 'Engineers': TH to JH, 26 Mar. 1889, 2.340; *LTH*, 2:231; Barton, 'Scientific Opposition'; E. R. Lankester, 'Huxley'.
54. Agnosco, 'Huxley'.
55. Denis, 'Brompton Barracks', 11.
56. J. R. Moore, 'Theodicy'; Moore, 'Crisis', 59–68; Moore, 'Freethought', 279–89; Moore, *Post-Darwinian Controversies*; Desmond, 'Author's Response'; Brooke, *Science*, 34; Turner, *Contesting*, 171; Barton, 'Evolution'. The war metaphor, as Barton so rightly says, was itself Huxley's major weapon.
57. Huxley, 'Schamyl', 491–517; TH to HAH, 8 Apr. 1854, HH 271; 'scientific': TH to JH, 5 Sept. 1858, HP 2.35; *LTH*, 1:160.
58. *LTH*, 2:46–7; Chatham: HM 1:4:131; Denis, 'Brompton Barracks', 12–22. The Forces' support of science is an unplumbed area (Brock, 'Patronage', 199; although Hearl, 'Military Examinations', has investigated one aspect). By contrast, much work has been done on the Navy's surveying voyages (Deacon, *Scientists*; Browne, 'Biogeography', 307–10; Desmond, 'Making', 229–30).
59. Gilley and Loades, 'Huxley', 287–9. Huxley's looking over the Permian *Protorosaurus* in Newcastle: A. Hancock to TH, 15, 20 Dec. 1869, HP 17.324–7; TH to CL, 4 Jan. 1870, HP 30.45.
60. J. R. Moore, 'Socializing Darwinism'; Briggs, *Age*, 488. The *Origin* as unfinished 1830s business: Desmond, *Politics*, 398–414; Desmond and Moore, *Darwin*, chaps 15–18; 'death': F. Darwin, *Foundations*, 52; 'Cooperative': Weikart, 'Recently Discovered'. Greene, 'Darwin', for an overview.
61. Huxley, 'Organization'; 'Lord Hartington on our Industrial Position', *Times*, 18 Mar. 1887; Ashworth, *Economic History*, 37; Roberts, *Europe*, 78, 101; Crook, *Darwinism*, chap. 3, esp. 65, 82–3.
62. TH to W. T. Stead, 21 June 1894, HP 27.32 draft; cf. *LTH*, 2:374–5; Crook, *Darwinism*, 103, and 99 on Stead's peace brokerage; Roberts, *Europe*, 113, 117–18.
63. Helfand, 'Huxley's "Evolution"', 160; but cf. Paradis, '*Evolution*', 6–7. Helfand was first to challenge the received wisdom that Huxley's lecture was 'a humanistic statement against the use of [Darwin's] authority' in science. He reinterpreted it contextually, as part of a six-year critique of Spencer and socialism by a reinvigorated Darwinian. Helfand made Wallace stand in for socialism, but I have tried to show that Huxley's exposure to socialism was in fact much more extensive in 1886–93.
64. Lang, 'Science'.

65. HAH to ES, 31 Dec. 1865, AD.
66. Undated fragment, HP 49.55; *LTH*, 2:16n, 56.
67. Hilgartner, 'Dominant View', 519; Cooter and Pumfrey, 'Separate Spheres', 248; Lightman, 'Voices'.
68. E. R. Lankester, 'Huxley'; Knight, 'Getting Science'; Turner, *Contesting*, 171ff.
69. *Daily News*, 1 July 1895; Stead: Lightman, 'Voices'.
70. TH to JH, 4 Dec. 1894, HP 2.454; *LTH*, 2:391.
71. Undated fragment, HP 49.55; see also the undated cutting, Huxley, 'Good Writing: A Gift or an Art', HP 49.58; L. Stephen to TH, 14 Oct. 1894, HP 27.66. Paradis, *Huxley*, 37, 42, on the 'dramatization'.
72. *Daily News*, 1 July 1895; *Illustrated London News*, 20 July 1895.
73. Huxley, 'On Species and Races' MS, HP 41, ff.51–6.
74. Huxley, early draft of Manchester Address 1887, HP 42.58–67, f.67.
75. Cooter and Pumfrey, 'Separate Spheres', 243.
76. Detrosier, *Lecture*, 5–8; Desmond, 'Artisan Resistance', 82–3, 89–92. While I have dealt with science at an ideological level, as seems appropriate with London's radical workers (Huxley's audience was composed of radical free-thinkers: J. P. A., 'Huxley', 2), Anne Secord ('Science in the Pub') has exquisitely investigated the relations of the non-radical artisan botanists in the Midlands.
77. Chilton, 'Geological Revelations'.
78. R. Carlile to F. Place, 5 Aug. 1841, BL Add. MS 35144, f.340.
79. J. P. A., 'Huxley', 2.
80. As such, Huxley had something of an older patron–client relationship as well as a newer canvasser–electorate alliance with his workers: Pickstone, 'Museological Science', 114 for discussions of lay patronage.
81. Davies, *Heterodox London*, 1:112; J. P. A., 'Huxley', 2; Cooter and Pumfrey, 'Separate Spheres', 249–50; Hilgartner, 'Dominant', 531.
82. Watts, 'Theological Theories', 134; nihilism: Kidd, *Social Evolution* 3.
83. Huxley, *Controverted Questions*, 52; HP 56.10; Laurent, 'Science', 595–7.
84. W. C. Meakin to TH, 25 Feb. 1894, HP 22.207; Richardson, *Death*, on the poor and dissection; G. Howell to TH, 1 Sept. 1880, 10 July 1883, HP 18.244, 248; *LTH*, 1:476; cabbies: Mivart, 'Reminiscences', 996; petitioned: HP 32.11–12.
85. Agnosco, 'Huxley'; 'hail': Kidd, *Social Evolution*, 3.
86. G. Sparks to F. G. M. Powell/TH, Feb.–Apr. 1894, HP 26.174–7 (also 'toy', telescope); Revd F. G. M. Powell to *Spectator*, clipping in HP 81.91; reproduced in *Eastern Morning News*, 16 July 1895; MF to TH, 1 Jan. [1894], HP 4.377; 'something', 'as': F. G. M. Powell to JD/TH, Jan. 1894–Jan. 1895, HP 24.179–190; *LTH*, 2:365–7, 382; Hollowday, 'Huxley', 437–8. Huxley tried to get Sparks a job in Foster's lab: L. Shore to TH, 3 Apr. 1894, HP 26.75.

    Donnelly, put on the search for Sparks (JD to TH, 5, 27 Jan. 1894, HP 14.165, 171, 175), offered to lend Huxley one of the Royal College's old Hartnack microscopes – a cheap student's instrument (Eric Hollowday, pers. comm.) – for the docker.
87. G. A. Gaskell to TH, 23 Jan. 1891, HP 17.20.
88. TH to unknown corres., 30 June 1894, APS; Hutton, 'Great Agnostic'. On his anonymous response to the Royal Society critics: Huxley, 'Criticism'.
89. Laurent, 'Science', 601–7; 'pauperism': Crane, 'Marriage'.

90. Wiener, *English Culture*, 10–14; cf. Edgerton, *Science*, 8, 19.
91. *Daylight*, 13 July 1895.
92. JD to HAH, 29 May 1893, HP 14.146; A. Geikie to TH, 31 May 1891, HP 17.39; 'over-rated': W. T. Thiselton-Dyer to TH, 24 Dec. 1894, HP 27.232; portraits: TH to JT, 8 Mar. 1891, HP 9.173. Athenaeum: H. E. Roscoe to TH, 22 Jan. 1891, HP 25.291.
93. Rose, 'Huxley', 23; Bowler, 'Holding'.
94. *Punch*, 13 July 1895; 'to': *Times*, 1 July 1895; 'warmed': *Saturday Review*, 6 July 1895.

Bibliography

Anonymous press articles are cited fully in the notes. Place of publication is London unless otherwise stated.

AMNH	*Annals and Magazine of Natural History*
ANH	*Archives of Natural History*
AS	*Annals of Science*
BJHS	*British Journal for the History of Science*
CR	*Contemporary Review*
CUP	Cambridge University Press
ER	*Edinburgh Review*
FR	*Fortnightly Review*
HS	*History of Science*
JHB	*Journal of the History of Biology*
NC	*Nineteenth Century*
NR	*National Reformer*
NRRS	*Notes and Records of the Royal Society*
OUP	Oxford University Press
QJGS	*Quarterly Journal of the Geological Society*
QR	*Quarterly Review*
UCP	University of Chicago Press
UP	University Press
VS	*Victorian Studies*
WR	*Westminster Review*

Adam, I., 'A Huxley Echo in "Middlemarch"', *Notes and Queries*, 209 (1964), 227.

Agnosco, 'Professor Huxley', *Agnostic J.*, 37 (1895), 1–2.

Alter, P., *The Reluctant Patron: Science and the State in Britain 1850–1920* (Oxford, Berg, 1987).

Amigoni, D., and J.Wallace, eds, *Charles Darwin's The Origin of Species. New Interdisciplinary Essays* (Manchester UP, 1995).

Argyll, Duke of, *The Reign of Law* (Strahan, 1867).

Ashforth, A., *Thomas Henry Huxley* (New York, Twayne, 1969).

Bibliography

Ashworth, W., *An Economic History of England 1870–1939* (Methuen, 1960).

Ball, W. P., 'Hebrew Prophecy', *NR*, 15, 29 Mar. 1891.

Barnes, B., and S.Shapin, eds, *Natural Order: Historical Studies of Scientific Culture* (Sage, 1979).

Barr, A., ed., *Thomas Henry Huxley's Place in Science and Letters: Centenary Essays* 2 vols. (Athens, Georgia, University of Georgia Press, 1997).

Barrow, L., *Independent Spirits: Spiritualism and English Plebeians 1850–1910* (Routledge & Kegan Paul, 1986).

Bartholomew, M., 'Huxley's Defence of Darwin', *AS*, 32 (1975), 525–35.

Barton, R., 'Scientific Opposition to Technical Education', in M. D. Stephens and G. W. Roderick, eds, *Scientific and Technical Education in Early Industrial Britain* (Department of Adult Education, University of Nottingham, 1981), 13–27.

—, 'Evolution: The Whitworth Gun in Huxley's War for the Liberation of Science from Theology', in Oldroyd and Langham, *Wider Domain*, 261–86.

—, 'The Creation of the Conflict Between Science and Theology', in C. Bloore and P. Donovan, eds, *Science and Theology in Action* (Palmerston North, NZ, Dunmore, 1987), 55–71.

—, 'John Tyndall, Pantheist', *Osiris*, 3 (1987), 111–34.

—, '"An Influential Set of Chaps": The X-Club and Royal Society Politics 1864–85', *BJHS*, 23 (1990), 53–81.

Bastian, H. C., 'Reply to Professor Huxley's Inaugural Address at Liverpool on the Question of the Origin of Life', *Nature*, 2 (1870), 410–13, 431–4.

[Baynes, T. S.], 'Darwin on Expression', *ER*, 137 (1873), 492–508.

Becker, B. H., *Scientific London* (King, 1874).

Beer, G., *Darwin's Plots: Evolutionary Narrative in Darwin, George Eliot and Nineteenth-Century Fiction* (Ark, 1983).

—, 'Travelling the Other Way', in Jardine, Secord and Spary, *Cultures*, 322–37.

Benson, K. R., 'American Morphology in the Late Nineteenth Century: The Biology Department at Johns Hopkins University', *JHB*, 18 (1985), 163–205.

—, 'From Museum Research to Laboratory Research: The Transformation of Natural History into Academic Biology', in Rainger, Benson and Maienschein, *American Development of Biology*, 49–83.

Besant, A., *The Law of Population* [1877] (Freethought Publishing Co., 1887).

—, *A Selection of the Social and Political Pamphlets* (New York, Kelly, 1970).

Bibby, C., 'The South London Working Men's College', *Adult Education*, 28 (1955), 211–21.

—, 'T. H. Huxley and Medical Education', *Charing Cross Hospital Gazette*, 54 (1956), 191–5.

—, 'Thomas Henry Huxley and University Development', *VS*, 2 (1958), 97–116.

—, *T. H. Huxley: Scientist, Humanist and Educator* (New York, Horizon Press, 1960).

Blake, C., *The Charge of the Parasols: Women's Entry to the Medical Profession* (The Women's Press, 1990).

Blake, R., *Disraeli* (University Paperbacks, 1969).

Blinderman, C. S., 'The Oxford Debate and After', *Notes and Queries*, 202 (1957), 126–8.

Bonner, H. B., *Charles Bradlaugh* 2 vols (Fisher, Unwin, 1898).

Bourdieu, *Outline of a Theory of Practice*, trans. R.Nice (CUP, 1977).

Bower, F. O., 'Teaching of Biological Science', *Nature*, 115 (1925), 712–14.

Bowler, P. J., *Fossils and Progress: Paleontology and the Idea of Progressive Evolution in the Nineteenth Century* (New York, Science History Publications, 1976).

—, 'Edward Drinker Cope and the Changing Structure of Evolutionary Theory', *Isis*, 68 (1977), 249–65.

—, *Theories of Human Evolution. A Century of Debate 1844–1944* (Oxford, Blackwell, 1986).

—, *The Non-Darwinian Revolution: Reinterpreting a Historical Myth* (Baltimore, Johns Hopkins UP, 1988).

—, 'Development and Adaptation: Evolutionary Concepts in British Morphology, 1870–1914', *BJHS*, 22 (1989), 283–97.

—, 'Holding your Head up High: Degeneration and Orthogenesis in the Theories of Human Evolution', in Moore, *History*, 329–53.

Bradlaugh, C., *The Channel Tunnel: Ought the Democracy to Oppose or Support It?* (Bonner, 1887).

Bravo, M. T., 'Ethnological Encounters', in Jardine, Secord and Spary, *Cultures*, 338–57.

Briggs, A., *The Age of Improvement 1783–1867* (Longman, 1979).

—, *Victorian Cities* (Penguin, 1990).

Brock, W. H., 'The Patronage of Science', in Turner, *Patronage*, 173–206.

—, 'School Science Examinations: Sacrifice or Stimulus?', in MacLeod, *Days of Judgement*, 169–88.

—, N. D. McMillan and R. C. Mollan, eds, *John Tyndall: Essays on a Natural Philosopher* (Royal Dublin Society, Historical Studies 3, 1981).

Brooke, J. H., *Science and Religion: Some Historical Perspectives* (CUP, 1991).

Brown, A. W., *The Metaphysical Society* (New York, Columbia UP, 1947).

Browne, J., 'The Charles Darwin–Joseph Hooker Correspondence: An Analysis of Manuscript Resources and their use in Biography', *J. Soc. Bibphy Nat. Hist.*, 8 (1978), 351–66.

—, 'Biogeography and Empire', in Jardine, Secord and Spary, *Cultures*, 305–21.

Buchanan, R., 'Are Men Born Free and Equal?', *Daily Telegraph*, 16, 27 Jan., 3 Feb. 1890.

Burkhardt, F., 'England and Scotland: The Learned Societies', in Glick, *Comparative Reception*, 32–74.

— and S. Smith, eds, *The Correspondence of Charles Darwin* 9 vols (CUP, 1985–94).

—, *A Calendar of the Correspondence of Charles Darwin, 1821–1882, With Supplement* (CUP, 1994).

Burrow, J. W., *Evolution and Society: A Study in Victorian Social Theory* (CUP, 1966).

Butler, S., *Evolution Old and New* (Hardwicke & Bogue, 1879).

Butler, S. V. F., 'Centers and Peripheries: The Development of British Physiology, 1870–1914', *JHB*, 21 (1988), 473–500.

Calderwood, H., 'The Present Relations of Physical Science to Mental Philosophy', *CR*, 16 (1870–1), 225–38.

Camerini, J. R., 'Evolution, Biogeography, and Maps: An Early History of Wallace's Line', *Isis*, 84 (1993), 700–27.

Cardwell, D. S. L., *The Organisation of Science in England* (Heinemann, 1972).

Carlyle, T., *On Heroes, Hero-Worship, and the Heroic in History* (New York, Chelsea House, 1983).

Caron, J. A., '"Biology" in the Life Sciences: A Historiographical Contribution', *HS*, 26 (1988), 223–68.

Carpenter, W. B., 'On the Doctrine of Human Automatism', *CR*, 25 (1875), 397–416, 940–62.

Catlett, S., 'Huxley, Hutton and the "White Rage": A Debate on Vivisection at the Metaphysical Society', *ANH*, 11 (1983), 181–9.

Chadarevian, S. de, 'Laboratory Science versus Country-House Experiments. The Controversy between Julius Sachs and Charles Darwin', *BJHS*, 29 (1996), 17–41.

Chilton, W., 'Geological Revelations', *Oracle of Reason*, 29 Aug. 1843.

Christie, J. D., 'A Working Man's Reply to Professor Huxley', *NC*, 27 (1890), 476–83.

Clark, R. W., *The Huxleys* (Heinemann, 1968).

[E.Clodd], 'The Right Hon. Thomas Henry Huxley', *Daily Chronicle*, 1 July 1895.

Cockshut, A. O. J., *The Unbelievers: English Agnostic Thought 1840–1890* (Collins, 1964).

Colbert, E. H., *Men and Dinosaurs* (Penguin, 1971).

Cole, G. D. H., and R. Postgate, *The Common People 1746–1946* (Methuen, 1966).

Coleman, D., and T. Mansell, 'Science, Religion and the London School Board: Aspects of the Life and Work of John Hall Gladstone (1827–1902)', *History of Education*, 24 (1995), 141–58.

Coleridge, S. T., *On the Constitution of the Church and State According to the Idea of Each* (Dent, 1972).

Collie, M., *Huxley at Work: With the Scientific Correspondence of T. H. Huxley and the Rev. Dr George Gordon of Birnie, near Elgin* (Macmillan, 1991).

Collier, J., *The Religion of an Artist* (Watts, 1926).

Collini, S., *Public Moralists: Political Thought and Intellectual Life in Britain 1850–1930* (Oxford, Clarendon Press, 1993).

Colp, R., *To Be an Invalid: The Illness of Charles Darwin* (UCP, 1977).

—, 'Notes on William Gladstone, Karl Marx, Charles Darwin, Kliment Timiriazev, and the "Eastern Question" of 1876–78', *J. Hist. Med.*, 38 (1983), 178–85.

Conway, M., 'Huxley', *South Place Magazine*, 1 (9) (1895), 73–5.

Cooter, R., and S. Pumfrey, 'Separate Spheres and Public Places: Reflections on the History of Science Popularization and Science in Public Culture', *HS*, 32 (1994), 237–67.

Cope, E.D, 'Descriptions of Extinct Batrachia and Reptilia from the Permian Formation of Texas', *Proc. Am. Phil. Soc.*, 17 (1878), 505–30.

—, 'Second Contribution to the History of the Vertebrata of the Permian Formation of Texas', *Proc. Am. Phil. Soc.*, 19 (1882), 38–58.

—, 'The Relations Between the Theromorphous Reptiles and the Monotreme Mammalia', *Proc. Am. Assoc. Adv. Sci.*, 33 (1884), 471–82.

Cosans, C., 'Anatomy, Metaphysics, and Values: The Ape Brain Debate Reconsidered', *Biology and Philosophy*, 9 (1994), 129–65.

Cowen, D. L., 'Liberty, Laissez-Faire and Licensure in Nineteenth Century Britain', *Bull. Hist. Med.*, 43 (1969), 30–40.

Crane, W. 'The Marriage of Science and Industry', *Pall Mall Gazette*, 20 Jan. 1887.

Crook, P., *Darwinism, War and History* (CUP, 1994).

Dale, P. A., *In Pursuit of a Scientific Culture: Science, Art and Society in the Victorian Age* (Madison, University of Wisconsin Press, 1989).

Darwin, C., *The Descent of Man, Selection in Relation to Sex* (Murray, 1877).
—, *The Autobiography of Charles Darwin 1809–1882*, ed. N. Barlow (New York, Norton, 1958).
Darwin, F., ed., *The Foundations of the Origin of Species. Two Essays Written in 1842 and 1844* (CUP, 1909).
—, ed., *The Life and Letters of Charles Darwin* 2 vols (Murray, 1887).
— and A. C. Seward, eds, *More Letters of Charles Darwin* 2 vols (Murray, 1903).
Davidoff, L., and C. Hall, *Family Fortunes: Men and Women of the English Middle Class, 1780–1850* (UCP, 1987).
Davies, C. M., *Heterodox London* 2 vols (Tinsley, 1874).
[Dawkins, W. B.], 'Darwin on the Descent of Man', *ER*, 134 (1871), 195–235.
Deacon, M., *Scientists and the Sea 1650–1900* (Academic Press, 1971).
Dean, D. R., 'Hitchcock's Dinosaur Tracks', *Am. Quart.*, 21 (1969), 639–44.
Denis, R. D., 'The Brompton Barracks: War, Peace, and the Rise of Victorian Art and Education', *Journal of Design History*, 8 (1995), 11–25.
Dennis, B., and D. Skilton, eds, *Reform and Intellectual Debate in Victorian England* (Croom Helm, 1987).
Desmond, A., *Archetypes and Ancestors: Palaeontology in Victorian London 1850–1875* (Blond & Briggs, 1982; UCP, 1984).
—, 'The Making of Institutional Zoology in London 1822–1836', *HS*, 23 (1985), 153–85, 224–50.
—, 'Artisan Resistance and Evolution in Britain, 1819–1848', *Osiris*, 3 (1987), 77–110.
—, *The Politics of Evolution: Morphology, Medicine, and Reform in Radical London* (UCP, 1989).
—, 'Foreword' to Ospovat, *Development of Darwin's Theory* (CUP pbk, 1995).
—, 'Author's Response' in Review Symposium: 'Huxley, A. D.', *Metascience*, 7 (1995), 27–55.
— and J. Moore, *Darwin* (Michael Joseph, 1991).
Detrosier, R., *Lecture on the Utility of Political Unions, for the Diffusion of Moral & Political Information Amongst the People; On the Necessity for that Information, and on the Political Influence of Scientific Knowledge* (Brooks, 1832).
Di Gregorio, M., *T. H. Huxley's Place in Natural Science* (New Haven, Yale UP, 1984).
—, 'A Wolf in Sheep's Clothing: Carl Gegenbaur, Ernst Haeckel, the Vertebral Theory of the Skull, and the Survival of Richard Owen', *JHB*, 28 (1995), 247–80.
Dockrill, D. W., 'T. H. Huxley and the Meaning of "Agnosticism"', *Theology*, 74 (1971), 461–77.
Draper, J. W., *History of the Conflict Between Religion and Science* (New York, Appleton, 1874).
Drower, M. S., *Flinders Petrie: A Life in Archaeology* (Gollancz, 1985).
Drummond, H., *The Lowell Lectures on the Ascent of Man* (Hodder & Stoughton, 1894).
Dubois, M. E. F. T., 'The Place of "*Pithecanthropus*" in the Genealogical Tree', *Nature*, 53 (1896), 245–7.
Duncan, D., ed., *The Life and Letters of Herbert Spencer* (Williams & Norgate, 1911).
Duncan, P. M., 'Anniversary Address', *QJGS*, 33 (1877), 41–88.

Dupree, A. H., *Asa Gray, 1810–1888* (New York, Athenaeum, 1968).
Durant, J., 'Scientific Naturalism and Social Reform in the Thought of Alfred Russel Wallace', *BJHS*, 12 (1979), 31–58.
—, 'The Ascent of Nature in Darwin's *Descent of Man*', in D. Kohn, ed., *The Darwinian Heritage* (Princeton UP, 1985), 283–306.
Edgerton, D., *Science, Technology and the British Industrial 'Decline' 1870–1970* (CUP 1996).
Eisen, S., 'Huxley and the Positivists', *VS*, 7 (1964), 337–58.
Ellegard, A., *Darwin and the General Reader: The Reception of Darwin's Theory of Evolution in the British Periodical Press, 1859–1872* (UCP, 1990).
Erskine, F., '*The Origin of Species* and the Science of Female Inferiority', in Amigoni and Wallace, *Darwin's Origin*, 95–121.
Escott, T. H. S., *Masters of English Journalism* (Westport, Conn., Greenwood, 1970).
Estes, J. W., *Dictionary of Protopharmacology. Therapeutic Practices, 1700–1850* (New York, Science History Publications, 1990).
Eve, A. S., and C. H. Creasey, *Life and Work of John Tyndall* (Macmillan, 1945).
Farley, J., *The Spontaneous Generation Controversy from Descartes to Oparin* (Baltimore, Johns Hopkins UP, 1977).
Fawcett, J. W., 'Thomas Henry Huxley', *Unity*, 95 (1925), 207–10.
Fiske, J., 'Reminiscences of Huxley', *Ann. Rep. Smithsonian Inst.*, (1901), 713–28.
—, *Darwinism and Other Essays* (Boston, Mass., Houghton, Mifflin, 1902).
—, *A Century of Science and Other Essays* (Boston, Mass., Houghton, Mifflin, 1902).
—, *The Personal Letters of John Fiske* (Cedar Rapids, Iowa, Torch Press, 1939).
Flexner, A., *Daniel Coit Gilman* (New York, Harcourt, Brace, 1946).
Flower, W. H., 'Introductory Lecture', *Medical Times and Gazette*, 1 (1870), 195–200.
Flürscheim, M., 'Professor Huxley's Attacks', *NC*, 27 (1890), 639–50.
Foot, M. R. D., and H. C. G. Matthew, eds, *The Gladstone Diaries* 15 vols (Oxford, Clarendon Press, 1968–1994).
Foote, G. W., *Defence of Free Speech: Being a Three Hours' Address to the Jury in the Court of Queen's Bench before Lord Coleridge on April 24, 1883* (Progressive Publishing Co., 1889).
Forgan, S., 'The Architecture of Display: Museums, Universities and Objects in Nineteenth-Century Britain', *HS*, 32 (1994), 139–62.
— and G. Gooday, '"A Fungoid Assemblage of Buildings": Diversity and Adversity in the Development of College Architecture and Scientific Education in Nineteenth-Century South Kensington', *History of Universities*, 13 (1994), 153–92.
—, 'Constructing South Kensington: The Buildings and Politics of T. H. Huxley's Working Environment', *BJHS*, 29 (1996).
Foster, M., 'A Few More Words on Thomas Henry Huxley', *Nature*, 1 Aug. 1895, 318–20.
Freeman, D., 'The Evolutionary Theories of Charles Darwin and Herbert Spencer', *Current Anthropology*, 15 (1974), 211–37.
French, R. D., *Antivivisection and Medical Science in Victorian Society* (Princeton, Princeton UP, 1975).
Friday, J., 'A Microscopic Incident in a Monumental Struggle: Huxley and Antibiosis in 1875', *BJHS*, 7 (1974), 61–71.
'Friend, A', 'Professor Huxley's Homes', *Illustrated London News*, 6 July 1895.

Galton, F., 'Statistical Enquiries into the Efficacy of Prayer', *FR*, 18 (1872), 125–35.

Gardiner, A. G., *The Life of Sir William Harcourt* 2 vols (Constable, 1923).

Gates, B. T., 'Revisioning Darwin, With Sympathy', *Hist. Eur. Ideas*, 19 (1994), 761–8.

Geddes, P., 'Huxley as Teacher', *Nature*, 115 (1925), 740–3.

Geison, G. L., *Michael Foster and the Cambridge School of Physiology* (Princeton UP, 1978).

Gilbert, S. F., 'Altruism and Other Unnatural Acts: T. H. Huxley on Nature, Man, and Society', *Perspectives in Biology and Medicine*, 22 (1979), 346–58.

Gillespie, N. C., 'The Duke of Argyll, Evolutionary Anthropology, and the Art of Scientific Controversy', *Isis*, 68 (1977), 40–54.

Gilley, S., and A. Loades, 'Thomas Henry Huxley: The War between Science and Religion', *Journal of Religion*, 61 (1981), 285–308.

Girouard, M., *Alfred Waterhouse and the Natural History Museum* (BM[NH], 1981).

Glick, T. F., ed., *The Comparative Reception of Darwinism* (UCP, 1988).

Godlee, R. J., 'Thomas Wharton Jones', *Brit. J. Ophthalmol.*, 93 (1921) 97–117, 145–56.

Goetzmann, W. H., *Exploration and Empire: The Explorer and the Scientist in the Winning of the American West* (New York, Norton, 1978).

Gooday, G., 'Precision Measurement and the Genesis of Physics Teaching Laboratories in Victorian Britain', *BJHS*, 23 (1990), 25–51.

—, '"Nature" in the Laboratory: Domestication and Discipline with the Microscope in Victorian Life Science', *BJHS*, 24 (1991), 307–41.

Gooding, D., T. Pinch and S. Schaffer, eds, *The Uses of Experiment* (CUP, 1989).

Gould, S. J., *Ontogeny and Phylogeny* (Cambridge, Mass., Harvard UP, 1977).

Grant, R. E., 'Lectures on Comparative Anatomy and Animal Physiology', *Lancet*, 1–2 (1833–4), 60 lectures.

—, *Tabular View of the Primary Divisions of the Animal Kingdom* (Walton and Maberly, 1861).

Green, L., '"Strange [In]difference to Sex": Thomas Hardy, the Victorian Man of Letters, and The Temptations of Androgyny', *VS*, 38 (1995), 523–49.

Greene, J. C., 'Darwin as a Social Evolutionist', *JHB*, 10 (1977), 1–27.

Greenwood, H, *General Booth and His Critics: Being an Analysis of the Scheme and an Enquiry into the Value of the Criticisms of Professor Huxley, Mr. C. S. Loch, "The Times" Newspaper, and Other Critics* (Howe, n.d.).

Grene, M., 'Recent Biographies of Darwin: The Complexity of Context', *Perspectives on Science*, 1 (1993), 659–75.

Gruber, H. E., and P. H. Barrett, *Darwin on Man* (New York, Dutton, 1974).

Gruber, J. W., *A Conscience in Conflict. The Life of St. George Jackson Mivart* (New York, Columbia UP, 1960).

—, 'The Richard Owen Correspondence: An Introductory Essay', in Gruber and Thackray, *Owen Commemoration*, 1–24.

—, 'Richard Owen and his Correspondents', in Gruber and Thackray, *Owen Commemoration*, 25–93.

— and J. C. Thackray, *Richard Owen Commemoration* (Natural History Museum Publications, 1992).

Haeckel, E., 'Scientific Worthies II. – Thomas Henry Huxley', *Nature*, 9 (1874), 257–8.

—, *The History of Creation* 2 vols (New York, Appleton, 1876).
—, *Freedom in Science and Teaching* (Kegan Paul, 1879).
—, *The Evolution of Man*, trans. J. McCabe (Watts, 1907).
Haight, G. S., *The George Eliot Letters* 9 vols (New Haven, Yale UP, 1954–6, 1978).
Hall, C., *Memoirs of Marshall Hall* (Bentley, 1861).
Hall, M. B., 'The Royal Society in Thomas Henry Huxley's Time', *NRRS*, 38 (1983–4), 153–8.
Hall, V. M. D., 'The Contribution of the Physiologist, William Benjamin Carpenter (1813–1885), to the Development of the Principle of the Correlation of Forces and the Conservation of Energy', *Med. Hist*, 23 (1979) 129–55.
Harris, J., *Private Lives, Public Spirit: Britain 1870–1914* (Penguin, 1994).
Harrison, B., 'Animals and the State in Nineteenth-Century England', *Eng. Hist. Rev.*, 88 (1973), 786–820.
Harrison, F., 'The Future of Agnosticism', *FR*, 45 (1889), 144–56.
Harte, N., *The University of London 1836–1986* (Athlone Press, 1986).
— and J. North, *The World of UCL 1828–1990* (University College London, 1991).
Hearl, T., 'Military Examination and the Teaching of Science, 1857–1870', in Macleod, *Days of Judgement*, 109–49.
Heimann, P. M., 'The *Unseen Universe*: Physics and the Philosophy of Nature in Victorian Britain', *BJHS*, 6 (1972), 73–9.
Helfand, M. S., 'T. H. Huxley's "Evolution and Ethics": The Politics of Evolution and the Evolution of Politics', *VS*, 20 (1977), 159–77.
Hepton, D., *Methodism and Politics in British Society, 1750–1850* (Hutchinson, 1984).
Heyck, T. W., *The Transformation of Intellectual Life in Victorian England* (Croom Helm, 1982).
Hilgartner, S., 'The Dominant View of Popularization: Conceptual Problems, Political Uses', *Social Studies of Science*, 20 (1990), 519–39.
Hodge, M. J. S., 'The Universal Gestation of Nature: Chambers' *Vestiges* and *Explanations*', *JHB*, 5 (1972), 127–51.
Hodges, S. H., *General Booth: 'The Family', and the Salvation Army* (Manchester, For the Author, 1890).
Hofstadter, R., *Social Darwinism in American Thought* (Boston, Mass., Beacon Press, 1955).
Hollowday, E. D., 'Thomas Henry Huxley and the Microscope', *Quekett Journal of Microscopy*, 37 (1995), 437–54.
Holyoake, G. J., 'The Priesthood of Science: Their Visit to Norwich', *Reasoner Review*, 1 Nov. 1868, 1–8.
Horne, A., *The Fall of Paris: The Siege and Commune 1870–71* (Pan, 1968).
Howarth, J., 'Science Education in Late-Victorian Oxford: A Curious Case of Failure?', *English Historical Review*, 102 (1987), 334–71.
Hull, D., *Darwin and his Critics* (UCP, 1983).
[Hutton, R. H.], 'The Great Agnostic', *Spectator*, 6 July 1895.
Huxley, Andrew, 'Grandfather and Grandson', *NRRS*, 38 (1983–4), 147–51.
Huxley, Leonard, ed., *Life and Letters of Thomas Henry Huxley* 2 vols (Macmillan, 1900).
—, ed., *Life and Letters of Sir Joseph Dalton Hooker* 2 vols (Murray, 1918).
[Huxley, Thomas Henry], 'Schamyl, the Prophet-Warrior of the Caucasus', *WR*, 61 (1854), 480–519.

[—], 'Contemporary Literature – Science', *WR*, 64 (1855), 240–55; 65 (1856), 261–71.
[—], 'Science and "Church Policy"', *Reader*, 4 (1864), 821.
—, 'The Natural History of Creation', *Academy*, 1 (1869), 13–14, 40–3.
—, 'The Forefathers of the English People', *Nature*, 1 (1870), 514–15.
—, 'The Deep-Sea Soundings and Geology', *Nature*, 1 (1870), 657–8.
—, 'To the Ratepayers of the Marylebone Division', (1870), flysheet.
—, 'The Royal School of Mines', *Times*, 11 Apr. 1871.
—, 'Kew Gardens', *Times*, 31 July 1872.
—, *Critiques and Addresses* (Macmillan, 1873).
—, 'Professor Huxley at Manchester', *Nature*, 10 (1874), 455–7.
—, 'Miss Jex-Blake and Her Examiners', *Times*, 8 July 1874.
—, 'Anthropogenie', *Academy*, 7 (1875), 16–18.
—, 'Notes from the "Challenger"', *Nature*, 12 (1875), 315–16.
—, 'The Article "Birds" in "Encyclopaedia Britannica"', *Nature*, 13 (1876), 247.
—, 'Professor Huxley on Lord Shaftesbury', *Times*, 26 May 1876.
—, 'Dinner to the Challenger Staff', *Nature*, 14 (1876), 238–9.
—, 'Evidences of Evolution', *New-York Daily Tribune*, 19, 21, 23 Sept. 1876.
—, *Physiography: An Introduction to the Study of Nature* [1877] (Macmillan, 1887).
—, 'A Modern "Symposium"', *NC*, 1 (1877), 536–9.
—, *A Manual of the Anatomy of Invertebrated Animals* (New York, Appleton, 1878).
—, [Speech], *Journal of the Quekett Microscopical Club*, 5 (1878), 47–9.
—, [On a New Arrangement of Lenses for Dissecting], *Journal of the Quekett Microscopical Club*, 5 (1878), 144–5.
—, 'Scientific Worthies XII. – William Harvey', *Nature*, 17 (1878), 417–20.
—, 'Prefatory Note' in Haeckel, *Freedom in Science*, v–xx.
—, 'On the Characters of the Pelvis in the Mammalia, and the Conclusions Respecting the Origin of Mammals which may be based on them', *Proc. Roy. Soc.*, 28 (1879), 395–405.
—, 'President's Address', *Journal of the Quekett Microscopical Club*, 6 (1879), 250–5.
—, 'On the Application of the Laws of Evolution to the Arrangement of the Vertebrata, and more particularly of the Mammalia', *Proc. Zool. Soc.*, 43 (1880), 649–62.
—, *The Crayfish: An Introduction to the Study of Zoology* (Kegan Paul, 1880).
—, 'The First Volume of the Publications of the "Challenger"', *Nature*, 23 (1880), 1–3.
—, *Twenty First Annual Report of the Inspector of Fisheries (England and Wales)* (1881).
—, 'Distribution of Awards, Normal School of Science and Royal School of Mines', *Nature*, 26 (1882), 233–5.
—, 'Prize Distribution at the Liverpool Institute', *Liverpool Mercury*, 17 Feb. 1883.
—, 'Unwritten History', *Macmillan's Magazine*, 48 (26 Apr. 1883), 26–41.
—, 'President's Address', *Proc. Roy. Soc.*, 36 (1883), 60–73.
—, ['Agnosticism', pirated letter], *Agnostic Annual*, (1884), 5–6.
—, 'President's Address', *Proc. Roy. Soc.*, 39 (1885), 278–99.
—, 'Proposed Fishery Board', *Times*, after 20 Mar. 1886.

—, 'The Home-Rule Bill', *Standard*, 13 Apr. 1886.
—, 'English Literature and the Universities', *Pall Mall Gazette*, 22 Oct. 1886.
—, 'The Queen's Jubilee', *Pall Mall Gazette*, 13 Jan. 1887.
—, 'The Imperial Institute', *Times*, 20 Jan., 19, 22 Feb. 1887.
—, 'The Organization of Industrial Education', *Times*, 21 Mar. 1887.
—, 'Royal Academy Address', *Times*, 2 May 1887.
—, 'On Free Libraries', *Daily Chronicle*, 8 June 1887.
—, 'From the Hut to the Pantheon', *Youth's Companion*, 23 June 1887, 281–2.
—, 'An Olive Branch from America', *NC*, 22 (1887), 620–4.
—, 'British Race-Types of To-Day', *Times*, 12 Oct. 1887.
—, 'On the Reception of the Origin of Species', in F. Darwin, *Life*, 2:179–204.
—, 'Bishop Wilberforce and Professor Huxley', *Times*, 1 Dec. 1887.
[—], 'M.P., P.R.S.', *Nature*, 37 (1887), 49–50.
—, 'How to Become an Orator', *Pall Mall Gazette*, 24 Oct. 1888, 1–2.
—, 'Spiritualism Unmasked', *Pall Mall Gazette*, 1 Jan. 1889, 1–2.
—, 'Sea Fisheries', *Times*, 4, 8 Jan. 1889.
—, 'Mr. Spencer on the Land Question', *Times*, 12 Nov. 1889.
—, 'Political Ethics', *Times*, 18 Nov. 1889.
—, 'The Ownership of the Land', *Times*, 21 Nov. 1889.
—, 'Are Men Born Free and Equal?', *Daily Telegraph*, 27, 29, 30 Jan. 1890.
—, *Social Diseases and Worse Remedies* (Macmillan, 1891).
—, [Letter on the Bus Strike], *Trade Unionist*, 20 June 1891.
—, *Essays upon some Controverted Questions* (Macmillan, 1892).
—, 'The Royal School of Mines', *Times*, 16 Jan. 1892.
—, 'An Apologetic Irenicon', *FR*, 52 (1892), 557–71.
—, 'Professorial University for London', *Times*, 7 July, 6 Dec. 1892.
[—], 'Criticism of the Royal Society', *Nature*, 47 (1892), 145–6.
—, *Collected Essays* 9 vols (Macmillan, 1893–4).
—, 'Professor Tyndall', *NC*, 35 (1894), 1–11.
—, 'Past and Present', *Nature*, 51 (1894), 1–3.
—, 'Mr. Balfour's Attack on Agnosticism', *NC*, 37 (1895), 527–40.
—, *The Scientific Memoirs of Thomas Henry Huxley*, ed. M. Foster and E. R. Lankester, 5 vols (Macmillan, 1898–1902).
— *et al.*, *School Board for London. First Report. The Scheme of Education Committee. 13 June 1871* (Yates & Alexander, 1871).
— and H. N. Martin, *A Course of Elementary Instruction in Practical Biology*, revised by G. B. Howes and D. H. Scott (Macmillan, 1888).
Irvine, W., *Apes, Angels, and Victorians: Darwin, Huxley, and Evolution* (Cleveland, Meridian, 1959).
Jackson, H., *The Eighteen Nineties* (Pelican, 1950).
Jacyna, L. S., 'Science and Social Order in the Thought of A. J. Balfour', *Isis*, 71 (1980), 11–34.
—, 'The Physiology of Mind, The Unity of Nature, and the Moral Order in Victorian Thought', *BJHS*, 14 (1981), 109–32.
—, 'Immanence or Transcendence: Theories of Life and Organization in Britain, 1790–1835', *Isis*, 74 (1983), 311–29.
Jann, R., 'Darwin and the Anthropologists: Sexual Selection and Its Discontents', *VS*, 37 (1994), 287–306.
Jardine, N., J. A. Secord and E. C. Spary, eds, *Cultures of Natural History* (CUP, 1996).

Jensen, J. V., *Thomas Henry Huxley: Communicating for Science* (Associated University Presses, 1991).
—, 'Thomas Henry Huxley's Address at the Opening of the Johns Hopkins University in September 1876', *NRRS*, 47 (1993), 257–69.
Jones, H. F., *Samuel Butler: A Memoir* 2 vols (Macmillan, 1920).
Jones, G., *Social Darwinism and English Thought: The Interaction Between Biological and Social Theory* (Brighton, Harvester, 1980).
—, 'Social Darwinism Revisited', *Hist. Eur. Ideas*, 19 (1994), 769–75.
Jones, G. S., *Outcast London* (Penguin, 1984).
J. P. A., 'Professor Huxley on Darwin's "Origin of Species"', *NR*, 31 Jan. 1863, 2–3.
Judd, J. W., *The Coming of Evolution* (CUP, 1911).
Kamil, J., *Luxor: A Guide to Ancient Thebes* (Longman, 1973).
Keith, A., 'Huxley as Anthropologist', *Nature*, 115 (1925), 719–23.
—, *An Autobiography* (Watts, 1950).
Kelly, A., *The Descent of Darwin: The Popularization of Darwinism in Germany, 1860–1914* (Chapel Hill, University of North Carolina Press, 1981).
Kidd, B., *Social Evolution* (Macmillan, 1895).
King, C., 'Catastrophism and Evolution', *Amer. Nat.*, 11 (1877), 449–70.
Kingsley, F., ed., *Charles Kingsley: His Letters and Memories of his Life* 2 vols (Kegan Paul, 1881).
Knight, D., 'T. H. Huxley: The Devil's Disciple?', *Dialogue*, 5 (1995), 31–4.
—, 'Getting Science Across', *BJHS*, 29 (1996), 129–38.
Kottler, M. J., 'Alfred Russel Wallace, the Origin of Man, and Spiritualism', *Isis*, 65 (1974), 145–92.
Kovalevskii, V., 'On the Osteology of the Hyopotamidae', *Phil. Trans. Roy. Soc.*, 163 (1873), 19–94.
Kropotkin, P., 'Mutual Aid among Animals', *NC*, 28 (1890), 337–54.
Lafargue, P., 'Primitive Communism', *Commonweal*, 6 (12 Apr. 1890), 114–15.
Lang, A., 'Science and Demonology', *Illustrated London News*, 30 Jan. 1894, 822.
Lankester, E., 'The Representation of Science at the School Board', *Nature*, 2 (1870), 509–10.
Lankester, E. R., 'On the Use of the Term Homology in Modern Zoology', *AMNH*, 6 (1870), 34–43, 342.
—, 'Instruction to Science Teachers at South Kensington', *Nature*, 4 (1871), 361–4.
—, 'On the Primitive Cell-Layers of the Embryo as the Basis of Genealogical Classification of Animals', *AMNH*, 11 (1873), 321–38.
—, 'Notes on the Embryology and Classification of the Animal Kingdom: Comprising a Revision of Speculations Relative to the Origin and Significance of the Germ-Layers', *Quart. J. Micros. Soc.*, 17 (1877), 399–554.
—, *Degeneration: A Chapter in Darwinism* (Macmillan, 1880).
—, *The Advancement of Science* (Macmillan, 1890).
—, 'The Right Hon. T. H. Huxley', *Athenaeum*, 6 July 1895.
Lansbury, C., 'Gynaecology, Pornography, and the Antivivisectionist Movement', *VS*, 28 (1985), 413–37.
Laurent, J., 'Science, Society and Politics in Late Nineteenth-Century England: A Further Look at Mechanics' Institutes', *Social Studies of Science*, 14 (1984), 585–619.
La Vergata, A., *Le Biografie Scientifiche*, *Intersezioni*, 15 (1995), 1–184.

Lester, J., ed. P. J. Bowler, *E. Ray Lankester and the Making of Modern British Biology* (Faringdon, British Society for the History of Science, 1995).
Lewin, L., *Phantastica: Narcotic and Stimulating Drugs* (Kegan Paul, 1931).
Lightman, B., 'Pope Huxley and the Church Agnostic: The Religion of Science', *Historical Papers* (1983), 150–63.
—, *The Origins of Agnosticism: Victorian Unbelief and the Limits of Knowledge* (Baltimore, Johns Hopkins UP, 1987).
—, 'Ideology, Evolution and Late-Victorian Agnostic Popularizers', in Moore, *History*, 285–309.
—, '"Fighting Even With Death": Balfour, Scientific Naturalism, and Huxley's Final Battle', in Barr, *Huxley's Place.*
—, '"The Voices of Nature": Popularizing Victorian Science', in Lightman, *Victorian Science.*
—, ed., *Victorian Science in Context* (UCP, 1997).
Lilly, W. S., 'Materialism and Morality', *FR*, 40 (1886), 575–94.
Linklater, E., *The Voyage of the Challenger* (Murray, 1972).
Litchfield, H., ed., *Emma Darwin. A Century of Family Letters, 1792–1896* 2 vols (Murray, 1915).
Livingstone, D. N., *Darwin's Forgotten Defenders: The Encounter Between Evangelical Theology and Evolutionary Thought* (Edinburgh, Scottish Academic Press, 1987).
—, 'Darwinism and Calvinism: The Belfast–Princeton Connection', *Isis*, 83 (1992), 408–28.
L.L.D., 'Professor Huxley as Schoolmaster', *NR*, 31 Dec. 1871, 422–3.
Lorimer, D. A., *Colour, Class and the Victorians: English Attitudes to the Negro in the Mid-Nineteenth Century* (Leicester UP, 1978).
—, 'Theoretical Racism in Late Victorian Anthropology, 1870–1900', *VS*, 31 (1988), 405–30.
Lyell, [K. M.], *Life, Letters and Journals of Sir Charles Lyell, Bart* 2 vols (Murray, 1881).
Lyons, S. L., 'The Origins of T.H.Huxley's Saltationism: History in Darwin's Shadow', *JHB*, 28 (1995), 463–94.
McCabe, J., *Prehistoric Man* (Milner, 1912).
McCready, T. L., 'The Worship of Istar', *Standard*, 17 Mar. 1888.
MacLeod, R. M., 'Government and Resource Conservation: The Salmon Acts Administration, 1860–1886', *Journal of British Studies*, 7 (1968), 114–50.
—, 'The Support of Victorian Science: The Endowment of Research Movement in Great Britain, 1868–1900', *Minerva*, 4 (1971), 197–230.
—, 'Science and the Civil List, 1824–1914', *Technology and Society*, 6 (1970), 47–55.
—, 'The Royal Society and the Government Grant: Notes on the Administration of Scientific Research, 1849–1914', *Historical Journal*, 14 (1971), 323–58.
—, 'Of Medals and Men: A Reward System in Victorian Science 1826–1914', *NRRS*, 26 (1971), 81–108.
—, 'The Ayrton Incident: A Commentary on the Relations of Science and Government in England, 1870–1873', in A. Thackray and E. Mendelsohn, eds, *Science and Values: Patterns of Tradition and Change* (New York, Humanities Press, 1974), 45–78.
—, 'Science and the Treasury: Principles, Personalities and Policies, 1870–85', in Turner, *Patronage*, 115–72.

—, 'Evolutionism, Internationalism and Commercial Enterprise in Science: The International Scientific Series 1871–1910', in A. J. Meadows, ed., *Development of Science Publishing in Europe* (Amsterdam, Elsevier, 1980), 63–93.
—, ed., *Days of Judgement: Science, Examinations and the Organization of Knowledge* (Driffield, Studies in Education, 1982).
—, *Public Science and Public Policy in Victorian England* (Variorum, 1996).
Magnus, P., *Gladstone* (Murray, 1963).
Maienschein, J., *Transforming Traditions in American Biology, 1880–1915* (Baltimore, Johns Hopkins UP, 1991).
—, '"It's a Long Way from *Amphioxus*": Anton Dohrn and Late Nineteenth Century Debates about Vertebrate Origins', *Hist. Phil. Life Sci.*, 16 (1994), 465–78.
Mairet, P., *Pioneer of Sociology: The Life and Letters of Patrick Geddes* (Lund Humphries, 1957).
Marsh, O. C., 'Discovery of a Remarkable Fossil Bird', *Am. J. Sci.*, 3 (1872), 56–7.
—, 'Notice of New Equine Mammals from the Tertiary Formation', *Am. J. Sci.*, 7 (1874), 247–58.
—, 'Notice of a New and Gigantic Dinosaur', *Am. J. Sci.*, 14 (1877), 87–8.
—, 'A New Order of Extinct Reptilia (Stegosauria) from the Jurassic of the Rocky Mountains', *Am. J. Sci.*, 14 (1877), 513–14.
—, 'Fossil Mammal from the Jurassic of the Rocky Mountains', *Am. J. Sci.*, 15 (1878), 459.
—, 'Notice of Jurassic Mammals Representing Two New Orders', *Am. J. Sci.*, 20 (1880), 235–9.
—, *Introduction and Succession of Fossil Life in America: An Address Delivered Before the American Association for the Advancement of Science, at Nashville, Tenn., Aug. 30, 1877*, offprint, pp.1–50.
—, *Odontornithes: A Monograph on the Extinct Toothed Birds of North America* (Washington, Government Printing Office, 1880).
—, 'Thomas Henry Huxley', *Am. J. Sci.*, 50 (1895), 177–83.
Meadows, A. J., *Science and Controversy: A Biography of Sir Norman Lockyer* (Macmillan, 1972).
Milner, R., 'Darwin for the Prosecution, Wallace for the Defence', *North Country Naturalist*, 2 (1990), 19–50.
Mitchell, P. Chalmers, 'Huxley', *New Review*, 13 (1895), 147–55.
Mivart, St G., *On the Genesis of Species* (Macmillan, 1871).
—, 'On *Lepilemur* and *Cheirogaleus*, and the Zoological Rank of the *Lemuroidea*', *Proc. Zool. Soc.*, (1873), 484–510.
—, 'On the Possibly Dual Origin of the Mammalia', *Proc. Roy. Soc.*, 34 (1888), 372–9.
—, 'Evolution in Professor Huxley', *NC*, 34 (1893), 198–211.
—, 'Some Reminiscences of Thomas Henry Huxley', *NC*, 42 (1897), 985–98.
Moore, A. L., 'Evolution and Christianity', in *Oxford House Papers* (Rivingtons, 1889), 148–182.
—, *Science and the Faith* (Kegan Paul, 1889).
Moore, J. R., *The Post-Darwinian Controversies: A Study of the Protestant Struggle to Come to Terms with Darwin in Great Britain and America 1870–1900* (CUP, 1979).
—, 'Charles Darwin Lies in Westminster Abbey', *Biol. J. Linn. Soc.*, 17 (1982), 97–113.

—, 'Evangelicals and Evolution: Henry Drummond, Herbert Spencer, and the Naturalisation of the Spiritual World', *Scot. J. Theol.*, 38 (1985), 383–417.

—, 'Socializing Darwinism: Historiography and the Fortunes of a Phrase', in L. Levidow, ed., *Science as Politics* (Free Association Books, 1986), 38–80.

—, 'Freethought, Secularism, Agnosticism: The Case of Charles Darwin', in G. Parsons, ed., *Religion in Victorian Britain. Volume 1* (Manchester UP, 1988), 274–319.

—, ed., *Religion in Victorian Britain. Volume 3: Sources* (Manchester UP, 1988).

—, ed., *History, Humanity and Evolution* (CUP, 1989).

—, 'Theodicy and Society: The Crisis of the Intelligentsia', in R. Helmstadter and B. Lightman, eds, *Victorian Faith in Crisis* (Macmillan, 1990), 153–86.

—, 'Crisis without Revolution: The Ideological Watershed in Victorian England', *Revue de Synthèse*, 4 (1986), 53–78.

—, 'Deconstructing Darwinism: The Politics of Evolution in the 1860s', *JHB*, 24 (1991), 353–408.

—, *The Darwin Legend* (Grand Rapids, Baker Books, 1994).

—, 'Metabiographical Reflections on Charles Darwin', in Shortland and Yeo, *Telling Lives*, 267–81.

—, 'Wallace's Malthusian Moment: The Common Context Revisited', in Lightman, *Victorian Science*.

Morley, J., *The Life of Richard Cobden* (Fisher Unwin, 1903).

—, *Recollections* 2 vols (Macmillan, 1917).

Morrell, J. B., 'The Patronage of Mid-Victorian Science in the University of Edinburgh', *Science Studies*, 3 (1973), 353–88.

Morris, J., *Heaven's Command: An Imperial Progress* (Penguin, 1979).

Nyhart, L. K., *Biology Takes Form: Animal Morphology and the German Universities, 1800–1900* (UCP, 1995).

—, 'Natural History and the "New" Biology', in Jardine, Secord and Spary, *Cultures*, 426–43.

O'Connor, W. J., *Founders of British Physiology* (Manchester UP, 1988).

Oldroyd, D., and I. Langham, eds, *The Wider Domain of Evolutionary Thought* (Dordrecht, Reidel, 1983).

Ophir, A., and S. Shapin, 'The Place of Knowledge: A Methodological Survey', *Science in Context*, 4 (1991), 3–21.

Osborn, H. F., 'Memorial Tribute to Prof. Thomas H. Huxley', *Trans. N.Y. Acad. Sci.*, 15 (1895), 40–50.

—, 'Enduring Recollections', *Nature*, 115 (1925), 726–8.

Ospovat, D., 'The Influence of Karl Ernst von Baer's Embryology, 1828–1859: A Reappraisal in Light of Richard Owen's and William B. Carpenter's "Palaeontological Application of 'Von Baer's Law'"', *JHB*, 9 (1976), 1–28.

—, *The Development of Darwin's Theory: Natural History, Natural Theology, and Natural Selection 1838–1859* (CUP, 1981).

Ostrom, J. H., and J. S. McIntosh, *Marsh's Dinosaurs* (New Haven, Yale UP, 1966).

Outram, D., 'New Spaces in Natural History', in Jardine, Secord and Spary, *Cultures*, 249–65.

Owen, A., *The Darkened Room: Women, Power and Spiritualism in Late Victorian England* (Virago, 1989).

Owen, R., 'Instances of the Power of God as Manifested in His Animal Creation', in *Lectures Delivered before the YMCA* (Simpkin & Marshall, 1864).

—, *On the Anatomy of Vertebrates* 3 vols (Longman, 1866–8).

—, 'The Fate of the "Jardin d'Acclimatation" during the late Siege of Paris', *Fraser's Magazine* (1872), 17–22.

—, *Descriptive and Illustrated Catalogue of the Fossil Reptilia of South Africa* (Taylor & Francis, 1876).

—, 'Evidence of a Carnivorous Reptile (Cynodraco Major, Ow.) about the Size of a Lion, with remarks thereon', *QJGS*, 32 (1876), 95–101.

—, 'Description of Parts of the Skeleton of an Anomodont Reptile (Platypodosaurus Robustus, Ow.) from the Trias of Graf Reinet, S. Africa', *QJGS*, 36 (1880), 414–25.

—, 'On the Order Theriodontia, with the Description of a new Genus and Species (Aelurosaurus Felinus, Ow.)', *QJGS*, 37 (1881), 261–5.

Owen, R.S., ed., *The Life of Richard Owen* 2 vols (Murray, 1894).

Padian, K., 'Pterosaurs and Typology: Archetypal Physiology in the Owen–Seeley Dispute of 1870', in W. A. S. Sarjeant, ed., *Vertebrate Fossils and the Evolution of Scientific Concepts* (Reading, Harwood, 1994).

—, 'A Missing Hunterian Lecture on Vertebrae by Richard Owen, 1837', *JHB*, 28 (1995), 333–68.

Pang, A. S.-K., 'The Social Event of the Season: Solar Eclipse Expeditions and Victorian Culture', *Isis*, 84 (1993), 252–77.

Paradis, J. G., *T. H. Huxley: Man's Place in Nature* (Lincoln, University of Nebraska Press, 1978).

—, '*Evolution and Ethics* in Its Victorian Context', in J. G. Paradis and G. C. Williams, eds, *Evolution & Ethics: T. H. Huxley's* Evolution and Ethics. *With New Essays on its Victorian and Sociobiological Context* (Princeton, Princeton UP, 1989), 3–55.

— and T. Postlewait, eds, *Victorian Science and Victorian Values, Ann. N.Y. Acad. Sci*, 360 (1981).

Parker, T. J., *William Kitchen Parker* (Macmillan, 1893).

—, 'Professor Huxley: from the Point of View of a Disciple', *Natural Science*, 8 (1896), 161–7.

Pauly, P. J., 'The Appearance of Academic Biology in Late Nineteenth-Century America', *JHB*, 17 (1984), 369–97.

Pedersen, S., 'Rathbone and Daughter: Feminism and the Father at the Fin-de-siècle', *Journal of Victorian Culture*, 1 (1996), 98–117.

Pelling, H., *A History of British Trade Unionism* (Penguin, 1971).

Perkins, H., *The Origins of Modern English Society 1780–1880* (Routledge, 1972).

Peterson, H., *Huxley: Prophet of Science* (Longman, 1932).

Pevsner, N., *The Buildings of England: London, except the Cities of London and Westminster* (Penguin, 1952).

Pfeifer, E. J., 'United States', in Glick, *Comparative Reception*, 168–206.

Pickstone, J., 'Ways of Knowing: Towards a Historical Sociology of Science, Technology and Medicine', *BJHS*, 26 (1993), 433–58.

—, 'Museological Science? The Place of the Analytical/Comparative in Nineteenth-Century Science, Technology and Medicine', *HS*, 32 (1994), 111–38.

Poore, G. V., 'Robert Edmond Grant', *University College Gazette*, 2 (34) (1901), 190–1.

Prospectus of the Normal School of Science, and of the Royal School of Mines (Science and Art Department, 1881).

Rainger, R., 'Paleontology and Philosophy: A Critique', *JHB*, 18 (1985), 267–87.

—, 'Vertebrate Paleontology as Biology: Henry Fairfield Osborn and the American Museum of Natural History', in Rainger, Benson and Maienschein, *American Development of Biology*, 219–56.
—, 'The Rise and Decline of a Science: Vertebrate Paleontology at Philadelphia's Academy of Natural Sciences, 1820–1900', *Proc. Am. Phil. Soc.*, 136 (1992), 1–32.
—, K. Benson, and J. Maienschein, eds, *The American Development of Biology* (Philadelphia, University of Pennsylvania Press, 1988).
Randel, W. P., 'Huxley in America', *Proc. Am. Phil. Soc.*, 114 (1970), 73–99.
Read, D., *England 1868–1914* (Longman, 1979).
Rehbock, P .F., 'Huxley, Haeckel, and the Oceanographers: The Case of *Bathybius haeckelii*', *Isis*, 66 (1975), 504–33.
—, *The Philosophical Naturalists: Themes in Early Nineteenth-Century British Biology* (Madison, University of Wisconsin Press, 1983).
—, ed., *At Sea with the Scientifics: The* Challenger *Letters of Joseph Matkin* (Honolulu, Univ. Hawaii Press, 1992).
Rice, A. L., 'Thomas Henry Huxley and the Strange Case of *Bathybius haeckelii*; A Possible Alternative Explanation', *ANH*, 11 (1983), 169–80.
—, 'Oceanographic Fame – and Fortune; The Salaries of the Sailors and Scientists on HMS *Challenger*', *ANH*, 16 (1989), 213–20.
Rich, P .B., 'Social Darwinism, Anthropology and English Perspectives of the Irish, 1867–1900', *Hist. Eur. Ideas*, 19 (1994), 777–85.
Richards, E., 'Darwin and the Descent of Woman', in Oldroyd and Langham, *Wider Domain*, 57–111.
—, 'A Question of Property Rights: Richard Owen's Evolutionism Reassessed', *BJHS*, 20 (1987), 129–71.
—, 'Huxley and Woman's Place in Science: The "Woman Question" and the Control of Victorian Anthropology', in Moore, *History*, 253–84.
—, 'Gendering the Romanes Lecture: The Sexual Politics of T. H. Huxley's "Evolution and Ethics"', paper delivered at Huxley Conference, Imperial College, London (April 1995).
—, 'Redrawing the Boundaries: Darwinian Science and Victorian Women Intellectuals', in Lightman, *Victorian Science*.
Richards, J. L., 'The Reception of a Mathematical Theory: Non-Euclidean Geometry in England, 1868–1883', in Barnes and Shapin, *Natural Order*, 143–66.
Richards, R. J., *Darwin and the Emergence of Evolutionary Theories of Mind and Behavior* (UCP, 1987).
Richardson, R., *Death, Dissection and the Destitute* (Penguin, 1989).
Ridley, M., 'Coadaptation and the Inadequacy of Natural Selection', *BJHS*, 15 (1982), 45–68.
Ritvo, H., *The Animal Estate: The English and Other Creatures in the Victorian Age* (Cambridge, Mass., Harvard UP, 1987).
—, 'Classification and Continuity in *The Origin of Species*', in Amigoni and Wallace, *Darwin's Origin*, 47–67.
Roberts, J. M., *Europe 1880–1945* (Longman, 1970).
Roderick, G. W., and M. Stephens, *Scientific and Technical Education in 19th Century England* (New York, Barnes & Noble, 1973).
Rolt, L. T. C., *Victorian Engineering* (Penguin, 1988).
[Romanes, E., ed.], *The Life and Letters of George John Romanes* (Longman, 1896).

Roos, D. A., 'Matthew Arnold and Thomas Henry Huxley: Two Speeches at the Royal Academy, 1881 and 1883', *Modern Philology*, 74 (1977), 316–24.

—, 'Neglected Bibliographical Aspects of the Works of Thomas Henry Huxley', *J. Soc. Biblphy Nat. Hist.*, 8 (1978), 401–20.

—, 'The "Aims and Intentions" of *Nature*', in Paradis and Postlewait, *Victorian Science*, 159–80.

Rose, P., 'Huxley, Holmes, and the Scientist as Aesthete', *Victorian Newsletter* 38 (1970), 22–4.

[Ross, W. S.], 'Professor Huxley and Agnosticism', *Agnostic J.*, 27 Apr. 1889, 261.

Royle, E., *Radicals, Secularists and Republicans: Popular Freethought in Britain, 1866–1915* (Manchester UP, 1980).

Rupke, N. A., '*Bathybius Haeckelii* and the Psychology of Scientific Discovery', *Stud. Hist. Phil. Sci.*, 7 (1976), 53–62.

—, *Richard Owen: Victorian Naturalist* (New Haven, Yale UP, 1994).

Ruse, M., *The Darwinian Revolution: Science Red in Tooth and Claw* (UCP, 1979).

—, 'Booknotes', *Biology and Philosophy*, 8 (1993), 249–54.

Sanderson, M., 'The English Civic Universities and the "Industrial Spirit", 1870–1914', *Historical Research*, 61 (1988), 90–104.

Schafer, E. A., 'William Sharpey', *University College Gazette*, 2 (36) (1901), 215.

Schuchert, C., and C. M. LeVene, *O. C. Marsh, Pioneer in Paleontology* (New Haven, Yale UP, 1940).

Schwartz, J. S., 'George John Romanes's Defense of Darwinism: The Correspondence of Charles Darwin and His Chief Disciple', *JHB*, 28 (1995), 281–316.

Secord, A., 'Science in the Pub: Artisan Botanists in Early Nineteenth-Century Lancashire', *HS*, 22 (1994), 269–315.

Secord, J. A., 'Behind the Veil: Robert Chambers and *Vestiges*', in Moore, *History*, 165–94.

—, 'Extraordinary Experiment: Electricity and the Creation of Life in Victorian England', in Gooding, Pinch and Schaffer, *Uses of Experiment*, 337–83.

Seeley, H. G., 'Note on a Femur and a Humerus of a Small Mammal from the Stonesfield Slate', *QJGS*, 35 (1879), 456–63.

—, 'The Ornithosaurian Pelvis', *AMNH*, 7 (1891), 237–55.

Seth, A., 'Man's Place in the Cosmos', *Blackwood's Magazine*, 154 (1893), 823–34.

Shapin, S., 'History of Science and its Sociological Reconstructions', *HS*, 20 (1982), 157–211.

—, *A Social History of Truth: Civility and Science in Seventeenth-Century England* (UCP, 1994).

Shortland, M., and R. Yeo, eds, *Telling Lives in Science: Essays on Scientific Biography* (CUP 1996).

Sloan, P. R., 'Darwin, Vital Matter, and the Transformation of Species', *JHB*, 19 (1986), 367–95.

—, ed., *Richard Owen. The Hunterian Lectures in Comparative Anatomy. May and June 1837* (UCP, 1992).

Smith, C., and M. N. Wise, *Energy and Empire: A Biographical Study of Lord Kelvin* (CUP, 1989).

Smith, F., 'Charles Darwin's Ill Health', *JHB*, 23 (1990), 443–59.

Smith, J. M., 'Thomas Henry Huxley in Nashville', *Tennessee Historical Quarterly*, 33 (1974), 191–203, 322–41.

Smith, R., 'The Background of Physiological Psychology in Natural Philosophy', *BJHS*, 6 (1973), 75–123.

—, 'Alfred Russel Wallace: Philosophy of Nature and Man', *BJHS*, 6 (1972), 177–99.

—, 'The Human Significance of Biology: Carpenter, Darwin, and *vera causa*', in U. C. Knoepflmacher and G. B. Tennyson, eds, *Nature and the Victorian Imagination* (Berkeley, University of California Press, 1977), 216–30.

Sopka, K. R., 'John Tyndall: International Populariser of Science', in Brock, McMillan and Mollan, *John Tyndall*, 193–203.

Spencer, H., 'Absolute Political Ethics', *NC*, 27 (1890), 119–30.

—, *An Autobiography* 2 vols (Williams & Norgate, 1904).

Stauffer, R. C., ed., *Charles Darwin's Natural Selection: Being the Second Part of his Big Species Book written from 1856 to 1858* (CUP, 1975).

Stearn, W. T., *The Natural History Museum at South Kensington* (Heinemann, 1981).

Stephen, J., 'William Wilberforce', in *Essays in Ecclesiastical Biography* 5th ed. (Longman, 1867), 469–522.

Stephen, L., 'Ethics and the Struggle for Existence', *CR*, 44 (1893), 157–70.

Stoddart, D. R., '"That Victorian Science": Huxley's *Physiography* and Its Impact on Geography', *Trans. Inst. Br. Geog.*, 66 (1975), 17–40.

Sulloway, F. J., *Freud: Biologist of the Mind* (Fontana, 1980).

Summerville, J., 'Albert Roberts, Journalist of the New South', *Tennessee Historical Quarterly*, 42 (1985), 18–38, 179–202.

Survey of London, The, Vol. 38: The Museums Area of South Kensington, ed. F. H. W. Sheppard (1975).

Tener, R. H., and M. Woodfield, eds, *A Victorian Spectator: Uncollected Writings of R. H. Hutton* (Bristol, Bristol Press, 1991).

Tennyson, A., 'Prefatory Poem', *NC*, 1 (1877), 1.

Thackray, A., 'Natural Knowledge in Cultural Context: The Manchester Model', *Am. Hist. Rev.*, 79 (1974), 672–709.

Thiselton-Dyer, W. T., 'Plant Biology in the 'Seventies', *Nature*, 115 (1925), 709–12.

Thomson, J. A., 'Huxley as Evolutionist', *Nature*, 115 (1925), 717–18.

Todes, D. P., 'V. O. Kovalevskii: The Genesis, Content, and Reception of his Paleontological Work', *Studies in History of Biology*, 2 (1978), 99–165.

—, 'Darwin's Malthusian Metaphor and Russian Evolutionary Thought, 1859–1917', *Isis*, 78 (1987), 537–51.

Tribe, D., *President Charles Bradlaugh, M.P.* (Elek, 1971).

Turner, F. M., 'Lucretius Among the Victorians', *VS*, 16 (1973), 329–48.

—, *Between Science and Religion: the Reaction to Scientific Naturalism in Late Victorian England* (New Haven, Yale UP, 1974).

—, 'Victorian Scientific Naturalism and Thomas Carlyle', *VS*, 18 (1975), 325–43.

—, 'The Victorian Conflict between Science and Religion: A Professional Dimension', *Isis*, 69 (1978), 356–76.

—, 'Public Science in Britain, 1880–1919', *Isis*, 71 (1980), 589–608.

—, *Contesting Cultural Authority: Essays in Victorian Intellectual Life* (CUP, 1993).

Turner, G. L. 'E., ed., *The Patronage of Science in the Nineteenth Century* (Leiden, Noordhoff, 1976).

Tyndall, J., *Fragments of Science*, 2nd ed. (Longman, 1871).

—, *Fragments of Science, II*, 6th ed. (Longman, 1879).
—, 'On the Political Situation', *Times*, 3 June 1886.
Van Riper, A. B., *Men among the Mammoths: Victorian Science and the Discovery of Prehistory* (UCP, 1993).
Veitch, J., 'Prof. Huxley's Hume', *Nature*, 19 (1879), 453–6.
Vorzimmer, P. J., *Charles Darwin: The Years of Controversy* (University of London Press, 1972).
[Wace, H.], 'Scientific Lectures – Their Use and Abuse', *QR*, 145 (1878), 35–61.
[Wallace, A. R.], 'Principles of Geology', *QR*, 126 (1869), 359–94.
—, 'Human Selection', *FR*, 48 (1890), 325–37.
—, *My Life: A Record of Events and Opinions* 2 vols (Chapman & Hall, 1905).
'Watchman', *In Darkest England. A Reply to 'General' Booth's Sensational Scheme for 'Social Salvation'* (Kensit, 1890).
Watts, J. 'Theological Theories of the Origin of Man', *Reasoner*, 26 (1861), 102–4, 119–21, 132–4.
Webb, B., *The Diary of Beatrice Webb. Vol. 1: 1873–1892*, ed. N. and J. MacKenzie (Virago, 1982).
Weikart, R., 'A Recently Discovered Darwin Letter on Social Darwinism', *Isis*, 86 (1995), 609–11.
Weindling, P. J., *Darwinism and Social Darwinism in Imperial Germany: The Contribution of the Cell Biologist Oscar Hertwig (1849–1922)* (Stuttgart, Gustav Fischer, 1991).
Wells, H. G., 'Huxley', *Science Schools Journal* (April 1901), 209–11.
—, *Experiment in Autobiography* 2 vols (Gollancz, 1934).
White, A. D., *A History of the Warfare of Science with Theology in Christendom* (New York, Free Press, 1965).
White, H. H., *Materia Medica Pharmacy, Pharmacology and Therapeutics*, ed. R. W. Wilcox, 3rd American ed. (Philadelphia, Blakiston, 1897).
Whitrow, G. J., *Centenary of the Huxley Building: Personalities and Events in the History of Imperial College* (1972).
Wiener, M. J., *English Culture and the Decline of the Industrial Spirit 1850–1980* (Penguin, 1992).
Wilberforce, R. G., 'Professor Huxley and the Life and Letters of C. Darwin', *Times*, 29 Dec. 1887.
Winsor, M. P., 'The Impact of Darwinism upon the Linnean Enterprise, with Special Reference to the Work of T. H. Huxley', in J. Weinstock, ed., *Contemporary Perspectives on Linnaeus* (Lanham, Md., University Press of America, 1985), 55–84.
—, *Reading the Shape of Nature: Comparative Zoology at the Agassiz Museum* (UCP, 1991).
Woodcock, G., *Anarchism* (Penguin, 1963).
Woodward, A. S., 'Contributions to Vertebrate Palaeontology', *Nature*, 115 (1925), 728–30.
Wynne, B., 'Physics and Psychics: Science, Symbolic Action, and Social Control in Late Victorian England', in Barnes and Shapin, *Natural Order*, 167–86.
Yeo, S., 'A New Life: The Religion of Socialism in Britain, 1883–1896', *History Workshop*, 4 (1977), 5–56.
Young, G. M., *Portrait of an Age*, 2nd ed. (OUP, 1989).
Young, R. M., *Darwin's Metaphor: Nature's Place in Victorian Culture* (CUP, 1985).

Index

Index

Index

Index

Index

Index

Index

Index

Index

Index

Index

Index